WK 4   1-5 , 8

9.3 TO - C
115 129 130

TO   TO
WK 5   12, 15 , 18
        ↓
   CRITIQUE

32
.99¢

D1242626

THE **SHAPE** *of* **PRACTICAL** THEOLOGY

Empowering Ministry with Theological Praxis

RAY S. ANDERSON

IVP Academic

An imprint of InterVarsity Press
Downers Grove, Illinois

InterVarsity Press
P.O. Box 1400, Downers Grove, IL 60515
World Wide Web: www.ivpress.com
E-mail: mail@ivpress.com

InterVarsity Press® is the book-publishing division of InterVarsity Christian Fellowship/USA®, a student movement active on campus at hundreds of universities, colleges and schools of nursing in the United States of America, and a member movement of the International Fellowship of Evangelical Students. For information about local and regional activities, write Public Relations Dept., InterVarsity Christian Fellowship/USA, 6400 Schroeder Rd., P.O. Box 7895, Madison, WI 53707-7895, or visit the IVCF website at <www.intervarsity.org>.

All Scripture quotations, unless otherwise indicated, are taken from the New Revised Standard Version of the Bible, copyright 1989 by the Division of Christian Education of the National Council of the Churches of Christ in the USA. Used by permission. All rights reserved.

Chapter five, "A Practical Theology of Ministry," is a revised version of the chapter "A Theology of Ministry," published in Theological Foundations for Ministry, ed. Ray S. Anderson (Grand Rapids, Mich.: Eerdmans, 1979), pp. 6-21, used by permission. Chapter ten, "Sociocultural Implications of a Christian Perception of Humanity," was previously published in Asian Journal of Theology 2, no. 2 (1988): 500-15, used by permission. Chapter eleven, "The Humanity of God and the Soul of the City—Where Is the Church?" is adapted from Ray S. Anderson, "The Soul of the City," in Ministry on the Fireline: A Practical Theology for an Empowered Church (Downers Grove, Ill.: InterVarsity Press, 1993), pp. 183-98. Chapter twelve, "Practical Theology as Paraclesis: Pastoral Implications," is a revised version of the chapter "Empowering Ministry: The Praxis of Pentecost," published in The Call to Serve: Essays on Ministry in Honour of Bishop Penny Jamieson, ed. Douglas A. Campbell (Sheffield: Sheffield Academic, 1996), used by permission. Chapter sixteen, "Homosexuality: Theological & Pastoral Implications," is a revised version of the article "Homosexuality: Theological and Pastoral Implications," published in Journal of Psychology and Christianity 15, no. 4 (1996). Chapter nineteen, "The Little Man on the Cross," was published in The Reformed Journal, November 1982, pp. 14-17, and is used by permission.

Cover photograph: ©Shinobu Hirai/Photonica

ISBN-10: 0-8308-1559-7
ISBN-13: 978-0-8308-1559-3

Printed in the United States of America ∞

Library of Congress Cataloging-in-Publication Data

Anderson, Ray Sherman.
   The shape of practical theology: empowering ministry with theological praxis/Ray S. Anderson.
      p. cm.
   Includes bibliographical references (p.)
   ISBN 0-8308-1559-7 (paper: alk. paper)
   1. Theology, Practical.   I. Title.
   BV3 .A47 2001
   230—dc21

00-047157

P   24   23   22   21   20   19   18   17   16   15   14   13   12   11

Y   23   22   21   20   19   18   17   16   15   14

Preface

The bridge connecting practical theology to the older discipline of "pure theology" was constructed for one-way traffic. While the discipline of practical theology was permitted as a necessary application of practice to theory, practical theologians ordinarily did not carry union cards admitting them to the theological guild.

The line between so-called academic theology and practical theology was first drawn by the faculties of the European universities, imported by the divinity schools of North American universities and imbedded in the curricula of most theological seminaries. The complaint that the more recent doctoral degrees in ministry (D.Min.) do not measure up to the rigor of academic standards is often heard among faculties who offer such degrees.

Listening to the play-by-play broadcast of a baseball game, one often gain insights hidden from the more sophisticated but readily apparent to their children. A close play at second base resulting in the runner being called "out" by the umpire often calls for colorful commentary when instant replay shows clearly that the runner was safe. When the batter strikes out to end the inning, the announcer will often say, "Well, that makes the play at second base academic." In other words, it had nothing to do with the outcome of the game.

Ouch! If that is what the concept of "academic" has come to mean in our culture, then "academic theology" may suffer from the ultimate irrelevance—it has nothing to do with the outcome of the game.

My thesis in this book is that the traffic on the bridge connecting theory and practice now flows both ways. As a theologian trained in the discipline of dogmatic theology, I first crossed over that bridge from the side of several years of pastoral ministry. Making a pathway for myself, I have endeavored to guide others in that journey through more than twenty-four years of teaching students and pastors who do have something to do with the outcome of the game.

A new breed of practical theologians is emerging and the shape of practical theology is rapidly changing. The line between "pure theology" and practical theology, as well as the demarcation between theory and practice, no longer is drawn so sharply and definitively. Distinctions are still to be made, but these are differentiations within a common task rather than separate disciplines.

My purpose in this book is threefold. First, I define more clearly the shape of practical theology as truly a theological enterprise rather than mere mastery of skills and methods. Second, I demonstrate the praxis of practical theology as critical engagement with the interface between the word of God as revealed through Scripture and the work of God taking place in and through the church in the world. Third, I offer some essays dealing with practical pastoral theology from the perspective of those who are on the "field of play" of life and ministry, where preaching, counseling and teaching does affect for many persons the outcome of the game. Readers will notice that the essays in parts two and three are placed in proximity due to common themes, but each remains a separate piece. Rather than attempt to create transitions between the chapters, I leave them as they were written so that one may go directly to a topic or subject according to a particular interest at a particular time.

The Christ proclaimed in the gospel through the church has a counterpart in the Christ clothed with the needs of the world. In one of his most eloquent missiological utterances, Thomas Torrance wrote, "The Church cannot be in Christ without being in Him as He has proclaimed to men in their need and with being in Him as He encounters us in and behind the existence of every man in his need. Nor can the Church be recognized as His except in that meeting of Christ with Himself in the depth of human misery, where Christ clothed with His gospel meets Christ clothed with the desperate need and plight of men."This is the praxis of practical theology. It is in this spirit that I offer this book as a primer in practical theology with the hope that it will stimulate discussion and inspire those who aspire to be practical theologians.

---

[1]Thomas Torrance, "Service in Jesus Christ," in *Theological Foundations for Ministry,* ed. Ray S. Anderson (Grand Rapids, Mich.: Eerdmans, 1979), p. 724.

Part 1

THE SHAPE OF
PRACTICAL THEOLOGY

1

INTRODUCTION TO PRACTICAL THEOLOGY

Before the theologian there was the storyteller. To say "Abraham, Isaac and Jacob" is not the recitation of a genealogical litany but the recapitulation of a theological legacy. To say "Abraham" calls to mind a personal encounter that demanded a walk of faith and a witness to divine promise. To say "Isaac" reiterates the gracious intervention of the God who brings forth the promised seed from Sara's barren womb. To say "Jacob" distinguishes Rebekah's revelation as divine Word from Isaac's natural inclination to honor a cultural custom.

These were all storytellers; it remained for Moses to become the first theologian. Following the encounter with God at the burning bush, and the revelation of the new name—Yahweh—Moses outlined the contours of the divine covenant of grace and mercy as revealed through the liberation of his people from Egypt and the journey toward the Promised Land. The inner logic of God's saving grace became the "spine" to which the stories lodged as fragments in the oral tradition could be attached as a coherent pattern of inspired and written Word of God. God's act of reconciliation is simultaneously God's Word of revelation. The God who accompanied the people on their journey through the wilderness walked with Adam and Eve in the Garden of Eden (Gen 3:8). To walk with God, from "bedlam to shalom," as John Swinton artfully put it, is to discover and know the Word of God.[1]

What makes theology practical is not the fitting of orthopedic devices to theoretical concepts in order to make them walk. Rather, theology occurs as a divine partner joins us on our walk, stimulating our reflection and inspiring us to recognize the living Word, as happened to the two walking on the road to Emmaus on the first Easter (Lk 24).[2]

I write this book as one who entered into pastoral ministry directly out of seminary with a major in systematic theology but, as I soon discovered, afflicted with PTDS—practical theology deficiency syndrome. I had a theology that could talk but that would not walk. What passed for practical theology in the seminary curriculum was a survey of the various forms of church polity unique to each tradition and some practical advice on how to make hospital calls—don't sit on the bed—and how to prepare sermons—spend at least one hour a week of preparation for each minute of the sermon! My sermons were strong on the attributes of God but weak on their application to the daily life of faith.

Finally a member of the congregation found the courage to tell me that it was easy to agree to the omnipotence of God—that he could do everything—but what was of more immediate concern was whether God could do anything in particular. If it is important to know and believe that God is omnipresent—that he is everywhere present—one could readily assent, but what one really longed for was to discover God present in the small space of one's personal life.

At that time I found no problem with those who had red letter editions of the New Testament, where every word that Jesus spoke was highlighted in color. I was taught that propositional truth in the form of that which was thought, spoken and communicated was "real truth," while the actions of Jesus were only descriptions and accounts of his ministry—as though ministry was only something Jesus did to prove that he was truly of God. One of my most revered seminary professors pointed me in this direction when he made the observation in a theology class one day that it was curious that the liturgical churches stood for the reading of the Gospels and sat for the reading of the Epistles. It should be the other way around, he opined. The letters of Paul constitute the truth of doctrine as the ground of our faith, while the Gospels are but anecdotes that provide the context for the teaching of Jesus. We should stand for the reading of the Epistles, he concluded. It never occurred to me that we had it upside down! Jesus himself had said, "Even though you do not believe me, believe

---

[1]John Swinton, *From Bedlam to Shalom: Towards a Practical Theology of Human Nature, Interpersonal Relationships and Mental Health Care* (New York: Peter Lang, 2000).

[2]Robert Banks calls the apostle Paul "the Walkabout Apostle" and suggests that the chief metaphor for Paul's vision of the Christian life was walking (*Reenvisioning Theological Education: Exploring a Missional Alternative to Current Models* [Grand Rapids, Mich.: Eerdmans, 1999], p. 138).

the works, so that you may know and understand that the Father is in me and I am in the Father" (Jn 10:38). Only later did I come to understand that what Jesus did was as authoritative and as much revelation of God as what he said and taught. I now hold that if one wishes to highlight what is revealed truth in the life and ministry of Jesus, one should better print his works in red! When Jesus healed on the sabbath, the act of healing became a criterion (text) by which a true theology of the sabbath was revealed.

My conversion to practical theology began early in my ministry. A woman member of the church had been divorced several years before joining. During her participation in our church fellowship she fell in love with a man who had also been divorced. Both of them were faithful and regular participants in the life of the church. One day she came to my office and said, "Pastor, I know what the Bible says concerning divorce and remarriage. According to the Bible I can never remarry. I am not the innocent party to my previous divorce. I contributed as much as my husband to the tragic failure of our marriage. I have sought and received God's forgiveness for the sin of divorce. Now I have met a man with whom I not only have a bond of love, but we share a strong bond of life in Jesus Christ."

She paused for a long time and then asked, "Where is God in our lives? Is God on the side of a law of marriage and divorce, or is he on our side as we experience forgiveness and renewal as his children seeking his blessing on our lives through marriage?"

She asked the right question. It was the question asked of Jesus by those who sought healing on the sabbath, who reached out to him from the ranks of those marginalized and scorned by the self-righteous religious authorities. It was not a question that sought to evade a biblical principle by finding a loophole through which one could drive a bargain with God. It was not a question of human pragmatism but of divine praxis. I was being asked to interpret the Word of God by the work of God in their lives. To use the Word against the work of God seemed dangerously close to the practice of those who crucified Jesus because he was judged to have violated the law of the sabbath by healing on the sabbath (Jn.9:16).

My response to this couple after meeting with them paraphrased the statement of Jesus concerning the sabbath: "Marriage is made for the benefit of humankind; humans are not made merely to uphold marriage as a law" (Mk 2:27-28). At their marriage, before the entire congregation, I said, "Bill and Sue [not their real names] want you to know that they have no right to be married today. But you are witnesses of the saving and healing work of Christ in their midst, and it is on that basis, as recipients of God's grace, that they stand before you as a testimony to the power of God to redeem and bless what is redeemed."

At that crucial point in my own ministry, I had a good deal of systematic theology but no preparation in practical theology. Since then I have come to understand that the core theology of the Bible, both Old and New Testament, is practical theology before it becomes systematic theology. This book attempts to define the contours of a biblical and practical theology as foundation for the theological task itself. I want to make clear the distinction between a theology grounded primarily in theory as compared to a theory of theology grounded in praxis. I also want to distinguish a theology made practical through a pragmatic approach—not everything that works is God's work—from a practical theology that reads Scripture in the context of ministry—what God does (works) honors and illuminates the purpose of God's Word.

This requires at the outset an analysis of the relation of theory to practice, including a brief survey of the factors that led to the splitting apart of theory and practice in the so-called modern period of theology following the Enlightenment in Europe. I confess that my own approach is from within a Western tradition and culture. I am a child of that culture. At the same time, I seek to lay bare the inner logic of God's self-revelation as directed to all of humanity, in every culture and across all ethnic and geographical boundaries. The first part of this book attempts to do this through an exploration of God's self-revelation in Christ as a form of Christopraxis, leading to a practical theology of ministry. The remainder of the book then takes up issues and questions that confront those who are on the frontlines of Christ's ministry through the church and in the world.

The Relation of Theory to Practice

At the center of the discussion of the nature of practical theology is the issue of the relation of theory to praxis. If theory precedes and determines practice, then practice tends to be concerned primarily with methods, techniques and strategies for ministry, lacking theological substance. If practice takes priority over theory, ministry tends to be based on pragmatic results rather than prophetic revelation. All good practice includes theory, some will say. Others will claim that theory without good practice is invalid theory.

Behind the massive work of Karl Barth lies the dynamic interrelation between theory and praxis. The task of theology as Barth construed it is to clarify the presuppositions of church praxis. Praxis comes first precisely because God is "no fifth wheel on the wagon, but the wheel that drives all wheels."[3] In his furious response to the Prussian churchman Otto Dibelius, Barth wrote:

> Dibelius characterizes the difference between us as if he was the representation of the Church, i.e. of praxis and love, and I the representative of theology, i.e. of a Christian theory. According to my view any serious undertaking makes that kind of opposition

---

[3]Karl Barth, *Der Römerbriefe,* 1st ed., p. 102, quoted in Timothy J. Gorringe, *Karl Barth: Against Hegemony* (Oxford: Oxford University Press, 1999), p. 9.

impossible. Praxis and theory, Church and theology, love and knowledge, simply cannot be set over against one another in this kind of abstract way.[4]

Barth, from the beginning, resisted all attempts to portray theory and praxis in opposition to one another. In his early *Church Dogmatics* he described any distinction between "theoretical" and "practical" as a "primal lie, which has to be resisted in principle."[5] The understanding of Christ as the light of life can be understood only as a "theory which has its origin and goal in praxis."[6]

To understand what lies behind this debate, we will look briefly at the historical process through which the division between theory and practice emerged.

The Premodern View of Reality

In the so-called premodern period prior to the Enlightenment in Europe, a philosophical and theological perception of reality was mediated through sacrament and myth. The medieval world viewed reality as basically metaphysical. The physical world as well as the world of sense experience and human behavior were regulated largely by appeal to abstract and well-defined concepts that transcend the ambiguous and uncertain temporal and historical order. This gave precision and universal status to what was considered to be both good and true. Moral character could be formed by acquiring the virtues of honesty, truthfulness and goodness through discipline, contemplation and devotion to these ideals. Moral values were grounded in this version of reality and moral character cultivated as one of the goals of an educated person.

From the human perspective, reality remained partially hidden and only indirectly accessible through signs, symbols and natural phenomena. When the physical world points away from itself to some ultimate reality, a theistic worldview is necessary to "hold things in place." Authority tended to be invested in tradition, religion, institutions and tribal hierarchy. This so-called precritical period in European intellectual history was quite congenial to an "uncritical" view of divine revelation as historical event simply because reality did not rest on historical authenticity but on metaphysical certitude contingent on the existence of God. With the ascendancy of metaphysical thought it only remained for the human thinker to claim autonomy and for the premodern adolescent to come into maturity, resulting in what has come be called modernity.

The Modern View of Reality

Historians generally date the birth of the modern mind to the Enlightenment of the

---

[4]Quoted in Gorringe, *Karl Barth*, p. 9.
[5]Karl Barth, *Church Dogmatics* (hereafter cited as *CD*) 1/2, ed. Geoffrey Bromiley and Thomas F. Torrance (Edinburgh: T & T Clark, 1955-1961), p. 787.
[6]*CD* 4/3, p. 79.

eighteenth century, but its foundation was laid two hundred years before in the Renaissance, which elevated man to the center of reality. The precise genealogy of the term *postmodern* is contested, but it first appeared in the 1930s, used, among others, by Arnold Toynbee. This social historian, writing in 1939, suggested that the modern age ended in 1914 and that the new era that emerged from the rubble of WWI should be described as *postmodern*.

Following the Enlightenment in Europe, and with the development of critical thought and autonomous reason, the physical world came to be viewed as self-existent and self-explanatory. The critical philosophy of Immanuel Kant (1724-1804) stripped "theory" of objective reality as an object of philosophical thought. For Kant, the real world was the noumenal, which is not subject to the determination that knowledge presupposes and thus cannot be known as a "thing-in-itself" (*ding an sich*). Kant's agnosticism concerning any objective knowledge of reality beyond experience did not lead to the collapse of theory. Rather, theory became lodged in structures of consciousness and "conventions" of human thought conditioned by experience rather than in abstract metaphysical concepts. His massive attack on speculative metaphysics as delusion led to a series of critical writings. Kant, however, confessed in the end that he did not quite succeed in banishing the metaphysical approach to reality. "We can therefore be sure that however cold or contemptuously critical may be the attitude of those who judge a science not by its nature but by its accidental effects, we shall always return to metaphysics as to a beloved one with whom we have had a quarrel."[7] The division between theory and practice was softened but not dissolved.

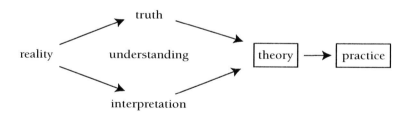

Figure 1.1. Modern approach to practical theology

In this modern period, theory continued to dominate practice, with epistemological and hermeneutical models laying the foundation for practical theology. Figure 1.1 depicts this view. In this diagram, truth and interpretation form the hermeneutical

---

[7]Immanuel Kant, *The Critique of Pure Reason*, trans. Norman Kemp Smith (London: Macmillan, 1929), p. 664.

bridge by which reality informs theory and theory determines practice. While theory precedes and determines practice, the way in which theory leads to practice is a matter of debate within contemporary forms of practical theology.[8] Ballard and Prichard favor the habitus/virtue model suggested by Stanley Hauerwas, who stresses the fact that truth is found in the community of shared meaning and is appropriated by a process of growth into wisdom.[9] The inherent weakness in this model, however, is the fact that practice only has access to truth through theory. What holds this construct in place is the modern view that truth stands above reality as objective, universal and fixed principles toward which all subjective interpretations must eventually lead. What modernity did not reckon with is that the autonomy of human reason logically entailed the demise of a theistic premise.

Dietrich Bonhoeffer (1906-1945) credited the Dutch philosopher Hugo Grotius (1583-1645) with the modern concept of natural law as existing independently of divine existence—*etsi deus non duretur*. "We cannot be honest," Bonhoeffer wrote, "unless we recognize that we have to live in the world *etsi deus non duretur* [even if there were no God]. And this is just what we do recognize—before God! God himself compels us to recognize it. . . . God would have us know that we must live as men who manage our lives without him. The God who lets us live in the world without the working hypothesis of God is the God before whom we stand continually. Before God and with God we live without God."[10] Bonhoeffer was prepared to abandon a theistic world view where God was merely a "working hypothesis," a *deus ex machina* to which people could turn as an explanation for evil and as a defender of the good. In his view, theology had no object for its reflection other than the personal reality of God revealed through concrete human social relations—Jesus Christ existing as community *(gemeinde)*.[11]

In this sense, Bonhoeffer was a forerunner of what later was to become the domain of practical theology. Seeking to overcome the individualism of Descartes (1596-1650) through his social anthropology, while accepting the Kantian critique of pure metaphysics, Bonhoeffer laid the groundwork for a praxis-oriented theology through an ethic of discipleship and obedience, where theory emerges only through engagement with truth as an ethical demand in the form of the claim of Christ through the

---

[8]Four different models of the relation of theory to practice have been elicited by Paul Ballard and John Pritchard: (1) the applied theory model, (2) the critical correlation model, (3) the praxis model and (4) the habitus/virtue model. Paul Ballard and John Pritchard, *Practical Theology in Action: Christian Thinking in the Service of Church and Society* (London: SPCK, 1996), p. 55.

[9]Ibid.

[10]Dietrich Bonhoeffer, *Letters and Papers from Prison* (New York: Macmillan, 1971), p. 360.

[11]This was the basic thesis of Bonhoeffer's dissertation at the University of Berlin in 1927. Dietrich Bonhoeffer, *Sanctorum Communio: A Theological Study of the Sociology of the Church* (Minneapolis: Fortress, 1998).

other person. In this sense also, Bonhoeffer can be considered to be a forerunner of what has come to be known as postmodernism.

The Postmodern View of Reality

In the post-Enlightenment period of European intellectual history, the scaffolding of a metaphysical view of reality suffered from a series of earthquakes. With the rise of scientific empiricism following Francis Bacon, the behavior of nature, when studied with scientific objectivity, was considered to be a revelation of the reality of things. Reality was viewed as now accessible and verifiable through the rigor of scientific method. While reality was now within the grasp of human self-understanding, theory continued to dominate with regard to practice. Truth, mediated through interpretive structures and paradigms, informed practice, which was largely relegated to the application of methods and skills based on theory.

In theological education, for example, this led to the division of the scientific study of biblical data (*Wissenschaft*) from its application through practical methods of preaching, religious education and pastoral care. Systematic and historical theology explored divine revelation from a purely theoretical perspective, leaving practical theology to devise methods and strategies of ministry based on the principles of efficiency and effectiveness. This division between theory and practice appeared to reinstate the former epistemological dualism where "truth" could be defined as theoretical and thus constitute an objective reality over and against "practice" as merely instrumental and methodological.

The rise of existentialism, following the rejection of Hegel's philosophy by the Danish philosopher Søren Kierkegaard (1813-1855), turned the metaphysical quest for reality upside down. The metaphysical version of reality posited essence as prior to and determinative of existence. As an object of philosophical thought, essence could be thought of as the objective reality that gave meaning and order to the subjective and fluid flow of personal existence. Kierkegaard regarded Hegel's concept of "absolute Spirit" to be sheer abstraction, lacking a compelling passion and a convicting presence. The existing person, Kierkegaard argued, defines and determines the essence of what is real. Hegel's dialectic, leading to ultimate synthesis, was replaced by the paradox between time and eternity, which only the existing individual could resolve through authentic decision in the dialectic of faith and reason. For Kierkegaard, theology was a "work of love" grounded in "edifying discourse" rather than "philosophical fragments."

Kierkegaard undermined the confidence of modern humanity by introducing anxiety (angst) as the deepest core of the human self. Faith is not only suspicious of rational certitude, it can only be genuine when it "leaps over" the chasm of irrational absurdity. Following Kierkegaard, the awakening of consciousness as the critical act of the human subject dislodged truth from its assured domain in the realm of universal truth established as pure concept. The moment of "decision" for Kierkegaard, while a subjective act, became the narrow pass through which one could grasp the objective reality God as the ground of faith. The concept of irony and skepticism introduced by Kierkegaard was quite congenial to the mood of postmodern thought.

While the modern mindset was optimistic, always looking for progress as knowledge increased—for knowledge was good—a postmodernist mood of irony and playfulness has arisen, expressing a deep-seated pessimism. The modern mindset valued objective certainty, based on rational rather than religious or mystical means of attaining truth. Against rational certainty a pluralist relativism has emerged—a relativism that questions even the existence of an objective reality to be known. The modern mindset looked for a totality and unity in all knowledge, believing that all rational minds operating independently would come to similar conclusions about what is universally true and good. In contrast, postmodernism values diversity with truth relative to each community's perspective and situation.

The modernist presumption of totality, universality and rational truth about the world is labeled a mere power play by some postmodern thinkers. There are no overarching, grand stories that explain reality. Such "metanarratives" are considered modernist ploys to legitimize the power of those in authority; they are nothing more than propaganda meant to impose particular preferences on others.[12]

Supreme among these consequences is the death of objective truth. We cannot stand outside the flux of our experience. There is no transcendent point from which to view the world. All grand statements of totality offered by reason are illusions, creations of our own language and a function of our own desire for power. Truth is no longer discovered; it is created. Such themes have become axiomatic among postmoderns.[13]

Richard Middleton and Brian Walsh comment on the shift from a modern to a postmodern view of reality:

> If the modern autonomous self sought to dominate the world . . . the postmodern . . . self fluctuates between the quest for a new form of autonomy and the experience of victimization. Compulsively seeking personal advancement. . . . [T]he postmodern/hypermodern self is nevertheless overcome by a sense of meaninglessness, powerlessness,

---

[12]Michel Foucault writes, "We cannot exercise power except through the production of truth" (*Power/Knowledge* [New York: Pantheon, 1980], p. 132, quoted in Jim Leffel and Dennis McCallum, "The Postmodern Challenge: Facing the Spirit of the Age," *Christian Research Journal* 19 [1996]: 37).

[13]For a discussion of the postmodern mindset, see Bill Kynes, "Postmodernism: A Primer for Pastors," *The Ministerial Forum* 8, no. 1 (1997). I have drawn upon this article from the National Evangelical Free Church Ministerial Association in this discussion.

rootlessness, homelessness and fragmentation, where the self is incapacitated before its infinite possibilities, reduced to an effect of its plural contexts and consequently haunted by a deep-rooted sense of anomie. The "I want it all" attitude is easily transmuted into "I'm paralyzed in the face of it all." The postmodern self thus exists in a perpetual state of dialectical self-contradiction.[14]

Several implications for practical theology emerge from this.

First, postmodernism is felt in the *celebration of diversity*. In reaction to the "totalizing" of modernism, unity is out and diversity is in. This celebration of diversity is reflected in a *moral relativism*. What is right is defined as "what I feel comfortable with" or "what is right for me." As Nietzsche sagely observed, if God is dead, anything is possible.

Second, a celebration of diversity leads to a demand for tolerance. In the words of one adherent, such universal claims have a "secretly terroristic function."[15] The antidote to such terror for the postmodernist is tolerance.

Third, the social implications of modernism included an expanding secularism, for to foster the freedom of human reason, the binding force of ecclesiastical authority had to be broken. Increased social planning reflected a confidence in human reason to correct social problems.

In response, we can see several positive effects of the shift from a modern to a postmodern view of reality, which fit well with a new paradigm of practical theology.

Postmodernism rightly rejects the myth that all knowledge is objective. We must concede that knowledge is not merely objective. We are involved as moral and personal agents in all that we know, and as Blaise Pascal pointed out long before the onset of the postmodern mindset, "The heart has its reasons which reason cannot know." Modernism is not Christian, and we can rejoice in its overthrow.[16]

Postmodernism rightly points to the importance of communities in perceiving reality. We who are ministers of the gospel can agree with postmoderns in acknowledging the importance of communities in our knowing. None of us is an autonomous individual, cut off from the influences of social traditions. We belong to communities that help shape our perception of reality. We offer a living community—the church. The distrust of reason means that truth must be experienced to be believed, and it is in the church that the truth of the gospel is to be lived out.

Postmodernism rightly emphasizes the significance of narrative and story. Though there is skepticism and even hostility toward metanarratives in our postmodern

[14]J. Richard Middleton and Brian J. Walsh, *Truth Is Stranger Than It Used to Be: Biblical Faith in a Postmodern Age* (Downers Grove, Ill.: InterVarsity Press, 1995), pp. 109-10.
[15]Terry Eagleton, quoted in Middleton and Walsh, *Truth Is Stranger*, p. 71.
[16]See also F. LeRon Shults, *The Task of Theology: A Postfoundationalist Appropriation of Wolfhart Pannenberg* (Grand Rapids, Mich.: Eerdmans, 1999).

world, that condition cannot last. Human beings cannot live without the meaning and purpose that such stories give. In deconstructing the false stories of modernism, postmodernism plays a useful function, "pulling the smiling mask of arrogance from the face of naturalism."[17] But it has no answers of its own for the future.[18]

Despite the problems with many forms of postmodern thought—its tendency toward to relativism, objective pluralism and continued traces of modernism—the postmodern vision of reality approaches more closely the biblical view than the vision of the so-called modern period. Doing practical theology in the present culture, in which modern and postmodern thought vie for allegiance, calls for critical and cautious reflection on the hermeneutics of divine revelation. To subsume divine revelation under the banner of modern thought with its claim to universal truth is outright arrogance from a theological standpoint. On the other hand, to allow culture and convention to determine what is normative apart from the compelling and convicting reality of God's self-revelation is only a thinly disguised form of modernism. Helmut Thielicke would call both attempts forms of Cartesian thought, whereby the human subject continues to serve as the criterion for divine truth. The Holy Spirit, says Thielicke, appropriates the human subject to the truth of the revealed divine Word.[19]

William Stacy Johnson, while pointing to the dangers of some forms of postmodern thought, has a more positive assessment when he points to the profoundly moral concern of postmodernity. "It points out the contradictions and hypocrisies in dominant cultural assumptions, and does so not to revel in the inconsistencies but to use them as leverage to call people to account for their own highest and best ideals."[20]

In the postmodern paradigm the relation of theory to practice is no longer linear but is interactive. Theory is no longer regarded as a set of mental constructs that can exist independently of their embodiment in the physical, psychological and social structures of life. Theory and practice inform and influence each other in such a way that all practice includes theory, and theory can only be discerned through practice. This interactive loop between theory and practice can be found in contemporary physics as well as in attempts to understand the interactive relation between the human spirit and the Spirit of God as a social-psychological experience.[21]

Robert Banks suggests that the older division between theory and practice, with

---

[17]James W. Sire, *The Universe Next Door: A Basic Worldview Catalog*, 3rd ed. (Downers Grove, Ill.: InterVarsity Press, 1997), p. 189.

[18]The above summary was drawn from Kynes, "Postmodernism."

[19]Helmut Thielicke, *The Evangelical Faith* (Grand Rapids, Mich.: Eerdmans, 1974), 1:3435, 135.

[20]William Stacy Johnson, *The Mystery of God: Karl Barth and the Postmodern Foundations of Theology* (Louisville, Ky.: Westminster John Knox, 1997), p. 5.

[21]See James Loder and W. Jim Neidhardt, *The Knights Move: The Relational Logic of Spirit in Theology and Science* (Colorado Springs, Colo.: Helmers & Howard, 1992); James Loder, *The Logic of Spirit: Human Development in Theological Perspective* (San Francisco: Jossey-Bass, 1998).

practical theology limited to reflection on practice, needs to be reframed as the relation of vision and discernment. "Unlike theory, vision is less likely to be regarded as 'irrelevant' or 'absolutist' in character. Unlike practice, discernment is less likely to appear 'pragmatic' and 'utilitarian.' Vision can incorporate the 'practical' contribution provided by the social sciences, and discernment the 'conceptual' clarification that comes from philosophy. There is a dialectical relationship between vision and discernment, with each informing and correcting the other."[22] What Banks calls vision I would label interpretation, and what he calls discernment I would call understanding.

While an interactive model demonstrates the dynamic interplay between theory and practice, it does not yet depict the relation between this dynamic and truth as an objective reality from which both understanding and interpretation can be validated. This lack will be taken up later in my discussion in the form of Christopraxis.

In summary, practical theology is a dynamic process of reflective, critical inquiry into the praxis of the church in the world and God's purposes for humanity, carried out in the light of Christian Scripture and tradition, and in critical dialogue with other sources of knowledge. As a theological discipline its primary purpose is to ensure that the church's public proclamations and praxis in the world faithfully reflect the nature and purpose of God's continuing mission to the world and in so doing authentically addresses the contemporary context into which the church seeks to minister.[23] In the next chapter we will look more closely at what is meant by practical theology as a discipline of study.

---

[22]Banks, *Reenvisioning Theological Education,* pp. 48-49.
[23]This summary has been adapted from Swinton, *From Bedlam to Shalom.*

2

THE DISCIPLINE
OF PRACTICAL THEOLOGY

The discipline of practical theology extends systematic theology into the life and praxis of the Christian community. While it includes cognitive reflection on truth as doctrine, practical theology takes into account the truth of experience. John Swinton comments, "Thus in contrast to models of theology which focus on the cognitive and rational aspects of theological knowledge, the understanding of theology that informs this book sees it in terms of *whole person knowledge*. Human beings are lovers and worshipers as well as thinkers, and all of these aspects are potential sources of theological knowledge. . . . Critical, analytical thinking is important, but it is not the only source of truth."[1] As Calvin stated at the very outset of his *Institutes,* knowledge of God entails knowledge of the human person; the two are distinct but intertwined.

Practical theology demands a very specific understanding of the nature of theology. It demands that the theologian hold the practitioner accountable to the truth of God's revelation in history and that the practitioner hold the theologian accountable to the truth of God's reconciliation in humanity. T. F. Torrance reminds us that the

[1]John Swinton, *From Bedlam to Shalom: Towards a Practical Theology of Human Nature, Interpersonal Relationships and Mental Health Care* (New York: Peter Lang, 2000), p. 11.

contemporary reality and presence of Christ is what makes theology a "living theology." "As the incarnate presence of the living God in space and time, he presents himself to our faith as its living dynamic Object. This has the effect of calling for a living theology, a way of thinking which is at the same time a way of living, that cannot be abstracted from the life-giving acts of Christ in the depths of human being and must therefore affect man radically in his daily life and activity."[2] Swinton reinforces this point:

> From this it can be seen that the task of practical theology is not simply to reiterate and apply dislocated theological truths, but rather to examine theological understandings in the light of contemporary experience, in order that their meaning within God's redemptive movement *in the present* can be developed and assessed. Theological truth is thus seen to be emergent and dialectical, having to be carved out within the continuing dialogue between the Christian tradition and the historical existence of church and world.[3]

Defining Practical Theology

In modern theology it was Friedrich Schleiermacher (1768-1834) who first developed the area of practical theology, being instrumental in the formation of a Protestant chair in that discipline at the University of Berlin in 1821. In this era practical theology first took the form of a "theology of the subject." The first practical theologian in an empirical sense was C. I. Nitzsch (1787-1868), who was a disciple of Schleiermacher. He defined practical theology as the "theory of the church's practice of Christianity." This led to a shift toward the social sciences and the second major emphasis in practical theology as a "theology in the way in which the church functions."[4]

Following Scheiermacher and Nitzsch, Philip Marheineke (1780-1846) began with faith as a unity of knowledge and action. He made a distinction between theoretical theology, which thinks from the perspective of the *possibility* of a relation between life and action, and practical theology, which is based on the *reality* of that relation. As a result, the theory-praxis relation became the object of reflection and practical theology received its own independent status. The focus for innovation had to be in the local congregation. Gerben Heitink identifies this third development as a "form of political theology."[5]

Drawing on certain emphases in the Protestant Reformation, a model of practical theology developed in the early twentieth century more along the lines of pastoral

---

[2]Thomas F. Torrance, *Reality and Evangelical Theology: The Realism of Christian Revelation* (1982; reprint, Downers Grove, Ill.: InterVarsity Press, 1999), p. 138.

[3]Swinton, *From Bedlam to Shalom*, p. 11

[4]Gerben Heitink, *Practical Theology: History, Theory and Action Domains* (Grand Rapids, Mich.: Eerdmans, 1999), p. 49.

[5]Ibid., pp. 63-65.

theology. Eduard Thurneysen, an early contemporary and lifelong friend of Karl Barth, produced his classic work *A Theology of Pastoral Care,* which focused on the role of preaching as mediation of God's Word to humans so as to effect healing and hope.[6] In North America A. T. Boisen founded what became known as the pastoral counseling movement, followed by the work of Seward Hiltner.[7] The shift from pastoral theology to practical theology took place under the leadership of Don S. Browning, who published a series of essays under this title in 1983.[8]

From a European perspective Gerben Heitink offers the most comprehensive survey of the history of practical theology and its most recent developments (since the 1960s) available up to the time of this writing. Heitink says that "practical theology deals with God's activity through the ministry of human beings." More specifically, he defines practical theology as a theory of action that is "the empirically oriented theological theory of the mediation of the Christian faith in the praxis of modern society."[9] He differentiates between the praxis of mediation of the Christian faith (praxis 1) and the praxis of modern society (praxis 2). The praxis of mediation has to do with the objective content, the core of the Christian conviction. This is a form of praxis for it has to do with how human ministry communicates the unique content of God's saving intention and actions as revealed dogma. The church is the foremost channel of mediation though the ministry of Word and Spirit. Practical theology in this sense is a theological subdiscipline having its place within theology as a whole.

The praxis of modern society (praxis 2) has to do with the domain of action where "individuals and groups, motivated by their personal ideals and driven by varying interests, make specific choices and pursue specific goals." This occurs, Heitink, says, in people's everyday life, in their mutual relations, marriage, family and the workplace. Praxis 1 and praxis 2, while differentiated in theory, can never be entirely separated, for "the exercise of practical theology does not have the church, but rather society, as its horizon."[10]

As a theology of action, practical theology, in the view of Heitink, draws heavily on the paradigm of the social sciences rather than the humanities for its method. From Jürgen Habermas, Heitink makes use of the paradigm of "communicative action," which safeguards the critical perspective. In the thought of Paul Ricoeur he finds a

---

[6]Eduard Thurneysen, *A Theology of Pastoral Care* (Richmond, Va.: John Knox Press, 1962).

[7]See Glenn H. Asquith Jr., ed., *Vision from a Littler Known Country: A Boisen Reader* (Decatur, Ga.: Journal of Pastoral Care Publications, 1991); Seward Hiltner, *Pastoral Counseling* (New York: Abingdon-Cokesbury, 1949), and *Preface to Pastoral Theology* (New York: Abingdon, 1958).

[8]See Don S. Browning, ed., *Practical Theology: The Emerging Field in Theology, Church and World* (San Francisco: Harper & Row, 1983).

[9]Heitink, *Practical Theology,* pp. 6-7 (emphasis in the original).

[10]Ibid., pp. 8-9.

model of interpretation that links the hermeneutical perspective of the human sciences with the empirical perspective of the social sciences. In his way Heitink shows how practical theology can successfully bridge the gap between understanding and explaining. Practical theology, then, is more than mere practice; it is a strategic perspective that links the hermeneutical with the empirical so as to achieve an integrative theological model that underlies the theological task as a whole.[11]

Practical theology too, as Ballard and Pritchard say, "must take on the characteristics of theology as such. It too is a descriptive, normative, critical and apologetical activity. It is the means whereby the day-to-day life of the Church, in all its dimensions, is scrutinized in the light of the gospel and related to the demands and challenges of the present day, in a dialogue that both shapes Christian practice and influences the world, however minimally."[12]

John Swinton suggests that at its simplest, "practical theology is critical reflection on the actions of the church in light of the gospel and Christian tradition."[13] He cites Don Browning's definition of practical theology as "the reflective process which the church pursues in its efforts to articulate the theological grounds of practical living in a variety of areas such as work, sexuality, marriage, youth, aging and death."[14]

The Browning Model of Practical Theology

In what has become a classic in the field of practical theology, Don Browning offers a compelling and critical model that is developed from what he calls practical reason. "I claim that practical reason has an overall dynamic, an outer envelope, and an inner core."[15] Browning's model is worth exploring as an attempt to integrate theory and practice in an ongoing process of action and reflection. The concept of practical reason, for Browning, places the theological task at the center of the social context, where the theologian stands with and alongside the church mediating the gospel of Christ from the center. This mediation begins with action-reflection prompted by critical incidents that ask how the gospel of Christ answers the questions What then shall we do? and How then should we live? Practical theology thus moves out from this center toward an "outer envelope" that includes interpretive paradigms, experimental probes, historical consciousness and communities of memory.

Figure 2.1 attempts to portray schematically the components of practical reason.

---

[11]Ibid., pp. 102-3.

[12]Paul Ballard and John Pritchard, *Practical Theology in Action: Christian Thinking in the Service of Church and Society* (London: SPCK, 1996), p. 12.

[13]Swinton, *From Bedlam to Shalom,* p. 7.

[14]Don S. Browning, *The Moral Context of Pastoral Care* (Philadelphia: Westminster Press, 1976), p. 14, quoted in ibid.

[15]Don S. Browning, *A Fundamental Practical Theology* (Minneapolis: Fortress, 1991), pp. 10-11.

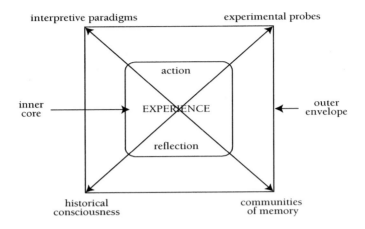

Figure 2.1. The components of practical reason

The inner core. This diagram should be read from the center outward, toward the four corners. At the center lies the "inner core," where experience raises the questions What then shall we do? and How then should we live? In the previous chapter I used the example of a divorced woman who sought answers to these two questions with regard to the possibility of remarriage. For more than simply a matter of applying church polity, this presented me with a profoundly theological issue: what is the relation between the work of Christ in redemption to the word of Christ in Scripture?

In reflecting on these questions I was forced to move outward to what Browning calls the "outer envelope"; I sought help through the larger context of historical consciousness, communities of memory and experimental probes. Browning describes the outer envelope in this way: "The outer envelope of practical reason is its fund of inherited narratives and practices that tradition has delivered to us and that always surrounds our practical thinking."[16] What systematic theology failed to resolve had become imbedded in the church's polity and practice so that rules and regulations imposed themselves on the situation. Biblical authority had become identical with interpretive paradigms and the historical consciousness of the tradition.

The woman reminded me that in our conservative theological tradition remarriage for divorced persons was considered to be unbiblical, except for certain cases, such as one being the "innocent party" of the divorce (an interpretive paradigm). My response was an "experimental probe." If one considered marriage to be somewhat

---

[16]Ibid., p. 11.

similar to keeping the sabbath, then we might consider that Jesus not only healed on the sabbath as one who had authority—"The Son of Man is Lord even of the sabbath" (Mk 21:28)—but that Jesus was also "Lord of marriage." This process is what Browning called the "overall dynamic."

Browning puts it this way: "When inherited interpretations and practices seem to be breaking down, practical reason tries to reconstruct both its picture of the world and its more concrete practices. The overall dynamic of practical reason is a broad-scale interpretive and reinterpretive process."[17]

Practical reason. Practical reason, as Browning defines it, may be what the apostle Paul used when he made the decision to circumcise Timothy in order not to hinder his ministry among Jewish Christians while, at the same time, refusing to circumcise Titus so as not to compromise his gospel of freedom from the law (cf. Acts 16:3; Gal 2:3). There was a critical incident in each case that demanded action as well as theological reflection. This can be viewed as the "inner core" in Browning's model.

Browning says, "By focusing on practical reason, I mean to point to the use of reason to answer the questions, What should we do? and How should we live? . . . the inner core functions within a narrative about God's creation, governance, and redemption of the world. . . . This narrative is the outer envelope of practical reason. It constitutes the vision that animates, informs, and provides the ontological context for practical reason."[18]

For Browning, practical theology must always be in touch with this "inner core" of human experience. Any theology that cannot respond to the questions "What should we do?" and "How should we live?" operates only within the confines of the outer envelope. At the same time, it is precisely when practical theology engages the outer envelope in its action-reflection process that it becomes a living and vital theology of the church and its mission in the world. Browning presents five levels where transformation can take place through strategic practical theology: (1) visional: a new or amended understanding of a person or community, (2) obligational: a new integration of old traditions and practices, (3) tendency-need: a more explicit way to allow people to deal with their needs in a conscious and intentional way, (4) environmental-social: a transformation of the community or the environment to more intentionally reflect theological convictions, (5) rules and roles: concrete patterns of living are changed.[19]

Objections and reservations have been voiced concerning Browning's model.

---

[17]Ibid., p. 10.
[18]Ibid., pp. 10-11.
[19]Ibid., pp. 105-8.

Ballard and Pritchard feel that Browning tends to subsume practical theology under ethics. They argue that practical theology's greatest concern is for the discovery of grace, with ethics being but one aspect of the task.[20] Todd Bolsinger also faults Browning for an overly anthropological bias in his approach, lacking sufficient focus on faith contents. Browning, according to Bolsinger, does not anchor his method sufficiently in Scripture.[21]

Browning Revised

While affirming Browning's model as one that enables practical theology to be viewed within the framework of postmodern thought, I suggest that there is a lack of christological concentration at the core and a trinitarian theology at the foundation. In my revision of Browning's model (figure 2.2), I have placed Christopraxis at the inner core. As I shall show in the next chapter, Christopraxis is the continuing ministry of Christ through the power and presence of the Holy Spirit.

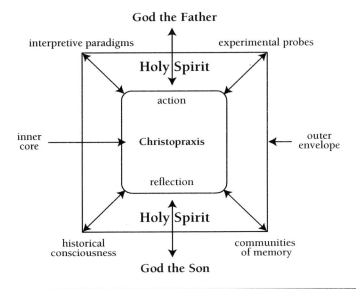

Figure 2.2. Browning's model revised

The only difference between figure 2.2 and my earlier depiction of Browning's model (figure 2.1) is that I have placed "Christopraxis" at the center rather than

---

[20]Ballard and Pritchard, *Practical Theology in Action,* p. 63.
[21]Todd Bolsinger, "The Transforming Communion: A Trinitarian Spiritual Theology" (Ph.D. diss., Fuller Theological Seminary, 2000).

"experience." While Browning would say that he does include Christology, he does so primarily as a component of systematic theology rather than at the inner core itself. In my response to the woman who was seeking an answer to the question as to "which side was God on" in her situation, I acknowledged that Christ was already present as a reality in her life and in the life of her friend. As members of our community these two demonstrated the concrete reality of the praxis of redemption through confession of sin and realized forgiveness, bearing the fruit of the Spirit. The praxis of Christ was already at work in their lives; theological reflection now took place between this praxis at work and the praxis of Christ as presented in the word of Scripture. The role of Scripture as a normative, apostolic deposit of truth remains critical for a hermeneutic of Christopraxis. This will be developed further in chapter four.

Even as the man who was born blind and healed on the sabbath became the text by which Jesus interpreted the Scripture regarding keeping the sabbath (Jn 9), so this woman and her friend constituted a "living text" by which I viewed the "written text" of Scripture and drew forth a conclusion leading to a decision. Every act of ministry teaches something about God, I tell the seminary students in my classes. Whether we are aware of it or not, each act of ministry will be interpreted by others as revealing something about the nature and purpose of God. The marriage of this couple, who had each been divorced, said something about the nature of God that I believed was consistent with what Scripture reveals about God. The ministry of Jesus, I have asserted, is as authoritative and revealing of God as the teaching of Jesus. Thus Christology as an academic discipline must also be correlated with Christopraxis as a discipline of practical theology.

This is the christological core that I feel is lacking in Browning's model. For Browning, Christology belongs to the "outer envelope" as part of the community of memory, with its historical consciousness expressed as creed and dogma. For the apostle Paul, it was the contemporary and present reality of Christ through the power of the Holy Spirit that stirred him to theological reflection. This trinitarian reality of God's ministry constitutes the threefold ministry of revelation and reconciliation.

Paul viewed the ministry of the Holy Spirit as the ministry of the risen and ascended Christ, determined to be the Son of God through resurrection from the dead (Rom 1:1-6). It was the presence of the Holy Spirit in the lives of uncircumcised Gentile believers that led Peter to baptize Cornelius and prompted Paul to declare that circumcision no longer should be a criterion of salvation through Jesus Christ (cf. Acts 10:47; Gal 5:6).

As a discipline practical theology has both a mission and ecclesial focus, set forth in that order. Mission precedes and creates the church. Mission is the praxis of God through the power and presence of the Spirit of Christ. As a result of this mission, the church comes into being as the sign of the kingdom of God in the world.

The Mission Focus of Practical Theology

Mission theology is an integral part of practical theology.[22] The mission and nature of the church have their source in the mission of God through the incarnate Messiah continuing in the world through Pentecost. This requires a theology that views the nature and mission of the church as a unity of thought and experience. Wolfhart Pannenberg supports the mission focus of practical theology.

> As a theory of the churches' activity which includes the history of the church, practical theology will have to recognise the fundamental importance of missiology to its general theme. The mission directed to all mankind is not simply the practice which originally created the church, but also the ultimate horizon on which the whole life of the church must be understood By its origin in mission the individual community is drawn into a history of divine election which looks towards a future in the kingdom of God—it is inserted into a Christian life-world which transcends its own particularity.[23]

The ongoing ministry of Christ through the power and presence of the Spirit of Christ constitutes the praxis of God's mission to the world through the church and its ministry. Thomas Groome suggests that the context of human praxis in ministry works as a social coefficient with the praxis of God in history as the context for doing theology.[24] Practical theology is a task belonging to the mission of the church and a function of those who are involved in that mission. The mission of the church is to embody in it corporate life and ministry, the continuing messianic and incarnational nature of the Son of God through the indwelling of the Holy Spirit. The nature of the church is determined in its existence as the mission of God to the world. For the church to exist as an end in itself, without a missionary praxis, is to sever its connection with the praxis of God's mission to the world. The apostle Paul's theology of the church was developed as a theology of the mission of Jesus as the praxis of the Holy Spirit.

When we grasp the heart of Paul's mission theology, we are struck by several things. First, Paul became the theologian of Pentecost, transforming it from a festival

---

[22]I have developed the concept of mission theology as a form of practical theology in my book, *Ministry on the Fireline: A Practical Theology for an Empowered Church* (Downers Grove, Ill.: InterVarsity Press, 1993), pp.114-18.

[23]Wolfhart Pannenberg, *Theology and the Philosophy of Science* (London: Darton, Longman & Todd, 1976), pp. 438-39.

[24]Thomas Groome, "Theology on Our Feet! A Revisionist Pedagogy for Healing the Gap Between Academia and Ecclesia," in *Formation and Reaction: The Promise of Practical Theology*, ed. Lewis S. Mudge and James N. Poling (Philadelphia: Fortress, 1987), p. 61.

into a foundation for the life and growth of the church. Second, Paul became the primary theologian of the apostolic church, defining the gospel of Christ as an imperative of mission before it becomes a subject of proclamation in the church. Third, Paul produced an authentic praxis theology, discovering anew the truth of the gospel in the context of Christ's ministry in the world.

Practical theology, while emerging from the inner life of the church in its mission to the world, has its praxis in the interaction of God's mission to the world. This enabled Paul to become a truly cosmic theologian, discarding the myopic lens through which one looks at God through a window on earth. Paul saw the whole cosmos, including this planet earth, as embraced by the incomprehensible love and grace of God, and all under the promise of redemption in Christ (Rom 8). Cosmic in vision, alive in praxis, apostolic in spirit and Pentecostal by nature, the church thrives where its mission theology flourishes freely. The boundaries of the mission focus of practical theology, as John Swinton reminds us, "are defined by the boundaries of God's continuing mission."[25]

The Ecclesial Focus of Practical Theology

The church, in its reflection on its existence as a missionary community, becomes the "base community" for practical theology. This provides the ecclesial focus for critical reflection on the church's nature with a view to its understanding of the nature of God and the triune life of Father, Son and Holy Spirit. As the church is involved in its mission, understood as the continuing mission of Jesus Christ through the praxis of the Spirit, its theological reflection opens up the more comprehensive discipline of exegetical and systematic theology.

At this point, Swinton cites James Fowler, who suggests that practical theology

> is critical and constructive reflection on the praxis of the Christian community's life and work in its various dimensions. As such practical theology is not self-sufficient as a discipline. Though it has and must exercise direct access to the sources of faith and theology in Scripture and tradition, it does not do so in isolation. Practical theology is part of a larger theological enterprise that includes the specialties of exegetical, historical, systematic and fundamental theological inquiry and construction.[26]

Fowler locates the axis of practical theology in the critical interface between the church and the world, which, he argues, is where the praxis of the church's life and mission should be focused. He makes the point that ecclesial praxis is located between the normative texts and practice of Scripture and tradition on the one hand,

---

[25]Swinton, *From Bedlam to Shalom,* p. 8.
[26]James Fowler, "Practical Theology and Theological Education: Some Models and Questions," *Theology Today* 42 (1985): 49.

and on the ongoing experience of the church's mission to the world on the other hand. This leads to his concept of practical theology as a form of *practical wisdom,* in which what the church does is informed by its understanding of what God is doing through its life and mission.[27]

The practical theologian seeks to interpret Scripture, tradition and praxis, in order that the contemporary praxis of both church and world can be transformed. Thomas Torrance says:

> In order to think out the relation of the Church in history to Christ we must put both these together—*mediate horizontal relation* through history to the historical Jesus Christ, and *immediate vertical relation* through the Spirit to the risen and ascended Jesus Christ. It is the former that supplies the material content, while it is the latter that supplies the immediacy of the actual encounter.[28]

Thus theory and practice are united within this form of practical knowledge which works itself out within the praxis of the church. This model of practical theology, with its emphasis on ecclesial praxis and the attainment of practical knowledge, goes a long way toward healing the rift between theory and practice. Torrance's insistence on the ecclesial context, where prayer, worship and obedient response to the Word of God take place, fits well within the scope of practical theology as we now understand it.

Practical theology, as envisioned by Torrance, therefore calls the church back to its roots as a fundamentally missionary church with a particular vision and a specific task to perform in the world. As a missionary church it is crucial that it remains faithful to its missiological task and vision. One of the primary tasks of the practical theologian is to ensure that the church is challenged and enabled to achieve this task faithfully.

In this chapter I have discussed the discipline of practical theology from both a historical and contemporary perspective. Don Browning's version of practical reason has been offered as a model of practical theology that fits well within the framework of a postmodern view of reality but at the same time preserves the principle of biblical authority and the relevance of tradition and historical consciousness.

---

[27]"In its efforts to interpret and respond to present context and issues of praxis, it draws on the hermeneutical aids of a variety of humanities and social scientific disciplines. In its own subdisciplinary foci, practical theology attends to various particular dimensions of ecclesial praxis as models of action in and interaction with persons and contexts of personal and social formation and transformation" (Fowler, "Practical Theology and Theological Education," p. 50, quoted in Swinton, *From Bedlam to Shalom,* pp. 9-10).

[28]Thomas F. Torrance, *Space, Time, and Resurrection* (Grand Rapids, Mich.: Eerdmans, 1976), p. 147 (emphasis in the original).

James Fowler led us to consider both the missiological and ecclesiological aspects of practical theology as a form of practical wisdom. What seems lacking in both Fowler and Browning is a christological core of praxis within a trinitarian structure of God's ministry as the basis for all ministry. The following chapters are intended to make up for this deficiency and to contribute a more adequate *theological* foundation for practical theology.

3

A TRINITARIAN MODEL
OF PRACTICAL THEOLOGY

Practical theology, as Don Browning has reminded us, begins with the inner core of the church's ministry where two questions arise out of a crisis of experience: What then should we do? and How then should we live?[1] While these are intensely practical questions, they are also profoundly theological.

In my encounter with pastors enrolled in continuing education seminars, I have found that for the most part they were inoculated with enough theology at seminary to provide lifelong immunity. As a generalization, I realize this is not fair. At the same time, despite theological controversies that rock the foundations of many denominations and some churches, the sources to which most pastors refer in seeking wisdom for their daily ministries are not usually found in theological books but in polity manuals. In many cases the question for the pastor becomes "What then should I do?" out of concern for his or her own theological integrity. The question "How then should we live?" as the practical question emerging out of the crisis of life is already contained in the answer to the first.

A pastor, whom I will call Larry, asked my counsel with regard to a situation in his

---

[1]Don Browning, *A Fundamental Practical Theology* (Minneapolis: Fortress, 1991).

church causing a great deal of anguish for him personally as well as for the members of the church. When a new choir was formed, a man from the congregation volunteered and was accepted as a regular member. While this man was a faithful attendee at the church, it was also well-known that he had been divorced and that he and the woman with whom he was living had never been legally married, though they presented themselves as a typical family, including the three children from her former marriage.

"The crisis came," Larry told me, "when I confronted the man with this situation and asked him to drop out of the choir. I told him that as long as he was living with a woman without legally being married to her, his presence in the choir compromised the ministry of the entire choir. He accepted this fact and withdrew, remaining in attendance at the church. When other members of the church found out about it, the thing blew up in my face. Even the choir director, who was a strong supporter of my ministry, accosted me the following week and said, 'Pastor, how could you do such a thing? Don't you have any compassion?'"

As Larry went on to describe the events of the following weeks and months, it became clear that he was also in a crisis, both theologically and personally. He had barely survived in his role as pastor with the help of a denominational official who intervened and stabilized the conflict.

Larry defended his action by saying that it was a matter of principle and that the character and integrity of his own ministry was at stake in allowing a man to participate in the morning worship service in the choir while living with a woman to whom he was not legally married. "I think that I do have compassion," he told me, "but how could I give approval to a relationship that was clearly wrong in the sight of God? I may have handled it wrong, and I have admitted that, but I am not able to approve of a relationship not consecrated by marriage."

I probed gently. Would he have permitted the man to remain in the choir if he had walked in a week later with a marriage certificate signed by a local justice of the peace and duly recorded with the proper legal authorities? "Yes," he replied, " that would have resolved the whole problem."

I pressed further. Does the civil authority have the power to consecrate what you called an unconsecrated relationship in God's eyes? He hesitated. "I don't like to think of it that way," he replied. "I think that it is a matter of obedience to God and that living together without being married is disobedience and thus a sin before God. I felt that allowing him to sing in the choir would compromise my own pastoral leadership and lower the spiritual quality of the church's ministry."

I have discovered that most pastors eventually feel caught in similar situations where they are expected to show compassion while at the same time uphold standards of holiness and biblical principle. It might be the matter of remarriage for persons who have been divorced or the marriage of a Christian believer to an unbeliever. It may be the issue of allowing a member of the church board who suddenly is revealed to be an alcoholic to continue in a leadership position. Whatever the circumstances, the issue of what constitutes a standard of holiness and what can be viewed as consecrated by God becomes a test of pastoral integrity and congregational maturity.

Larry thought that the issue was between the human quality of compassion and his theology of sanctification. He discovered that the real issue was his own theology of holiness in tension with the praxis of the Spirit of Jesus at work in the lives of the people in his congregation. He had attempted to be a prophet in the sense that the self-righteous Pharisee used the term. In so doing, he failed to be a pastor in the sense of the ministry as Jesus defined it. In effect, Larry answered Browning's first question in such a way as to defend his own pastoral role and to satisfy his theological conscience. How then should I live? became for him the only question. The question for the couple, How then should we live? was not considered as a basis for his theological reflection. As it turned out, he was caught between his systematic and biblical theology and the demands of practical theology.

A more helpful approach would have been to have quietly counseled the couple to have their union blessed by the affirmation of the congregation and for their "common law marriage" to be legally certified. Paul's counsel is apropos at this point: "Let us therefore no longer pass judgment on one another, but resolve instead never to put a stumbling block or hindrance in the way of another" (Rom 14:13). The questions raised by practical theology are hermeneutical questions, questions that seek the mind of Christ through Scripture as applied in a concrete situation.

The Hermeneutics of Practical Theology

Practical theology is essentially a hermeneutical theology. That is to say, theological reflection that begins in the context and crisis of ministry seeks to read the texts of Scripture in light of the texts of lives that manifest the work of Christ through the Holy Spirit as the truth and will of God. Present interpretation of Scripture must be as faithful to the eschatological reality and authority of Christ as to scriptural reality and authority. This is why the hermeneutics of practical theology is a theological hermeneutic and not merely a spiritual hermeneutic.

Jürgen Moltmann suggests that a "hermeneutics of origin," which grounds theology in Scripture alone (*sola Scriptura*) must understand that Scripture is grounded in Christ, not only historically but eschatologically. "The hermeneutics of christology's origin must therefore be complemented by the hermeneutics of its effects."[2] The

---

[2]Jürgen Moltmann, *The Way of Jesus Christ: Christology in Messianic Dimensions* (San Francisco: Harper

hermeneutics of practical theology seeks what is normative in Jesus Christ, as the inspired source of the written Word and the objective reality of Christ as the praxis of the Holy Spirit in the context of ministry.[3]

The criterion for the praxis of the Spirit as discerned in the ministry context is not determined by cultural relevance or pragmatic expediency. It is the work of the risen Jesus Christ that becomes the criterion in the praxis of the Holy Spirit. It is this contemporary work (praxis) of Christ through the Holy Spirit that becomes normative and calls the church into repentance, where it has imposed its own normative and binding rules. We, of course, are not apostles, nor is Scripture replaced as a normative text by our own experience of the Holy Spirit. Rather, as will be shown in later chapters, the risen Christ as the true and continuing apostle, through the ministry of the Holy Spirit, binds the word of Christ in Scripture to the work of Christ through the Spirit.

The claim that the praxis of the Spirit revealed the truth of Jesus Christ was, for Paul, the basis for his mission theology. He could no longer require circumcision when he saw that the Spirit of Jesus worked equally among the circumcised and the uncircumcised. He could no longer require the observance of sabbath and cultic laws of the Old Testament when he saw that Christ himself is the substance of that righteousness to which these laws pointed (Col 2).

Having the Spirit of Christ is to have the substance of Christ, Paul argued. In this way theological reflection upon the law and prophets became a christological hermeneutic. The law was now interpreted through Christ, so that those who have the Spirit of Christ cannot be judged by anyone—for "we have the mind of Christ" (1 Cor 2:15-16). "Do not let anyone condemn you in matters of food and drink or of observing festivals, new moons, or sabbaths. These are only a shadow of what is come, but the substance belongs to Christ" (Col 2:16-17).

Paul viewed the ministry of the Holy Spirit as the ministry of the risen and ascended Christ, determined to be the Son of God through resurrection from the

---

& Row, 1990), pp. 43-44. This follows closely my own suggestion that Christopraxis has hermeneutical significance in relating the effects of Christ's contemporary work with the inspired word of Christ in Scripture.

[3]The hermeneutical significance of the Holy Spirit is argued by Douglas Hall when he writes, "It is particularly the Holy Spirit who provides the dogmatic basis for the insistence that theological reflection necessarily means engagement with the historical context. The corrective to a theology which has neglected or dismissed the context by means of a rationalized and doctrinaire concentration on the second person of the Trinity is a theology which is goaded into engagement with the worldly reality by a fresh apprehension of the Holy Spirit. For the Spirit will permit us to rest neither in the church nor in doctrinal formulations that know everything ahead of time. The Spirit will drive us, as it drove Jesus, to the wilderness of worldly temptation and the garden of worldly suffering" (Douglas John Hall, *Thinking the Faith: Christian Theology in a North American Context* [Minneapolis: Augsburg, 1989], p. 105).

dead (Rom 1:1-6). It was the presence of the Holy Spirit in the lives of uncircumcised Gentile believers that led Peter to baptize Cornelius and led Paul to declare that circumcision no longer should be a criterion of salvation through Jesus Christ (cf. Acts 10:47; Gal 5:6).

Having his own apostolic authority grounded in the Spirit of Christ, which encountered and taught him, and having followed the Spirit in his mission itinerary and strategy, he had to argue the essential unity of the Spirit, of Christ and of God. The nature of God, if we are to use that language, was not for Paul a matter of specifying three natures contained within one deity. Rather, the nature of God is manifested in God's working through the Spirit and through the Son, Jesus Christ. God is one, not as a mathematical point but as the unity of being present in the threefold activity of Father, Son and Holy Spirit.

The Trinitarian Foundation of Practical Theology

The Spirit poured out at the first Pentecost provides the theological praxis for a doctrine of the Trinity. Paul argued passionately and profoundly for the unity of God in his work as Spirit within us, Christ with us and the Father around us. A practical theology cannot be truly evangelical and trinitarian without also being a Pentecostal theology. Nor can a Pentecostal theology be effective in mission without also being trinitarian in nature.

Paul's profound grasp of the trinitarian relations between Holy Spirit, Christ and God the Father is the ground for his teaching and ministry. His theological reflection is more substantive than merely ethical instruction. What was at stake was the very heart of the revelation of God through the law and the prophets, as well as through the incarnation of God in Christ.

Here we see the trinitarian foundation for practical theology emerging. When we remember that Paul's ministry and the writing of this letter preceded the writing of the four Gospels, we see the emergence of a trinitarian theology from within mission theology. To be sure, what came to the early disciples following Easter as a commission directly from the risen Lord was part of the oral tradition that Paul would have learned immediately following his conversion. Yet more than any other witness to the resurrection, it was Paul who carried out this commission of Christ and so was led to develop a theology of the continuing mission of Christ through the Spirit.

The praxis of the Spirit of the risen Christ constituted the "new school of theology" for Paul. As he proclaimed the gospel of a crucified and resurrected Messiah, he witnessed the convicting and transforming power of the Holy Spirit. He reminded the church at Thessalonica of this compelling testimony to the power of the gospel when he wrote, "Our message of the gospel came to you not in word only, but also in power and in the Holy Spirit and with full conviction; . . . you turned to God from idols, to serve a living and true God, and to wait for his Son from heaven, whom he raised from the dead—Jesus, who rescues us from the wrath that is coming" (1 Thess 1:5, 9-10).

A theology of Pentecost is the beginning point for a theology of Jesus Christ because the Holy Spirit reveals to us the inner life of God as the Father of Jesus and of Jesus as the Son of the Father. To receive the Spirit of God, wrote the apostle Paul, is to "have the mind of Christ" (1 Cor 2:10, 16). Jesus said, "All things have been handed over to me by my Father; and no one knows the Son except the Father, and no one knows the Father except the Son and anyone to whom the Son chooses to reveal him" (Mt 11:27).

The practical theologian is the theologian of the Holy Spirit, who points to and participates in the creative indivisibility of the God who holds all things together.[4] The Holy Spirit is the revelation to us of the inner being of God as constituted by the relations between Father and Son. For this reason, practical theology is grounded in the intratrinitarian ministry of the Father toward the world, the Son's ministry to the Father on behalf of the world and the Spirit's empowering of the disciples for ministry.

Jesus' Ministry to the Father on Behalf of the World

The conversation on the airplane became somewhat more intense when my seatmate discovered that I was a teacher of theology at a Christian seminary. "You Christians are always trying to get converts," he said. "I served for six years in the Peace Corps helping people learn how to grow their own food using more effective farming techniques. We contributed directly to the physical welfare of these people. As I recall, Jesus called himself a servant too. What's the big difference?"

"If you are a servant," I replied, "it might make a difference who it is that you are serving. Servants have masters. Who is your master?"

"I knew it," he said, shaking his head, "You are trying to convert me!" He was good natured about it and, as the plane was beginning its descent, we settled back, each in our own thoughts.

My own thoughts carried over into the pastors' seminar I was teaching. I broached the subject to them, each of whom was a seminary graduate. "When you think of Jesus' ministry as a servant, what is the most distinctive aspect of that ministry?" I asked. The responses were what I expected. His service was done in love, it was indiscriminate with regard to race and religion, it was entirely without regard for his own needs, and it ended up costing him his life.

"What was the primary motivation for his service?" I prodded. Again the answers

---

[4]A saying of John V. Taylor, quoted by Paul Ballard and John Pritchard in *Practical Theology in Action: Christian Thinking in the Service of Church and Society* (London: SPCK, 1996), p. 41.

were predictable. He was moved with compassion for those in need, he had a mission to accomplish, and as the Scripture says, "Having loved those who were in the world, he loved them to the end" (Jn 13:1). I was reminded that the towel with which he girded himself as he assumed the role of the servant in washing the feet of his disciples was the primary biblical metaphor of servanthood.

"Would you then agree," I said, "that Jesus was the servant of the world on behalf of God?" The agreement was unanimous, and I noted several writing this statement down in their notes, assuming that this was the first point in the lecture.

"Well I don't agree," I replied. "I think that way of stating it misses the crucial point in the servanthood of Jesus. It is not the ministry of Jesus to the world on behalf of God that made him a servant, but his ministry to the Father on behalf of the world."

"Find a need and fill it" is a popular maxim meant to motivate Christians for a ministry of service. But the needs of the world did not set the agenda for the ministry of Jesus. It is true that wherever the needs of the world impinged on him, he reached out to heal the sick and feed the hungry. But hunger, sickness and even death did not set the agenda for his ministry.

When Lazarus was sick and dying, his two sisters, Mary and Martha, sent word to Jesus. "Lord, he whom you love is ill" (Jn 11:3). The context is clear and compelling. Mary and Martha, along with their brother, Lazarus, had often provided hospitality for Jesus in the little village of Bethany. As the sisters indicated, there was an unusual bond of love between Jesus and Lazarus.

If we could place their request in the vernacular of today's language, we might hear them say, "Jesus, Lazarus your beloved friend is sick unto death, and you have the pills in your pocket to cure him." Indeed he did! He had earlier interrupted a funeral and raised a widow's son from death (Lk 7:12), and had healed many from various diseases and infirmities. Yet, we are told, "Accordingly, though Jesus loved Martha and her sister and Lazarus, after having heard that Lazarus was ill, he stayed two days longer in the place where he was" (Jn 11:5-6).

What do we make of this? Some commentators hold that the chronology suggests that Jesus knew that Lazarus was already dead by the time that he received the message and that this accounts for his delay. From the perspective of the sisters, however, any delay was unforgivable. Each of them in turn accused Jesus when he arrived: "Lord, if you had been here, my brother would not have died" (Jn 11:21, 32).

This much is clear. The love of Jesus for Lazarus and the desperate plea of the two sisters did not set the agenda for the ministry of Jesus. This need from the side of the world did not take precedence over his commitment to serve the Father. It is the Father who loves the world and sends his Son (Jn 3:16). Jesus does not have to love Lazarus more than the Father.

The inner logic of Jesus' ministry is grounded in his obedience as the Son to the Father. Consequently, the first priority of Jesus is to serve the Father who sends him into the world.

When Jesus did arrive and found Lazarus had been dead for several days, he asked that the stone be removed. The sisters protest and attempt to stop his ministry! Martha said to him, "Lord, already there is a stench because he has been dead four days" (Jn 11:39). Jesus replied, "Did I not tell you that if you believed, you would see the glory of God?" (Jn 11:40). And Lazarus came forth.

The sisters had a concept of Jesus' ministry that was based on response to human need. They knew that as long as their brother was only sick, he might still be healed if only Jesus could arrive in time. Death, however, is not a need that a physician can meet. Death, to their minds, was a reality that required its own ministry: respect and care for the one who has died, and sealing the tomb as a boundary between life and death. This is why they attempted to stop the ministry of Jesus. The boundary of death set limits to their expectation. Jesus crossed that boundary as one sent by the Father in order that the glory of God might be revealed in the raising of Lazarus. Lazarus was restored to life and to other needs that would demand attention. The difference between a ministry founded on the meeting of needs and one directed by the will and wisdom of God is worth discovering. The ministry of Jesus to the Father on behalf of the world is the inner logic of all ministry. Every aspect of the ministry of Jesus is grounded in the inner relation of mutual love and care between the Father and the Son. On behalf of the world, Jesus offers up to the Father a ministry of prayer, worship, obedience and service. His ministry is first of all directed to God and not to the world. The needs of the world are recognized and brought into this ministry but do not set the agenda.

In the incident with Lazarus we can see the inner logic present in every act of Jesus' ministry. He understood clearly that he could only do what the Father sent him to do. "Very truly, I tell you," said Jesus, "the Son can do nothing on his own, but only what he sees the Father doing; for whatever the Father does, the Son does likewise. The Father loves the Son and shows him all that he himself is doing" (Jn 5:19-20). Jesus drew human need into his own ministry of service to the Father. In this ministry to the Father, all ministry on behalf of the world is taken up and fulfilled. There is no ministry that belongs to the church or to members of the body of Christ that is not already grounded in the ministry of Jesus. [5]

Jesus' Ministry in the Spirit for the Sake of the Church

There is no ministry of Jesus recorded in Scripture prior to his anointing by the Spirit

---

[5]I have discussed this at greater length in The Soul of Ministry: Forming Leaders for God's People (Louisville, Ky.: Westminster John Knox, 1997), chap. 9.

of God at his baptism. It is by the power of the Spirit that he heals the sick, proclaims the good news and casts out demons. "But if it is by the Spirit of God that I cast out demons, then the kingdom of God has come to you" (Mt 12:28). As the Messiah sent by God, Jesus fulfilled the prophetic promise that pointed forward to the coming of the Spirit as the source of healing and hope (Is 61:1; Lk 4:16-19).

Jesus was sent into the world on behalf of the Father to create a true form of humanity in the midst of the world. In the face of all that is inhuman, whether in secular or religious form, Jesus lived a truly human life. As he was sent into the world, Jesus took up both sides of the ministry of the Father. Jesus brought to the world the good news of the gospel of love for the world. At the same time, Jesus came forward from the side of the estranged and broken world to be healed to reconcile humanity to God. Thomas Torrance says it eloquently when he writes, "The Church cannot be in Christ without being in Him as He is proclaimed to men in their need and without being in Him as He encounters us in and behind the existence of every man in his need. Nor can the Church be recognized as His except in that meeting of Christ with Himself in the depth of human misery, where Christ clothed with His Gospel meets with Christ clothed with the desperate need and plight of men."[6]

Jesus is the incarnation of the divine Logos and, as such, stands with humans offering up to God the true ministry of service on their behalf. At the same time, Jesus stands among humans as the very presence of God bringing to bear the reality of divine mercy, grace and love for persons in their need.

Having completed his ministry to the Father on behalf of the world and having prepared in his own body a dwelling place for the Spirit of God, Jesus, following his resurrection, promised the gift of the Spirit to his followers as a continuation of his ministry on earth. With the coming of the Holy Spirit at Pentecost, the believers were constituted as the gathered body and empowered to become the serving and ministering body. Called out of the world in conformity to Christ, the early church was sent into the world on his behalf empowered by the Holy Spirit.

While the disciples and early believers were followers of Jesus and witnesses to his resurrection, they were powerless until the Spirit came on them at Pentecost. Incarnation without baptism in the Spirit would leave Jesus powerless, even though he was the Son of God. Resurrection without Pentecost would leave believers powerless even though through faith they had become children of God.

The Church's Ministry to the World on Behalf of Jesus
Pentecost is the pivotal point from which we can look back to the incarnation of God

---

[6]Thomas Torrance, "Service in Jesus Christ," in *Theological Foundations for Ministry*, ed. Ray S. Anderson (Grand Rapids, Mich.: Eerdmans, 1979), p. 724.

in Jesus of Nazareth and look forward into our contemporary life and witness to Jesus Christ in the world. Pentecost is more than a historical and instrumental link between a theology of the incarnation and a theology of the institutional church. Pentecost is more than the birth of the church; it is the indwelling power of the Spirit of Christ as the source of the church's life and ministry.

Figure 3.1 depicts the continuity of spiritual empowerment and the ministry of Jesus. Prior to his death and resurrection Jesus ministered in the power of the Spirit. Following his resurrection and the coming of the Holy Spirit on the day of Pentecost, the early church experienced the power of the Spirit in ministry.

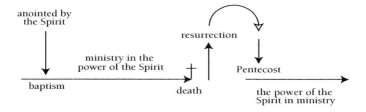

Figure 3.1. Continuity of spiritual empowerment and the ministry of Jesus

Reading the diagram in figure 3.1 from left to right, we see how the Spirit of God anointed Jesus for his ministry. Following his death and resurrection the Spirit now descends on the believers empowering them to be his witnesses in the world. In Jesus, prior to his resurrection, we see his ministry in the power of the Spirit. Following Pentecost, we see the power of the Spirit in ministry through the church, thus ensuring continuity between the ministry of God in Jesus, the ministry of Jesus in service to God, and the ministry of the Spirit as the ministry of Christ in the world.

While the disciples and early believers were followers of Jesus and witnesses to his resurrection, they were powerless until the Spirit came on them at Pentecost. Incarnation without baptism in the Spirit would leave Jesus powerless, even though he was the Son of God. Resurrection without Pentecost would leave believers powerless even though through faith they had become children of God.

A Practical Theology of Spiritual Empowerment

Pentecost has more to do with empowering through the Spirit than being filled with the Spirit. While this may surprise us, let us consider how the New Testament views the relation of the Spirit to empowering. Luke, in the book of Acts, says that the 120 in the upper room were "filled with the Holy Spirit" on the day of Pentecost (Acts 2:4). Subsequently, certain individuals and gathered people were said to be "filled with the Holy Spirit" (Peter, Acts 4:8; the believers, Acts 4:31; Stephen, Acts 7:55;

Saul of Tarsus, Acts 9:17; 13:9; the disciples, Acts 13:52). While these are quite specific instances, they are relatively few considering the importance Luke gives to the Holy Spirit in the book of Acts.

At the same time, Luke made it clear that it was power that the Holy Spirit was to bring, not merely "fullness." "But you will receive power when the Holy Spirit has come upon you; and you will be my witnesses in Jerusalem, in all Judea and Samaria, and to the ends of the earth" (Acts 1:8). Stephen was "full of grace and power" and thus performed great wonders and signs prior to Luke's description of Stephen being "filled with the Spirit" (Acts 6:8; 7:55). Overall, Luke's emphasis is on what I have called empowerment rather than simply an experience of being filled with the Spirit (cf. Acts 2:11, 22; 4:7, 33; 8:10, 19; 10:38).

In a study of Paul's writings, however, it becomes clear that his emphasis was not on the "filling of the Spirit," as such, but on the "power of the Spirit." In only one place does Paul explicitly speak of the filling of the Spirit. "Do not get drunk with wine, for that is debauchery; but be filled with the Spirit" (Eph 5:18). A better translation of the Greek verb (*plēron*) used in this verse might be, "seek the fullness that the Spirit gives." The Greek word *plērōma* has more the idea of moving into fullness rather than a container being filled to capacity.

On the other hand, when we read Paul's letters looking for his reference to power and the power of the Spirit, we find more than two dozen references. For example, "I pray that, according to the riches of his glory, he may grant that you may be strengthened in your inner being with power through his Spirit" (Eph 3:16); "for God did not give us a spirit of cowardice, but rather a spirit of power and of love and of self-discipline" (2 Tim 1:7; cf. Rom 15:13, 19; 1 Cor 2:4; 1 Thess 1:5).

The promise and expectation leading to the Pentecost event was in the context of a community of ministry, not personal edification as an end in itself. It was for the purpose of being witnesses of the power of the resurrection "to the ends of the earth" that the promise of spiritual empowerment was given (Acts 1:8). Empowerment for ministry is the express purpose for which one seeks the "filling of the Holy Spirit." Where there is empowered ministry, there is also the filling of the Spirit. The evidences for the Spirit's presence are found in the manifestation of the Spirit's power. This is why Paul appealed to the power of the Spirit manifest in his ministry rather than to his own experience of being "filled with the Spirit" in defense of his apostolic credentials (e.g., Rom 15:19; 1 Cor 1:17; 2:4-5; 14:13; 2 Cor 12:9).

The evidence of empowerment is not always in the obvious results but in the unswerving commitment and the inexplicable devotion to a task. The empowerment of the Spirit did not diminish in the life and ministry of Jesus as he moved relentlessly toward the cross. It was only then that the true nature of empowerment became clear. When the other disciples wavered and abandoned him, his own pathway became clear and compelling (Lk 13:33; 18:31-34).

With the death of Jesus the disciples concluded that the mission was over and that there was nothing left to do but return to their former lives. Even when they were told of his resurrection, they were unable to translate this good news into personal empowerment. The final words of the resurrected Jesus gave them their clue: "But you will receive power when the Holy Spirit has come upon you; and you will be my witnesses in Jerusalem, in all Judea and Samaria, and to the ends of the earth" (Acts 1:8).

He did not leave with them a manual with techniques and skills gained through equipping. Rather, he promised them the empowerment of the Spirit. This began at Pentecost and continues to this very day as the Spirit's ministry through Jesus for the sake of the church.

Practical theology needs a solid theological foundation in order that the "practical" not overwhelm and determine the theological. At the same time, the subject matter of theology is not embedded in the historical consciousness of the community in the form of its creeds and dogma alone. Rather, theology must continue to reflect on the contemporary work of the Holy Spirit as the praxis of the risen Christ. This will be developed further in the chapter that follows.

4

PRACTICAL THEOLOGY
AS CHRISTOPRAXIS
Hermeneutical Implications

The word *praxis* as I intend its meaning must be distinguished from *practice,* which is ordinarily understood as the application of theory. *Practice* tends to refer to tasks which carry out a plan or actions that relate theory to a task. Thus, we often speak of physicians having a *practice,* or the *practice* of a psychotherapist as the task of providing therapy in a clinical setting. *Praxis,* on the other hand, also involves tasks, but in the performing of the tasks, meaning is discovered, not merely applied. It is in this sense that Don Browning discusses the kind of practice that is "theory-laden."

> By using the phrase theory-laden, I mean to rule out in advance the widely held assumption that theory is distinct from practice. All our practices, even our religious practices, have theories behind and within them. We may not notice the theories in our practices. We are so embedded in our practices, take them so much for granted, and view them as so natural and self-evident that we never take time to abstract the theory from the practice and look at it as something in itself.[1]

---

[1]Don Browning, *A Fundamental Practical Theology: Descriptive and Strategic Proposals* (Minneapolis: Fortress, 1996), p. 6. Swinton says that "Browning goes on to develop a model of practical theology that emphasizes the concept of phronesis: it begins with praxis, moves to reflection on praxis and returns to praxis. For Browning the task of the practical theologian is to excavate the hidden layers of meaning that indwell the praxis of the church community. Browning presents a framework that will

John Swinton says that "praxis is relective because it is action that not only seeks to achieve particular ends but also reflects on the means and the ends of such action in order to assess the validity of both in the light of its guiding vision. Praxis is theory-laden because it includes theory as a vital constituent. It is not just reflective action but reflective action that is laden with belief."[2]

Praxis as Truth in Action

When we speak of praxis, says Swinton, we are

> referring to a practical form of knowledge which generates actions through which the church community lives out its beliefs (holistic, theory-laden action). . . . The act of friendship is a form of praxis. It is the embodiment of particular theological understandings. What at first glance appears to be a simple relational practice, on reflection in the light of the gospel, proves to contain deep levels of theological meaning. In a very real sense belief is embedded within the act itself. The act is found to be expressive of particular beliefs and as such is an appropriate subject for critical theological enquiry.[3]

> In this sense, praxis finds its biblical foundation in the actualization of John 3:21: "But whoever lives by the truth comes into the light, so that it may be plainly seen that what he has done has been done through God."[4]

> Praxis then reveals theology in a very tangible form. In this sense, *actions are themselves theological* and as such are open to theological reflection and critique. Thus the praxis of the church is in fact the embodiment of its theology.[5]

> Christian praxis is understood as the medium through which the Christian community embodies and enacts its fundamental vision of the gospel. Theology is properly conceived as a performative discipline in which the criterion of authenticity is deemed to be orthopraxis, or authentic transformatory action, rather than orthodoxy (right belief).[6]

The word *practice* ordinarily refers to the methods and means by which we apply a skill or theory. This tends to separate truth from method or action so that one assumes that what is true can be deduced or discovered apart from the action or

---

[1] enable congregations to engage in critical moral reasoning in order that the authenticity and moral appropriateness of their praxis can be assessed and tested. Browning's work is a good example of the contemporary movement within practical theology, away from the applied model toward a more praxis-centered model" (John Swinton, *From Bedlam to Shalom: Towards a Practical Theology of Human Nature, Interpersonal Relationships and Mental Health Care* [New York: Peter Lang, 2000] pp. 14-15).

[2] Swinton, *From Bedlam to Shalom,* p. 11.

[3] Ibid.

[4] Ibid., p 15.

[5] Ibid., p.11

[6] Elaine L. Graham. *Transforming Practice: Pastoral Theology in an Age of Uncertainty* (New York: Mowbray, 1996), p. 7, quoted in Swinton, *From Bedlam to Shalom,* p. 11.

activity that applies it in practice. I mean by praxis something of what Aristotle meant when he distinguished between *poiēsis* as an act of making something where the telos lay outside of the act of making and praxis as an act that includes the telos within the action itself. The telos of something is its final purpose, meaning or character.[7] Praxis is an action that includes the telos, or final meaning and character of truth. It is an action in which the truth is discovered through action, not merely applied or "practiced." In praxis one is not only guided in one's actions by the intention of realizing the telos, or purpose, but by discovering and grasping this *telos* through the action itself.

A schematic diagram of the difference between *poiēsis* and praxis can be seen in figure 4.1.

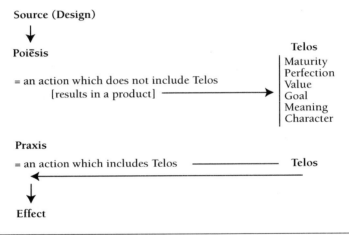

Figure 4.1. The difference between *poiēsis* and praxis

In this diagram note that the action of *poiēsis* begins with a theoretical design and through the action produces a product. The telos of that action, however, is not included in the action nor in the product. With praxis however, while the theoretical design would also be the source from which the action begins, by including the telos as the ultimate goal and purpose of the action, the action not only produces a product

---

[7]See Aristotle *Nichomachean Ethics* 9.6.5. The use of the term *praxis* in contemporary theology has been greatly influenced by the quasi-Marxist connotation given to it by some Latin American liberation theologians. My own attempt in using the word is to recover the authentically biblical connotation of God's actions which reveal his purpose and truth. I appreciate the concept of praxis as used by Orlando Costas (see *The Church and Its Mission: A Shattering Critique from the Third World* [Wheaton, Ill.: Tyndale House, 1974]). I have discussed this further in Ray S. Anderson, "Christopraxis: Competence as a Criterion for Theological Education," *Theological Students Fellowship (TSF) Bulletin,* January-February 1984.

but the action is accountable to the telos and, in moving toward the telos, is informed by the telos as to the kind of action required in order to produce the intended effect. Through the prophet, God points to the effect that the Word intends to produce as an ultimate result: "So shall my word be that goes out from my mouth; it shall not return to me empty, but it shall accomplish that which I purpose, and succeed in the thing for which I sent it" (Is 55:11).

For example, a builder might be asked to build a house in accordance with a specific design and blueprint. When the house is finished, the builder is paid in full if the building has been constructed according to the design. If, after several years, persons living in the house commit illegal or immoral acts, the builder of the house cannot be held liable for these actions. In other words, the ultimate use, or telos, of the house was not part of the builder's responsibility. This is *poiēsis* and not praxis. In praxis the telos of the action includes the ultimate purpose or goal of the action so that not only is one held accountable for the final purpose, but through the action the truth of the action becomes revealed.

Consider the task of constructing a sermon from the Bible. If the sermon manuscript itself, based on exegetical methods faithful to the text, becomes the goal with no regard for its effect when read, this is *poiēsis*. If when the manuscript is read, the heart of no person is convicted of sin and turns to God, then the telos of the sermon as an event of the Word of God preached is not reached. The production of a sermon manuscript and the mere verbalization of its content does not constitute praxis, for praxis necessarily involves the realization of an intended result or effect. The homiletics professor in seminary might award an A grade to the sermon manuscript, but from the standpoint of the purpose of the Word of God, the sermon has not realized its telos until the Word of God has had an effect (Is 55:11). Praxis includes the effect of the Word as well as a presentation of it.

The preparing and preaching of a sermon from the Word of God ought to include praxis as well as *poiēsis*. It follows then that the *effect* of the Word of God is bound to the authority and power of the Word in the same way as its source is inspired by the Spirit of God. What the Word of God creates in its proclamation belongs to the truth and authority of the Word, and not to the human act of proclaiming.

In the case of a sermon the truth of the Word of God resides in the Scripture text as originally inspired by the Holy Spirit through the human author. The praxis of the preaching event, however, goes beyond the preparation of a sermon manuscript and includes the power of the inspired Word to accomplish God's purpose in the human heart. The truth and authority of the inspired text thus finds its completion (telos) in producing a truthful response. This is what I mean by praxis as the "inner logic" of the relation of the written Word to the preached word.

A theology of preaching thus emerges from within the context of the preached

Word and not in abstraction from it. This means that there are truths contained within the inspired Word of Scripture that are only discovered and revealed through the praxis of teaching and preaching. This does not mean that careful exegetical methods of determining what the biblical text says can be disregarded. On the contrary, we must take up the biblical text with full commitment to its intrinsic character as the Word of God written. At the same time, by the authority of the Scripture itself, we must take with the same seriousness the praxis of the Holy Spirit by which our preaching and teaching reaches God's purpose in the transformation of human hearts and lives. Within such a context, one might define ecclesial praxis as a *dynamic human process of critical reflection carried out.*

In praxis, God's truth is revealed through the structures of reality by which God's actions and presence are disclosed to us through our own actions. It is not our human actions that constitute the praxis of God. Rather, God acts through our human actions to reveal the truth. The truth of God's Word, for example, is not something that can be extracted from the Bible by the human mind so that one can possess this truth as a formula or doctrine without regard to its purpose of bringing us "into the truth." There is also true doctrine as opposed to false doctrine. But God's truth does not end with our concept of truth, nor is the human mind the absolute criterion for God's truth. God is the authority for what is true of God. How could it be otherwise? "Let God be proved true," wrote Paul, "although every one is a liar" (Rom 3:4).

Ballard and Pritchard include praxis as one of their four models of doing practical theology. "The term praxis points to the fact that all practice reflects the inner dynamic that informs it. . . . Out of the practice comes a new praxis which, hopefully, enables creativity and growth."[8]

When Jesus experienced the work of God through a miraculous healing on the sabbath (Jn 9), he argued that the truth of the sabbath was to be found in the restoration of humanity, not in keeping the law of sabbath. When challenged by the Pharisees as to his view of the sabbath, he responded, "The sabbath was made for humankind, not humankind for the sabbath; so the Son of man is Lord even of the sabbath" (Mk 2:27). This is what is meant by praxis. The work of God in our midst discloses to us the word of God, even as the Word of God reveals its truth in producing God's work. God's Word of truth reaches its telos in healing, making whole, and restoring God's created purpose. This is the praxis of God's Word as truth.

Christopraxis: From the First Century to the Last Century
The continued presence and work of the Holy Spirit constitute the praxis of Christ's

---

[8]Paul Ballard and John Pritchard, *Practical Theology in Action: Christian Thinking in the Service of Church and Society* (London: SPCK, 1996), p. 81.

resurrection. This means that the truth of resurrection is not only the fact of an historical event but the presence and power of a resurrected person, Jesus Christ. The means by which Christ's work of making peace between humans and God does not take place through the application of methods, ideologies or even theories derived from Scripture. It is Christ himself who "makes peace" through the praxis of his Spirit in a dialogical relationship with our truth and methods.[9]

The praxis of Christ's ministry in the first century was completed (telos) in his resurrection and continued through the gift of the Holy Spirit at Pentecost. Following Pentecost the early church interpreted the praxis of the Holy Spirit as the continued ministry of the risen Christ, thrusting the community into the world as a mission community and preparing the church to be the church for the last century—the century when Christ returns. With Scripture as its authority, the church engages in the hermeneutical task of interpreting the Word of Christ in the context of the work of Christ.

Practical theology is thus grounded in Christopraxis as the inner core of its encounter with the Spirit's ministry in the world. With this in view, one can then adopt Browning's model as depicted in chapter one and as modified in chapter two. The questions "How then should we live?" and "What should we do?" are inherently theological questions when asked with respect to what God has revealed through his Word and what God is doing through the Spirit. This is the ongoing hermeneutical task given to the church in its practice of practical theology.

Christopraxis and Holy Scripture

Theological reflection has the task of disarming the skill of hiding behind practiced piety on the one hand and pedantic scholarship on the other. The Pharisees "traverse sea and land to make a single proselyte," scolded Jesus, and "when he becomes a proselyte, you make him twice as much a child of hell as yourselves" (Mt

---

[9]James Will offers a helpful comment: "If incomplete and ideologically distorted persons nevertheless have the dignity of participation with their Creator in the preservation and completion of the creation, then praxis is a necessary dimension of theology. But praxis must not be misunderstood as practice. Practice has come to mean the use of external means to attain a theoretically defined end. It suggests that finite and sinful persons may so understand the meaning of God's peace as to be able to devise economic, political, diplomatic, and even military means to attain it. The end of peace is thought to be a transcendent value that appropriate external means may effect. Praxis, on the other hand, is a dialectical process of internally related events from which a result dynamically emerges. Given the finite and ideological character of our preconceptions of peace, they cannot be treated as sufficient definitions of an eternal value to guide our practice. Rather, we need a praxis; that is, peace must be allowed to emerge from a dialogical and dialectical process that may continuously correct our ideological tendencies. Praxis is thus a process of struggle, negotiation, and dialogue toward a genuinely voluntary consensus" (*A Christology of Peace* [Louisville, Ky.: Westminster John Knox, 1989], pp. 24-25).

23:15 RSV). Strong language! But those of us involved with the responsibility of preparing others for ministry must not mistake education for proselytizing. Christopraxis is a ministry of making disciples—how else could it be? However, the particular competence demanded of a maker of disciples is that Christ himself be revealed as the discipler.

Christopraxis, I have argued, is the normative and authoritative grounding of all theological reflection in the divine act of God consummated in Jesus Christ and continued through the power and presence of the Holy Spirit in the body of Christ. Practical theology is an ongoing pursuit of competence through critical theological reflection. This competence does not arise merely through repetition and practice of methods but is gained through participation in the work of God in such a way that accountability for the judgments made in ministry situations are congruent with Christ's own purpose as he stands within the situation and acts through and with us.

Those who have followed the argument to this point and are "almost persuaded" will still be uneasy over what might appear to be a shift from the objective role of Scripture as the sole depository of revealed truth to the subjective discernment of the mind of Christ amidst the hopeless and ambiguous labyrinth of human feelings and impulses. Nothing that I have said should be construed as being sympathetic with such a movement from objective to subjective truth. I grant that the objectification of divine truth in the form of rational propositions deduced from Scripture appears to be a safeguard against the relativizing of truth to what seems to be right in each person's eyes. But all idolatry has its source in the desire to make the way to God more certain and more manageable. Consequently, I myself am not persuaded that we can legitimately detach the truth of God from the being of God and make out of it an abstract standard of correctness.

Christopraxis, as I have attempted to present it, upholds the full authority and objectivity of the divine Word as written in holy Scripture but only because Scripture itself is contingent on the being of God as given to us through the incarnate Word. Should one wish to dissolve this contingency into a Word of God that exists as a sheer objectification of truth detached from God's being, it would be done at the peril of idolatry, in my judgment.

I do not hold that the objective reality of God over and against his own creature is ever surrendered to an objectified Word that comes under the control of the mind of the creature. This would be a subjectivism of the worst kind. Christopraxis, as I have attempted to present it, upholds the full authority and objectivity of the Spirit of Christ as present and active in the creating and sustaining of his body, the church. The tormenting question as to how we can ever be sure of knowing what the purpose and work of Christ is through our own actions of ministry must push us to apprehend the objective reality of God himself, rather than cause us to comprehend the truth in categories more susceptible to our control. Rather than this causing confusion and anxiety, the apostle Paul held that the objective reality of the Spirit in the body of Christ is the source of true knowledge and unity of thought and action (1 Cor 2:6-16; Eph 4:1-6).

Even as Christ himself did not act against the commandments of God but integrated them into his own act of revelation and reconciliation, so the Spirit of Christ in the church does not act against the teachings of Christ in Scripture but integrates them into his own actions of revelation and reconciliation. Theological competence is the ultimate theological examination. "Examine yourselves," says apostle Paul, "Do you not realize that Jesus Christ is in you?—unless indeed you fail to meet the test! . . . For we cannot do anything against the truth, but only for the truth" (2 Cor 13:5, 8).

Christopraxis as Theological Existence in Ministry

Within the community of the church in the broadest sense, Christopraxis is itself the continuation of Christ's own ministry of revelation and reconciliation. Christians, therefore, exist by virtue of this ministry and are empirical evidence of this ministry that takes place through the power of the Holy Spirit in connection with the authority of the revealed Word of holy Scripture. To have Christian existence is, therefore, to have theological existence. It is to have both a presence and practice in the world that reveals Christ through a ministry of reconciliation. There are forms of ministry that appear to be comforting and even reconciling, but if they do not reveal Christ, these ministries are not of God. That is, these ministries are not actions of God. For God has acted in Jesus Christ and continues to act in him in such a way that Christ is revealed in all of God's actions.

For example, there certainly are many forms of caring for people that alleviate genuine human distress and result in the restoration of human lives to functional health and order. These forms of ministry can take place in such a way that "creature comforts" are maintained, but without enacting the reality of God's revelation and reconciliation through Jesus Christ. A social worker or a psychiatrist may be able to "make" people better or to "make" the conditions of human existence better. But the end result tends to be just that—a result, a product from which the "maker" can detach himself or herself with no consequent loss of identity or meaning. However, in Christopraxis the act itself becomes the embodiment of a life of community and wholeness that is derived from God himself through Christ. Thus we know that reconciliation is more than making people or conditions better; it is inextricably involved with revealing the power and presence of God through the act.

In the same way, we can also say that there are forms of ministry that purport to proclaim revealed truths of God and to indoctrinate disciples in those truths, but if they do not also touch broken and alienated human lives with liberating and healing power, they are not of God. This assertion is certainly more troublesome, especially for many Christians. The implication of the statement is that when preaching the truth about God in a completely orthodox fashion from the pulpit or in personal witness and no effect takes place in the form of saving faith, renewed life and fellowship in the community of God's own people, then this ministry is not of God. Obviously this assertion must be immediately qualified by the concession that we have no infallible way of determining what the effect of God's Word and Spirit might be in any person's life. Thus there may be a hidden work to which we are not privy. However, as a general rule the biblical witnesses to God's truth were not content to leave aside the question of response and not only looked for response as evidence of the power of the Word of truth but built their own confidence as true ministers of God on such evidence (cf. Paul, in 1 Thess 1—2). One could only argue that the true Word of God is proclaimed in the absence of response by appealing to the possibility of a hidden, secret response. For to assert that the Word of God remains true without accomplishing its true purpose is to argue against the very revealed Word itself: "So shall my word be that goes forth from my mouth; it shall not return to me empty, but it shall accomplish that which I purpose, and succeed in the thing for which I sent it" (Is 55:11).

Theological reflection is the activity of the Christian and the church by which acts of ministry are critically and continually assessed in light of both revelation and reconciliation as God's true Word. Thus truth cannot be abstracted from personal faith and knowledge, nor can personal faith be detached from the objective truth of God's own being and Word. Theological reflection as a critical exercise leads to competence in ministry by which the one who ministers unites both proclamation and practice in the truth of Jesus Christ. It is not only reflection on the nature of ministry from the perspective of biblical and theological truths but also on the nature of divine revelation from the perspective of its saving and reconciling intention in the lives of people.

It must be said also that theological reflection does not lead to new revelation, for God has spoken once and for all in the revelation of Jesus Christ, and holy Scripture is the normative and infallible truth of that revelation. However, theological reflection takes note of the presence of the One who is revealed in his continuing ministry of reconciliation through the Holy Spirit. The same Jesus who inspired the true account of his own life and ministry through the Holy Spirit in the form of Scripture continues to be present in the act of reading, hearing and interpreting the Scriptures. Thus Scripture is not merely a product that was "made" by the inspiration of the Holy Spirit and from which the maker can be detached, but Scripture continues to be the particular form of Christopraxis that provides a normative and objective basis for the life of the church. But because Scripture is a form of Christopraxis, its infallibility is located in the Christ of Scripture as the only true Word of God and not merely in Scripture as a product of inspiration that could somehow be detached from Christ.

In this way, it can be said that Jesus is not only the subject of proclamation (the one about whom we preach), but he is himself the proclaimer in every act of proclamation (the one who proclaims himself through the event of preaching). Theological reflection does not ask the question "What would Jesus do in this situation?" because this question would imply his absence. Rather, it asks the question "Where is Jesus in this situation and what am I to do as a minister?" When the Scripture is interpreted in such a way that direction is sought for lives who need to be conformed to the true and healing power of God's Word, we must remember that Jesus is not only the "author" of Scripture through the power of the Spirit, but he himself is a "reader" and interpreter of Scripture in every contemporary moment. Thus to be a competent teacher or interpreter of Scripture, one must allow the purpose of Scripture and the authority of Scripture to come to expression as Christopraxis. This requires a particular kind of competence.

Theological Competence in the Practice of Ministry

The particular competence resulting from theological reflection is evidenced by discernment, integration and credibility.[10] Combined, these qualities in a minister produce an authentic spiritual authority and competence rather than an authoritarian posture.

Discernment is the recognition of the congruence between the Christ of Scripture and the Christ in ministry. This discernment is thus both exegetical and practical, and arises where the Holy Spirit has control over both the mind and the heart. Discernment can only be tested "in ministry," for it is a judgment rendered on behalf of persons in need of Christ's presence as much as it is true information about Christ. This is not meant to imply that there actually are "two Christs," one objectified in the propositions of Scripture and the other a subjective perception on the part of the interpreter of Scripture. Rather there is but one Christ who in his own objective being and authority unites the truth of divine revelation with the truth of divine reconciliation in the objective structure that we have called Christopraxis. Scripture anchors divine revelation in the infallible authority of the incarnate Word as enacted through the historical person Jesus of Nazareth. However, Scripture itself is anchored in the normative and objective reality of Christ who continues to enact the truth of God

---

[10]In developing this section I have drawn on material that first appeared in Anderson, "Christopraxis."

through his reconciling presence and ministry in the contemporary situation.

An exegetical or hermeneutical decision regarding a scriptural teaching that is not also a judgment on behalf of the saving and gracious purpose of Scripture has not yet entered into the sphere of Christopraxis. There is, of course, a preliminary searching of the mind of Christ in Scripture that requires careful attention to textual exegesis and basic hermeneutical principles. However, the authority of the text cannot pass over directly into the assured results of such exegetical study, for in this case the text has been used to "make" the truth appear in such a form that it can stand independently of the "maker of truth." When this happens, infallibility and authority can become detached from the objective reality of Christ himself and can be used against the truth.

This is precisely what happened when the Old Testament revelation becomes objectified in the form of infallible interpretation and used to condemn Jesus himself, who was the incarnation of the Word of God: "This man is not from God, for he does not observe the sabbath" (Jn 9:16). The "orthodoxy" of the Pharisees came to stand outside the Christopraxis of the incarnate Word as the divine act. Instead of the proper kind of theological reflection enabling them to discern the act of God in their midst, they became incompetent to judge the truth and hopelessly blind. To have one's eyes opened to "see the truth" is to be able to discern the work of God in the present context and thereby to hear the Word of God as delivered by the inspired witnesses. In this way, the early preaching in the book of Acts called for this kind of theological reflection and discernment. "You killed the Author of Life," proclaimed Peter. But God raised him from the dead. "To this we are witnesses. And by faith in his name, his name itself has made this man strong, whom you see and know; and the faith that is through Jesus has given him this perfect health in the presence of all of you" (Acts 3:15-16). It is in this same sense that I have suggested that a particular kind of competence is represented by the discernment that is able to see the congruence between the Christ of Scripture and the Christ at work in the ministry of the church.

Integration is the second aspect of competence produced by theological reflection. Integration is the application of discernment where God's Word is both proclaimed and practiced in ministry with the result that Christ as truth both touches and is touched by human need. An integrated ministry overcomes the ambivalence that results from two levels of truth, one purely theoretical and the other merely functional. Integration, therefore, is a form of competence, not a theoretical component of a curriculum. Within the structure of Christopraxis the "presence-in-action" mode of revelation stands as a barrier to all attempts to view the truth of God in abstraction from the work of God. "Do not, for the sake of food, destroy the work of God," wrote the apostle Paul (Rom 14:20). The eating or not eating of meat had become for some an absolute principle of the law in abstraction from the work of God in building up a body of people who existed in the mutuality of peace and love. The particular kind of competence represented by integration is demonstrated by Jesus who healed on the sabbath. This act of reconciliation became a normative interpretation of the law of the sabbath as a revelation of God. The sabbath does not lose its authority as a command-ment because it is drawn into the work of God, but rather its true authority as a com-mand of God comes to expression in the objective reality of the work of God.

The particular kind of competence represented by integration is demonstrated by the apostle Paul when he withstood the attempts of the Judaizers to force circumci-sion on the Gentile converts and to enforce a separation between the practice of Gen-tile Christians eating with Jewish Christians. The authority of Christ as the revealed Word of God is enacted in the table fellowship at which he himself is present. The table fellowship of Christopraxis, therefore, becomes a normative criterion for dis-cerning and judging the truth of Christ. When Peter fell prey to the wiles of the Judaizers, Paul reproaches him openly in the church at Antioch for the sake of the "truth of the gospel" (Gal 2:11-21). The integration of the Jew and Gentile is first of all, for Paul, an ontological reality grounded in the objective person of Jesus Christ. It is the Word of revelation, therefore, that contains the structure of integration, not the practice of reconciliation. Christopraxis grounds the criteria for competence in the very being of the truth as the personal being of God revealed through the historical and contemporary person and presence of Jesus Christ.

The competence of integration, therefore, is a special competence demanded of the theologian and the biblical scholar. Only when this competence is present as an essential component of theological education can the task of preparing men and women for ministry include the developing of competence for ministry. It is hard to see how this competence can be certified with the granting of a degree, unless the narrower scope of the curriculum with its focus on abstract knowledge is set within the broader curriculum of discernment and integration. But if there is to be such a broader curriculum through which competence can be produced, it will entail cir-cumstances in which judgments will have to be made as to the work of God in his own ministry of reconciliation.

A third form of competence is credibility. Credibility is the transparency of method and lucidity of thought that makes the presence of Christ self-evident and worthy of belief in every event of ministry. Christ is ultimately believable only in terms of his own unity of being in word and deed. It is the task of theological reflec-tion to press through to this criterion at the expense, if necessary, of every claim of self-justification on the part of the minister (and teacher).

"You know what kind of persons we proved to be among you for your sake," wrote Paul to the Thessalonian Christians, "And you became imitators of us and of the

Lord" (1 Thess 1:5-6). Paul was not conceding to others the authority to make judgments on him. In another context he can say, "It is a very small thing that I should be judged by you or by any human court. I do not even judge myself. . . . It is the Lord who judges me" (1 Cor 4:3-4). However, the Lord who is coming as the judge of all ministry (then what is true will be finally revealed) is also revealed in this present time through actions of reconciliation. Christopraxis, therefore, demands a particular kind of competence that manifests in being credible as a presentation of Christ himself, not merely as an infallible interpreter of Christ. This is a subtle distinction that eludes analysis but that becomes razor sharp when viewed from the perspective of the one who is truly seeking the truth and grace of God in Christ.

For the Pharisees, the official interpreter of the law and the possessor of the official interpretation became identical with the giver of the law. But for Jesus, the distinction was absolutely clear. Jesus told them, "If you were Abraham's children, you would be doing what Abraham did, but now you trying to kill me, a man who has told you the truth. . . . If God were your Father, you would love me, for I came from God" (Jn 8:39, 42). For all of their erudition concerning the law, they were basically incompetent with regard to the truth and reality of God. Their eyes were opaque, and they could not see the transparency of Jesus as the one who revealed the true God in his words and deeds (cf. Jn 9:40-41). On the other hand, the common people, despised by the Pharisees as unlearned, found Jesus to be truly credible as a "man of God."

Ecclesial Praxis

Practical theology as

> critical and constructive reflection on ecclesial praxis is the process of ongoing critical reflection on the acts of the church in the light of the gospel and in critical dialogue with secular sources of knowledge with a view to the faithful transformation of the praxis of the church-in-the-world. Secular sources are drawn upon not only to improve technique, but also to clarify the nature of the ecclesial praxis, to uncover the meanings that lie behind and are present within the praxis of the church and even to challenge and clarify particular understandings of theological concepts. Contrary to models of theology which suggest that theology is done primarily within the faculty, a model of practical theology that focuses on ecclesial praxis points towards the fact that ecclesial praxis is the place where theology is done.

> This model of practical theology, with its emphasis on ecclesial praxis and the attainment of practical knowledge, goes a long way towards healing the perennial rift between theory and practice. By focusing on critical reflection on ecclesial praxis, the practical theologian will seek to examine the meaningful acts of the church and to critically assess, challenge and seek the transformation of particular forms of praxis in the light of the mission of God and in critical dialogue with the Christian tradition and the world. The practical theologian seeks to interpret Scripture, tradition and praxis, in order that the

contemporary praxis of both church and world can be transformed. An adequate under-standing of the theological validity of Christian praxis as a form of practical knowledge allows practical theology to hold in constructive tension theory and practice, church and world, normativity and transformation . . . [and] enables a constructive, mutual dialogue to take place between all of these elements and other sources of knowledge.[11]

The next chapter will draw forth the assumptions set forth thus far and develop a practical theology of ministry as foundational for the practice of ministry in the church, by the church and by members of the church in the world.

---

[11]Swinton, *From Bedlam to Shalom,* p. 12.

5

A PRACTICAL THEOLOGY OF MINISTRY

T he recent spate of "adjectival" theology concerns those who question the utilitarian basis for such movements. Has theology succumbed totally to the prevailing winds of praxis, where movements write their conceptual basis for existence as revolutionary manifestos meant to justify as much as to compel? Or to put it another way, does a political theology or a black theology appropriate revelation to a concrete situation in such a way that the immediate occasion becomes the authoritative "text"? Has theology virtually become hermeneutics—where self-understanding incorporates the data of revelation into one's own experience and action? At the core of these questions is a concern that the center of gravity has shifted from revelation as determinative of truth in action, to action as determinative of truth in revelation.

Yet, do we want to return to the concept of "pure" theology as distinguished from "applied" theology, a dichotomy that continues to plague the curriculum of theological education in the guise of "practical" theology? To take another approach in questioning, can the church tolerate the separation of the theoretical task from the concrete situation of its own existence? Will theologians be permitted to work in cool absentia while pastors sweat out their existence in the steamy space of the church in the world? Does theological training end where practice begins?

Obviously, these questions prejudice the case by exaggerating the options. However, the point has been made. In too many cases the seminary graduate considers his theoretical task to be finished and his education for ministry to take place through the relentless and unforgiving demands of feeding, healing and above all pleasing the sheep. The danger in this is twofold: first, when theological thinking is practiced in abstraction from the church in ministry, it inevitably becomes as much unapplied and irrelevant as pure; second, when the theological mind of the minister is being educated primarily through experience, an ad hoc theology emerges that owes as much (or more) to methodological and pragmatic concerns as to dogma. The task of working out a theology for ministry begins properly with the task of identifying the nature and place of ministry itself.

The Nature of Ministry

One fundamental thesis will control this discussion—the thesis that ministry precedes and produces theology, not the reverse. It must immediately be added, however, that ministry is determined and set forth by God's own ministry of revelation and reconciliation in the world, beginning with Israel and culminating in Jesus Christ and the church.

All ministry is God's ministry. Jesus came not to introduce his own ministry but to do the will of the Father and to live by every word that proceeds out of the mouth of God. God's initial act, and every subsequent act of revelation, is a ministry of reconciliation. Out of this ministry emerges theological activity, exploring and expounding the nature and purpose of God in and for creation and human creatures. Theology thus serves as the handmaid of ministry, proclaiming it as God's ministry and making known the eternal being of God. This knowledge of God, as Calvin reminds us in the opening paragraphs of his *Institutes,* leads us to a knowledge of ourselves. We cannot contemplate the nature of God in his revelation without contemplating our own nature and purpose.

Ministry cannot be construed solely as the practical application (or technique) that makes theological knowledge relevant and effective. Theological activity must emerge out of ministry and for the sake of ministry if it is to be in accordance with the divine modality. The "practice" of ministry, then, is not only the appropriate context for doing theological thinking, it is itself intrinsically a theological activity.

To say that all ministry is God's ministry is to suggest that ministry precedes and determines the church. The ongoing ministry of Jesus Christ gives both content and direction to the church in its ministry. Jesus is the minister par excellence. He ministers to the Father for the sake of the world, taking the things of God and disclosing them faithfully to sinners, and taking sinners to himself and binding them graciously into his own sonship to the Father. This ministry is as extensive as it is intensive. As the eternal Word that goes forth from the Father, Jesus continually discloses the depths of divine being as purposeful and loving in its relationship to the creature. This ministry continues through the inspired witness of the apostles, whose own ministry is foundational for this very reason. Thus God's ministry becomes the dogma from which all insight into the nature and strategy of ministry issues and to which the church must return in every generation to test its own concept of ministry.

The church has no existence apart from being called into being through this ministry and equipped for it by the gift of the Holy Spirit. For the church to seek a ministry of its own is to deny Christ's ministry and to turn aside to spurious activities that can never justify its own existence or redeem the world. Consequently, unless ministry takes a purely pragmatic turn, it is necessarily led to the theological activity of exploring the dogma of divine revelation given to us as the Word of God in holy Scripture. This theological activity will be both exegetical and experiential.

The Holy Spirit unites the doing of ministry to the ministry already accomplished in Christ, establishing a reciprocity between dogma and experience that continually discloses and disciplines. There is disclosed to the church the nature of ministry in the context of its own situation. There are different ministries even as there are different gifts to the church, but all ministries are forms of Christ's ministry, even as all gifts of the Spirit come from one Spirit. The experiential component in ministry is necessary to identify and confirm gifts for ministry.

As Christ's own ministry is unfolded and proclaimed, the church discovers its own ministry, and its members discover their own particular ministry. Christ continually discloses his ministry in concrete situations. This disclosure is the source of all true innovation and creativity in ministry. Thus dogma does not stifle but stimulates creativity.

Christ's primary ministry is to the Father for the sake of the world, not to the world for the sake of the Father. This means that the world does not set the agenda for ministry, but the Father, who loves the world and seeks its good, sets this agenda. This christological, and actually trinitarian, basis for ministry rules out both utilitarianism, which tends to create ministry out of needs, and pragmatism, which transforms ministry into marketing strategy. It links the church and the theological seminary in a mutual commitment to learning and healing. For God's ministry is at once revealing and reconciling with respect to the world.

Ministry as Reconciliation and Revelation

It is common in contemporary theology for Cartesian and Kantian assumptions to demand that revelation be appropriated to the human subject. It was the distinguished French philosopher René Descartes in the middle of the seventeenth century who formulated the dictum "I think, therefore I am." This principle not only led to the objectification of that experienced outside of the mind itself but located the only source of certainty in the subjective act of thought. As applied to theology this principle dictated the conclusion that the objectification of God as a phenomenon of experience necessarily shifted the decision with regard to the reality of God to the human subject.

But it remained for Immanuel Kant a century later to cut the connection between the act of thinking and the ultimate being of that which is thought. Pure reason, said Kant, can be extended only to objects of possible experience and can never be extended beyond the objects of sense perception to "things in themselves." In his *Critique of Pure Reason* Kant expounded a "rational faith," which was expressed in terms of the moral law. By placing the source of the moral law in the pure principle of reason, that is, in the noumenal realm, he made revelation inaccessible to reason and therefore unverifiable. Kant thought that in effectively "disobjectifying" God (revelation), the reality of God would no longer be conditioned by the relativism and doubt that the Cartesian principle entailed.

This agnosticism concerning objective knowledge of God set the agenda for modern theology. Holding that a determination of the truthfulness or objective validity of divine revelation is impossible and yet that revelation should continue to be normative for theological discussion, modern theologians made distinctions between truth and meaningfulness and between knowledge and faith, and they viewed these distinctions as advances rather than losses for theological thought. While denying that revelation is true and can be objectively experienced (i.e., can be known), they nevertheless affirmed that revelation is meaningful, that is, it leads to coherence and authentication of the self. They viewed faith, then, simply as a means to self-understanding. Their position was really one of theological solipsism, for it referred all statements about God to the judgment of the human person.

The point in this all-too-brief excursion into philosophical theology is to establish a critical reference point for the discussion of ministry as God's ministry. Given the assumptions of a Cartesian approach to revelation coupled with a Kantian agnosticism concerning objective truth, it would be impossible to sustain the thesis that God's ministry is determinative for and is the dogmatic basis for the ministry of the church. Rather, one would be compelled to assert, as do many contemporary theologies, that the ministry of the church is determinative for God's ministry. Reconciliation thus becomes the dogmatic basis for revelation. The world sets the agenda for the church, and all things become true to the extent that they are useful and actually work. Hence, utilitarianism and pragmatism become prevalent in the literature of the church concerning its ministry in the world.

It is the objective of this essay to offer an alternative to this methodology and these conclusions, without pausing to demonstrate the fallacious and unfortunate assumptions underlying the Cartesian paradigm as a basis for a theology of divine revelation.[1] The development of this alternative will properly be a dogmatic task. That is, it will require us to set forth the nature of revelation and reconciliation as God's giving of himself to us in Jesus Christ. As such, our task will be what Karl Barth calls "scientific theology." It will require us to allow the nature of reality, as it discloses itself to us, to determine our method of knowing that reality. It will necessitate our viewing the object of knowledge as free to disclose itself to us on its own terms. Thus, by subordinating or relativizing the knowing subject to that which is known, our scientific theology will present an alternative to the Cartesian paradigm. It will be the reader's responsibility to determine which paradigm is more compelling.[2]

Based on a reading of the account of God's self-disclosure through the history of salvation as given to us in holy Scripture, it can be stated as an axiom that revelation and reconciliation are reciprocal movements of a single event. This is to assert that God reveals himself to the creature in such a way that a knowing relation is established and upheld from both sides by God. This axiom precludes the possibility that divine self-revelation occurs in such a way that it presupposes a creaturely capability and disposition to grasp it and complete it by way of a response that is not itself produced by the event of revelation. Or put another way, to say that revelation produces the appropriate response on the part of the human creature is to say that humans bear the image and likeness of God (Gen 1:26-27). It is a dogmatic assertion of biblical theology that the imago Dei is an endowment rather than an innate disposition of the creature. Adam does not bear the divine image because he is human; he becomes human as a result of the divine fiat, portrayed as a divine inbreathing (Gen 2:7).

If reconciliation is supposed to represent that movement by which humans are conformed to the Word of God and through which humans are constituted as possessing health and holiness, then it would be meaningful also to suppose that this is what is meant by ministry—the reconciling of humanity to God. However, in asserting axiomatically that reconciliation is reciprocal to revelation, it must be made clear that reconciliation is not a movement that originates with the Fall. That is, the fundamental paradigm of revelation includes reconciliation as an original movement of response. This can be expressed more clearly in the diagram in figure 5.1.

The diagram shows that the word is creative of the response. As such, the word of God is self-authenticating in its demand for recognition and response. Adam ought to

---

[1] I have set forth a more systematic critique of Cartesian theology in Ray S. Anderson, *Historical Transcendence and the Reality of God* (Grand Rapids, Mich.: Eerdmans, 1975), pp. 39-77. Cf. also Helmut Thielicke, *The Evangelical Faith*, vols. 1-2 (Grand Rapids, Mich.: Eerdmans, 1976-1977).

[2] For a helpful discussion of an alternative to the Cartesian paradigm in the form of a more heuristic approach, see Richard Gelwick, "Discovery and Theology," *Scottish Journal of Theology* 28, no. 4 (1975): 301-21.

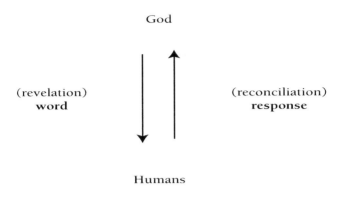

Figure 5.1. The word is creative of the response

respond because he can respond. Because the divine word posits a correspondence of
the creature to God in the form of a divine image and likeness, the word reveals God
in terms that are creaturely and human. The word does not need to be appropriated
by a human action; it becomes a human word while retaining its transcendence. The
human response does not condition or determine the divine word, for the word has
itself a divine correspondence by virtue of the image of God through which Adam
knows himself. This is what Calvin meant when he said that knowledge of God necessarily involves knowledge of self.

The temptation story (Gen 3) suggests that deviation from the word occurs when
an independent criterion is adopted as a basis for making a judgment concerning the
divine word. The temptation comes in the form of a question: Has God said? What
the question implies is that the concrete word of God for which obedience is the
proper response, is now conditioned by a verdict based on an abstract knowledge of
truth to which the divine word must correspond. In deciding to eat the forbidden
fruit, a decision against the self-authenticating word is made in favor of the universal
principle that holds that the good, the true and the beautiful can be established independently of one's experience of the divine word. The word, which comes through a
historically and temporally conditioned event of revelation, is set aside in favor of a
nonhistorical and timeless truth that appears accessible through human thought
alone. The Cartesian principle of the primacy of the human mind is taken up over
and against the historical word. This act is the Fall.

The fact that God does not abandon the creature who attempts to establish an
autonomous existence is a testimony to the original grace that underlies the creative
act. Reconciliation, as a movement initiated by God, does not originate outside of the

event of revelation itself. Because the divine word and the human response are recip-rocally related, so that one cannot be considered apart from the other, revelation and reconciliation participate in the same fundamental paradigm. Because the fallen expe-rience is the typical experience by which all persons experience their selfhood (this too is a dogmatic assertion, though it appears also to be experientially validated), God's word of revelation involves the ministry of reconciliation. That is, the word is saving in its revelatory nature. This is not to deny that there is a general revelation. But as Paul makes clear in Romans 1, a revelation of God through creation only serves as an indictment against unbelief. The word that saves as it reveals does not presup-pose a positive attitude but a negative one, which must be overcome. To assert that the word is revelatory without also producing reconciliation violates the fundamental paradigm. Furthermore, it tends to sustain the autonomy of the fallen self in its attempt to render a verdict over the word itself, based on something other than the word. It is the paradigm of revelation and reconciliation that establishes the nature of ministry as God's ministry and brings that ministry as both an act of judgment and grace to the human situation.

Ministry as Judgment and Grace
We have established the postulate that all ministry is God's ministry, for the word of revelation is always a creation ex nihilo. The word of God that goes forth to create, brings into being that which is from that which is not (Heb 11:3). The creative word does not presuppose existing substance or capability outside of itself. In the divine fiat "Let there be," there is the implied negation of all that would seek to exist outside this word. What then comes into existence rests solely on the creative and sustaining word. Herein is both the grace and judgment of the word.

Out of his freedom, God moves to create. This is his grace—to bring into being what had no possibility of being, that is, to make possibility out of impossibility. But this grace militates against any encroachment on God's freedom. For the creature to assert a possibility based on some creaturely or created nature, independently of this word, would cause it to come into opposition to and under judgment of the word. To assert that ministry is both a word of judgment and grace, then, is to follow faithfully this paradigm and to assess critically every motivation toward ministry that seeks some possibility outside of the revealing and reconciling word.

The original possibility of a human response to the divine word is posited by the Word itself. In the creation narrative (Gen 1—2) the human creature emerges as a result of a divine initiative that bestows an image or likeness of the divine Word itself (Gen 1:26-27). While other creatures are created "after their own kind," the first human, Adam, knows himself only as he knows the Creator and responds to him. There is no humanity of a creaturely sort that has the "choice" of responding to the divine word.

The very response, which can be considered to be reflexive in nature, is itself the endowment of humanity. Adam speaks with God because he is human, and he is human because he speaks with God. To this extent, Adam's humanity is self-authenticating. It is not as though an independent criterion exists by which Adam can verify his humanity in terms of likeness to God. Adam is free to know himself for what he is as he knows himself in relation to God the Creator. The dignity he possesses, which marks him off from all other creatures, is an alien dignity. It is a dignity that has its antecedent in something other than a creaturely nature, though it can only be known and experienced as a creaturely nature.

In the second creation narrative (Gen 2) the human creature is presented as a solitary being—the male. Despite the fact that the Creator provides a supportive environment and a meaningful task, the verdict of God himself is that "it is not good for the man to be alone." But then it is as though some possibility is sought within creatureliness to fill this void. God creates and brings the other creatures to Adam, one by one, so that he can name them. Certainly in this act of naming there is also implied a search on the part of Adam for a counterpart to his own being. And yet not even the Creator himself could find a suitable counterpart within the possibilities of existing creation. It is as though at the very outset we are warned against an overly optimistic reliance on some technique or some technician that could intensify or alter existing creaturely being so that it could fulfill and complete itself. God as the master technician is unable to find sufficient possibilities within the creature for the human self to complete itself. It is only when the single male is put to sleep and the creative word itself operates in such a way that the divine likeness and endowment is divided into a complementary existence, that such a possibility is actualized. Out of impossibility God's word becomes God's ministry. Adam responds, "At last, this is bone of my bone and flesh of my flesh." This grace of God is a verdict rendered on every attempt to circumvent that word and to provide an alternative response. It is revelation that provides the reconciliation. God's ministry takes what is impossible and creates possibility. But it does this in such a way that the creature himself is incorporated into the new possibility. It is "bone of my bone and flesh of my flesh." Adam is not himself set aside. There is no judgment against him but a judgment for him and against all that would only inevitably betray and fail him.

This fundamental paradigm is reiterated in the event of Abraham. There is no hint given as to how Abraham verifies the divine summons that leads him to leave his kindred and homeland for a land unknown to him (Heb 11:8). Because this paradigm suggests that the word of God is self-authenticating, one suspects that he hears and obeys the word because it is the word of God. Implicit in this word is a judgment against all the questions that could be raised in hopes of verifying the word on some basis independent of the word itself.

But there is more. To Abraham and Sarah the promise is given that through their heir a blessing will come on them and on all nations (Gen 12:1-4; 15:1-6; 17:1-8). However, it is seemingly impossible for this promise to be fulfilled. Sarah is not only barren but past childbearing age. Yet Abraham and Sarah believe the promise and attempt to appropriate it to their situation, that is, to understand it as meaningful and attempt to live by it. It seems reasonable to Abraham that the means by which the promise could be effected would legitimately take into account the human possibilities. Thus Abraham views the opportunity to have an heir of his own loins through the servant-maid Hagar as a means of acting in obedience, given the imperative of the revelation itself. So, from the union of Abraham and Hagar, Ishmael is born, and for thirteen years Abraham lives with assurance that the promise is being fulfilled and that the word is completed by this response.

However, the word of the Lord again comes to Abraham, saying that his wife, Sarah, who by this time is ninety years old, will conceive a child who will be the true heir of the promise. To Abraham this is incredible and unnecessary. For thirteen years Abraham has taught Ishmael that he is the answer to the promise, the heir that can fulfill God's word. "O that Ishmael might live in your sight!" cries Abraham. But the response is "No, but your wife Sarah shall bear you a son" (Gen 17:18-19). All that Ishmael has been taught must now be untaught. The word of grace that will enable Sarah to conceive supernaturally is also a judgment against the natural possibility. Isaac is the son of promise and the divinely provided response to the word itself. True enough, Abraham and Sarah must come together in an act of human love in order that the child be conceived, and Sarah must carry and nourish the child in her own womb. But this only establishes again the truth that the divine word is not a judgment against the creature but against that presumption of the creature that will inevitably lead to failure. The human act is given a place in the new creation of God and thereby finds the completion of its own authentic being.

Israel itself becomes the historical paradigm for this truth. In Israel's election to be the people of God, the word that reveals is also the word that reconciles—but it is a word of both judgment and grace. For the sake of the covenant that Yahweh has established, there is a judgment against the presumption by which a human possibility is viewed as a means to the fulfillment of Israel's goal. Again and again the strategy of survival that depends on military alliances, cultural assimilation and religious syncretism is disowned by God. Israel is the chosen one who must suffer and die in order that it might be created anew and given a response to the word, which will not fail. The remnant will come as a "root out of dry ground" and as a green shoot from the stump of the tree. The barrenness of Israel must be demonstrated in order that the promise may be shown to rest on divine aid. God's ministry of reconciliation comes as a judgment against everything that would condition this divine word.

From creation ex nihilo, from the barren womb of Sarah and from the impotency of Israel, the paradigm moves through the virgin womb of Mary and the grave of Jesus, where it reaches its final utterance in the resurrection. The miracle of the virgin birth is a judgment against the possibility of the creature producing its own word of revelation and reconciliation. For Jesus himself, the argument rages. "Take this cup from me," says Jesus, but only if it is thy will. Implicit in this prayer is the plea, "Cannot my Ishmael live before you? Is not there sufficient reason in all of my good works to warrant a verdict of righteousness?" But the answer is the same: "No, for this purpose I have come to this hour" (Jn 12:27 RSV). There can be no resurrection without a death. God's ministry of reconciliation brings a judgment against the possibility of a creaturely response that can complete the word of revelation. When Jesus stands outside of his own tomb on Easter morning, there is only discontinuity with that which stood against the word. Continuity is maintained with all that he was, is and shall be. His new humanity does not disannul the original humanity but completes it.

The sabbath of God is a summons and permission for the creature elected by God to stand free of the tyranny of the sixth day. In the sixth day nature determines destiny, and what *is* becomes the verification of what *shall be*. Bound up in the "solidarity of the sixth day" (a fine phrase of Thielicke's), the human person experiences the word of God as a liberating word. It is a word that gives permission to escape the determinism of the sixth day, of nature alone, and to receive a new destiny, that of eternal fellowship with the Creator. In bringing this sabbath to its completion, Jesus, through his resurrection from the dead, provides the hermeneutical paradigm for all understanding of divine revelation. To seek to appropriate divine revelation to the understanding and situation of the creature is hopelessly to imprison it within the determinism of the sixth day and to subject it to futility. It is against this fatal tendency toward appropriation of the revealed Word that Helmut Thielicke inveighs. For in the act of appropriating revelation to the self-understanding of the human creature, the revelation is not only altered in its content and character but is stripped of its reconciling power. The act of appropriation as an epistemological movement incorporates revelation into a human situation and then seeks to render a verdict on it from a finite, creaturely perspective. This act, as Thielicke points out, is Cartesian in form, whether it takes place as a rationalist or existentialist movement. The moment that revelation is only a possibility that must be actualized by the believing subject, the believer is left without an objective basis for a life of faith.[3]

While Ishmael seems more objective to Abraham than the word, which still insists on its own incarnation on its own terms, the child is hopelessly subjective with respect to the divine word itself. Ishmael is not the ministry of God and therefore

---

[3]Thielicke, *Evangelical Faith*, vol. 1.

cannot be the revelation of God. What the word produces becomes the actuality that verifies what the word says. Isaac is God's actuality and therefore becomes Abraham's possibility. Thus Isaac can never really betray Abraham in being subject to the inevitable threat of death. In being received supernaturally from a barren womb he can be received again from the dead (Heb 11:19). Because Abraham's faith has already taken into account a human impossibility, Abraham does not stagger in unbelief at the seeming impossibility of offering Isaac as a sacrifice. The word of God is not only self-authenticating, it is self-actualizing. It brings into being what it demands.

Ministry as Actuality and Possibility

It ought to be clear at this point that to introduce a creaturely and human possibility as the basis on which the word of God can actually be heard and obeyed is to violate the fundamental paradigm of revelation and reconciliation itself. The implications of this fact for a theology of ministry ought also to be quite obvious. If ministry is viewed as the actualizing of the possibilities that exist because the gospel reveals to us a new order of being, it will inevitably flounder in the shallow waters of its own impotence. But ministry, as our thesis originally stated, precedes and determines not only theological reflection but the very existence and life of the church.

To elaborate on this thesis is to enlarge the scope of Christology as a discipline of theological reflection. A christological perspective of ministry is that of ministry that has been accomplished and that continues to be accomplished through the Holy Spirit, who indwells and actualizes the life of the church. To say that actuality precedes possibility is to say that God has actually given and upheld both sides of the ministry of the word.

Through the incarnation of the divine Logos (Jn 1:14), ministry of bringing the word of God to human creatures was accomplished as well as the bringing of the human creature into conformity with that word. In his ministry of revealing the word, Jesus stands among us as the God who is for humanity. He discloses the depth of divine love and grace in terms that are fully accessible to finite, human creatures. To know Jesus is to be confronted with the reality of God himself. This fact was the concern of the fourth century doctrine of the *homoousion* as argued against the Arians, who denied the essential deity of the incarnate Logos. To confess anything less than that Jesus of Nazareth is of the same essence as the Father, with respect to his deity, is to deny the actuality of revelation as a divine Word that stands on the creaturely side with us. The concern of Arius was to make the divine Logos more understandable from the perspective of created rationality, but as the orthodox theologians at Nicaea clearly saw, this concern betrayed Christian faith at its very core by substituting a possibility for an actuality, with respect to the saving effect of the word. A divine revelation that awaits appropriation to a contemporary worldview or metaphysical structure of reality, achieves recognition and acceptance at the cost of sacrificing its objective and transcendent content.

In bringing the Word fully into human flesh, the incarnation unites the finite and creaturely with the infinite and uncreated reality of God himself. That is, revelation does not exist between God and humanity as an abstract entity that is something else than either God or human, but exists as God himself exists—personally and concretely in relation with humanity. The possibility of knowing and expressing the word of God in human thought forms and in historical events follows on the actuality of that event in the incarnate life of Jesus. The fact that the incarnate Word inevitably acquires a human language and culture may be considered by some to be an embarrassment and limitation for that Word. But those who follow this line of thinking will only be confronted by the embarrassment and limitation of being unable to grasp a divine revelation that has been stripped of its humanity and temporality. The ministry of proclamation, for example, will be radically determined by how we understand the incarnation. If the Word of God stands only as an abstract or existential possibility, separated from the historical context in which it originally came, then the ministry of proclamation will have no dogmatic basis for its content. Scripture will necessarily be appropriated to the latest style of cultural interpretation and hermeneutics; the act of making meaningful will itself be the primary source for revelation. Proclamation will seek to actualize all possibilities in hope of producing an event of revelation.

On the other hand, for those who take the incarnation seriously, proclamation has already occurred in the Word made flesh. All subsequent proclamation has its possibility based on this actuality. The event of revelation does not rest on the inspiredness of the proclaimer or the existential moment for the hearer, but exists in human language and historical event as the dogma of Jesus Christ incarnate. As Karl Barth so well put it, "It is not He that needs proclamation, but proclamation that needs Him."[4] If the hermeneutical task is that of ascertaining the meaning of that which is revealed, then one could say that revelation has incorporated (appropriated) the human situation into its own occurrence as historical event. Revelation is not just the word of God to Abraham; it is Abraham. As Abraham becomes drawn into the sphere of the word, no distinction can be made between the word of God that came to Abraham, and Abraham's history as a history of that word. Thus the written record of this history is revelatory precisely because it is revelation's history.

Surely this is what it means to say that the Holy Spirit will take the things of Christ and make them known to us (Jn 16:13-14). As a theological discipline the hermeneutical task of the church is to continue searching out and seeking to be conformed to the hermeneutical stricture of revelation itself as given in holy Scripture. Thus the

---

[4]*CD* 4/1, p. 227.

ministry of the church necessarily involves theological reflection and a correction of its own inevitable tendencies to create ministry for its own justification.

But if actuality can be asserted concerning revelation as a word of God for humans, what of reconciliation as response to that word? Here too, a christological understanding of ministry is helpful. Not only is Jesus the God who is for humanity, but he is also the Man who is for God. Not only is he the one who brings the word and bears the word fully in his own humanity, but he is also one who bears the word and faithfully lives in obedience to it. At every point he is tempted, such as we are (Heb 4:15), but he steadfastly lives by every word that proceeds from the mouth of God (Mt 4:4). With regard to a human will disinclined to conform to the will of God, Jesus bends that will back into conformity to the divine will at every point. Coming not to destroy the law but to fulfill it, he completes all of the demands of the divine word through his life of obedience and faith. Being conceived of the Spirit in the virgin and anointed by the Spirit at his baptism, he sanctifies the humanity, which he assumes as his own, and creates the actual sanctification of that humanity through his atoning death and resurrection.

The good news he announces is based on his own self-testimony as the faithful servant of Yahweh. His gospel invitation—"Come unto me"—is no burden to be applied to weak humanity and no yoke to be thrown on the necks of struggling disciples but rather is an offer to assume his burden and his yoke. It is easy because he actually has borne it and continues to bear it.

In preaching the gospel of the kingdom Jesus opens up his own life of fellowship with the Father as the avenue on which the weary, the crippled, the blind and sinners can walk in grace and glory. He breaks down partitions between races and ideologies, and creates new bonds of fellowship for old enemies. Through him the reconciliation of the world to God actually occurs (2 Cor 5:19). The ministry of reconciliation given to the church has its possibility firmly rooted in this actuality. Otherwise, it would be a cruel hoax.

Thus God upholds the event of revelation from both sides. The ministry of disclosing the Word to the world is upheld by the reality of the incarnate presence of Christ in the world. All exegetical, hermeneutical and homiletical work as the proper theological activity of the church is supported and made possible by this incarnation. The ministry of reconciling the world to this word of revelation is upheld by Jesus' incarnate life of obedience and faithful response to this word. All of the healing, teaching and saving ministry of the church is supported and made possible by this incarnation.

In this way it can be said that ministry precedes and creates the church. All ministry is Christ's ministry of faithfulness to the Father on behalf of the world. The sending of the Holy Spirit continues this ministry; it does not constitute the creation of another ministry (Jn 16:7-15). To the extent that the church understands this ministry of God, it will understand its own existence and ministry in the world.

Every Ishmael struggles for recognition, however. And in a sense, as long as Ishmael stands before us we will have difficulty hearing and believing the Word of God. "The discovery of truth," said John Macmurray, "must be from the subjective side a process of disillusionment. . . . We all confess to the desire to get at the truth, but in practice the desire for truth is the desire to be disillusioned."[5] Illusions die hard. Theological illusions have the strongest resistance.

Every pragmatic principle of ministry must be subjected to the critical dogmatic test: has it gone through the death and resurrection process? Have we allowed the ministry as such to reveal to us its impossibility before we have assumed its possibility? Does the church understand that it only exists because of Christ's ministry? Does Christ's ministry continue to exist in our ministry as both the presupposition and the goal?

It is always the task of the church, admonished Barth, to give account of its theology in light of the contemporary situation and the dogma of Christ's ministry of reconciliation. Who better is prepared to do that, and who can less afford to ignore that task, than those who are ministers of the gospel of Christ?

---

[5]John Macmurray, *Reason and Emotion* (London: Faber & Faber, 1935), p. 22.

Part 2

THE PRAXIS OF
PRACTICAL THEOLOGY

6

THE RESURRECTION OF JESUS AS HERMENEUTICAL CRITERION

Is Jesus not only the author of inspired Scripture but, as the resurrected and living Lord of the church, also a contemporary reader and interpreter of Scripture?" I recently asked this question of a class of pastors in a doctor of ministry seminar with dramatic results.

Some, who said they had not thought of that before, were carried away with possible implications for hermeneutical method. Others, apprehensive and troubled, suggested that this could be dangerous, for it would tend to undermine the place of Scripture as an objective revelation of God's truth for us and as the "sole rule of faith and practice."

But if it is true that the living Lord Jesus is present in the hermeneutical task of reading and interpreting Scripture, what would this mean for the task of hermeneutics? In this chapter I will probe that question further, and theoretically and practically explore its implications.

As a foray into the thicket of contemporary hermeneutics, this project is more of a probe than a pronouncement. It is meant to be a programmatic essay rather than a monograph. My purpose is to stimulate discussion and to elicit a response.

I write with a sense of conviction that hermeneutics belongs high on the agenda of the contemporary theological task, particularly for those of us who hold the Scriptures to be the inspired and infallible Word of God. Whatever we mean by hermeneutics, the task is unavoidable. As Friedrich Schleiermacher once said, "Every child arrives at the meaning of a word only through hermeneutics."[1]

But seriously, the responsibility to interpret faithfully and accurately the word of God as given in holy Scripture is more than child's play. It is a task that demands both rigor of mind and the wonder of a child. Interpreting Scripture is akin to standing where Moses stood on the holy ground in the presence of the burning bush, where his first meaningful act was to remove his shoes.

As a theologian I assume that my task is a hermeneutical one. I agree with David Tracy when he says that "systematic theologies are principally hermeneutical in character" and that it is "imperative for each theologian to render explicit her or his general method of interpretation."[2] My own commitment to the theological task as a hermeneutical one is represented by what one might call a "praxis hermeneutic." This follows closely the direction suggested by Peter Stuhlmacher in his "hermeneutics of consent." We are concerned to find a method of interpretation of Scripture that seeks conformity to the biblical text, while at the same time seeks authenticity with regard to the "praxis of faith." However, as Willard Swartley rightly cautions:

> The incorporation of understanding (interpretation) into our lives through meditation, through worship and through living accordingly functions as an empirical, validating criterion. But while this validates the claim to understanding, the incarnation of interpretation in life and praxis of itself does not validate the *rightness* of the interpretation. For this reason the call to praxis—living it out—must be put into critical and creative tension with the other aspects of the validating process.[3]

---

[1]Heinz Kimmerhe, ed., *Hermeneutics: The Hand-Written Manuscripts,* trans. James Duke and Jack Forstman (Missoula, Mont.: Scholars Press, 1977), p. 52. For a discussion of contemporary issues in hermeneutics, see Anthony C. Thiselton, *The Two Horizons: New Testament Hermeneutics and Philosophical Description* (Grand Rapids, Mich.: Eerdmans, 1980). The theme of the "two horizons" has been set forth by Hans-Georg Gadamer in *Truth and Method,* trans. Garrett Borden and John Cumming (New York: Continuum, 1975). I might mention also Paul Ricoeur's "hermeneutics of suspicion," in his *Freud and Philosophy: An Essay on Interpretation,* trans. Denis Savage (New Haven, Conn.: Yale University Press, 1970), p. 32; or Peter Stuhlmacher's "hermeneutics of consent," in his *Historical Criticism and Theological Interpretation of Scripture: Towards a Hermeneutic of Consent,* trans. Roy A. Harrisville (Philadelphia: Fortress, 1977); or Geoffrey Wainwright's suggestion that hermeneutics be considered as doxology, in his *Doxology: The Praise of God in Worship, Doctrine and Life* (New York: Oxford University Press, 1980), pp. 175-76; or David Tracy's "paradigmatic hermeneutic," following Mircea Eliade's contention that "only the paradigmatic is the real," in Tracy, *The Analogical Imagination: Christian Theology and the Culture of Pluralism* (New York: Crossroads, 1981), p. 193.
[2]Tracy, *Analogical Imagination,* pp. 58-59.
[3]Willard M. Swartley, *Slavery, Sabbath, War and Women* (Scottsdale, Penn.: Herald, 1983), p. 223.

I have argued elsewhere that Christopraxis, as the act of God in Christ, is one way of understanding how the authority and the presence of truth can be located in the creative tension between the Word of God written as inspired and the Word of God living as inspiring. This act of God in Christ may now be understood as the present working of the risen Lord in the church by the Holy Spirit. Understood in this way, Christopraxis as a criterion for biblical interpretation seems preferable to the concept of the "praxis of faith."[4]

The Resurrection of Jesus as Hermeneutical Criterion

This brings us directly to the thesis of this chapter: the resurrection of Jesus to be the living Lord of the church constitutes a continuing hermeneutical criterion for the church's understanding of itself as under the authority of Scripture. It is the risen Lord himself who is the criterion, not the event or idea of resurrection. For this chapter take the expression "resurrection of Jesus" to mean "the resurrected Jesus."

First, we will explore the way in which the resurrection of Jesus served as a hermeneutical criterion for apostolic authority, the experience of salvation and the "rule of faith." I will argue that the resurrection as hermeneutical criterion was not totally replaced by other criteria, following the inspiration of the New Testament documents and the reception of the canon by the church. Rather, the resurrection of Jesus continues to function as a criterion within the process of interpreting Scripture as a "rule of faith." I will then conclude by suggesting several areas where the resurrected Jesus as hermeneutical criterion may be helpful.

I will select three areas to demonstrate how the criterion was applied: the questions of what constituted genuine apostolic authority, what constituted legitimate grounds for a saving relation to God, and what constituted a new understanding of what it meant to live by the will of Christ as a "rule of faith." I will not treat these areas exhaustively but only enough to demonstrate how in each case the resurrection served as a criterion.

The Resurrection as a Criterion for Apostleship

With regard to apostolic authority, the critical issue centered on historical continuity, coupled with witness to the resurrection. At first it seemed simple. The criteria for selecting a replacement for Judas included the necessity of having shared in the pre-

---

[4]See Ray S. Anderson, "Christopraxis: Competence as a Criterion for Preparation for Ministry," *TSF Bulletin*, January-February 1984. Paul D. Hanson suggests something quite similar when he says, "In the life, death, and resurrection of Jesus Christ, a new breakthrough occurred in God's activity which in its uniqueness still serves as the master paradigm in the Christian's understanding of Dynamic Transcendence" (*The Diversity of Scripture: A Theological Interpretation* [Philadelphia: Fortress, 1982], pp. 66-67).

resurrection witness to Jesus of Nazareth, as well as having witnessed his resurrection from the dead and his ascension (Acts 1:22). The early apostolic preaching centered on the announcement of the resurrection as an interpretation of the life and death of Jesus as both providential and salvific (Acts 2:32).

It was not so simple in the case of Saul of Tarsus. Not only was he not a witness to Jesus of Nazareth prior to Jesus' crucifixion and resurrection, but he was in active opposition to the testimony of the early Christians that Jesus had been raised. Yet Saul, now presenting himself as Paul the apostle, made the claim to apostolic authority based solely on his encounter with the risen Jesus (Acts 9:1-9; 1 Cor 9:1). In his argument to the church at Galatia, against those who impugned his credentials as an apostle, he stated that he was an apostle "sent neither by human commission nor from human authorities, but through Jesus Christ and God the Father, who raised him from the dead" (Gal 1:1). Paul argued that he had not received his gospel from man, but "through a revelation of Jesus Christ" (Gal 1:12).

Against those who appear to have questioned Paul's apostolic authority on the grounds that he was not a follower of Jesus from the baptism of John to the ascension (Acts 1:21-22), Paul counters with the claim that it is the living Jesus who constitutes the source of apostolic authority. If having been among the followers of Jesus prior to his crucifixion is an indispensable criterion for apostolic authority, Paul has no case. But Paul could well have argued, How can one's history of following Jesus prior to his resurrection become a criterion when the chief apostle himself has died? The crucifixion put an end to the history of human actions as a criterion. The risen Lord, who is also the incarnate Word, is the new criterion. And as Paul makes quite clear, the resurrected Jesus appeared to him as well as to the others (1 Cor 9:1; 15:8). Paul does not deny that the disciples, commissioned by Jesus to follow him, also have grounds to be apostles through the new commission of the resurrected Jesus, but he refuses to allow historical precedent to be the determining criterion.

For the apostle Paul there is discontinuity at the level of a claim for apostolic authority "from below," so to speak, as a historical precedent or criterion. But there is continuity "from above" because the resurrected Jesus is the same Jesus who lived, taught, died and was raised by the power of God. Paul did not reinterpret apostleship in terms of his own experience. This is not a "praxis of faith" as hermeneutical criterion. Rather, it was Jesus himself who became the criterion for Paul. Thus he did not argue that his claim to apostleship was the *only* valid claim but that his apostleship was constituted by the *only paradigm* for apostleship—that which is based on encounter with the risen Jesus as its criterion. It is the living Christ present and at work through the power of the Spirit who constitutes the criterion. This is Christopraxis. It was the power of God in the resurrected Christ that seized Paul and constituted for him the criterion for interpreting the life and death of Jesus of Nazareth as the "gospel."

The Resurrection as a Criterion for Salvation

A second crucial issue for the early Christian community was that of the legitimate grounds for salvation as relation to God. For the Jews, circumcision had been established as a sign of the "everlasting covenant" between Abraham and God (Gen 17:7, 10-14). This was meant to serve as a decisive and normative "hermeneutical criterion." Paul argued, to the consternation of Jewish Christians, that circumcision was no longer necessary as a sign of salvation and covenant relation. Paul could have argued that the Gentiles were excused from circumcision because they were not true descendants of Abraham, but he argued that the Gentiles were descendants of Abraham through their relation to Jesus Christ, the true "seed" of Abraham (Gal 3:23-29), and yet not required to be circumcised! The Gentiles do not constitute the criterion; the crucified and risen Christ is the criterion for both Jew and Gentile.

As in the case of apostolic credentials the issue of continuity with a historical criterion again appeared to be at stake. But, as the early Christian community came to see, Jesus was the "end of the law" for those who have faith in the resurrected one (Rom 10:4). Jesus was circumcised in the flesh as a sign of the everlasting covenant (Lk 2:21). Yet his circumcision did not save him. The circumcised man died on the cross. This calls into question the validity of circumcision as a continuing criterion and covenant sign. Yet in being raised from the dead this same Jesus was regenerated in the flesh. Thus his regenerated flesh as the new humanity became the criterion of covenant relation, a point that even the Old Testament prophets anticipated (Jer 31:31-34; Ezek 36:26-27). It is in this sense that one can say that the cross is the "end of circumcision" as a criterion (1 Cor 7:17-19; Gal 5:6; 6:15).

If this can be said about the attempt to continue circumcision as a necessary criterion for salvation, would not the same apply to every attempt to circumvent Jesus' death and resurrection by imposing a criterion lodged in a natural or even a religious law? If Jesus the Jew died, does not Jewishness as a racial criterion for understanding election to salvation also have to surrender its exclusive claim as a criterion of covenant and give way to the criterion of the resurrected Christ in whom there is "neither Jew nor Gentile"? If Jesus the male died, does not the male prerogative as a sexist criterion also surrender its exclusive claim for role status and authority in the kingdom of God to the new criterion of the resurrected Christ, in whom there is "neither male nor female" (Gal 3:28)? Or to put it another way, can the work of the resurrected Jesus in the church, by the power of his Spirit, be set aside in favor of another criterion or principle that has not also been "crucified with him?" Hardly. Paul's hermeneutical criterion at this critical point seems clear enough.

The Resurrection as a Criterion for the Rule of Faith

If there was a third critical issue in the New Testament church, surely it was the question of what constituted a valid interpretation of the will of God for the community of believers. What constitutes appropriate behavior, lifestyle and the practice of faith in personal, social and civic life? If Jesus is the "end of the law," can there be any criteria left by which to determine a "rule of faith?"

Again the criterion for Paul was the resurrected Christ as an experienced presence. As the new criterion the living Lord does not displace the Old Testament nor the apostolic witness as criteria, but he establishes the hermeneutical criterion for these witnesses.

Here too, however, this new criterion of the resurrection of Jesus as an experienced presence represents both a discontinuity as well as a continuity with respect to the ethical demands of the kingdom of God. "The kingdom of God is not food and drink," wrote Paul to the Roman church, "but righteousness and peace and joy in the Holy Spirit" (Rom 14:17). This reminds us of Jesus' teaching that it was not what entered a person that constituted uncleanness, but what came out of a person (Mk 7:14-23).

In this regard, it is interesting that this teaching of Jesus seemed to have no real effect as a criterion until after his resurrection and appearance to Peter and after a personal vision in which the Lord spoke to him in preparation for his visit to the Gentile centurion Cornelius (Acts 10:9-16). Also instructive is the mention of the fact that Peter was still uncertain as to what the vision meant until there was a knock at the door with the invitation from Cornelius to come and preach to him.

This is a fine example of Christopraxis as a hermeneutical criterion. There was the remembered teaching of Jesus, there was the mystical vision in which the Lord spoke to him, but the interpretation actually came when Peter went to the house of Cornelius and preached the gospel of Jesus to him. Only then, when the Spirit of Jesus came upon the Gentile gathering with convincing power and effect, did Peter grasp the full implications of the command of the Lord, and he baptized them in the name of Jesus Christ (Acts 10:44-48). This event was a "preparing of the way of the Lord" to the Gentiles, an incredibly radical and difficult hermeneutical decision—but this is how Christopraxis becomes a hermeneutical criterion.

One cannot forbid a work of the risen Christ through the Holy Spirit for the sake of a law or principle that itself points to this work. The interpretation of the law comes through its fulfillment; but Christ himself is the fulfillment of the law, not another principle or law. The law always was meant to point to the grace of Yahweh as the sole criterion for salvation. It was the *use* of the law as a criterion that wrongly led the Jews to reject the new criterion of the living Lord. Thus the cultic law, even though it was enshrined in the sacred writings as the very word of God, gave way to the new criterion of the living Word through whom the kingdom of God is present in power.

Freedom from the law is not the new ethical criterion but rather "the law of the Spirit of life in Christ Jesus" that sets us free from the law of sin and death (Rom 8:2). To live according to the flesh is to live by the old criterion, which is to reject the Spirit of the resurrected Lord as the new criterion. To live according to the flesh is not only to surrender to licentiousness but to seek to achieve righteousness by conformity to a criterion lodged in the flesh. Only a wrong interpretation of the Old Testament law could see the regulation of the "flesh" as being the criterion for righteousness. Now that the criterion *himself* is present, Paul argues in his letter to the Galatians that the regulations "written in the book of the law" have their true interpretation, which is freedom from the works of the law (Gal 3:10, 13). Paul argues that the law of God is not against the promise of God. But when that promise is present in the form of Christ, these regulations no longer have their "custodial" function (Gal 3:23-29).

Jesus' crucifixion and resurrection put an end to these old regulations and established a new basis and a new criterion for the ethics of the kingdom of God in the experienced presence of the resurrected one (Rom 8:3-11).

Of course, Christians still live in this world with its roles, structures and relationships, even though they have been "raised with Christ" (Col 3:1). But these existing relationships are not to be the place for Christopraxis—"Christ's practice," if you please. Thus Paul's epistles are pastoral in tone and generally include a "domestic code," or *Haustafel,* in which existing cultural and domestic relationships are to be brought within the sphere of Christ that he may be revealed (see Eph 5:21-33; Col 3:18—4:1).

In these situations and social structures, there is a "command of Christ" too. Often the command is expressed in such a way that the person who receives it is expected to glorify Christ through an existing order, even though that order has already "come to an end" in the death and resurrection of Christ. Thus Paul can say as a direct consequence of the command, "Let the word of Christ dwell in you richly" (Col 3:16); "Wives, be subject to your husbands. . . . Children, obey your parents in everything, . . . Slaves, obey in everything those who are your earthly masters. . . . Masters, treat your slaves justly and fairly" (Col 3:18—4:1). The criterion in each of these cases is not a "chain of command" that functions as a legalistic principle but rather the "command of the risen Lord" that functions as a spirit of peace and freedom.

There is, then, a "pastoral hermeneutic" that Paul applies in dealing with the practical matters of determining the rule of faith. In deciding issues for the churches, Paul based his rulings on the claim that he has the "command of the Lord" (1 Cor 14:37). "I received from the Lord what I also handed on to you," wrote Paul (1 Cor 11:23). In certain cases he appears to distinguish between having a direct teaching of Jesus to impart and a word that he himself speaks, which is meant to have the same effect. "To the married I give this command—not I but the Lord. . . . To the rest I say—I and not the Lord" (1 Cor 7:10, 12). He concludes by embracing both what he feels has been a direct teaching by Jesus (concerning the marriage vows) and a teaching that Jesus communicated through Paul's pastoral words (concerning living with an unbelieving spouse) by saying, "I think that I too have the Spirit of God" (1 Cor 7:40). In this case we have the interesting situation of a teaching by Jesus while on earth prior to his crucifixion and resurrection placed alongside of a teaching of Jesus that comes through his presence in the life of the apostle Paul.

This shows us two things: first, there is continuity with the historical Jesus in determining the rule of faith for the postresurrection Christian community; second, there is also equal authority claimed for the pastoral ruling made by Paul out of the experienced presence of the risen Christ. The fact that Paul's pastoral rule has the authority of Christ himself informs us that the presence and authority of the resurrected Jesus served as a hermeneutical criterion for the early church. That is, Jesus himself continues to instruct Christians as to the will of God in practical matters of the life of faith. Jesus has not simply left us a set of teachings. He has done that. But in addition, he continues to teach. Discerning this teaching is itself a hermeneutical task, not merely an exercise in historical memory.

Through sound principles of literary and historical criticism, one can examine more accurately the *syntactical* or structural relation and meaning of words in the inspired texts. But if there is also a *semantical* or referential relation between the words of Scripture and the living Lord of the church, is this relation not a proper area of hermeneutical concern?[5] And if so, is it not the living and present Lord who upholds that referential relation for the sake of the inspired word accomplishing its purpose? And if this is so, then Christopraxis will continue to lead us into his Word, and Jesus' prayer will be completed: "Sanctify them in the truth; your word is truth" (Jn 17:17).

The Eschatological Nature of a Hermeneutical Criterion

Because faith as experience of the risen Christ is not the criterion, but the resurrected Lord himself, there is an eschatological tension in the pastoral hermeneutic of Paul. Christopraxis as a hermeneutical criterion never surrenders the inherent infallibility and authority of the living Word as the resurrected, ascended and present Lord to a human experience, teaching, regulation or tradition. Paul is quite explicit about this regarding his own teaching:

---

[5]Thomas F. Torrance likes to say, "No syntactics contains its own semantics" (*Reality and Evangelical Theology* [Downers Grove, Ill.: InterVarsity Press, 1999], p. 116). "It is in the semantic relation between the human word and the divine Word that the basic clues to understanding will be found, for the higher level of God's Word comprehends the operation of the human word at the lower level and forms its meaningful reference to itself" (p. 117).

Think of us in this way, as servants of Christ and stewards of God's mysteries. Moreover, it is required of stewards that they be found trustworthy. But with me it is a very small thing that I should be judged by you or by any human court. I do not even judge myself. I am not aware of anything against myself, but I am not thereby acquitted. It is the Lord who judges me. Therefore do not pronounce judgment before the time, before the Lord comes, who will bring to light the things now hidden in darkness and will disclose the purposes of the heart. Then each one will receive commendation from God. (1 Cor 4:1-5)

According to this caution from Paul, there is a hermeneutical criterion anchored in the eschatological event of the final parousia of Christ. This does not evacuate the present Word of God of its authority, for "the Lord is the Spirit, and where the Spirit of the Lord is, there is freedom" (2 Cor 3:17). On this basis Paul equates the word that he teaches and writes with the word of the Lord himself (1 Cor 14:37). Yet even as the inspired words of Moses and the prophets are interpreted by the hermeneutical criterion of the incarnate Word, and even as the human and historical life of Jesus is interpreted by the hermeneutical criterion of the resurrected Jesus, so the words taught by the Spirit and inspired by the Spirit will be interpreted in the end by the hermeneutical criterion of the risen and coming Jesus Christ. Does this diminish the authority of the apostolic and inspired Scripture? Paul does not think so.

However, it does mean that the resurrection as hermeneutical criterion points forward to the coming Christ as well as backward to the historical Christ. In this present age, meanwhile, there is a tension between the ever-present demands of the former criteria and the already-present criterion of the resurrected Lord. The word of the Lord came through cultural, social and religious forms that persisted in spite of the radical new criterion of the resurrected humanity of Christ.

Where these forms were not a direct threat to the existence of the freedom of the Lord to form a new humanity, they were permitted to exist by the pastoral hermeneutic of the apostle. "Were you a slave when called?" asked Paul. "Do not be concerned about it. Even if you can gain your freedom, make use of your present condition now more than ever" (1 Cor 7:21). Thus Onesimus is sent back to Philemon not only as a Christian but also as a fugitive slave. Paul leaves it to Philemon to apply the hermeneutical criterion of the resurrection in this situation (cf. Philem 8-10). From this we can infer that Paul's letter to Philemon, which is the inspired Word of God, has authority not merely by virtue of what it said but in its effect to produce a modification of the behavior and life of Philemon (the interpreter).[6] Paul did not "liberate"

---

[6]Cf. Scott Bartchy, who says, "The authority of a New Testament text dealing with human behavior lies first of all in the *direction* in which any aspect of first century behavior is being modified by the text in question (i.e., *from* wherever Christ encountered the new behavior toward maturity in Christ)" ("Jesus, Power and Gender Roles," *TSF Bulletin,* January-February 1984, p. 3).

Onesimus by command of the divine word. Rather, he sought the liberation of Philemon from his old ways of thinking as a slave owner, so he could be free to receive Onesimus as a full Christian partner and brother. In the same way, the authority of Scripture is evidenced by its effect in producing the intention and purpose of Christ in the liberation of men and women to become full partners in every aspect of the life and work of God's kingdom.

There ought to be general agreement as to the essential thrust of the argument thus far. The resurrection of Jesus Christ is the hermeneutical criterion for determining the content of the apostolic gospel, for establishing the ground for salvation as relation to God and for giving direction to the church in living out the life of Christ in this present age. The resurrected Jesus has usually been seen as the decisive criterion marking the emergence of the early Christian church as a distinct community of faith in which both Jew and Gentile found unity in Christ. Our purpose has not been to develop a new criterion but to demonstrate the resurrection of Jesus as the criterion. Before we continue, it might be helpful to list the steps we have taken in demonstrating this criterion as a foundation on which we can build our case.

1. To say that Jesus died and was raised up by the power of God is to say that the law, tradition, nature, culture and history must give way to the new criterion of his presence as Lord in the world.

2. To say that Jesus is Lord is to bring the old order, which is passing away, under the sphere of the healing and liberating power of the command of God.

3. To say that "the Lord commands" in the context of a pastoral ruling on Christian faith and practice is to unite the teaching of Christ with the presence of Christ for the purpose of modifying the direction of Christian behavior toward maturity in Christ, whatever one's situation is at the beginning.

4. To say that one is obedient to Christ and moving toward maturity in him is to interpret Christ's teaching and will through faith and practice that looks toward commendation at his coming.

5. To say that Scripture is the Word of God is to bind the interpreters of Scripture to Jesus Christ as the living Lord, who is the infallible One.

6. To say that the resurrected Jesus is the hermeneutical criterion for understanding the Word of God is to give holy Scripture the unique status of being the Word of God without making the authority of Scripture dependent on literary, historical or confessional criteria alone.

7. To say that the responsibility of the contemporary church is to exercise this pastoral hermeneutic in the power of the Holy Spirit is to recognize Christopraxis as the sign of "preparing the way of the Lord" in every sphere of domestic, social, political and religious life; this is to say, "For freedom Christ has set us free" (Gal 5:1).

The Living Lord: A Contemporary Hermeneutical Criterion

We now have come to the critical task in the development of the thesis: *the resurrected Jesus as the living Lord is a continuing hermeneutical criterion for interpreting the Word of God.*

Once holy Scripture is written and the canon closed, is it still possible to say that Jesus Christ as risen Lord is the hermeneutical criterion for interpretation of Scripture?

To put it another way, having the living Lord in the church through the Holy Spirit, does the church today stand in the same hermeneutical relation to the New Testament Scriptures as did the New Testament church with respect to the Old Testament Scriptures?

I would answer no, for two reasons. First, the coming into being of the church following Pentecost was an absolutely unique event. In a sense one could say that the emergence of the church was a divinely inspired interpretation of the Old Testament Scripture with respect to God's redemptive purpose. The first church did not so much interpret the Old Testament using the resurrected Jesus as hermeneutical criterion as it was the result of this interpretation through the "acts of the Spirit" and the faithful work and witness of the apostles. Second, the apostolic foundation for the church is itself unique and no other foundation can one lay but that which is built on the cornerstone, Jesus Christ (1 Cor 3:10-15).

At the outset it must be clearly stated that we are not talking about adding to the canon of Scripture or suggesting a new canon but merely interpreting rightly the canonical Scriptures, given the assumption that interpretation is a two-edged sword. One edge is the truth of *God's holy Word*, which is "living and active . . . piercing until it divides soul from spirit, joints from marrow; it is able to judge the thoughts and intentions of the heart" (Heb 4:12). The other edge is the truth of *Christ's holy work* by which he is active to do God's will in setting captives free and breaking down dividing barriers, preparing in his church, his body, a people who are and will be his brothers and sisters. "Examine yourselves," wrote the apostle Paul. "Do you not realize that Jesus Christ is in you?—unless, indeed, you fail to meet the test! . . . For we cannot do anything against the truth, but only for the truth" (2 Cor 13:5, 8).

Can we say that Jesus is not only the living Word who inspires the New Testament and thus insures its trustworthiness but that he is also present in the contemporary reading and interpretation of the New Testament? Can we affirm that the living, glorified Jesus Christ, even now preparing to come out of glory to this world and for his church to consummate all things, is the already-present Lord who upholds his word in Scripture as true and directs its purpose to his own creative ends? And can we affirm that the very words of Scripture, inspired as they are, continue to speak to us out of the very being of the One present with us? Can we dare to say with Ricoeur, though with a different point of reference, "I believe that being can still speak to me"?[7]

I think we can and we must. For if we cannot, we will find ourselves in the position of the Grand Inquisitor in Dostoyevsky's classic story, who, surprised to confront Jesus himself in the roundup of heretics to be condemned, refused to allow him to contribute to what had been written. "The old man has told him He hasn't the right to add anything to what He has said of old," said Ivan in telling the story.[8]

Certainly there are dangers here! We are well aware of the final words of warning in the New Testament about taking away from or adding to the inspired prophecy (Rev 22:18-19). But it must also not be forgotten that the very next words contain the promise, "Surely I am coming soon" (Rev 22:20).

Let it be clearly understood that no confusion must blur the sharp line between revelation that has taken the form of the inspired writings of holy Scripture and interpretation that depends on that revelation for its infallible source and norm.

The first-century horizon, which is the occasion for the Scripture text in the New Testament, cannot be fused with our contemporary horizon to make revelation dependent on our self understanding (such as Rudolf Bultmann tended to do). This would confuse hermeneutics with revealed truth itself. Nor should we attempt to push our contemporary horizon back into the first century, for we cannot do this. We can only create an abstraction of this first horizon that, if used as the sole criterion for revealed truth, makes out of divine Logos an impersonal and abstract logos as a criterion for the truth of God himself (such as Carl Henry tends to do).[9]

What we are suggesting here—if we wish to continue to speak of the hermeneutical task in this way—is that the two horizons are not resolved into a single, contemporary meaning, nor into a principle of abstract reason. As the criterion for both the original and contemporary meaning of the text, the Lord himself sustains these two points in a creative and positive tension. In this way the horizon of the original occasion of the text and the horizon of the contemporary interpreter are not really fused at all but remain quite distinct. Paul is permitted to say what he said as the command of the Lord in his pastoral hermeneutic, without forcing the text to be read in a way alien to the original context.

When we take seriously the fact that the resurrection of Jesus Christ continues to be the criterion for our hermeneutical task, we do not fuse the present horizon of our experience to the text as an abstract law, nor do we fuse the text to our present hori-

---

[7]Paul Ricoeur, *The Symbolism of Evil*, trans. Emerson Buchanan (Boston: Beacon, 1967), p. 352.

[8]Fyodor Dostoyevsky, *The Brothers Karamazov* (New York: Random House, Modern Library, 1950), p. 297.

[9]See Rudolf Bultmann, *Jesus Christ and Mythology* (London: SCM Press, 1958); Carl F. H. Henry, *God, Revelation and Authority* (Dallas: Word, 1976-1983), 3:221-22, 364.

zon as a relativization of revelation to culture. Rather we submit our present horizon of experience as well as the horizon of the text to the Lord himself, who is the living and coming One, before whom all of our understanding and actions must be judged. Only in this way can obedience to Scripture uphold both the truth and the purpose of Scripture.[10] And to those who protest that the reality of the living Lord cannot be objectively discerned and known in the context of our own subjective experience, we must in turn protest that this is a denial of the sheer objective reality of the being of the risen Lord who presents himself to us both as an object of knowledge and as experience through the Holy Spirit's encounter of us. To be sure, this objective reality of Christ does not dissolve into our experience as the criterion of truth, for Christ has bound himself to Scripture and to its propositional form of revelation. But neither is the living Lord dissolved into the impersonal abstractness of revelation as the objectification of truth, with our own logic (logos) as the hermeneutical criterion.

Because the criterion of the living Lord in the church is not a different criterion from the same Lord who inspired the apostolic teaching and not different from the same Lord who taught his disciples while on earth, this hermeneutical criterion does not stand in contradiction or opposition to Scripture itself. There is a tension, but it is the creative and redemptive tension between the "now" and the "not yet." It is the tension between the new humanity and new order, which is always and already present through the Holy Spirit, and the old order, in which we have received the command of God but which must give way to the new.

While the entire Scriptures are subject to the resurrected Jesus as a hermeneutical criterion, there appear to be areas within the New Testament where this tension between the "now" and the "not yet" is more pronounced than in other areas. These areas are noted by the fact that a particular text or passage can be used to support a practice or teaching that appears quite different from a teaching derived from another set of texts, using in both cases sound principles of historical and grammatical exegesis.

Where a New Testament teaching appears unanimous and consistent in every pastoral situation, I am not suggesting that the presence of the living Lord in the church can be understood in such a way that this "single voice" can be silenced or

---

[10]See the helpful suggestion by Geoffrey Bromiley to the effect that God is not identical with the Bible, though God teaches what the Bible teaches (preface to *God and Marriage* [Grand Rapids, Mich.: Eerdmans, 1981]). In this same connection Thomas F. Torrance helpfully comments, "In order to think out the relation of the Church in history to Christ we must put both these together—*mediate horizontal relation* through history to the historical Jesus Christ, and *immediate vertical relation* through the Spirit to the risen and ascended Jesus Christ. It is the former that supplies the material content, while it is the latter that supplies the immediacy of actual encounter" (*Space, Time and Resurrection* [Grand Rapids, Mich.: Eerdmans, 1976], p. 147).

"made to sing a different tune." But where apostolic teaching and practice is clearly governed by the readiness or openness of the situation to experience full freedom in Christ, the hermeneutical criterion of the resurrected Christ as a continuing presence in the church is, in my judgment, indispensable. For it is here that the tension between the now and the not yet is most evident. This is not to suggest that we have here a kind of "God of the exegetical gaps!" All exegesis of Scripture must finally be accountable to the resurrected, always present and already coming Lord. For the purpose of this discussion, we are focusing on those areas most clearly in this eschatological tension and that require unusual sensitivity to the hermeneutical criterion we are advocating.

It is not difficult to find instances within the New Testament Scriptures where such a hermeneutical criterion is especially relevant. For example, consider the matter of the Christian's relation and responsibility to the state. In certain situations we are encouraged to "obey God rather than man." In other situations we are reminded that we are subject to the governing authorities as instituted by God himself (Rom 13:1-7)! Or consider the issue of Scripture's teaching on divorce and remarriage when viewed in the context of a personal failure and confession of sin in this area. Does the living Lord offer grace and forgiveness when it is sought on the basis of the promise and teaching of Scripture?

One contemporary issue for the church is the proper role of women in positions of pastoral leadership and service. Are Christian women who testify to God's calling to receive ordination and serve as pastors of the church in disobedience to the teaching of Scripture, or are they in obedience to the Spirit of the resurrected Christ at work in the church? This issue is surely one that requires a patient and careful hermeneutical approach that honors the Word of God and makes manifest the will and power of Christ in his church in our present situation. The following section will take up the issue of sexual parity in pastoral ministry as a case in which the resurrection of Jesus might serve as a hermeneutical criterion.

A Case for Sexual Parity in Pastoral Ministry

Can we say that Jesus not only is the living Word who inspires the words and teaching of the New Testament and thus insures its trustworthiness but that he is also a contemporary reader and interpreter of Scripture? We answered this question in the affirmative earlier in this chapter and argued the following thesis: *the resurrection of Jesus to be the living Lord of the church constitutes a continuing hermeneutical criterion for the church's understanding of itself as under the authority of Scripture.*

We saw that the resurrection of Jesus served as a criterion by which the early church determined questions of apostolic authority, the experience of salvation and the "rule of faith." I also suggested that the risen Lord continues to serve as a criterion for interpreting the purpose of Scripture in the contemporary church. Where there is a tension within Scripture between the now and the not yet, I argued that a proper interpretation of scriptural authority as a rule of faith must take into account the presence and work of the risen Christ within his church. This is not an appeal to experience over and against the authority of Scripture. Rather this is a recognition that Jesus himself continues to be the hermeneutical criterion by which the authority of Scripture is preserved in its application to a concrete and present situation.

The purpose of this section is to apply this thesis in one specific area of concern for the contemporary church: the role of women in pastoral ministry.

In choosing the case of sexual parity in pastoral ministry for the purpose of working through an application of our thesis, I am well aware that this is one of the most complex and vital issues facing the church today. There are, of course, many facets of the issue, not least of which is the issue of a critical exegesis of the primary New Testament texts that deal with the role of women in society, marriage and the church. There is no way to review the extensive exegetical and theological literature that has recently emerged concerning this question in the short space of this chapter.[11]

What is clear is that while the New Testament speaks with an emphatic voice concerning a restriction on the role of women in certain teaching and ministry situations, in other situations the emphasis is as clearly on the side of full participation and full parity. One only has to compare the insistent commands issued by the apostle Paul that women be "silent in the churches" and not be permitted "to teach or to have authority over a man" (1 Cor 14:34; 1 Tim 2:12), with the rather matter-of-fact instruction that a woman who prophesies (in public worship) should keep her head covered (1 Cor 11:4). Even more significant is the same apostle's practice of identifying women as coworkers [synergoi] along with men (Phil 4:2-3) and his commendation of Phoebe in the church at Rome as a "deaconess," which is a dubious translation in the RSV of the masculine noun diakonos (Rom 16:1-2). Paul goes on to describe Phoebe as his "helper" (RSV), which again is a weak translation of prostatis, which is a noun form of the verb used in 1 Timothy 3:5 that designates a leadership activity or "managing" one's household.[12] The apostle's overt recognition of the role of women serving as coworkers alongside other apostles is worthy of note. There is a strong possibility, according to many scholars, that the Junias mentioned along with Andronicus

---

[11]A helpful bibliography of recent literature on the issue of the Bible and the role of women can be found in Swartley, *Slavery, Sabbath, War and Women,* pp. 342-45.

[12]For a full discussion of these exegetical issues, see Scott Bartchy, "Power, Submission and Sexual Identity Among the Early Christians," in *Essays on New Testament Christianity,* ed. C. Robert Wetzel (Cincinnati: Standard, 1978). See also the discussion of these issues by David Scholer, "Women in Ministry," *A Covenant Companion* 72, nos. 21, 22 (1983): 8-9, 14-15; ibid., 73, nos. 1, 2 (1984): 12-13, 12-15.

as being "among the apostles" was actually a woman—Junia (Rom 16:7).[13] "Only an extraordinary Biblical assumption that a woman could not be an apostle keeps most commentators from reading Junias as Junia," says Don Williams. Williams goes on to cite the church father Chrysostom as saying, "And indeed to be Apostles at all is a great thing. . . . Oh! How great is the devotion of this woman, that she should be even counted worthy of the appellation of Apostle!"[14]

The point is this: with recent scholarship demonstrating that the New Testament evidence is not unanimous as to a teaching forbidding women to exercise pastoral leadership and ministry in the church, the issue cannot be settled on textual exegesis alone. When all the exegesis is done, a decision still must be made as to which set of texts demand priority or serve as a normative criterion for determining the role of women in the church.[15]

It is in cases like this that the resurrected Jesus as the living Lord of the church can serve as a hermeneutical criterion. For surely he knows what his will is for the church in the particular situation of the contemporary church. And there are many of us who feel that he has already shown us what his will is by calling and anointing women for pastoral ministry in full parity with men.

The situation is not unlike that which confronted Peter. On the one hand he had the Old Testament teaching that God's gracious election was restricted to the Jews and that the Gentiles were excluded. On the other hand he had the teaching of the Lord himself that pointed toward offering Cornelius and his household full parity in the gospel. The issue was decided for him when the Spirit fell on the assembled people while he was yet speaking. "Can anyone withhold the water for baptizing these people who have received the Holy Spirit just as we have?" he exclaimed (Acts 10:47).

Can the church today recognize and affirm female members as having the same calling and gift of pastoral ministry as male members, without being disobedient to the Lord's teaching in Scripture? Or perhaps we should formulate the question as a paraphrase of Peter's rhetorical remark: "Can anyone forbid ordination for those women who give evidence of being called forth and gifted for pastoral ministry in the church?"

---

[13]See Bernadette Brooten, "Junia . . . Outstanding Among the Apostles," in *Women Priests*, ed. L. and A. Swidler (New York: Paulist, 1977), pp. 141-44. Also Bartchy, "Power, Submission and Sexual Identity," pp. 66-67.

[14]Don Williams, *The Apostle Paul and Women in the Church* (Glendale, Calif.: Regal, 1978), p. 45. The original form of the Chrysostom quote can be found in *Epistolum ad Romanus* 31.2.

[15]Bartchy, in his helpful essay cited above, suggests that there are at least three broad categories of texts that deal with the place and role of women in the New Testament communities. "Normative" texts declare the way things are to be; "descriptive" texts report the activity of women without making any comment for or against activities; and "problematic" texts point to where a disorder had occurred or was occurring and needed correction ("Power, Submission and Sexual Identity," p. 56).

If Christ is at work through his Holy Spirit setting apart women for pastoral ministry with the evident blessing of God in their ministries, then there will be full sexual parity in pastoral ministry. By pastoral ministry we mean all that a person assumes when receiving the gift and calling of ordained ministry within the church, by whatever form of polity it is recognized. By parity we mean a full share in pastoral ministry. This, of course, entails equality, but parity implies a full share in that distributed by Christ, while equality tends to focus first of all on rights, power and privilege.

Can there be parity between men and women in pastoral ministry? Only if the Lord himself intends that there shall be and only if he acts within his church to distribute the gift of pastoral ministry to women and men alike.

For some of us, at least, it has become imperative to recognize and not deny that the Lord calls forth women within his church to receive and exercise the gift of pastoral ministry as a full share of Christ's own ministry. To deny this, for some of us, would be to deny that the Lord, through his Spirit, has so acted. To refuse to ordain women to pastoral ministry would be to refuse to recognize the freedom of the Lord as manifested through his work of calling, gifting and blessing the ministry of women in the church today. It is Christ himself working in this continuing ministry, as T. F. Torrance reminds us:

> Not only did he pour out his Spirit upon the Apostles inspiring them for their special task, and not only did he pour out his Spirit in a decisive and once for all way, at Pentecost, constituting the people of God into the New Testament Church which is the Body of Christ, but within that Church and its Communion of the Spirit he continues to pour out special gifts for ministry, with the promise that as the Gospel is proclaimed in his Name he will work with the Church confirming their ministry of Christ to others as his own and making it the ministry of himself to mankind.[16]

In taking this position we are mindful of the objections raised.[17] There is the objection based on precedent. Jesus himself was male, and all of his disciples were male. We have already seen how this objection loses its power based on the resurrection of Jesus as a hermeneutical criterion. The criterion of maleness, as the criterion of Jewishness and the criterion of circumcision, came to an end with the crucifixion of the Jewish, circumcised male named Jesus of Nazareth. No longer can the non-Jewish, the uncircumcised and the female members of the believing community of faith be systematically discriminated against. We are not surprised to discover that

---

[16]Torrance, *Space, Time and Resurrection,* p. 121.

[17]For a discussion of the objections raised against women's ordination, along with a perceptive argument for ordination of women, see Paul K. Jewett, *The Ordination of Women* (Grand Rapids, Mich.: Eerdmans, 1982).

the early New Testament church carried forward these criteria as part of its tradition. The new wine was put into old wineskins with predictable tensions and torments (Mt 9:17). What is surprising is to discover that even here there are evidences of an incipient recognition of the hermeneutical criterion of the resurrection with regard to the role and status of women in the church.[18] I have made reference above to the recognition the apostle Paul gave to women as coworkers with the apostles and not merely followers.

There is the objection that argues from church history. From the early church "fathers," through the medieval period and even forward through the Reformation into modern church history, has the church ever officially recognized and affirmed the full parity of women in the pastoral office? As a rule the answer is no, even allowing for some exceptions. It should be noted, however, that Dean Alford records the interesting fact that "women sat unveiled in the assemblies in a separate place, by the presbyters, and were ordained by the laying on of hands until the Church Council of Laodicea forbade it in 363 A.D.—three hundred years after Paul had written the epistle to the Corinthians."[19]

But here too we have seen that historical precedent cannot be a determinative criterion for validating the present and future work of Christ. For he, as the living Lord, is the one who is the criterion himself. We have argued that the resurrection of Jesus and his already present eschatological power in the church is the criterion for interpreting the command of the Lord. If this is true, does not the new work of Christ in the church today really suggest that Christ is continuing to give gifts to his church and prepare it for his own coming? Ought we not at least have a sense of fear and trembling about such a possibility instead of appearing to be "dead certain" when we may really be "dead wrong?"

For many serious Christians the foremost objection to the ordination of women is based on an argument from certain scriptural texts. We have already cited some of these above. In 1 Timothy 2:8-15 Paul sets forth what he considers to be appropriate behavior for men who pray and for women who practice piety. In this context he addresses a specific charge: "I permit no woman to teach or to have authority over men; she is to keep silent" (1 Tim 2:12).

In 1 Corinthians 14:34-36 Paul says much the same to the Corinthian church, adding that not only is it a shame for women to speak in church, but they are to be subordinate (presumably to their husbands). In chapter 11 of this same letter, again

---

[18]For a helpful discussion of the new role of women as portrayed in the New Testament, see Williams, *The Apostle Paul and Women in the Church*.

[19]Quoted by Jessie Penn-Lewis, *The Magna Carta of Woman* (Minneapolis: Bethany Fellowship, 1975), pp. 45-46.

in the context of public prayer, he states that the head of a woman is her husband, the head of a man is Christ, and the head of Christ is God (1 Cor 11:3-5).

Only a casual survey of recent literature dealing with these texts would be necessary to convince a reader that no amount of exegetical cunning can rescue Paul in these cases from the appearance that he taught in certain circumstances that women should not have full parity in ministry with men.[20] What is not as clear is what Paul's teaching and practice is universally, without regard to the capacity of the particular situation to bear responsibly the full measure of Christ's gift of freedom. It is well known that in the Corinthian society of Paul's day, women were suspected of being immoral when not abiding by the local customs regarding manner of dress and behavior. For this reason, Paul seems to have accommodated his pastoral teaching to this cultural factor in addressing some problems in the Corinthian church. While Paul clearly held that women were equal to men and had the freedom to minister along with the apostles, he nevertheless urged the Christian women in Corinth to abide by the local custom concerning the style of their hair. The freedom of women in Christ apparently did not give them license to act in such a way that they would be viewed as "immoral" (cf. 1 Cor 11:4-16).[21]

Yet when it comes to the churches of Macedonia and the church at Rome, Paul is not only silent concerning the need for women to be silent but actually encourages and recognizes the role of prominent women such as Lydia, Euodia, Syntyche and Phoebe. Beyond this argument from these "descriptive" texts, there is the normative text in Galatians 3:28 where Paul explicitly states that "there is no longer Jew or Greek, there is no longer slave or free, there is no longer male or female; for all of you are one in Christ Jesus."

Here again, if we approach the texts without regard to the historical situation, we create a textual "standoff." If one leans to the side of Paul's specific pastoral injunctions as the criterion, then one will conclude that the Galatians text does not in fact have a bearing on the role of women in ministry, only to their full equality as children of Abraham. On the other hand, if one leans to the side of the Galatians text as a "Magna Carta" of women's liberation, then the teaching of Paul in the specific situation cannot be a criterion as a command of God. Willard Swartley says, "In Paul's

---

[20]For an excellent discussion of the various exegetical approaches to these passages, see Swartley, *Slavery, Sabbath, War and Women,* pp. 150-91, 256-69.

[21]See Alan Padgett, "Paul on Women in the Church: The Contradictions of Coiffure in 1 Corinthians 11:2-16," *Journal for the Study of the New Testament* 20 (1984): 69-86. Padgett discusses the three traditional exegetical arguments that seek to account for the apparent contradiction between Paul's harsh restrictions upon women in 1 Corinthians 11:4-7 and his emphasis in 1 Corinthians 11:10-12 on the equality of women with men. Setting aside these solutions, Padgett argues for a new interpretation of this section, reading Paul as stating the position the Corinthians themselves held in verses 4-7 and then correcting this position with his own in verses 10-12.

writings we find texts which give different signals. Some appear to prescribe specific roles for men and women; others appear to grant freedom from these roles."[22]

I realize that not all will agree that there appear to be unresolved differences between certain scriptural texts relating to the role of women in the church. Some will argue that these are only "apparent" differences and that Scripture speaks with "one voice" in all matters because that is the nature of Scripture as the Word of God. It is true that Scripture testifies to its own intrinsic unity. But if this unity becomes a "principle of harmonization" of texts, this imposes a criterion of consistency on the exegetical and hermeneutical task that serves more as an a priori principle than a theological insight. After all, the phenomena of Scripture in its own cultural, historical and literary context constitute the primary source for our doctrine of Scripture, not the reverse. One aspect of the phenomena of Scripture, surely, is the freedom of the Word of God in its specific and concrete variety of expression and application to communicate authoritatively and infallibly the truth of God to us.

For this reason, we do not feel that the freedom of an author of Scripture, say, the apostle Paul, to express the command of God in ways quite different in specific situations contradicts the essential unity and consistency of the Word of God itself. What does contradict the Word of God, in my judgment, is to force it into a logical straitjacket of conformity to a principle of consistency. In this case, the criterion has shifted from the Word of God itself to a hermeneutical principle that controls the exegetical task. In our case, we argue that it is the resurrected Lord himself who is the criterion of continuity and consistency in the freedom of his own self-witness to the truth of God.

If one takes Paul's various statements on the role and status of women in the church in a way that abstracts them from the historical context in which they are uttered, a kind of "textual standoff" will occur, as stated above. This then compels the interpreter to attempt a kind of Hegelian synthesis through an exegetical exercise by which thesis and antithesis are resolved through a "higher principle." But this approach tends to dissolve particular texts of their full weight for the sake of a theological principle that becomes the criterion.

This can work two ways. One could take the position that Paul's christological statement in Galatians 3:28 concerning the status of male and female in Christ has a theological priority over his occasional teaching in 1 Timothy 2, where he forbids women to exercise the role of teaching or having authority over men. The theological principle of "equality in Christ" thus becomes the criterion by which one text is played off against another for the sake of resolving the apparent contradiction. This approach obviously makes the apostolic teaching to Timothy of dubious quality with

---

[22]Swartley, *Slavery, Sabbath, War and Women*, p. 164.

regard to its being the word of God for the church. In the end, one will wonder whether or not Timothy should have followed Paul's instructions if he applied the theological principle of equality as Paul himself taught in his letter to the Galatian church.

One can also see this same tendency to synthesize contrasting texts in the attempt to harmonize Paul's teaching in Galatians 3 with 1 Timothy 2 by interpreting the Galatians 3:28 passage as referring only to the spiritual unity and equality between male and female in Christ, and not as an attempt to eliminate these distinctives as role functions in the church. This approach succeeds in resolving the apparent impasse in interpreting the Pauline texts regarding the role of women through an exegetical surgery whereby the spiritual benefits of being in Christ are excised from the role functions of serving Christ in the church. Gender identity coupled with physical sex differentiation becomes the criterion for ministry. Male and female continue to operate as criteria outside of the benefits of Christ. Nature determines the extent to which grace can go in bringing the benefits of Christ into the historical and temporal order. In this case, the synthesis has been at the expense of the full weight of the Galatians text as a christological basis for the order of the church's ministry.

Let us assume, for the moment, that what Paul meant for his readers to understand in the above texts was exactly what he wrote in the context of their own time and place. Rather than attempting to fuse the horizon of these texts with a contemporary horizon and so interpret them in a way that renders their meaning more congenial to our modern views of egalitarianism, suppose we let them stand as the command of the Lord to the churches to which they are addressed.[23] What do we then have?

---

[23] For a penetrating critique of the problem of "presenting" New Testament texts, see Dietrich Bonhoeffer, "The Presentation of New Testament Texts," in *No Rusty Swords,* trans. E. H. Robertson (London: Collins/Fontana, 1970), pp. 302-20. Rather than bringing the text to the present situation in hopes of making it relevant, Bonhoeffer suggests that one must bring the present situation to the text and remain there until one has heard Christ speak through the text. This changes the present to the future: "*The Present* is not where the present age announces its claim before Christ, but where the present age stands before the claims of Christ, for the concept of the present is determined not by a temporal definition but by the Word of Christ as the Word of God. The present is not a feeling of time, an interpretation of time, an atmosphere of time, but the Holy Spirit, and the Holy Spirit alone. The Holy Spirit is the subject of the present, not we ourselves, so the Holy Spirit is also the subject of the presentation. *The most concrete element of the Christian message* and of textual exposition is not a human act of presentation but is always God himself, it is the Holy Spirit. . . . 'Presentation' therefore means attention to this future, to this that *is outside,* and it is a most fatal confusion of present and past to think that the present can be defined as *that which rests upon itself and carries its criterion within itself.* The criterion of the true present lies outside itself, it lies in the future, it lies in Scripture and in the word of Christ witnessed in it. Thus the *content* will consist in something outside, something 'over against,' something 'future' being heard as present—the strange Gospel, not the familiar one, will be the present Gospel. A scandalous 'point of contact!' " (p. 309).

The church in Corinth has an apostolic command that is equivalent to the command of the Lord himself. Timothy has an apostolic command that is also tantamount to the word of the Lord. But what must be remembered is that the *command* of the risen Lord through the apostle, expressed in the form of a pastoral rule, does not automatically become a *criterion* that can be used independently of the authority of the Lord himself. That is to say, the Lord himself is the head of the body. He is the criterion by which the church as the body of Christ defines its existence and seeks its true order. The command of the Lord comes as a specific command in the particular situation in which the church exists and is meant to teach the church how to exemplify Christ in its present state and how to grow up into Christ in all things (cf. Eph 4:1-15). The "basic teaching of Christ" that the author of Hebrews suggests should be left behind for the sake of going on to maturity is also a command of God in its own time (Heb 6:1).

This same relationship between a specific rule and the command of God was made quite clear in our earlier examination of the way in which the resurrection of Jesus served as a hermeneutical criterion to interpret the teaching concerning the "everlasting" covenant sign of circumcision. The Old Testament law concerning circumcision was the command of God for Abraham and remains the inspired word of God but not the criterion for determining salvation as relation to God. When the Judaizers sought to invoke circumcision as a criterion and a formal principle by which Gentile Christians were not given full parity in the church, Paul rebuked them vehemently (cf. Gal 1—2).

Certainly it is true that the Bible is normative and infallible in that it is the word of God. The Bible teaches many helpful and instructive principles for Christian faith and practice. The problem comes when any principle is made into a normative criterion and imposed as a rule or law that excludes the Spirit of Christ as the criterion that upholds the normative teaching of the Scriptures.

Can a Scripture text remain intact as an inspired word of God when a *principle abstracted* from that specific command no longer serves as a normative rule in the church? I believe that it can and does. The "law of circumcision" was replaced by the "law of the Spirit of Christ" as the absolute criterion. To insist that circumcision as a principle or law defines the status of human persons before God is to deny the work of Christ who broke down that barrier and gave full parity to Gentiles along with Jews (cf. Eph 2:11-22). Yet this does not destroy the validity and authority of the Old Testament Scriptures as the Word of God, for these Scriptures served as the revelation of God to the people of their time, and so to us, because they point to Christ, as Jesus himself testified (Jn 5:45-47).

In somewhat the same way, I am suggesting that those who feel it necessary to deny the very possibility (if not also the actuality) that Christ has distributed the gift of pastoral ministry to women as well as to men in his church will be forced to make out of one group of texts an absolute criterion that excludes women from pastoral ministry. This will have the effect of forcing other texts that describe full parity for women to be concealed or suppressed. Even more serious, it will create a law that restricts Christ from exercising that freedom here and now. In a sense, this fuses the horizon of the present church to the horizon of the early church and results in a hermeneutical criterion that gives primacy to the letter rather than the spirit, to law rather than grace and to the past rather than to the future.

I think that I can understand why some would want to do this. For I too do not wish to sacrifice the authority of the inspired text to cultural relativism and "prevailing winds of doctrine." I suspect that those who feel it necessary to deny the possibility of Christ's contemporary gift of pastoral ministry to women do so because they see this as the only alternative to an approach to certain parts of Scripture that appear to relativize the text to contemporary cultural values or ideological convictions.

It is the purpose of this chapter to suggest that these are not the only two alternatives. One does not have to (and ought not) make out of an inspired text of Scripture a universal and everlasting law of the church that deprives half the members of the church from full parity in the gift and calling of pastoral ministry. Nor does one have (and ought not) to use as a hermeneutical criterion the prevailing impulses and ideological currents for the sake of making Scripture meaningful or acceptable to the present age.

When we allow that the resurrection of Jesus is a hermeneutical criterion (not the only one but the supreme one), Scripture can be interpreted fairly and the word of God that Scripture proclaims and is can be experienced freely. It is the task of biblical exegesis to assist us in determining as closely as possible what the exact meaning of the text is with respect to the single intention of the author. Critical methods of textual study as well as basic principles of exegesis must be employed so the text can speak for itself and have its own "distance" from the interpreter. In teaching and preaching these texts, as we have referred to above, one can show that the texts say what they were intended to say by the author. However, if doctrines or principles are abstracted from these texts and applied to the church and the life of faith as the command of God for today, without regard to the work of God in the church today, the resurrection no longer serves as a hermeneutical criterion. This separates the word of God from the work of God, a practice against which the apostle Paul warned in his letter to the Roman church (Rom 14:20).

In teaching and preaching the scriptural texts there is also a pastoral hermeneutic that must be joined with textual exegesis in order to be faithful to Christ as the living Word. This is what Willard Swartley seemingly means when he calls biblical interpretation a "co-creative event" and goes on to say, "The task is not merely applying a learning to a given situation. To be sure, it includes that but it involves much more;

the interpretive event co-creates a new human being, a new history, and a culture."[24]

It must be made absolutely clear that what I am suggesting here as an argument for the freedom of the church to recognize and affirm full parity for women in pastoral ministry does not give permission to set aside the normative role of the Bible in favor of some contemporary criterion. This is true for several reasons. First, all Scripture is subject to the hermeneutical criterion of the risen Lord. This binds the text of Scripture to the purpose of God's word as a construct of truth and infallibility. Second, the Spirit of the risen Lord is not just another "contemporary" spirit but is the Spirit of the incarnate Word, whose authority is vested in the apostolic witness and communicated through the inspired word as holy Scripture.

Third, there is an eschatological tension between the now and the not yet within which Scripture stands as the Word of God written. In certain areas, of which the role of women in the pastoral ministry of the church is one, we can find the resurrection of Jesus as a critical and helpful hermeneutical criterion. Apart from that criterion, as we have noted above, there will be a tendency to impose on Scripture a hermeneutical criterion that "wrestles" the exegetical task into submission to a priori principles. This eschatological tension does not allow the camel's nose under the tent, as some might fear, so that Scripture loses its binding authority on the church. Certainly Swartley does not himself mean to open the door to any and all claims to freedom from the teaching of Scripture by his suggestion that interpretation is not only the application of what we learn from Scripture but is a "co-creative" event.

For example, in areas of moral behavior, personal holiness in thought and life, and the intrinsic differentiation of male and female as created in the image of God, there is no thought of suggesting that the Spirit of Jesus as manifest in the church will lead to reinterpretation of the clear scriptural teaching. The resurrection of Jesus as hermeneutical criterion is a criterion that must be used to judge critically all contemporary claims for a "new moral order" for human relations, as well as a criterion to interpret critically and responsibly the Scriptures as an infallible guide to glorifying God in Christ, through a life of Christian faith and love.

The issue of the role of women in pastoral ministry is not an issue that strikes at the heart of a biblically based moral and spiritual order. Nor does this issue violate a fundamental natural order of creation, as Stephen Clark suggests in his book *Man and Woman in Christ*. To argue, as Clark does, that the subordination of female to male is "created into the human race" is of such dubious exegetical worth that it can be accounted for only by a theological predisposition to subordinate grace to nature.[25]

Nor does the ordination of women, in recognition of the work of Christ in his

---

[24]Swartley, *Slavery, Sabbath, War and Women,* p. 225.

[25]Stephen Clark, *Man and Woman in Christ* (Ann Arbor, Mich.: Servant, 1980). The sexual difference

church today, set up a new criterion of "human rights" as a principle that seeks to reinterpret Scripture in line with contemporary cultural and ideological passions.

Those who would seek to use the resurrection of Jesus as a hermeneutical principle that gives permission to reinterpret Scripture in order to make it more congenial to "modern" or "contemporary" concerns will find no basis in what has been said above. Quite the opposite. The resurrected Jesus is *himself* the criterion—there is no new principle of interpretation presented here. Where the Spirit of the Lord is, there is freedom, said the apostle Paul (2 Cor 3:17). But it is the "Spirit of the Lord," not the spirit of the age, that gives this freedom. Paul is quite emphatic about that. But he is equally emphatic that where the Spirit of the Lord Jesus is present and manifest in his works, one must recognize and confess the truth and authority of that Spirit. It is the Spirit of the resurrected Jesus, working in his church, who is the criterion. And failure to exercise this criterion could well lead to "quenching the Spirit," a word of caution addressed by Paul to the church at Thessalonica (1 Thess 5:19).

We must remember that the living Christ is Lord of Scripture as well as Lord of the church. The resurrected Jesus is not a criterion of new revelation that replaces Scripture; rather he is the hermeneutical criterion for interpreting Scripture in such a way that his present work of creating a new humanity fulfills the promise of Scripture. We believe that he now chooses to call both women and men into the task of co-creating the new humanity through pastoral ministry by the gift of his Holy Spirit.

Can the church be trusted to exercise the criterion of the resurrected, coming and already present Christ as a "hermeneutical community" of faith and practice, under the authority of Scripture?

If it cannot be trusted, what is to be trusted? For every reading of Scripture is already an interpretation of Scripture. And the inability to interpret Scripture as the word of God that seeks to accomplish our salvation and freedom in Christ is already a reading of Scripture that has failed.

Let the church become the community of the resurrected and coming one, and then we shall experience that which the prophet Joel spoke of and that which Peter saw happening at Pentecost:

> And in the last days it will be, God declares, that I will pour out my Spirit upon all flesh, and your sons and daughters shall prophesy, and your young men shall see visions, and your old men shall dream dreams. Even upon my slaves, both men and women, in those days I will pour out my Spirit; and they shall prophesy. (Acts 2:17-18)

---

between men and women, says Clark, has been "created into the human race" (p. 440) and thus reflects human nature as God's creative purpose (p. 447). The benefits of Christ thus cannot alter this fundamental "nature" with its sexual differentiation and hierarchical structure. The merits of this theological assumption need to be debated before it can be allowed to become a hermeneutical criterion in the way Clark wishes to use it.

7

THE PRAXIS OF THE
SPIRIT & A THEOLOGY
OF LIBERATION

In discussion with South African theologians during a visit to that country in the late 1980s, I was accused on several occasions of espousing a kind of "liberation theology." My use of the word *praxis,* combined with an emphasis on doing theological reflection in the context of the work of the Holy Spirit, raised their suspicions. It soon became clear that any theology that raised questions about the practice of apartheid was viewed as liberation theology by many who were defending the concept on theological and biblical grounds.[1]

Following my visit I wrote an article subsequently published in the *Journal of Theology for South Africa* in which I pointed out the need for a post-apartheid theology in the event of the end of apartheid.[2] Thankfully, a significant paradigm shift has now occurred among many theologians and church leaders in South Africa, so that the dismantling of apartheid is not only part of a political process but also the result of a new theological hermeneutic.

The concept of praxis has often been associated with a quasi-Marxist component

---

[1]In writing this chapter I have drawn heavily on Ray S. Anderson, "The Praxis of the Spirit as Liberation for Ministry," in *The Soul of Ministry: Forming Leaders for God's People* (Louisville, Ky.: Westminster John Knox, 1997).
[2]Ray S. Anderson, "Toward a Post-Apartheid Theology in South Africa," *Journal of Theology for South Africa,* June 1988.

of some contemporary liberation theology. My own use of the concept of praxis is more in the tradition of Aristotle, who defined the word as action that took into account the *telos*, or goal and purpose of the act. In biblical theology it is not the *telos* of a historical or human process that constitutes the goal of praxis but the *eschaton,* or final revelation of God in history through the coming of Christ.

It is not only in South Africa, however, where points of contention and confrontation arise when the praxis of the Spirit appears to collide with deeply entrenched traditions and theological convictions. In our contemporary situation, for example, the issue of the role of women in ministry, or the ordination of homosexuals, can be viewed as a critical matter of biblical interpretation where both a vision of the Spirit's leading and the context of the Spirit's ministry demand a new theological paradigm.

Revisioning and Rethinking Our Theological Paradigm

Theology must be as contextual as it is metaphysical, and it must be as visual as it is cerebral. Another way of putting it is to say that theological reflection must be done in the context of the Spirit's ministry in the world. Theological reflection must also be a "way of seeing" as well as a way of thinking. Let me give an example.

When Peter was visiting in the house of Simon in the seaside village of Joppa, he went up on the roof to pray while waiting for a meal to be prepared. He fell into a trance and had a vision of a large sheet being lowered with all kinds of animals on it, both clean and unclean. A voice from heaven said, "Get up Peter; kill and eat." But Peter protested. "By no means, Lord; for I have never eaten anything that is profane or unclean." The voice came again, "What God has made clean, you must not call profane" (Acts 10:9-15).

One might account for this vision by the fact that Peter was hungry and that this stimulated his vision. But we are told that immediately when he awakened from the trance, there was a knock on the door, and servants of Cornelius, a Roman centurion who lived in nearby Caesarea, were there asking for Peter. It seems that Cornelius, too, had received a vision in which he was instructed by an angel to send for Peter in order to receive a message from God, for Cornelius, while a Roman soldier, was also a devout man who "prayed constantly to God" (Acts 10:1-8).

The scene now shifts to the house of Cornelius in Caesarea, where Peter said to the centurion, "You yourselves know that it is unlawful for a Jew to associate with or to visit a Gentile; but God has shown me that I should not call anyone profane or unclean. So when I was sent for, I came without objection" (Acts 10:28-29). As Peter began to proclaim the ministry of Jesus under the power of the Spirit, his death and resurrection, the Holy Spirit came upon all who heard this good news. With such compelling evidence before him, Peter immediately baptized Cornelius and his household (Acts 10:34-48).

It is difficult for us to grasp the significance of this "paradigm shift" in Peter's theology without understanding both the context and the visual perspective. God prepared Peter through the vision by presenting him with what I might call a "visual parable." In much the same way as Jesus attempted to portray the true nature of the kingdom of God by placing a child in the midst of his followers (Mt 18:1-5), the Spirit of Jesus placed before Peter a visual object that shifted his theological focus from the law to the giver of the law. "What God has made clean, you must not call profane."

But the context was also an important factor in this paradigm shift. Despite his earlier theological training Peter was obedient to the vision and put himself in the context of the Spirit's ministry to the Gentile household of Cornelius. When Peter confronted the evidence of the Spirit's presence upon these Gentiles, Peter not only made an exception in this case, he made a fundamental shift in his way of thinking and baptized the uncircumcised Gentiles!

Of course he was challenged by this action when he returned to Jerusalem by the "theologians in residence." His defense was not based on clever exegetical reading of the Scriptures but on the compelling praxis of the Spirit revealed through his ministry of witness to the resurrection power of Jesus. Recounting the promise of Jesus, Peter told them. "And I remembered the word of the Lord, how he had said, 'John baptized with water, but you will be baptized with the Holy Spirit.' If then God gave them the same gift that he gave us when we believed in the Lord Jesus Christ, who was I that I could hinder God? When they heard this, they were silenced. And they praised God, saying, 'Then God has given even to the Gentiles the repentance that leads to life' " (Acts 11:16-18). As a matter of fact, Peter later appeared to have recanted this conversion to a theology of freedom through the Holy Spirit under the influence of the leaders of the church in Jerusalem. This led to formidable opposition to Paul's ministry at a later day (cf. Gal 2:11-21).

Paul also had his encounter with the Spirit of Jesus on the Damascus road and, through the praxis of the Spirit's ministry among the Gentiles, developed a theology of liberation from the rigid confinement of legal Judaism. Paul's liberation theology, however, was grounded in the praxis of the Spirit, not in historical processes and sociopolitical agendas. It is by "the law of the Spirit of life in Christ Jesus" that we are set free from the law of sin and death, argued Paul. "For all who are led by the Spirit of God are children of God" (Rom 8:2, 14).

Which Century Is Normative for Our Theology?

I have suggested that theological reflection is best done where both vision and context inform the interpretation and application of biblical truth. The incident with

Peter in the house of Cornelius provided one example of how this was done in the first century.

"Which century is determinative as a context for our understanding of biblical truth?" I ask my students, who are all seminary graduates and practicing pastors. Without fail they respond, "The first century, of course." They remind me that biblical scholars go to great lengths to recover contextual factors in the period in which the Bible was written in order to aid in our understanding of it.

That is well and good. Accurate exegesis of Scripture requires cultural and contextual factors as well as linguistic analysis. We are told that in ancient times where fire was scarce, to give someone burning coals to carry back to their residence in a basket on top of their head was a good thing to do. With this information we can read the proverb quite differently: "If your enemies are hungry, give them bread to eat; and if they are thirsty, give them water to drink; for you will heap coals of fire on their heads, and the Lord will reward you" (Prov 25:21-22). Heaping coals of fire is a friendly and neighborly thing to do, even to an enemy!

Does this mean that the context of first-century Christianity is normative for our understanding of what it means to live and minister according to biblical truth? Not at all, as I hope to show. Look at the figure 7.1 with me. (Remember that theological reflection must be visual as well as metaphysical!)

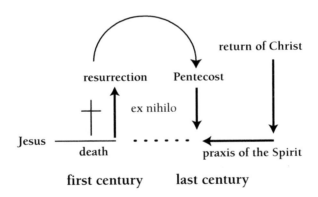

Figure 7.1. The Spirit comes to the church out of the future

The Spirit that comes to the church comes out of the future, not the past. The presence of the Spirit is the anticipation of the return of Christ. Paul makes this clear when he writes to the church at Ephesus reminding them that in receiving the Holy Spirit they were "marked with the seal of the promised Holy Spirit; this is the pledge of our inheritance toward redemption as God's own people, to the praise of his glory" (Eph 1:13-14). The "pledge" is literally "the first installment" or the "down payment" (Greek *arrabōn*) on the inheritance promised as the eschatological fulfillment of God's promise.

When Christ returns to bring to consummation this pledge made by the gift of the Holy Spirit, it will be the "last century." The Spirit is thus preparing the people of God for this "last century." While the first century of the church is normative for the revelation of Christ as the incarnation of God and the redemption of humans from sin and death, the return of the same Christ and the resurrection from the dead constitute the normative praxis of the Spirit.

If this century should be the century in which Christ returns and this age comes to an end, then this will be the "last century." If this return does not occur until the next century, then that will be the "last century." The praxis of the ministry of the Holy Spirit can be understood in light of that which God desires to become a reality at the end, not merely to replicate that form of ministry during the first century.

This is the perspective that Paul had even during the "first century." He looked toward the coming of Christ as the final word of approval on his own teaching and ministry. While the historical Jesus and the cross were central to Paul's theology of redemption and creation, the Spirit of the resurrected and coming Christ was normative for interpreting the past events in light of the coming ones.

This was the argument Paul used in defending his own apostolic authority in the face of those who claimed historical precedence based on their relation to Jesus of Nazareth: "It is the Lord who judges me. Therefore do not pronounce judgment before the time, before the Lord comes, who will bring to light the things now hidden in darkness and will disclose the purposes of the heart. Then each one will receive commendation from God" (1 Cor 4:4-5).

Eschatological Preference and Historical Precedence

The early Christians used the principle of historical precedence to find a replacement for Judas. As there were originally twelve disciples, so there must be twelve apostles following the resurrection. As these were all male, so gender was thought to be a criterion for apostleship after the resurrection as well. Only those who had been followers of Jesus from his baptism to his crucifixion were eligible, according to historical precedence (Acts 1:21-22). Regardless of what one makes out of the selection of Matthias by lot as the replacement for Judas, it is clear that the Holy Spirit used the criterion of eschatological preference rather than historical precedence in calling Saul of Tarsus to be an apostle!

If the same Holy Spirit is active in the world today as then, should we not expect the praxis of the Spirit in our day to operate with the same freedom?

From the theological paradigm outlined above, we should expect that the Spirit will more and more prepare the church to be the church that Christ desires to see when he returns, not the one that he left in the first century. Until we have made this theological paradigm shift, we are in danger of forcing the Spirit into the constraint of historical and traditional precedence, as some in the early church attempted to do.

With the first-century church largely bound by its understanding of the traditional role of women in society and the synagogue, for example, we are not surprised to discover first-century Christianity in conflict over the role of women in the ministry of the church. Indeed, though Pentecost itself brought forth a vision and praxis of ministry that was only anticipated in the Old Testament, it never was fully realized in the first-century church.

When the Spirit came upon both men and women in the upper room on the day of Pentecost, Peter rightly concluded that the prophetic utterance of Joel had come to pass: "In the last days it will be, God declares, that I will pour out my Spirit upon all flesh, and your sons and your daughters shall prophesy, and your young men shall see visions, and your old men shall dream dreams. Even upon my slaves, both men and women, in those days I will pour out my Spirit; and they shall prophesy" (Acts 2:17-18).

In this case, eschatological preference was seen to prevail over historical precedence. Did the first-century church succeed in carrying out the eschatological agenda of the Holy Spirit? Hardly, even though Paul labored valiantly to bring it about. In the end he had to make concessions due to expediency, fully assured that the Spirit would lead the church beyond what even he was able to see in his lifetime.

At critical points Paul placed theological anchor points for this eschatological preference, such as the one in the third chapter of his letter to the Galatians: "As many of you as were baptized into Christ have clothed yourselves with Christ. There is no longer Jew or Greek, there is no longer slave or free, there is no longer male and female; for all of you are one in Christ Jesus" (Gal 3:27-28).

While he permitted the circumcision of Timothy (Acts 16:3) out of expediency, he refused to have Titus circumcised (Gal 2:3) as a sign of liberation from this historical and physical sign of membership in the covenant community. While he apparently restricted the role of women in the church at Ephesus (1 Tim 2), he openly acknowledged the ministry of Lydia in the church at Philippi, of Phoebe, a *diakonos,* and Junia (apparently a woman) who was "prominent among the apostles" (Rom 16:1, 7).

Paul allowed for the eschatological preference of the Holy Spirit where it could be implemented without causing disorder and confusion in the church. Giving way to expediency where it was necessary for the ministry in special situations apparently was not considered by Paul to establish a principle and precedent for all time. To make what was merely expedient normative would have supplanted the eschatological freedom of the Spirit of Jesus to prepare the church for the last century. Regarding circumcision, Titus—not Timothy—represents what was normative. With regard to the role of women in church leadership and apostolic ministry, Lydia and Junia—not the women in the church at Ephesus—represent what is normative.

In figure 7.2 I have attempted to depict the liberation that occurred through the death and resurrection of Christ, with the praxis of the Spirit following Pentecost. Here again we see the ex nihilo, which separates historical and natural determinism from the creative and liberating power and grace of God.

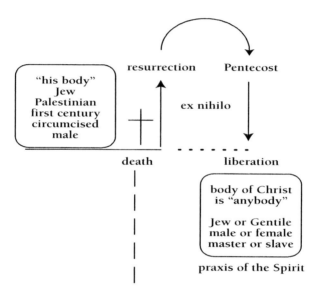

Figure 7.2. Praxis of the Spirit following Pentecost

Note in particular in figure 7.2 the specific limitation represented by the physical body of Jesus as the incarnation of God. Jesus was a Jewish, circumcised male, speaking his mother tongue of Hebrew (or Aramaic) and possibly Greek, in a first-century Palestinian cultural context. With the death of Jesus, all of these limiting factors were "put to death," so to speak. Though chosen by God as the temporal form in which the revelation of the Word occurred, these biological, cultural and historical forms came to an end on the cross. In the resurrection we have the continuity of the person of Jesus without the continuation of these factors.

Whereas Jesus was a Jew, "anybody"—Jew or Gentile—can now be gifted with the Spirit. In conformity to tradition and practice, the twelve disciples were male. Following the gift of the Spirit at Pentecost, "anybody"—male or female—can now be anointed with the Spirit of Jesus for ministry. How do we know this? Because the praxis of the Holy Spirit in the church following Pentecost provided the context for the new theological paradigm.

It is worth noting that the action of the eleven men following the resurrection and ascension of Jesus in selecting a replacement for Judas preceded Pentecost. Anxious to establish their own credentials and to maintain historical continuity, they probably were premature. When Jesus took his leave of his followers, he instructed them to "wait there for the promise of the Father," not to develop criteria for leadership and lay down administrative guidelines.

How Does It Work in Practice?

But some will ask, Does this mean that we are free to justify *everything* which claims to be done in the name of the Spirit?

This is a good question! Does eschatological preference mean that there is nothing normative in the history of divine revelation as given to us in the Bible? If that were the case, we would be close to spiritual anarchy, a situation not uncommon in some movements found within Christianity today. Let me respond in this way.

As nearly as I can see, for every case in which eschatological preference was exercised by the Spirit in the New Testament church, there was a biblical antecedent for what appeared to be revolutionary and new. For example, Paul's argument in support of treating circumcision as no longer necessary was not based on the visitation of the Spirit on uncircumcised Gentiles alone. When Paul faced the reality of the Spirit's praxis in this context, he looked again at the Scriptures and found an antecedent for his position in the case of Abraham. Within the tradition of the Jews following Abraham and Moses, there was no precedent for allowing uncircumcised males to enjoy the full privileges reserved for the people of promise (i.e., descendants of Abraham, Isaac and Jacob). This was the position taken by those Christian Jews who opposed Paul.

In going back to the story of Abraham, however, Paul discovered that it was before Abraham was circumcised that he received the promise and was declared righteous before God (Gen 15:6; 17:10). "Faith was reckoned to Abraham as righteousness," Paul reminded his readers. "How then was it reckoned to him? Was it before or after he had been circumcised? It was not after, but before he was circumcised" (Rom 4:9-10; cf. Gal 3). Paul thus found the biblical antecedent for the Spirit's ministry with the Gentiles.

Similarly, in the case of the role of women in the church, when the Holy Spirit set aside certain women for ministry, including that of diaconal and apostolic leadership, a biblical antecedent can be found for women who served God in the Old Testament.

While these cases were exceptional and did not set an historical precedent, they nonetheless constitute a biblical antecedent. We need only to recall women who were called prophets, such as Huldah (2 Kings 22:14; 34:22), Deborah (Judg 4:4-5), Miriam (Ex 15:20) and Noadiah (Neh 6:14).

There was a strand of tradition in the first-century church that clung to historical precedent as the criterion for establishing the ministry of the church. Those today who seek to justify certain forms of first-century Christian life and ministry rely strongly on the passages in the New Testament that represent this tradition. For those who cling to historical precedent, Pentecost and the power of the Holy Spirit were constrained by institutional forms and doctrinal formulas.

At the same time, there was another movement in the first century that followed the leading of the Holy Spirit and looked back into historical revelation for antecedents rather than precedence. Such a movement as made by the apostle Paul.

I suggest that these represent two theological paradigms, one oriented by first-century Christianity and historical precedent, and the other oriented to eschatological precedence, biblical antecedent and a vision for the "last century" church.

Every pastor will sooner or later be confronted by the issue of divorce and remarriage of divorced persons. On exegetical grounds alone the issue of whether the Bible ever allows for remarriage or on what conditions is a subject of debate and division. Many pastors have chosen to practice mercy and grace in such situations rather than to consign persons who have failed in one marriage to live as a casualty of that failure for the rest of their lives. But how many practice this ministry with an uneasy if not an anxious conscience?

I believe that the two theological paradigms developed above provide some basis for making pastoral decisions in some of these cases that are theologically sound and biblically grounded. For example, if a failed marriage and subsequent divorce is considered to be a form of the ex nihilo in which the grace of God can create a situation in which "everything has become new" (2 Cor 5:17), one could understand that the praxis of the Holy Spirit frees the individuals from historical determinism and opens them up to eschatological fulfillment of God's promise. A remarriage can then be viewed theologically as a gracious recovery of the biblical *antecedent* that marriage itself is given by God as a possibility within the divine image (Gen 2:24).

In this case, there is precedent for a remarriage in the divine institution of marriage itself. It would seem that the response of Jesus to the quarrelsome question put to him by the Pharisees was of this kind. "From the beginning of creation, 'God made them male and female.' " And Jesus then quotes the passage from Genesis 2: 'For this reason a man shall leave his father and mother and be joined to his wife, and the two shall become one flesh.' . . . Therefore what God has joined together, let no one separate" (Mk 10:2-9).

Cutting through the casuistry that they traced back to Moses, Jesus reminded them that when they deal with marriage "they deal with God." And the God that we encounter when dealing with failure and sin is the one who meets us as Jesus Christ, who forgives, renews and restores. Certainly it was God's intention that those joined together in marriage stay together and that no human principle or law can justify this separation. But as we have seen throughout the Bible, where barrenness and death occur—and tragically, they do—God's grace operates out of this ex nihilo to create something entirely new. Historical precedence, even as a consequence of sin, is canceled by eschatological preference.

But What About the Ordination of Homosexuals?

The question always arises at this point: If the church can accept women as pastors and bless the remarriage of divorced persons through the praxis of the Spirit, can it not also accept the homosexual person, bless homosexual unions and ordain homosexuals to ministry where the same Spirit is evident?

Many churches have done just that, setting aside the biblical passages that appear to forbid this sexual practice as irrelevant in our present understanding of same-sex relationships. At the same time, it should also be noted that many churches refuse to ordain women to pastoral ministry and refuse to bless the remarriage of divorced persons on biblical grounds. For these churches the refusal to affirm positively homosexual relationships is consistent with their understanding of biblical teaching.

The position advanced in this chapter, however, is that eschatological preference is grounded in the praxis of the Holy Spirit in such a way that God's original purpose for humanity be realized. This means that the church must recognize and affirm the work of the Spirit in the present time in anticipation of the reconciliation of the world to God as promised through Jesus Christ.

The issue of homosexuality is one that requires a book in itself, and many are available. It would take us far beyond the purpose of this chapter to review this literature and to discuss the exegetical issues involved. Later, in chapter fourteen, I will discuss the issue of homosexuality at greater length. For now I only intend to use this issue to illustrate my use of the concept of a biblical antecedent.

While it might seem logical to assume that acceptance of women as pastors and blessing the remarriage of divorced persons establishes a precedent, we must remember that it is not precedent that permits the church to move with the freedom of the Spirit but a biblical antecedent. Where the church has recognized the role of women in ministry, it has a biblical antecedent for affirming this as the praxis of the Spirit. Where the church has blessed the remarriage of divorced persons in recognition of the renewing work of the grace of God, it has a biblical antecedent for this ministry grounded in marriage itself as part of God's created order. Some who argue that even as the first-century church struggled over the issue of including the Gentiles and finally accepted them, so the church today must accept homosexuals. The issue is not the same, however, for in the case of the Gentiles, there is a biblical antecedent in the promise to Abraham, a point Paul clearly made in his argument to the Galatian church (Gal 3:8).

What can we say about the issue of homosexuality in this regard? Even if one should dismiss all of the biblical texts that appear to forbid homosexuality (in both the Old and New Testaments) as not relevant for our present understanding of same-sex relationships, we are left with absolute silence from the Bible in this regard. Those who argue for the validity of homosexual relations as fully equivalent to heterosexual relations do, in fact, argue from silence with regard to a biblical view of sexuality.

I have carefully laid the foundation for eschatological preference and the praxis of the Spirit in the need for a biblical antecedent, even without a clear precedent in the biblical tradition. The Bible, however, is not silent regarding human sexuality and the image of God. "So God created humankind in his image, in the image of God he created them; male and female he created them" (Gen 1:27).

If one reads this text as intending that the image of God be understood to include sexual differentiation as male and female, male or female, as does Karl Barth, among others, then the biblical antecedent is clearly one of heterosexual orientation and practice as God's preference. The antecedent for homosexual relations does not appear to be found in Scripture. As a consequence, those who argue for the normalizing of homosexual relationships and full acceptance by the church must do so on other grounds.

The main purpose of this chapter is to present a biblical and theological paradigm for ministry based on the liberating praxis of the Holy Spirit. I have argued that this is exactly what Peter first experienced in the house of Cornelius with regard to the Gentiles and what Paul later developed as the foundation for the church of the first century. The church is created and re-created through the praxis of the Spirit, liberating it from its conformity to nature and culture and its tendency to institutionalize the Word. The church is empowered by the Spirit and each member is equipped for ministry through the liberating praxis of the Spirit, as we shall discover in the next chapter.

8

THE CHURCH
& ITS MINISTRY
The Latreia of Christ

The vocation of Jesus was grounded in his nature as Son of the Father. This recurring theme in the theology of H. R. Mackintosh suggests that Jesus did not first of all awaken to self-consciousness as the Messiah but as the Son of God. His unswerving faithfulness in word and deed to the kingdom of God, his obedience unto death on the cross, and his glorious presence as the risen Lord issue out of his nature as the Son of the Father. He did not become a son through his obedience but because he was a son, he learned obedience, and thus became the source of salvation for others (Heb 5:8-9).[1]

In a similar way one could say that the vocation or mission of the church is grounded in its nature as the community of the children of God, whose lives have ontological grounding in the very being of Christ. Mackintosh certainly learned from Herrmann the crucial content of the inner life of Jesus as the core ontological reality that gave meaning to the events and facts contained in the story of Jesus' life. So too, Mackintosh could say, "Christianity loses its moral nerve if it be made independent of the historical stream of believing life."[2] As the inner life of Jesus in his relation to the Father is constitutive of Christology, so the inner life of the church in its experience of Jesus Christ is constitutive of ecclesiology.

---

[1]See, for example, Hugh Ross Mackintosh, *The Doctrine of the Person of Jesus Christ* (Edinburgh: T & T Clark, 1912), pp. 30, 84.

[2]Hugh Ross Mackintosh, *The Divine Initiative* (London: SCM Press, 1921), p. 92.

My concern in this chapter is to explore this christological and ontological basis for the nature of the church and its ministry in two parts. First, I examine the nature of the church as an incarnational community and then the church as a ministering community. There is only one incarnation, that of the divine Logos in the person of Jesus of Nazareth. The church is not a continuation of this incarnation, nor is the church another incarnation. To speak of the church as an "incarnational community" is to describe the church as formed by the incarnate One, Jesus Christ, in its life, character and ministry.

The Church as Incarnational Community

The incarnation of God as Jesus of Nazareth can be said to be the ontological ground for the moral life of Jesus as well as for his messianic ministry of proclaiming the kingdom of God. This incarnation, interpreted by John in the formulation "the word became flesh," is more than an act of moral condescension and obedience; it is an act of self-emptying, or "kenosis." In the same passage where Paul speaks of "obedience unto death," he first says of Jesus that he "emptied himself" (*ekenosen*) and took the form of a servant (Phil 2:7). Obedience by itself is the most insidious of all temptations. It is the ontological source and motive behind obedience that gives it its character. Thus obedience is not the central motive in the life of Jesus as sheer ethical demand. Rather, it is the inner life of sonship that comes to expression through his obedience that characterizes Jesus. And it is in this sonship that we find the motif of self-emptying carried out through his identification with both the sinner as the object of divine love as well as with the Father as the source of love. Indeed, it may be said that in this sonship there is displayed not only the love of the Father for the world but the love of the Son for the Father who loves the world.

This self-emptying, or kenotic act, can be considered as the central ontological reality of the existence of Jesus. In this view kenosis does not represent a functional or moral act of condescension of a temporary nature but an ontological reality that exists as the core of divine being itself, revealed to us in terms of the inner relation of the Son and the Father as a differentiated order of equality. The Son is no less God than the Father but is essentially divine precisely in the differentiation between Father and Son.[3]

---

[3]My use of the kenotic motif in this essay takes a different course from that which preoccupied theologians who pursued a more traditional "kenotic Christology" in the sixteenth and seventeenth centuries in Germany and in the latter part of the nineteenth century in Britain. I have made this distinction in my *Historical Transcendence and the Reality of God* (Grand Rapids, Mich.: Eerdmans, 1975), pp. 149-50. Mackintosh himself struggled to retain the ontological care of a kenotic Christology by stressing the unequivocal humanity of Christ but also attempting to avoid the speculative pitfalls of the older kenotic Christologies. See Mackintosh, *Doctrine of the Person of Jesus Christ*, pp. 463-507.

When the self-emptying (kenosis) of Jesus is considered as an essential relation of the Son to the Father as divine being, we are involved in far more than a style of life or a principle by which an ethical imperative can be added to Christian life as such. What the incarnation reveals to us through the condescension of God to become flesh is the actual content of divine being itself. Thus Jesus does not empty himself into the world, nor does he pour himself out first of all into the needs of the world as an ethical imperative that is added to his love for the Father. Rather his act of self-emptying is a primary one with regard to his relation to the Father. The community that exists as the life of the Father to Son and Son to the Father, in the Spirit, is the community that becomes the reconciling community of salvation history.

The Trinitarian Basis for Christ's Ministry in the World

It follows from this that the doctrine of the incarnation must be explicated in terms of the doctrine of the Trinity. At the very heart of the divine ministry of reconciliation, there is a receptivity and self-emptying that, in its depth of divine being, is capable of assuming a human "estrangement" that does not result in what Barth once called an "ontic cleft" within God himself. In his identification with sinners, even to the point of the experience of "Godforsakenness" on the cross, Jesus does not move outside of the "Godness" of his own being in order to fulfill a moral intention located merely in the freedom of God to act outside of his own being. There is within his own divine sonship a relation with the Father that has a depth of humility and condescension that grasps what is essentially human precisely in its situation of being under the judgment of God as Father. The "identity" between God and humanity under the condemnation of sin is thus established in the incarnation, not merely in the atonement on the cross. The atonement is therefore grounded in the core of God's own being rather than in a moral or legal act *ad extra,* as an operation outside of God's own being.

In positing an equivalence between the economic trinity disclosed to us in salvation history and the immanent Trinity of God's eternal self-existence, we need also to make a distinction between the two for the sake of showing the logical relation between creaturely humility and divine humility. The preexistence of Christ as a doctrine of Christology is not then a mere apologetic for his divinity, but it is the ontological basis on which community as self-emptying love is explicated.[4] By preexistence then is meant an ontological continuity between the act of love that stands with and in the place of humanity under judgment with the love that constitutes the inner being of God himself as Father of the Son and Son of the Father. It is the knowledge

---

[4]See the helpful essay on this theme by Donald M. MacKinnon, "The Relation of the Doctrines of the Incarnation and the Trinity," in *Creation, Christ, and Culture,* ed. W. A. McKinney (Edinburgh: T & T Clark, 1976), pp. 92-107.

of the Father that only the Son possesses and the knowledge of the Son that only the Father discloses that constitute the "inner logic" of incarnational community (cf. Mt 11:25-27).

"Incarnational community" means that community in which the life of Jesus continues to exist through the ontological reality of his indwelling Spirit. The apostle Paul saw clearly that the Spirit who constitutes the community of the resurrected Christ is the Spirit of Christ himself. Thus Paul can view the historical community of believers in Christ as "saints" and quite literally as the "body of Christ" (cf. 1 Cor 1:2; 12:1-31; Eph 1:15-22). As Jesus exists in a community of relation with the Father characterized by self-emptying, so does the church exist as a community of self-emptying, or kenotic presence, in the world. It is this nature of the church, as we shall see, that determines the form of its ministry. Jesus expresses this quite specifically in the prayer "As you have sent me into the world, so I have sent them into the world" (Jn 17:18). The "as" and the "so" constitute the hinge on which the existence of God as revealer and reconciler turns outward into the world. Ministry thus precedes and determines the existence of the church as the ministry and existence of Christ.

Paul can thus appeal to Christians to "let the same mind be in you that was in Christ Jesus, who, though he was in the form of God, did not regard equality with God as something to be exploited, but emptied himself, taking the form of a slave, being born in human likeness" (Phil 2:5-7).

The Formation of Christ in the World

This kenosis, or self-emptying, is the form of Christ in the world because it is the content of the life of the Son to the Father. This is also the form of incarnational community. It is a community called into existence as the "little flock" surrounding Jesus as he makes his way to the cross in faithful obedience to the Father's will and in true affirmation of his own being.

Jesus said, "You are those who have stood by me in my trials; and I confer on you, just as my Father has conferred on me, a kingdom" (Lk 22:28-29). They were more and more being bound into the "body of his sufferings," conformed to his own intimate communion with the Father, which, as a life of divine selflessness, produced a total indifference to institutional or formal "religion," in order that the Father's love may be affirmed redemptively for the "lost sheep of the house of Israel." Preparing them through both example and teaching by receiving and bestowing the Spirit, finally, in the Last Supper, he gives them his own body and blood as constitutive of their own participation in his life and mission. On Easter day Jesus meets the same confused and confounded group and "breathes upon them," giving them his own Spirit, inspiring them with his "last breath" so that they now become "his body" in the world. They are not to be conformed to the world but transformed to conform to his own existence (Rom 12:2).

The kenotic community, as the formation of Christ in the world, must first of all be the re-formation of humanity into the human existence of Jesus Christ. The world does not know itself, says Barth: "It does not know God, nor man, nor the relationship and covenant between God and man. Hence, it does not know its own origin, state, or goal. It does not know what divides, nor what unites. It does not know either its life and salvation, or its death and destruction."[5] Human existence as fallen humanity cannot be the form of Christ in the world because it does not know its own destruction or its own hope. Through his own humanity Jesus brings all humanity under judgment and therefore under grace. In the cross all human possibility was brought to an end—not just the humanity of the disciples, who struggled against the implications of this kenosis, but the human possibilities of Jesus himself. The cross cuts through all presumption based on the intrinsic ability of the creature apart from the Creator. This is a judgment against human ideologies as well as human institutions.

For the world to find its true humanity in Jesus Christ is to know itself as brought under judgment for the sake of its healing and its hope. In this sense, as Dietrich Bonhoeffer pointed out, the incarnation has already taken up the humanity of all people in the body of Christ. And it is precisely this truth that must be announced to the world.[6] He goes on to say, however, that this testimony will always be foreign to the world and threatening to its existence, for it serves to consolidate the humanity of the world to the humanity of God on the cross, not the humanity of God to the humanity of the world. This reconciliation of humanity into the community of Christ as the life of the Son with the Father carries as its presupposition a judgment against human possibilities. Everyone wants a resurrection but not the death it necessarily presupposes! Grace must first kill and then make alive. This is the reformation of human existence into the humanity of Christ. And it is the nature of the incarnational community to bring the world under the same judgment and therefore into the same hope; this is what the church, as the community bound to Christ, affirms.

Along with the *re-formation* of humanity to the human existence of Christ, the kenotic community exists as the *formation* of Christ in the world. This formation does not take place as an act of separation from the world for the sake of exemplifying certain characteristics or virtues that may be thought to portray an ideal of Christ. Rather it takes place as Christ himself continues to have both a presence and practice in the world. The church thus becomes the form of Christ in the world through Christ's

---

[5] *CD* 4/3, p. 769.
[6] Dietrich Bonhoeffer, *Ethics* (New York: Macmillan, 1965), p. 206.

own ministry of reconciliation. The church does not "possess Christ," as Bonhoeffer said. "Everything would be ruined if one were to try to reserve Christ for the Church and to allow the world only some kind of law, even if it were a Christian law. Christ died for the world, and it is only in the midst of the world that Christ is Christ."[7]

It is not only that the world needs the church in order to have Christ. The church also needs to be in relation to the world in order to know Christ and in order to be the body of Christ. Formation of Christ in the world does not take place apart from the world. This can be seen as the thrust of the teaching of Jesus in Matthew 25, where the formation of Christ in the world occurs through ministering to those who are outcasts, visiting the imprisoned, ministering to the poor and clothing the naked. When the Christian goes to the prison to visit the one judged to be an outcast by society, Christ will be found already there, though the formation of Christ occurs when two or three come together "in the name of Christ." The Christian mission does not bring Christ to the world. That is not its power. Rather, Christians witness by their own presence in the world that Christ has come to the world and has taken up the cause of the afflicted, the oppressed and the estranged as his own cause. Solidarity between the community of Christian believers and the world has already been established through the incarnation. This incarnational solidarity is the theological presupposition of all Christian mission in the world. This solidarity between the church and the world is one not of substance but of grace. It is by the grace of God that all humans bear God's image, even as sinners. It is by the grace of God that the church exists in the world and for the sake of the world as those who bear witness to the transforming power and life of Christ.

It must immediately be added, however, that the incarnational community in its kenotic life does not mean conformity to the world in the practice of solidarity. We have already established that solidarity cannot mean conformity by asserting the reformation of humanity to the human existence of Christ as the theological ground for existence in the world and yet as not of it (Jn 17:16).

Yet as Barth points out, the formation of Christ in the world must take place with a "good conscience":

> Since Jesus Christ is the Savior of the world, the church can exist in worldly fashion, not unwillingly or with a bad conscience, but willingly and with a good conscience. It consists in the recognition that its members also bear in themselves and in some way actualize all human possibilities.[8]

Strategic withdrawal or separation from the world for the sake of conscience aban-

[7]Ibid., pp. 205-6.

[8]*CD* 4/3, p. 774. Barth's treatment of the concept of solidarity is worthy of a more extended quotation. "Solidarity with the world means that those who are genuinely pious approach the children of the

dons the world to its own condition. The incarnational community may need to practice tactical withdrawal for the sake of nurturing its own "life-support" system, but it can never justify strategic withdrawal (cf. Mk 6:31-32; Lk 4:42-43). Its conscience must be controlled by the Christ who is himself in mission and thus seeks only for the glory (*doxa*) that comes from God, rather than the praise (*doxa*) of men (Jn 5:41, 44). In its solidarity with the world the incarnational community dare not abandon the world to itself but has an obligation to remain bound to the world, even as Christ himself has bound the world to him. This obligation is the responsibility for the world, or to the world, that Christ assumed in coming to the world. One cannot discharge obligation to God and be irresponsible to the world.

The Diaconal Ministry of Christ in the World

This responsibility can be positively construed as *diakonia*. Jesus was in the world as "one who serves" (Lk 22:27). He assumed the role of the servant in the feet washing of the disciples (Jn 13:5). He condescended to share and absorb human hurt, taking on himself the sicknesses and weakness of humanity. He allied himself with sinners against evil as their advocate. He hazarded his own existence, placing himself in the judgment that falls on the sinner, serving the creature from below. He places himself in concrete situations of human existence where he serves God by extending mercy and serves human beings by raising up a response of prayer and faith. He creates a healing reconciliation in his body, uniting both judgment and mercy, creating one new person out of old estrangements. All of this is the incarnational nature of diaconal existence. He drew his disciples into this diaconal life and made *diakonia* the essential mark of the community, which is his continued existence in the world. There is intercession through prayer and the struggle with humanity against the sin that entraps it. There is witness, declaration of the gospel, evangelical address and yet a word that must be enfleshed as love incarnate. The incarnational community does not come to the world offering what it has to those who have not, but comes as those who have not of themselves, as receiving for and with all others what God gives abundantly and without favor through Jesus Christ.

---

world as such, that those who are genuinely righteous are not ashamed to sit down with the unrighteous as friends, that those who are genuinely wise do not hesitate to seem to be fools among fools, and that those who are genuinely holy are not too good or irreproachable to go down 'into hell' in a very secular fashion. . . . Hence it does not consist in a cunning masquerade, but rather in an unmasking in which it makes itself known to others as akin to them, rejoicing with them that do rejoice and weeping with them that weep (Rom 12:15), not forming and strengthening them in evil nor betraying and surrendering them for its own good, but confessing for its own good, and thereby contending against the evil of others, by accepting the fact that it must be honestly and unreservedly among them and with them, on the same level and footing, in the same boat and within the same limits as any or all of them" (ibid., pp. 774-75).

It becomes quite clear in this exposition of the kenotic life of Christ as incarnational community that there is both an "onlook" by which the community takes the world seriously, as well as an "outlook" in which the world is summoned to consider and expect deliverance and freedom. This is portrayed briefly but significantly in the incident recounted by Luke, where Peter and John are about to enter the temple for prayer. Suddenly they are accosted at the gate of the temple by a man, lame from birth, who asks them for alms. "Peter looked intently at him, as did John, and said, 'Look at us.' And he fixed his attention on them, expecting to receive something from them. But Peter said, 'I have no silver and gold, but what I have I give you; in the name of Jesus Christ of Nazareth, stand up and walk' " (Acts 3:1-6). When Peter "looked intently" at the man, there is the engagement of the eyes, the most vulnerable and thus most implicating of all contacts. It immediately transforms a casual, impersonal encounter into one that now has unavoidable implications for one who understands solidarity of common humanity. The incarnational community dares to make eye contact! Its "onlook" is personal and therefore contractual. One can only "buy out" of this contract with a few alms or step into it and "enflesh intentionality" by taking up the cause of the afflicted man as one's own limitation. The kenotic community as the body of Christ sees and takes seriously the humanity of others. This is its "onlook" with respect to the world.

But we are also attracted to the second movement in this vignette. When Peter said, "Look at us," the man "fixed his attention upon them." Certainly the man's own expectation had been painfully conditioned by experience to wager little on the outcome—perhaps a few alms. And yet we sense a boldness in Peter's spirit that evokes a new "outlook" that Peter himself has brought to the situation. And here the point must be pressed. The incarnational community brings a certain eschatological crisis into the human situation by which the reality of the kingdom of God as God's reign in and through and over all that is both natural and unnatural is proclaimed and promised. The bearing of the sins of the world in his own body was an eschatological act on the part of Jesus. It was both a final judgment against the evil that stands against God's reign with his own people, as well as a final gift of the reconciliation that offers liberation and restoration to those who are the slaves of the evil one, Satan.

And so the incarnational community exists as an eschatological-sacramental presence in the world between the evangelical word of forgiveness and the restoration and liberation of all things. In the healing of the paralytic (Mk 2:1-12), Jesus first of all pronounces the word of forgiveness of sin and then only subsequently the word of liberation and healing. During this interval the paralytic had only the presence of Jesus as an eschatological reality of hope and faith within his vision. Between the word of the kingdom and its power of healing lies what T. F. Torrance once called an "eschatological reserve," in which the Word is borne in hope and faith.[9] The incarnational community lives and functions between these two moments, between the cross and the parousia, between the evangelical word of forgiveness and the final act of restoration and reconciliation.

In a certain sense the church in its incarnational mission is also sacramental. That is to say, the humanity of the incarnational community binds itself to the One to whom the evangelical word of forgiveness has been announced, not removing its presence or turning away its face until the parousia of the Lord and the resurrection of the body occurs. In another sense the incarnational community assembles to celebrate its life in Christ in its liturgical and kerygmatic service as the church, with its own appropriate expression of order and sacrament. But this liturgical and sacramental celebration must have a vicarious significance on behalf of the total incarnational community, which in its very mission is both evangelical and eschatological.

There should be no concern at this point over the fact that the relation between the incarnational community and the church in its more institutional sense is ambiguous. There is both a provisional nature and an ambiguous character to the church that resists precise delineation at the point of its relation to the world. The ambiguity itself evidences the incarnational character of Christ's continued presence in the world and thus is more hopeful as a way of uniting the church in its mission to the world with its identity as the body of Christ.

It would be a mistake to assume that a communal existence or lifestyle is equivalent to an incarnational existence of Christ. Many attempts to establish communal projects of existence may well have valid incarnational intentions and to a certain extent may realize certain objectives of an incarnational community. It seems difficult for communal projects to escape the inherent fallacies of any realized eschatology, where the ambiguity between the kingdom of God and the church is resolved into a single reality, and where expectations become absolutized to the point where the community becomes a polemic against both the institutional church and the world. The presence of a communal lifestyle could be considered an eschatological sacrament in the same sense as a miraculous physical healing. When one person is healed, it is a sign that points everyone, including the one healed, to the eschatological reality of the resurrection. The healed person is still part of the larger body, which is awaiting its final redemption. Thus the incarnational community suffers the same limitations and kenotic existence in the world, of which it is a part, including an inveterate inability to purify itself. Where the grace of common life does exist, it summons the larger body to a renewed hope of the coming of the kingdom of God in power.

---

[9]Thomas F. Torrance, *The Ministry and the Sacraments of the Gospel*, vol. 11 of *Conflict and Agreement in the Church* (London: Lutterworth, 1960), p. 159.

The Church as Ministering Community

The mission of the church, I have asserted above, is grounded in the nature of the church. It is the nature of the church to experience the forgiveness of sins and reconciliation with God that is actualized through the incarnation and the atonement of Christ. As the incarnational community in which Christ himself is present and through which he continues his ministry in the world, the church has its existence grounded in this divine ministry or service of the Son to the Father on behalf of the world.

The church as community is more than a social entity; it is the corporate body of Jesus Christ. It is a presentation of his own personhood, his own service (*latreia*) as the Son to the Father in the power of the Spirit. Thus *latreia* is the root paradigm of community. Or, one could say that community is the liturgical paradigm by which incorporation and edification of the self is experienced in terms of fellowship and union with God.

But this means that community exists as an eschatological as well as an incarnational reality in the world. It exists as Jesus Christ himself exists in the world as the end of the world, as the *eschatos* of the world. He is the one who brings restoration, relation and sabbath rest into the world. This *latreia,* or service of Christ, is a primary event in the sense that it is the actuality of community between human beings and God from which all possibility of community proceeds. In this way our discussion of the possible as well as the permissible functions of the incarnational community must proceed dogmatically out of the actuality of the christological (trinitarian) community, and yet with the proper eschatological tension between the now and the not yet.

The questions that arise in any discussion as to the nature and function of the church as community are basically the questions of authority, order and praxis. These questions are anticipated and answered in the christological priority that the incarnation sets before us. In the *latreia* of Christ as the man who exists for God, there is the priority of the Word that precedes and determines the human response—that is the authority of community. As the God who exists for man, there is revealed the priority of divine ministry that precedes and determines that the church is the body of Christ—that is the order of the community. And finally, as the God-man who exists in the power of the Spirit, there is demonstrated the priority of belonging that precedes and determines believing—that is the praxis of the community.

The Question of Authority

When we ask by what authority the community carries out the ministry of Christ, we are asking the question of accountability as to the source of the ministry. Not all forms of community that might attract one's interest or even allegiance can be said to be incarnational community. It is quite natural that there should be some apprehension over this matter. Even Jesus was challenged by this question: "Tell us, by what authority are you doing these things? Who is it who gave you this authority?" (Lk 20:2). It is not the case that community has its authority by virtue of its own existence any more than Jesus had his authority by virtue of his own existence. He appeals to his relation with God as the One who sent him and who has witnessed to him through the mighty works that he performed.

The mere fact of social community, or solidarity, is not evidence of incarnational community. There are certainly human societies quite perverse in their common cause and common life. The church quite rightly asks the question of authority when it asks to what or to whom is a movement accountable when it purports to exist as a community of reconciliation between God and human beings.

Yet the question of authority is one that also includes a temptation. It is a temptation to put the question in such a way that the one questioned is brought under accountability to the one who questions. The Pharisees questioning the authority of Jesus did not think to question their own! If the church as a legal or institutional entity places itself in the position of calling into question a community or ministry that it has not authorized, it has momentarily forgotten that the question must first of all be addressed to itself. Under and by what authority does any human community function as the community of Jesus Christ? It can do so only by the authority of the Word enfleshed and present in it as a "ministering Spirit."

The enfleshment of the Word along with its presence as a ministering Spirit removes it from the domain of an idea or a principle or even an "authority" in the abstract sense. As the man who exists for God, Jesus brings humanity into the service of God in the concrete sense of his own social life of obedience and conformity to the will of God. He is "authorized" for this service because he himself is recognized as the Son by the Father. In him authority is manifested as *exousia*, the power of divine being through which community between Son and Father becomes at the same time a community of human response and reconciliation. In Christ the priority of word that precedes and creates human response invests his every action with *exousia*—the authority of the divine word itself.

For this reason the social relations that existed between Jesus and his disciples became a liturgical paradigm of the community that exists between the Son and Father. In binding word and deed together, the community established by the incarnation can only be accountable to its own self-existence as the paradigm of Christ's *latreia*—his own service of man to God. This, of course, is a kenotic service, and its fundamental structure is self-emptying existence and ministry. Thus its accountability to self-existence as determined by the divine Word is the mark of its transcendent power and authority. If it should seek to accredit itself by any other external standard or "authority," it would compromise this transcendent source and so lose its incarnational power. The very existence of an incarnational community and *latreia* is thus qualified by the ontological status of the "being" of the community itself.

This is why the manifestation of divine *exousia* often took the form of exorcism, the exposing and driving out of the demonic for the sake of the authentic *latreia* in which there is healing, unity of selfhood and true commonality of life. The "principalities and powers," to use Paul's language, are challenged as authorities that enslave the human spirit. The *exousia* of Jesus is an apocalypse of divine being, which becomes united with the life of human beings over and against the dehumanizing and tormenting "powers" of evil. This exorcism is basically an "ordinary" ministry of the incarnational community that only becomes "extraordinary" in critical situations. The tormenting and crippling powers of alienation, self-will, bitterness, unbelief and anger against God are crowded out in the incarnational community by the power of the new being that the Word of God itself creates. As a result, wholeness, psychically, somatically and spiritually results from authentic liturgical communal life under the power of Christ as ministering Spirit.

What the incarnational community knows is the power of an ordinary exorcism by which the word becomes more fully human as the paradigm of God's own true humanity in Jesus Christ. The forgiveness of sins gives authority to be free of mental oppression due to an estranged mind as well as spiritual oppression due to a guilty conscience. "The Church is in the world," Mackintosh once wrote, "that within the circle of mutual placability people may breathe an air which gives them courage to believe in the pardoning grace of the Father."[10] The church, argued Mackintosh, is a kind of "family of families," in which love, friendship and forgiveness are practiced as the context in which the reality of God's love and forgiveness can be appropriated. When the evil that I practice and that has its power over me is challenged by a love that will not forsake my own humanity, he asserted, then I have the freedom to experience the fullness of God's grace.[11]

Here too one might consider the role of the social and behavioral sciences as means by which the incarnational community practices the ordinary exorcism of enabling authentic humanity to emerge through the authority of the divine word. The church does not compromise the authority of the gospel of Christ in being open to all means by which the true service, or *latreia,* of Christ can be reenacted through community. It is in rendering this service that the church finds its authority to be the church as the community of Christ.

When we ask concerning the true order of the church in its ministry, we are seek-

---

[10]Mackintosh, *Divine Initiative*, p. 96.
[11]Ibid., p. 97.

ing to discover the channels through which the *latreia* of Christ flows as a ministering Spirit. Because every concrete Christian community inherits and absorbs from its culture sets of values that are relatively uncriticized, the question of order often constitutes a crisis of community. Indeed it might be said that the crisis of the contemporary church is a crisis of order, often confused with the question of authority. In the face of cultural relativity, where community can often assume the form of prevailing social structures, ideologies may provide strong sanctions and order, for they are usually narrowly conceived, rigorously logical and thoroughly demanding. They are also simplistic, but this may account for their appeal. Ideologies also tend to create and focus on a concept leadership that is tyrannical and dictatorial rather than serving and sustaining. As a consequence a disposition toward provincialism and protectionism can result, with a strong polemic against other forms of order.

The classic case in the New Testament is the conflict between the Pauline concept of order grounded in Christ as ministering Spirit and the Jerusalem concept of order grounded in historical continuity with the apostolic office coupled with a hierarchical concept of "church" over "mission." Unable to sense the priority of community over office, of humanity over ethnic privilege and of the ministering Spirit over the legal commandment, the Jerusalem church sought to bring order to what was perceived as disorder through the principle of circumcision. Only reluctantly did they concede to Paul his own apostolic authority, and only by this concession did they recognize the Gentile and uncircumcised Christians as sharing in the messianic reign and realm of Christ.

While this conflict has been recognized for its historical and ecclesiological importance as to a doctrine of the church, the deeper issue at stake is not merely how the church determines its order in being the church but how the church finds its order in the *latreia* of Christ. If we allow that the christological axiom also holds for the ecclesiological axiom, then we must return to the statement that the nature of the church determines its mission, even as the nature of Christ determined his vocation. The fundamental *latreia* of Jesus was not conditioned by his messianic anointing, but rather his messianic mission was grounded on his essential nature as divine Son of the Father. He did not become Son of God through the filling of the divine Spirit at his baptism but as the divine Son he became incarnate in the person Jesus of Nazareth. It was as this incarnate Word that he received the messianic office and carried out the messianic mission. In being raised from the dead he was declared to be the Son, not merely the resurrected Messiah, as Paul makes clear at the outset of his letter to the church at Rome (Rom 1:4). His messianic office and apostolic ministry will be completed at the eschaton, according to Paul, when he delivers the kingdom to the Father. Yet he remains subject to the Father as the Son for all eternity (1 Cor 15:24-28).

As the *leiturgos* in the heavenly sanctuary (Heb 8:2), Christ continually fulfills his divine *latreia* on behalf of both the Father and his community on earth. The true order that exists as the structure of community as his body, and he being the head, continues through the agency and power of the Holy Spirit as the Spirit of Christ himself. The nature of this order is a sanctifying one, so that those who constitute the community can be called *hagioi,* sanctified one's. The factors of human culture, race, ethnic identity, ideologies, as well as the principalities and powers are now radically conditioned by the priority of the enfleshed Word, which sanctifies by inclusion rather than by exclusion. This thought lies at the center of much that H. R. Mackintosh wrote with respect to the atonement. He credits John McLeod Campbell, whom he calls "the greatest of all Scottish theologians," with providing him this insight. Mackintosh saw in Jesus a fusion of love and holiness that severely judged the evil that dehumanized humanity but at the same time tenderly sought the good of humanity even in its sorry condition. "It was a condemning holiness; yes, but also it was a tender and merciful holiness, and it was essentially both."[12]

The original structure of sanctification as the holiness of God that determines the true order of community is now revealed as a polemic against the exclusiveness that marks the old order. Jesus is recognized as the "holy one of God" even by the demons (Lk 4:34). But it is a holiness that goes out seeking the lost, and it is a holiness that sanctifies by an act of inclusion rather than by a principle of exclusion. The inner power of sanctification is relatedness, experienced immediately by Jesus as the koinonia that he shares with the Father and the Spirit. This "exclusivity" that properly belongs to the holiness of God has become opened out into the world through the incarnation so that humanity now too can share in this koinonia of holiness. Through Jesus Christ the holiness of God is perceived in the context of the love of God.

The new order of the incarnational community is thus a priestly order through which humanity is grasped by the divine word for the sake of bringing it into the order that the Son himself experiences in his life with the Father. Here we might recall the somewhat controversial passage in Paul's letter to the Corinthian church concerning the consecration of the unbelieving spouse, not to mention the children, through the believing partner (1 Cor 7:12-14). Here we see one facet of the order that belongs to the incarnational community as the "communion of saints." The filial unit becomes the "holy ground" on which a believing husband or wife stands as a "Moses," binding those others with whom there is relation to the sanctifying order of God himself. We could say that there is a certain complicity established by which the unredeemed stand within the order of ministry that God himself established through the incarnation, which provides itself the context for the priestly act of reconciliation.

---

[12]Hugh Ross Mackintosh, *The Christian Apprehension of God* (London: SCM Press, 1929), pp. 158-60.

The incarnational community thus functions as a priestly community. The believing spouse is the priest for the unbelieving partner. The believing parents are the priest for the children, all because of the priority of the ministry of Christ as a divine *latreia* through which sanctifying grace becomes embodied in the community. To be sure, this priesthood must also be understood as an ordinary priesthood, rather than an extraordinary one. But as such, it is itself part of the liturgical paradigm that is the nature of the incarnation community. In the extraordinary priesthood of Christ, after the order of Melchizedek (Heb 5:6), the members of his body are all constituted priests in the ordinary sense. The ontological ground for priesthood is seen by the author of Hebrews as sonship, not natural descent or religious office (Heb 5:8).

So we can say that the order of ministry that belongs to the incarnational community is given to all members of the body, who are like "living stones" in the temple, a "holy priesthood," to offer "spiritual sacrifices" to God in Christ (1 Pet 2:5). This holiness, expressed as divine *latreia* that belongs exclusively to God and is experienced in the inner relation that Jesus has with the Father, is incommunicable as either a moral virtue or religious office. Holiness can only be found where there is the presence of the living God—it is a rational and thus a concretely social reality. The incarnational community is the primary social reality through which the *latreia* of Jesus takes place as a priestly ministry of reconciling sinners to God. The concrete reality of the church then, as a social community in which Jesus dwells through his Spirit, is the true order of ministry by virtue of its nature, not merely as its calling. The church lives out its calling to ministry by expressing its true nature as the "communion of saints."

We can therefore say that it is ministry itself as the divine *latreia* of Christ that constitutes the true order of the church. This is exactly what the apostle Paul argued in stating his case before the Jerusalem elders. Ministry, as the divine work of reconciliation whereby sinners are brought into the sanctifying fellowship of Christ's body, thus creates and sustains the church in its true order. The church does not first of all exist through some historical or religious order and then seek to find its ministry. If the church exists at all, it exists as the result of Christ's ministry through Word and Spirit. The *latreia* of Christ did not take place first of all in heaven and then was mediated to earth in the form of a principle. Rather it took place on earth for and on behalf of sinners and then is mediated in heaven as the ongoing service of Christ on behalf of his body.

The Question of Praxis

It is true then to say that the order of ministry is that of doing the truth, not merely applying the truth. Thus the *latreia* of Christ is first of all revealed as praxis. In praxis, as Aristotle pointed out, the telos of the action is contained within the act. This is quite different from the act of "making" a product, where the *telos* lies outside of the act. Both authority and order are disclosed through the act of ministry.

This is clearly seen in Jesus' own ministry while on earth. His act of ministry through word and deed brought the eschatological end, or telos, within the action itself. Thus he announces the forgiveness of sins to the paralytic and thereby raises the question of both authority and order (cf. Mk 2). His authority to forgive sin as an eschatological reality is itself the praxis of God alone, and his authority to perform this divine *latreia* is demonstrated in the physical healing of the paralytic.

The incarnational community is not merely the "practical theology" department of the church, where truths learned in seminary are put into practice. Rather the praxis of ministry is itself the context in which both the authority and true order of theology is grounded. The theological task is that of interpreting the praxis of Christ, both in its revealed sense as the "dogma" of the gospel of Christ and in its contemporary form as divine *latreia*, or reconciliation, as the ministry of the church. It is noteworthy that the primary theological documents of the New Testament were produced by the apostle Paul from the itinerant centers of his own praxis of ministry. Theologians who are first of all recognized as academic scholars and technicians may not be the theologians that the church needs in carrying out its own theological task as the *latreia* of Christ.

The incarnation did not occur as a result of a series of human decisions, nor was it something that God simply "made" as a product, awaiting its *telos* through human actions. God's enfleshment in Jesus Christ creates the place and the space in which believing is now possible as a gift of God through grace. The true freedom to believe only results from the actuality of belonging, which the incarnational community signals by its own existence in the world as the gracious *latreia* of Christ. And this is done with authority and as the true order of ministry. That is to say, there are signals and signs, as well as relationships and structures that point to the exorcism by which unbelief is cast out and the priesthood by which sanctifying relations are established.

In drawing out the implications of the nature of the church and its ministry considered as praxis, I will look at only one aspect of the church's larger ministry, that of evangelism. In the praxis of ministry the church carries out the task of evangelization through an incarnational presence in the world whereby the social structure of individual persons is intercepted and related to the kingdom of God. In evangelism the presentation of the good news that Jesus Christ is Savior of humanity must also address the core social structures rather than attempting to alter the individual's self-perception through the mind alone. A theology of evangelism must be developed that is indigenous to the social and cultural context in terms of the social structures that the gospel seeks to address.

This means that evangelism must not be construed as merely adding members to the church in such a way that the humanity of those evangelized is left unconsecrated. The sanctification of humanity is grounded in the humanity of Christ as a vicarious humanity, by which his priestly ministry includes all who are suffering in their own humanity. Formation of Christ in the world through the Spirit does not take place apart from the world. This can be seen as the thrust of the teaching of Jesus in Matthew 25, where the presence of Christ in the world occurs through ministry to those who are outcasts, through visiting the imprisoned, through ministry to the poor and clothing the naked.

The Christian mission does not bring Christ to the world. That is not its power. That is the power of Pentecost, where Christ returns in the power of the Holy Spirit. Rather, Christians who are the temple of the Holy Spirit witness by their own presence in the world that Christ has come to the world and has taken up the cause of the afflicted, the oppressed and the estranged as his own cause. The mandate for theological reflection is pressed on those who minister to give account of that which is done in the name of Christ and for the sake of "humanizing humanity" in its estrangement from Christ. Pastoral decisions with regard to human persons who suffer loss and estrangement demand this kind of practical theology.

Christopraxis is the continuing Pentecost event that takes place through the growth of the church in the world. Even mere numerical church growth, if it is the growth of those who participate in God's mission through Christopraxis, is a Pentecostal mission theology event. The church growth movement, which tends to rely overly much on sociological principles and strategies for its success, could well find in the praxis of Pentecost its theological mandate as well as its spiritual muscle.

The emphasis on signs and wonders as a methodology for evangelism and church growth does not grasp the holistic thrust of the church's life and mission. The miraculous does not violate the natural means by which God's mission finds its way through Christ into the world for the salvation of all. Feeding the hungry, liberating the oppressed, bringing peace and reconciliation to people and between people is never accomplished by the miraculous alone—not in Jesus' ministry, not in Paul's ministry and not in the church's ministry to the world.

When the church is defined in terms of historical institution, as an object, the church fails to view evangelism as a Pentecost event and its relation to the mission of God in the world. No longer existing primarily as a missionary people of God empowered and directed by the Holy Spirit, the church struggles to formulate a theology of evangelism when it is reminded of the Great Commission (Mt 28). Concerns for orthodoxy in its doctrinal confession produced a rich but sometimes puzzling tradition of theological reflection. Evangelism becomes a means to add members to the church. Expressed concerns for social and political justice, for the poor and the oppressed, for peace and reconciliation between persons not in the church are weak in theological substance.

To this day there rages a debate over the so-called priority of the evangelistic mandate over the cultural mandate, or the relation of evangelism to social action.[13] The root of this problem, as I see it, is the traditional formation of a theology of the church along institutional lines in contrast to the New Testament process of theological development. As a result the church tends to become inward directed rather than outward focused.

Implicit to the mission theology of the church grounded in Christopraxis is a theology of evangelism that is *numerically commissioned*—"make disciples of all nations", (Mt 28:19)—*geographically mandated*—"to the ends of the earth" (Acts 1:8)—*Pentecostally empowered*—"you will receive power when the Holy Spirit has come upon you" (Acts 1:8)—and *ecclesially multiplied*—"and day by day the Lord added to their number those who were being saved" (Acts 2:47). Church growth, as a movement, must become part of church growth as mission, with Christopraxis once more becoming the basis for the theology and praxis of the church as the missionary people of God.

The praxis of the incarnational community not only includes exorcism and sanctification as the ordinary functions of its daily life but the act of naming as the fundamental paradigm of salvation. It is taken for granted that this act includes the naming of Jesus Christ as the name in which the community has its authority and order. But we need as well to recognize the act of naming by which those who participate in the order of the community itself are named as belonging to Christ and are thus summoned to their own confession of faith in Christ. In this way, evangelism as a specific ministry of the church has its theological basis in the very nature of the incarnational community itself. The witness of the community cannot be abstracted from the question of the existence of the community in the world. The multiple modes by which the incarnational community functions in its witness and service must be appreciated, utilized and critically judged from the perspective of this order of ministry.

The primary sanction for the order and authority of the incarnational community is thus the *latreia* of Jesus Christ. The community functions as the liturgical paradigm in which this service is reenacted in the world, as both a sign of the presence of God in the beginning of our salvation and as a sign of the coming of God in Christ as the

---

[13]The issue of the relation of an evangelism that is directed toward individual salvation as contrasted with a gospel of the kingdom that seeks social justice and transformation of society has been a continuing debate within the Lausanne Conference movement, with John Stott as a primary spokesperson. See Consultation on the Relationship Between Evangelism and Social Responsibility (June 19-25, 1982), *Evangelism and Social Responsibility: An Evangelical Commitment* (London: Paternoster, 1982). A more recent discussion between John Stott and David Edwards can be found in David Edwards and John Stott, *Evangelical Essentials: A Liberal-Evangelical Dialogue* (Downers Grove, Ill.: InterVarsity Press, 1988), pp. 273-331.

end and completion of our salvation. The community thus functions as an "eschato-logical reserve," to use the words of T. F. Torrance, in which the announcement of the kingdom of God is made with authority and boldness, and yet with patient and hopeful human presence sustained until the realization of this kingdom in power and glory. The community will claim as its members more than can be healed, but it will not be willing to abandon them, having once enfleshed the word of forgiveness. This is not the least that it can do—it is the most that it can do for the sake of Christ.

9

THE CONCEPT OF NEIGHBOR IN THE ETHICS OF KARL BARTH

The purpose of this chapter is to explore some aspects of Karl Barth's theological anthropology for the purpose of showing that Barth's concept of grace as judgment against all human natural goodness does not destroy the structure of human life as the concrete and ethical criterion for perceiving and seeking to establish the good of human life. Christopraxis, as developed in earlier chapters, will now be developed as a form of Christian social ethics, drawing on Barth's concept of the neighbor as the material content of the command of God through Jesus Christ.

In the furious exchange between the two Swiss theologians Emil Brunner and Karl Barth over the issue of natural theology, Brunner, almost in an aside, aimed a telling blow at Barth when he wrote, "This much is clear: the theologian's attitude to *theologia naturalis* decides the character of his ethics."[1]

In his response Barth summarily dismissed the discussion of ethics as being one more attempt to establish a point of contact as "the other task of theology." For Barth, ethics should never be considered outside of the single task of theology itself, which is to expound the grace of God as given in Jesus Christ and the command of God as the sole ground on which theology as well as anthropology rest. Even with his

---

[1] Emil Brunner and Karl Barth, *Natural Theology,* trans. Peter Fraenkl (London: Geoffry Bles/Centenary, 1946), p. 5. For a recent discussion of the Barth-Brunner debate, see Trevor Hart, "A Capacity for Ambiguity? The Barth-Brunner Debate Revisited," *Tyndale Bulletin* 44, no. 2 (1993).

emphasis on the "neighbor" as the concrete occasion for the ethical dimension of the command of God in his later *Dogmatics*, Barth did not wish to surrender ethics to a criterion outside of the particular and concrete demand of God on one's personal existence.[2]

If Brunner was correct, then Barth's rejection of the supposed "point of contact" *(anknüpfungspunkt)* as a basis for natural theology appears to undermine Barth's theology as ethical address, particularly as an appeal for social justice and moral responsibility in the public and political sphere.

It is my thesis that Brunner's concern was a valid one but that he failed to recognize in Barth's theological anthropology, particularly in Barth's concept of the neighbor, an ethical criterion that is not only accessible to all people but that confronts all human beings with the command of God as the basis for ethical and moral concerns. In developing this thesis I will not attempt to reconcile Barth with Brunner on the issue of natural theology, nor will I show how Barth's denial of point of contact does not in fact lead him to deny an ontological relation between God and human beings.[3]

After looking briefly at Barth's critique of general ethics, from which one might conclude (mistakenly) that Barth's theological ethics has no grounding in human life itself, we will examine more carefully Barth's theological anthropology and his concept of the neighbor as ethical criterion. From this we will draw forth some implications for theological ethics today.

Barth's Rejection of Ethics

At the very outset of his major work on theological anthropology (*Church Dogmatics* 3/2), Barth warns that an abstract, philosophical ethic is at one with the naturalistic in viewing human beings as self-contained, both in external conditioning and human freedom. Both the naturalistic and ethical as well as the biological and idealistic views of humans must be transcended, argues Barth. The self-contained subjectivity of the human person as the basis for ethics must be overcome and radically shattered by seeing people as the object of divine grace and therefore under divine judgment and constituted as a totally new subject—the subject who is established as the object of God's grace. From this it is clear that Barth sets aside general ethics as an independent and autonomous moral law grounded in human moral reason.[4]

---

[2]Karl Barth, *Ethics,* ed. Dietrich Braun, trans. Geoffrey W. Bromiley (New York: Seabury, 1981), pp. 94-95.

[3]For a discussion of Barth's view of ethics with respect to the "other person" and the shift of his focus from a negative to a positive view of the "other" person as ethical responsibility, see Steven G. Smith, *The Argument to the Other: Reason Beyond Reason in the Thought of Karl Barth and Emmanuel Levinas* (Chico, Calif.: Scholars Press, 1983), pp. 44-46, 158.

[4]*CD* 3/2, pp. 109-10.

In his earlier work on theological ethics (1928), Barth has already warned that the theologian who enters the sphere of ethical reflection cannot "regard the supposedly original inhabitants of the land as a court to which he is commanded or is even able to give account."[5] To be sure, ethics can be found in the phenomena of the human, agrees Barth, but just to that extent it has no common ground with theological ethics any more than phenomenological aspects of human existence can become criteria for theological anthropology.

The criterion for "real man," counters Barth, can only be found in Jesus Christ as the one man in whom true humanity is realized. The one Archimedian point given us beyond humanity and therefore the one possibility of discovering the ontological determination of all persons, says Barth, is the man Jesus.[6]

This christological criterion for Barth's theological anthropology has become well known. What is not so well known is that Barth's view of Christ is in no way an ideal-ization of humanity cloaked in christological rhetoric. Rather, because Barth takes the humanity of Christ as the incarnate form of the divine Lord itself, Adam, as the source of natural humanity, becomes bound to Christ as the source of real humanity. It is, after all, the humanity of Adam as sinful humanity that Christ assumes as the form of real humanity.[7] The solidarity between Christ and Adam has thus been estab-lished through incarnation. It has already been established for Barth, however, that the incarnate Christ is the express image of the God the Father, in whose image Adam and all human beings are created. It is the image of God in Christ that grounds both creation and reconciliation in the Word of God as election and command. As a result, though Barth did not make this connection expressly, one might say that the ethics of reconciliation can now be seen as the basis for the ethics of creation.

It would be a mistake to assume that Barth has drawn a dichotomy between gen-eral ethics and theological ethics, leaving each to its own sphere. Rather he has attempted to show that ethics has to do with real humanity, not with pseudohuman-ity, nor even ideal humanity. There can only be one real form of humanity, argues Barth, and Jesus Christ has revealed that form of humanity as it was originally and finally determined to be. If we have discerned the true form of humanity, Barth con-cludes, then we will have discovered the criterion for theological ethics. This is so because the form of humanity is called into being originally by the determination of the Lord of God, which, through the incarnation of God in Jesus Christ, establishes the ethical response of hearing and obedience. God becomes the neighbor to humans

---

[5]Barth, *Ethics,* p. 21.
[6]*CD* 3/2, pp. 132-33.
[7]I have drawn out the implications of Barth's theological anthropology further in my book *On Being Human: Essays in Theological Anthropology* (Grand Rapids, Mich.: Eerdmans, 1982).

as creature and summons persons to become the neighbor to God and to fellow humanity.

Let us now turn to an examination of some aspects of Barth's theological anthropology to delineate further the form of humanity in its concrete and historical existence.

Theological Anthropology as a Basis for Theological Ethics

The critical issues having to do with life and death that confront us in the rise of modern science and technology are fundamentally anthropological before they are ethical. What one decides as to the nature and state of a human person will ordinarily determine the weight and relevance of ethical imperatives. As Barth has pointed out, ethical imperatives issue from the command of God by which real humanity is set forth as a created order and an eschatological goal in Christ. Thus "wrongdoing" is disobedience to the divine command, not merely violation of an abstract ethical principle. The same divine order that graciously summons forth the true order of humanity as a command of God calls for judgment against that which is contrary to this order. To place humanity under some other order as having ultimate authority is idolatry in Barth's view. That there is a basic form of humanity, for Barth, is first of all a christological statement. We must view true humanity as essentially found in Jesus Christ and only secondarily in Adam.

The Basic Form of Humanity

If there is a basic form to humanity, suggests Barth, it must be understood as that determined and upheld by God in its historical and concrete existence. This form of humanity is constant and inviolable, even through the changes produced by sin. The constant factor in the creaturely form of humanity is "man himself" as the subject of a theological anthropology.[8] No phenomenological depiction of humanity can assert this constant factor at the historical and creaturely level without surrendering the form of the human to natural determinism on the one hand, or abstracting away from the historical level into an idealization of humanity on the other hand. True, Jesus himself was recognized as "human" by his contemporaries at the phenomenological level. Yet, Barth would say, his common humanity, shared with all others, did not define his humanity as "sinless humanity." The humanity of Jesus was "real" humanity not merely because it corresponded to the humanity of all others but because it was under the divine determination of original humanity. This is not a phenomenological determination, argues Barth, any more than the content of the imago Dei can be deduced from the phenomenon of the human.

---

[8]*CD* 3/2, p. 208.

It is through the humanity of Jesus, which is concrete, historical and fully crea-turely, that Barth finds the basic form of humanity as fellow humanity (*mitmenschlich-keit*). Jesus is the "man-for-others" in a relationship of ontological and historical solidarity with all human beings.[9]

This, of course, is first of all a christological assertion before it is an ethical asser-tion. Real humanity is a historical reality that has constancy as well as concreteness. The emergence and existence of humans is necessarily determined by the word of God, first as a creative act and then as a redemptive act. The incarnation takes hold of the humanity of Adam, even in its partiality and falseness due to sin, and gives to par-ticular humanity as the object of divine grace ontological and ethical existence as a concrete relation of fellow humanity or cohumanity.

But this also then becomes an anthropological statement, though Barth makes it clear that when we turn from Jesus as real humanity to other persons, we cannot expect to find in general humanity the humanity of Jesus.[10] In other words, we can-not use the humanity of Adam to define and determine the humanity of Jesus. Rather, it is the reverse.

Theological anthropology, argues Barth, seeks to delineate the basic form of humanity in solidarity with the humanity of Christ as a condition of fellow humanity, in which all persons exist for and with the other, even in their sinful humanity.[11] Far from a total loss of the image of God due to sin, as Barth had earlier suggested, sinful humanity retains the full form of the image of God in the concrete construct of cohu-manity. This construct, however, contrary to Brunner's search for a "point of contact," is not a positive possibility out of which some ethical sense of responsibility can be drawn but is the occasion for sinful humanity out of which real humanity can be dis-covered.

There is no "claim" or "worth" of any kind that can be grounded in this construct of cohumanity, continues Barth. The fact that humans are covenant partners with God, even in their sin, and are inescapably bound up with fellow humanity points not toward some residual moral knowledge but rather toward the determination of God himself that all human beings shall be grasped and upheld in an ontological rela-tionship with him and with each other. There can be no neutrality found in general humanity that stands in an ethical relation, either negatively or positively, to the cre-ative word of God. This is especially true of the original construct of humanity before

---

[9]Ibid., p. 212.

[10]Ibid. "If the humanity of Jesus consists in the fact that He is for other men," says Barth, "this means that for all the disparity between Him and us He affirms these others as beings which are not merely unlike Him in His creaturely existence and therefore His humanity, but also like Him in some basic form" (pp. 222-23).

[11]Ibid., p. 227.

the Fall and thus is all the more true after the Fall. The common factor that binds humanity together in historical and concrete existence is the positive determination of God to uphold humanity in its particularity as fellow humanity and as the covenant partner of God.

What Barth means by this is that persons do not possess some kind of intrinsic moral criteria independent of their relation to God. Barth does not deny that being human entails moral knowledge. He simply denies that such moral knowledge stands autonomously over and against God.

The divine decision for humanity in creation and the divine decision for humanity through incarnation are both rooted in the common factor of the divine upholding of humanity in the form of fellow humanity. It is the humanity of Jesus that provides theological anthropology with the primary text by which this is known of all humanity.[12]

It is impossible for humans to break free from this determination to exist in fellow humanity, argues Barth. "He can forget it. He can misconstrue it. He can despise it. He can scorn and dishonor it. But he cannot slough it off or break free from it. . . . Man is in fact fellow-human. He is in fact in the encounter of I and Thou. This is true even though he may contradict it both in theory and in practice; even though he may pretend to be man in isolation and produces anthropologies to match."[13]

This construct of fellow humanity is concretely experienced as encounter with the other, as male and female, male or female, and is the only structural differentiation that exists, claims Barth. "The so-called races of mankind are only variations of one and the same structure, allowing at any time the practical intermingling of the one with the other, so that they cannot be fixed and differentiated with any precision but only approximately."[14]

One is not the neighbor of the other simply through fellow humanity. The "middle term" in the construct of neighbor for Barth is Jesus Christ, whose own humanity is the concrete manifestation of the express image of God, and thus the common factor in fellow humanity is grounded in the "inner essence of God, which has its creaturely correspondence and similarity in His fellow-humanity, in His being for men." How then, asks Barth, "can this be denied to those for whom He intervenes. How can they be creatures which completely lack this image?"[15]

Here then is the connection between the form of humanity as fellow humanity and the concept of the neighbor. It is in the basic form of humanity that the ethical crite-

---

[12]Ibid., pp. 223-24.
[13]Ibid., p. 285.
[14]Ibid., p. 286.
[15]Ibid., p. 225.

rion of the other emerges. "If we do not realize and take into account from the very outset, from the first glance and word, the fact that he has a neighbor, we do not see him at all."[16] The neighbor becomes real humanity through the incarnation. No new ethical criterion has been introduced through the humanity of Jesus. The original and basic form of humanity as fellow humanity has been renewed and brought under the saving determination of God. The neighbor is not first of all an ethical construct based on some general ethical principle of duty or even of love. The neighbor is both God and the other. To deny the other as neighbor is to deny God. To recognize the other as neighbor is to recognize the good and the right as the demand of God on me through the neighbor.

The "Humanization" of Humanity

In the basic form of humanity as fellow humanity (*mitmenschlichkeit*), we see Barth positing a common form of humanity as a creaturely and historical construct, based on the solidarity of the humanity of Jesus with the humanity of Adam. In Jesus Christ, God himself has become the "neighbor" to Adam through his own humanity. The incarnation is the embodiment of God as the true form of humanity, not the embodiment of an ethical ideal.

Real humanity, then, is humanity as a determination of human being by God himself; it is humanity in the form of a being of one with the other, and it is humanity as the covenant partner with God and the other.[17]

The incarnation does not produce another form of humanity but can be understood as the "humanization" of humanity (*Vermensohlichung*). The ethical content of love as a criterion for theological ethics is not just "Christian love," as distinct from non-Christian love, but it is "human love," as distinct from inhuman love. Humanity under the conditions of sin remains fully human as a concrete relation of cohumanity and, as such, constitutes an "ethical event." But the concrete situation of cohumanity can also produce inhumanity, where there is violence, oppression and lack of love. It is, after all, says Barth, "not ethics, but an ethical event that takes place between two persons."[18]

The love that constitutes the ethical event in cohumanity is common to all forms of humanity. When divine love becomes the content of the event of cohumanity created through incarnation, what results is the "humanization" of humanity. Or to put it another way, the true form of humanity made manifest through the humanity of Jesus serves to ground moral responsibility not in moral reason alone as an abstraction but in cohumanity as determined by God and as experienced in the concrete, historical

---

[16]Ibid., p. 227.
[17]Ibid., pp. 243-44.
[18]Barth, *Ethics*, p. 354.

existence of persons. What is common between Christian and non-Christian is not a universal moral law or reason as an abstract principle, but a common humanity, in which no ultimate differentiation can be allowed except the encounter of the I and Thou in the ethical event of love.[19] This, of course, is the material basis for the formal structure of moral reason.

Even outside the Christian sphere, argues Barth, and quite apart from the concept of Christian love, humanity, for all of its perverse and unfounded forms, is *genuinely there*. As a result, theological anthropology possesses a criterion that enables it to move quite directly and with final consistency in the direction of the conception of humanity and therefore of human nature as constituted in the primary ethical relationship of fellow humanity.[20]

This means that true elements may be found in general ethics, but not as independent ethical criteria standing alongside of and apart from a "critical comprehensiveness" grounded in our knowledge of God as Creator. "To speak with universally binding force is an obligation from which it [theological ethics] cannot possibly seek exemption. It has to take up the legitimate problems and concerns and motives and assertions of every other ethics as such. . . . To that extent its attitude to every other ethics is not negative but comprehensive. But just because it is comprehensive, it is fundamentally critical and decidedly not one of compromise."[21]

The incarnation of God does not take place in a privileged sphere nor in something less than real humanity. In the humanity of Jesus Christ the actual humanity of every person has been taken up, judged, put to death and justified. Jesus Christ is not only the Son of the Father, he is at the same time the brother of every brother and sister. Through the incarnation it is determined that humanity, in its concrete and particular form as cohumanity, is a more fundamental and authentic humanity than that which exists merely as "nature," including all racial and cultural forms. In this form of humanity as cohumanity, the creaturely and natural aspect of human personhood is "humanized" without the need to appeal to "orders of preservation" or "institutions of sanctification."

Wherever people are found, says Barth, whatever the racial or cultural factors, there will be found the inescapable and unavoidable ethical responsibility of living freely for and with the other. The incarnation did not "Christianize" humanity, it "humanized" humanity. Humanity in its concrete and historical form as creaturely existence is brought back into its contingent relation to God and to the other as the concrete neighbor.

---

[19]*CD* 3/2, pp. 276-77.
[20]Ibid., pp. 277-78.
[21]*CD* 2/2, p. 527.

The Falsification of Humanity as Social and Political Problem

Every supposed form of humanity that is not radically and from its very first fellow humanity, says Barth, is inhumanity. There is a false form of cohumanity as well as an authentic form. The false community is exposed and judged for its inhumanity by the real humanity of Jesus. The eschatological judgment will take the form of a question concerning what has been done in the way of true humanity. "Has the community been first and foremost human in all that it has done? The question may be comforting or disconcerting but there can be do doubt that it is crucial, and where it is heard it can hardly fail to be incisive and therefore admonitory. This is the Magna Carta of Christian humanitarianism and Christian politics."[22]

The falsification of humanity, with a resulting inhumanity as measured against the true form of humanity, can even take the form of a natural theology. This is what Barth felt he saw coming in Brunner's appeal to a "point of contact" and the grounding of the ethical in humanity as a construct of nature, with an ethical norm that is not contingent on God's determination of humanity through his special Word of revelation.

Where a natural theology is based on the intrinsic "rights" of nature, or the inviolable freedom of individual personhood, the ethical dimension is already conditioned by "natural rights" or "created orders." On the other hand, where a natural theology is rejected in favor of grace as a contingence "away from" the ontological relation between God and human personhood, an ethical void emerges between Christology and the doctrine of God, between reconciliation and creation.

There is a positive contingence "toward God," as T. F. Torrance likes to put it, that grounds created reality in the act and being of God. There is also a negative contingence "away from God" through which creaturely being seeks to stand in an autonomous and independent reality of its own determination.[23]

It is humanity in its contingence away from God that seeks to reify nature, race and culture under the religious rubric of "orders of creation." It is humanity in its contingence away from God that thinks of justice in terms of natural rights and fairness in terms of sharing what one would otherwise have for oneself. It is humanity in its contingence away from God that becomes vulnerable, weak and exploitable. It is humanity in its contingence away from God that surrenders to the state the prerogatives for determining what is best for the "common good." There is here a danger of abstracting even cohumanity away from its grounding in Christ and establishing a principle based on a doctrine of creation alone by which ethical mandates are upheld. What Barth correctly saw as a fatal plunge into ethical ambivalence in Brunner's opti-

---

[22]*CD* 3/2, p. 508.
[23]Thomas F. Torrance, *Divine and Contingent Order* (New York: Oxford University Press, 1981), p. 82.

mism concerning "orders of creation" came to pass in the Nazi regime of the 1930s. But what Brunner saw as a fatal chasm between Barth's sheer christological event of revelation and the natural goodness of life continues to challenge protestant theological ethics.[24]

It is to Barth's credit that he saw the dangers of a natural theology that lent its support to the ethical arrogance of "blood, race and soil." But those who think that they follow Barth in creating a chasm between the ethics of reconciliation and the ethics of creation fail to understand how he grounds the ethics of neighbor and the authentic form of humanity as cohumanity in the determination of humans as covenant partners, and as such, the inner and eternal reality of creation.

Theological anthropology, as Barth saw it, had as its task the development of a material content for theological ethics as grounded in the command of God. The election of persons to be covenant partners and the determination of persons to be neighbors in the form of fellow humanity does not exhaust the ethics of creation for Barth but is surely a significant component. I should make it clear at this point that I do not wish to construct a general concept of humanity or even an abstract principle of cohumanity, but a theological ethic that takes radically and seriously the concrete existence of humanity as neighbor as one form of the command of God. It is now to the neighbor as ethical criterion that we look for one important component of theological ethics.

The Neighbor as Ethical Criterion

Karl Barth's insistence that theological ethics ought to be firmly grounded in dogmatics is clearly seen in the development of his lectures on ethics at Münster and Bonn in 1929 and 1930. Following the dialectical period of the early twenties in which Barth drove a hiatus between the Word of God and the word of man, he began the task of constructing a dogmatic theology in his lectures at Göttingen (1921-1925). Here we find already that Barth can say, "The Word of God is the basis of ethics."[25] Here too we find that theological ethics is set squarely within the task of dogmatic theology, which begins to assume the form of God as Creator, Reconciler and Redeemer. Though Barth will revise and rework these early Göttingen lectures on dogmatics as well as the Münster lectures on ethics, the foundations have been laid.

Barth appeared to sense, long before others were to raise objections to the radical otherness of the Word of God, that the Word is the command of God expressly to

---

[24]These comments have appeared in another context in Ray S. Anderson, "Karl Barth and a New Direction in Natural Theology," in *Theology Beyond Christendom: Essays on the Centenary of the Birth of Karl Barth,* ed. John Thompson (Alison Park, Penn.: Pickwick, 1986).

[25]Karl Barth, *The Göttingen Dogmatics: Instruction in the Christian Religion*, ed. Hannelotte Reiffen, trans. Geoffrey W. Bromiley (Grand Rapids, Mich.: Eerdmans, 1991).

human beings in their concrete situation. It is the right hearing of the Word and the obedient response to the claim on one's personal and social life this Lord brings that constitute the basis for a theological ethics. This is brought out more clearly in his later treatment of ethics as dogmatics, where the *hearing* of the Word of God involves the *doing* of the Word of God, and where the command of God upholds the practice of doing the will of God.[26]

His opening paragraph in his 1929 lecture puts this matter quite plainly: "Ethics as a theological discipline is the auxiliary science in which an answer is sought in the Word of God to the question of the goodness of human conduct. As a special elucidation of the doctrine of sanctification it is reflection on how far the Word of God proclaimed and accepted in Christian preaching effects a definite claiming of man."[27] Here the *proclaiming* of the Word precedes the *claiming,* reminding us again of the grounding of ethics in the Word of God.

The Neighbor as Criterion

Because the Word of God becomes the command of God in its concrete social and historical occasion of being heard and obeyed, Barth quickly saw that the command of God unites love of God and love of neighbor in a single ethical movement. The question of God could not be raised independently of the command of God to love the neighbor, and the question of ethical relation to the neighbor could not be raised independently of the command of God to know and love him as he gives himself in his self revelation. While the two commands cannot be separated, neither can one be subsumed under the other.[28]

Barth viewed Schleiermacher as attempting to ground both dogmatics and ethics in the religious form of self-consciousness. Barth rejected this methodological starting point. Instead he grounded both dogmatics and ethics in the divine self-revelation that has as its object the goodness of humans in their social, political and historical existence. Barth preferred to view the concrete human relation of cohumanity as an ethical event by which the command of God was experienced first as a material reality rather than as a formal demand. As God assumed humanity in the person of Jesus of Nazareth, the human person becomes the neighbor to whom God turns in his freedom as Creator, Reconciler and Redeemer. Even here we see the broad outlines of the earlier Göttingen dogmatics and what will become the basis for a revised discussion of ethics in *Church Dogmatics.*

Barth moves from his ethics of creation, under which he discusses humanity, to

---

[26]Cf. *CD* 1/2, pp. 782–96; *CD*, 2/2, pp. 509–51.
[27]Barth, *Ethics,* p. 3.
[28]Cf. *CD* 1/2, p. 402.

the ethics of reconciliation, where the ethical question is now formulated in terms of the neighbor. The neighbor becomes the concrete form of the Word of God with respect to the question, How does the Word of God lay its claim on me as a true knowledge of God and as a true knowledge of my own humanity?

The neighbor is (1) a criterion for the command of God itself. Even as the command of God comes to us as the command of the Creator who has bound us to him in covenant partnership, so the command of God comes to us as the command of God the Reconciler, who binds us to the other as our neighbor.[29]

"How do I really stand each moment of my life in relation to my neighbor?" asks Barth. "Among the many, near and far, whom I see around me, who is the Thou to whom my I is now bound and must do what God wills within this bondage? And what precisely shall I do? What is my place within the system of human relationships that can and does change each moment? . . . The more urgently we ask this, or realize that we are asked it, the better."[30]

The neighbor, thus, is (2) a criterion of conduct: "In all that we do the question arises whether we do it with that opening up of our naively egocentric will to our fellow man, who is posited fundamentally by the fact that we are created as neighbors, as neighbors in soul, so that from the very outset we are on the lookout for the other who is of interest to us only because of his invisible soul."[31]

It is not just this or that person, says Barth, but in this or that person as our fellow human that we find the criterion for what it means to love our neighbor. This criterion cuts across but does not obliterate the responsibilities we have to others in terms of sexuality and kinship. It is the neighbor who breaks through the egocentricity of the self by his or her own concrete existence in fellow humanity that demands my conduct be such that the command of God is heard and obeyed.

The sin of egocentricity is especially difficult to bring under judgment when kinship, ethnic solidarity or national identity becomes a criterion for who is neighbor. In his earlier section on ethics of creation, Barth had some sobering words in this regard: "In a way that is fundamentally just as sure and specific as in our own nationhood, we now live inside and progressively outside state boundaries in relation to other nations too." Drawing the implications out even further, Barth adds:

> Even if in fact this were not so, even if someone could be as sure of the national purity of his descent as probably only very few can be, and even if he could seal himself off hermetically from other peoples in his own state, by what basic insight could he ward off the implications of the truism that we are all related to one another in Adam? Is the human

---

[29]Barth, *Ethics*, pp. 94–95.
[30]Ibid., pp. 350, 421.
[31]Ibid., p. 190.

bond in which we stand any less a given factor because it is that of a broader circle than that of kin and people? And if the latter is a criterion of our conduct, why should not this, as a longer extension of the same line, but no less urgently on that account, be a criterion too? Who would deny this after considering the remarkable role played by the stranger within thy gates (Ex 20:10) in the law of the Old Testament? . . . Behind the relative is the fellow countryman and behind the fellow countryman is "the stranger that is within thy gates," and it is precisely the last of these who tells us, if we have not heard it before, that the true concern even in blood relationship is *humanity.*[32]

The neighbor then becomes (3) a criterion for repentance. There can be no Christian humility, argues Barth, "which exhausts itself in repentance before God and will not become ministry to the neighbor as well."[33] While the two are not identical, and repentance toward God has a fundamental priority, there would be no real content in repentance toward God without genuine love of and service to the neighbor. The neighbor is the "brother whom God has set there for me." The sin of the neighbor, against God and even against me, is the obstacle over which I must leap "with a Nevertheless in order to understand him as what he is, namely, the bearer of the divine command."[34]

I cannot make genuine repentance before God, Barth tells us, nor can I exist in true humility before God and the divine command when I ignore the neighbor who is unrepentant. I am bound up in my neighbor's sin and unrepentance to the extent that I cannot abandon my neighbor to the fate of his sin as though it were of no concern to me. This does not mean that I cannot live in humility and repentance before God until my neighbor repents. But it means that my repentance toward God *includes* seeking reconciliation with my neighbor, costly though that may be.

Therefore, the neighbor becomes (4) the criterion for what is lawful and right for me to do. By right, says Barth, we understand the order of human life in society that is publicly known and recognized and protected by public force. Theologically, Barth argues, the concept of right (or law), falls under the concept of reconciliation, not that of creation.[35] At this point, while still wishing to hold to some form of orders of creation, a concept he later rejected, Barth clearly sees this order as grounded in God's determination that humans exist as fellow humans and that rights are contingent on this divine determination. In Barth's view, human rights are not rights of natural humanity as abstract principles that become embodied in the state or society as an impersonal authority. What is right is grounded in what actually is in fact the case—though this can only be known with certainty and clarity through revelation—that

---

[32]Ibid., p. 195.
[33]Ibid., p. 419.
[34]Ibid., p. 421.
[35]Ibid., p. 376.

human beings exist for and with the other as neighbor.

Unlike education, where teachers seek our agreement, right as embodied in the neighbor comes sometimes with pain. We must either submit to what is right with regard to our neighbor or bear the pain of the consequences. Thus there is a certain indifference, says Barth, in the way in which my neighbor, through the authority that properly belongs to the good of fellow humanity, must sometimes coerce and punish disorder as a destructive act against fellow humanity.

There is, then, no natural goodness of humanity that can be counted on always to do the right, observes Barth. Original sin does not disqualify the neighbor from serving as a criterion of the right (lawful) but certainly makes painful the administration of the right. "We are forced to say," Barth concludes, "that the dogma of original sin is much better preserved by the police than by teachers and even by modern pastors."[36] I will not speculate as to how Barth felt about that ten years later!

Finally then, the neighbor is (5) a criterion of Christ for me. He who was God's eternal Lord but also who assumed our humanity, our human nature, "fundamentally reveals—whether we see and hear it or not is another question—each of our fellows to be a question, a promise, a supremely living reminder of his humanity. . . . The one that stands over against me—can and must and will become for me a witness, a messenger, a reminder and confirmation of revelation, of Christ himself."[37]

We must not miss Barth's point here. Christ is not present in the general form of humanity, but he can and will be present to me in the form of my neighbor. He and not I says Barth, decides when and where and how he wills to meet me in the neighbor. This is certainly the basis for recognizing that the church as the body of Christ is the presence of Christ in the world despite the disobedience and unfaithfulness of the church. I cannot refuse to recognize that a fellow member of the church is my neighbor and thus one who serves as a criterion of Christ for me. If I determine that Christ is not present in this neighbor, it will not be because the neighbor is not in agreement with me nor because the neighbor is himself or herself disobedient to Christ (in my judgment). Rather, when other neighbors, in whom I recognize Christ as making a claim on me, are rejected and denied by those who claim to be my Christian neighbor, I must be open to the possibility that even my Christian neighbor may stand outside of Christ's demand. In Barth's way of thinking, the ethical event in which Christ's demand is recognized and experienced takes place first of all between humans, not between "Christians."

The church, says Barth, must always be a missionary community. By that he means that the church must be an open circle, not a closed one. The neighbor as cri-

---

[36]Ibid., p. 378.
[37]Ibid., p. 335; cf. also pp. 432–34.

terion of Christ for me cannot be identified only as a fellow member of the church. It may be that the one who stands outside of the church is precisely the neighbor of the church and therefore the criterion of Christ for the church as well. If I refuse to meet this neighbor, even though he may appear to be ungodly to me, says Barth, I may deny the Christ living in me.[38]

We have seen here how thoroughly and how radically Barth uses the concept of neighbor to develop his theological ethics. It is helpful to remember that this was developed by Barth prior to the church struggle in Germany from 1933 to the end of the war, though the specter of German nationalism and the development of the radical politics of what later became the Nazi movement were already in view. It is quite obvious that Barth found clear direction from his theological ethics in taking a course of resistance to Hitler and even in giving direction to the delegates at Barmen in 1934 as to what the church should be in living by the command of God. In refusing to take the oath of loyalty to Hitler, he lost his teaching position at Bonn but gained proximity to his neighbor—the Jew.

We can also now see that the development of his theological anthropology, published after the war in 1948 (*Church Dogmatics* 3/2), and particularly his ethical section on the doctrine of creation, published in 1951 as "Near and Distant Neighbors" (*Church Dogmatics* 3/4, pp. 285-324), is solidly grounded in his earlier work on ethics. One should also remember his earlier sections on neighbor in *Church Dogmatics* 1/2, pp. 402-64, and in 2/2, pp. 575-630.

Near and Distant Neighbors

The command of God, says Barth, binds each person to distant neighbors as well as to near neighbors. The near neighbors are defined in terms of those who stand close to us in terms of the sexual differentiation of fellow humanity, those who belong to us through bonds of kinship, marriage and family, as well as those who comprise the immediate social community of our historical existence. But beyond this circle of nearness there is a larger circle of the distant neighbor, which includes our own particular race or people, as well as people of other races.

For every person, says Barth, there are "distant neighbors, an innumerable company of those who are foreigners to him as a member of this people, yet not altogether foreigners, the whole sum of humanity. As he belongs to this or that group he stands consciously or unconsciously on the borders of so many others."[39]

We have no choice but to live out the command of God with those near and quite specific neighbors with whom we share our human existence. I cannot evade the

---

[38]Ibid., pp. 432-34.
[39]*CD* 3/4, p. 287.

command of God that comes to me through the neighbor who shares my space and with whose life I am bound up in common personal and social identity. Though all differentiations are ultimately overcome, in the concrete form of existence in this world there remain specific differentiations that must be brought under the command of God and lived out in terms of the ethical category of neighbor.

In his early lectures on ethics, under the discussion of the ethics of creation, Barth says that the neighbor is a given factor and not merely an idea. This raises questions, says Barth, not only for the ancient problem of anti-Semitism but for the modern phenomenon of nationalism.[40] Barth has sniffed out already the ominous signs of discrimination against those who are not "racially" approved or of "pure" Aryan stock.

Necessarily, my life impinges on others who are not family or kin, who do not share my own racial or ethnic identity. Those who are foreign to me on the terms of near neighbor are also neighbor. We must, says Barth, understand the concept of people dynamically and not statically, even from the standpoint of geographical or racial determination. "One's own people in its location cannot and must not be a wall but a door. Whether it be widely opened or not, and even perhaps shut again, it must never be barred, let alone blocked up."[41]

In light of the divine command, says Barth:

> we cannot speak of natural and necessary antitheses. These exist in the relationships of man and woman and parents and children. Even here there is to be fellowship according to the command. . . . Between the peoples, however, everything is basically fluid. There may for a time be Iron curtains. But that is all. And no such curtain has every proved to be impenetrable or fixed. Indeed, it is the function of a curtain not only to fall but also to rise again. This being the case, we must not confuse the contrast of near and distant neighbors with the creation of God and its immutable orders."[42]

Here we see Barth clearly dissociating himself from the concept of created orders. The irreversible relations of man and woman, parent and child, continue to function as "orders," though they are under the mandate of fellowship and do not stand as orders of creation and, as such, ethical criteria. The ethical responsibility to live under the command of God must be fulfilled through these irreversible relations, but the relations do not constitute a separate "created order."

While he allows for the relative fact of differentiation between neighbors on the basis of race, national identity, language or identity as a "people," he allows for no permanent or absolute differentiation at this level. The distant neighbor is always a frontier that must be crossed. It is even heretical, suggests Barth, to hold to a

---

[40]Barth, *Ethics,* p. 195.
[41]Barth, *CD* 3/4, p. 214.
[42]Ibid., p. 301.

"national god" or a concept of a people of God with national identity. "This national god is thus a strange god, his service a sacrificing on alien altars, and therefore this doctrine a false doctrine which can only disturb and disrupt the proclamation of the Christian Church, and therefore spell ruin rather than salvation for the world."[43]

Barth clearly has in mind the historical context of the "German Christians" during Hitler's rise to power. In an extended addendum to his treatment of the near and distant neighbor, Barth recalls the tragic events that took place in Germany during the two world wars. He refers specifically to the elevation of the concept of "people" to the front rank of theological and ethical concepts, and the underlying assumption that in this concept we have a national identity that supersedes all other bonds. The near neighbor became the exclusive right and place of the loyal German Christian, and all of this argued under the theological construct of order of creation.[44]

Barth confesses that he is at a loss to trace the theological origin of this tragic movement but allows that it was a genuine innovation. In neither the field of biblical scholarship, religious and ecclesiastical history, nor systematic theology, observes Barth, were there any preparations for what was to come.

There was, however, following World War I a resurgence of nationalism with a strong theme of the divinely ordered foundation of race, family and blood, according to Barth. Nationality as the common soul of a people, revealed in its language and culture, was bound to Luther's confession that God has created us with a specific identity and a specific nationality. Out of this spontaneous movement, theologians began to create a basis for a national church. In these writings the German prophets of culture and enlightenment replaced the prophets of the Old Testament. The practical life of the church now consciously embodies the national customs and rituals.

Barth hardly feels it necessary to repudiate what, from his perspective in 1950, he calls simple "nonsense." He reminds us that the main theme of the Bible is not the history of nations or peoples, but the history of God's covenant partnership with humanity, which strikes across all national and racial divisions. These divisions and boundaries are not obliterated but relativized to the ethical demand to live under the command of God as neighbors. He concludes his discussion with a reminder of the miracle of Pentecost, where both near and distant neighbors were encountered by one and the same Spirit of Jesus Christ.

Here we see that God as Redeemer (Holy Spirit), empowers and sustains the humanity of God as Reconciler (Jesus Christ) in seeking the goodness of human beings as constituted by God as Creator. The neighbor, as ethical criterion, is not a

---

[43]Ibid., p. 305.
[44]Ibid.

Christianized form of humanity accessible only to the private sphere of Christian ethics but is a humanized form of humanity itself, making an absolute claim on us through the concreteness and factuality of fellow humanity. If there are irreversible forms of human relations as Barth holds—sexuality, parent-child relations—as well as differentiations of a more subtle character—color of skin and national origin—these all must be brought under the "critical comprehensiveness" of a theological ethic. No human relation can be exempt from the form of the command of God that comes in the form of the neighbor. The neighbor presents us with the only absolute ethical demand, other than God himself. And, as Barth has shown, God and the neighbor constitute the ethical event.

Implications for Theological Ethics Today

It will have become quite apparent that we have refrained from addressing specific contemporary situations in our exposition of Barth's concept of the neighbor as ethical criterion. Our purpose was primarily to show that Barth's radical judgment against natural human goodness did not entail a hiatus between an ethics of reconciliation and an ethics of creation. In the concept of neighbor, both near and distant, we see that Barth's theological ethics are open to all that moral reason itself wishes to call good and right for humans. This means that ethical concepts of justice, honesty, the sanctity of life and so on are bound up in theological ethics. It also means that what ethics defines as human good from a secular perspective defines the same "good" as that approached through theological ethics.

To be sure, there is a methodological check in Barth's dogmatic inquiry with regard to the true ethical subject. Setting aside the ethical self-consciousness of individual and universal moral reason (both religious and secular) as the subject for ethical reflection, he posits the concrete existence of the other as the object for ethical reflection.

If Barth appears to have surrendered ethical objectivity in the form of abstract moral principles, he has gained it back in the form of the objectivity of the ethical demand on the subjectivity of the ethical person himself or herself. Only thus has Barth felt that the egocentricity that lies concealed in natural and idealistic ethics is disclosed, judged and redeemed.

While Barth allows for the relative ethical structures that comprise the "orders of society," including the state and civil law, he defines an ethical order and structure intrinsic to the human good itself—the ethical structure of fellow humanity, with the neighbor as ethical criterion. If my assessment of Barth's attempt to ground ethics in fellow humanity is positive, and for the purpose of this chapter let us assume that it is, what implications then arise for our own ethical responsibility as Christians and neighbors?

The Public Nature of Moral Issues

It has long been assumed that Barth's theological ethics fail precisely at the point of the public discussion of moral issues. Robin Lovin has recently charged Barth with exactly this failure: "For all its theological integrity, Barth's position is impossible for a public ethics. If we are to choose our actions by reason and defend them publicly by argument, we must either limit the freedom of God or abandon the metaethics that bases all moral meanings on God's will."[45]

The attempt in this chapter has been to show that Barth's construct of neighbor as a christological and ethical criterion can be understood in terms of his theological anthropology. That is, through fellow humanity as the basic form of humanity, the command of God as the basis for ethical responsibility can be heard in a universal and public sense as that which determines the basis for moral reason. Lovin's point is true to the extent that the *motivations* for moral decisions and moral actions cannot be based on universal moral principles according to Barth. But what is argued here is that the *content* of the moral agenda as well as the *consequence* of moral action can be a matter of common discussion and action between Christian and non-Christian when the issue of human life is at stake. I would argue against Lovin that Barth's theological ethics are not derived out of "metaethics based on God's will." Rather theological ethics are derived out of the concreteness of human life, and especially the concreteness of the neighbor, as a form of the command of God.

Here I may well be going beyond Barth himself but not, hopefully, contrary to Barth. We do well to remember that for Barth bad ethics means bad theology and that good ethics requires good theology. The position I take here does not go contrary to that. To argue that the concept of neighbor as ethical criterion opens the moral agenda to public moral discussion does not abandon Barth's own criterion of "critical comprehensiveness," by which all that is considered as a universal and public basis for human good is subject to theological and critical assessment.

The incarnation can be viewed as the single ethical event that destroyed the "dividing wall of hostility" between persons (Eph 2:14). Moral goodness, as the material content of a life in union with Jesus Christ, means that one is accountable not only for what is honorable in the sight of Christ but "also in the sight of others" (2 Cor 8:21; cf. Rom 12:17; 14:18).

No longer can there be both sacred and secular spheres that permit Christians to claim ethical exemption from the moral good of the neighbor. Rather, as Bonhoeffer put it, "Christ, reality and the good" comprise a single sphere of moral and spiritual

---

[45]Robert W. Lovin, *Christian Faith and Public Choices: The Social Ethics of Barth, Brunner and Bonhoeffer* (Philadelphia: Fortress, 1984), p. 42.

unity.[46] This means that an agenda for moral discussion can be established that takes priority over specific doctrinal, ideological, ecclesiological and political commitments. We are making a distinction here between the theological foundation for ethics and specific doctrinal formulations of that theology.

To say that the moral good of the neighbor constitutes an ethical criterion from which no one is exempt by virtue of doctrinal, ideological, ecclesiological or political commitments is itself a theological statement. Thus far we are attempting to preserve the grounding of ethics in dogmatic theology. It is our understanding that this was the intent of Bonhoeffer as well, even in his most radical "worldly" and "secular" forms of obedience to the Word of God.

This does not mean that these commitments are not of significance to those who hold them. But they cannot intrude into the moral agenda in such a way that they circumvent the moral issues of human goodness. When they do, consistently and inevitably the moral agenda becomes blurred and moral action paralyzed. Only when there is the freedom to move beyond ideological and religious agendas to constructive engagement at the moral level of human good will the right prevail and justice be done. To paraphrase Bonhoeffer, we are speaking here of a nonreligious theological ethic. Where doctrinal commitments and ecclesiastical polity and practice block right moral actions, then all the more the need for a better theology.

Two examples can be seen in recent events on the American scene. In the decade of the sixties concerted efforts were made at the political and social level to set aside discriminatory laws with regard to the participation of blacks in public and civil life, including educational rights, right to vote and right to have equal access to public facilities. The moral agenda seemed clear enough when viewed abstractly. However, when concrete situations were addressed at the level of local communities and state-controlled educational facilities, ideological and doctrinal commitments created for some a paralysis of action at both the political and social level.

Martin Luther King became the visible center of a civil rights movement that set a moral agenda and demanded concrete action and even resistance to laws deemed contrary to the basic human rights of blacks to participate freely in the society in which they lived. Many Christians found it difficult to support such a moral agenda because of certain theological ambiguities and certain ideological tendencies perceived at the center of the movement. Those who felt free to move into the discussion and participate in the actions had to set aside deeply felt ideological and theological commitments for the sake of ethical integrity in treating the black Americans as neighbors. A price was paid, in many cases, by experiencing rejection from the very segments of the society in which those who participated had their theological and ideological roots.

---

[46]Dietrich Bonhoeffer, *Ethics* (New York: Macmillan, 1955), p. 188.

We do not mean to suggest here that all theological commitments are to be set aside for the sake of moral action. Rather, a theological ethic grounded in the command of God as represented by the human situation of the neighbor seizes the moral issue as a true "confession" of theological integrity. The specific point is that one can act in such cases with both moral and theological integrity without demanding that those who are participants in joint moral discussion and action share explicitly in one's own religious or doctrinal commitments. The public nature of moral issues is not merely because human goodness is a universal ethical category but because human goodness is an object of divine concern and action.

Karl Barth himself was called the "Red Parson" while a pastor at Safenwil, where he committed himself to the cause of the workers who were suffering from exploitation. Barth later was to struggle with the tensions involved here between resistance to political authority and the state, and the command of God as expressed in concern for the neighbor. For Barth the freedom of God came also to mean the freedom to act with God and for the neighbor, even in taking up force as resistance to the tyranny of evil.[47] Yet in fairness to Barth, we must also say that he would not go so far as we have gone here in arguing that the goodness of humanity as understood in terms of cohumanity and under the category of neighbor constitutes an ethical mandate for moral action unless prompted clearly by the command of God.

A second example can be drawn from the history of struggle for full equality of women with regard to voting rights and participation in the marketplace of business and commerce, not to mention education and the church. Here too the moral agenda of public discussion was clouded with theological and ideological commitments. Some argued from an ethics of creation against granting women equal rights as a violation of a divine ordering of the sexes and as a fatal undermining of the integrity of the home and family.

Those who took up the front line of moral protest against such discrimination often argued out of an ideological view of human rights which was unacceptable to others who desired more freedom for women, but could not agree to a direction which seemed to destroy the ideological foundation of society itself. Here too, we see how difficult it is to have a moral vision and moral agenda which is not ideologically, politically or even theologically biased.

The argument, admittedly, appears to be circular. We have said that theological ethics, grounded in a theology of God as Creator, Reconciler and Redeemer, can be the basis for putting a moral goal—the good of the neighbor—ahead of theological commitments. The difficulty is in making a clear distinction between what might be

---

[47]See Karl Barth, *The Knowledge of God and the Service of God,* trans. J. L. M. Haire and Ian Henderson (London: Hodder & Stoughton, 1938), pp. 217-32.

called theological commitments, which arise in a systematic or doctrinal form, and a dogmatic theology, which stands as a critical and comprehensive basis for these commitments.

God's freedom is not understood as a capricious or arbitrary relation to the human situation. Rather, following Barth we hold that God's freedom is expressed in his freedom to elect and sustain individuals in covenant partnership with himself and in a relation of neighbor, one to the other. This is a theological understanding of the command of God as the basis for ethical actions as well as a theological basis for the continuity and relatedness of issues that relate to the good of people—that is, to moral issues.

To say that one is led to ethical action by the command of God alone is meaningless in light of God's command bound up in his determining of humans to be in the form of fellow humanity. For the apostle to say that we "must obey God rather than any human authority" (Acts 5:29) does not mean that God's commands are arbitrary and totally subjective but that God's purposes for humankind already revealed through Jesus Christ take precedence over religious commitments and religious authority.

It seems consistent with Barth's theological ethics, then, grounded in the concept of neighbor as ethical criterion, for Christians to be able to move with courage and good conscience toward a moral agenda that places human goodness as an ethical goal ahead of all other commitments, if necessary.

In saying this, one realizes that this is a direction fraught with complexities and hazards. Human goodness as an ethical goal is many textured and layered, rather than simple and self-contained. Yet, one cannot really find out where the points of tension are until the moral agenda is defined in terms of the moral goodness of humanity as determined by God as a concrete reality of fellow humanity. That is to say, when the injured person lies beside the road on which the religious person travels, the question as to what constitutes the ethical action of a "neighbor" takes precedence over the more abstract fine points of theological difference. Isn't this the point of the parable told by Jesus?

Only when the ethical issue is defined in these terms will one have a measure of what ideological, political, theological and ecclesiological commitments are at stake. Only when the participants in moral discussions committed to moral action recognize and assess these commitments in light of the moral goodness of humanity itself will progress be made.

One implication of Barth's theological ethics is that Christians can and ought to be able to participate in the setting of moral agendas and even in morally committed actions that affect the social and public lives of human beings, side by side with those committed to a different theology of the church and with a different ideological view of political and economic structures.

It was largely the work of Karl Barth that produced the Barmen Confession in 1934. Yet, for all of the emphasis on the Word of God and Jesus Christ as ethical criteria by which the true church was defined over and against the German church as co-opted by Hitler, there was no mention of the Jew as the neighbor. The fate of the Jew as neighbor was subordinated to the concern for the theological integrity of the church. The fate of the church appeared to be the primary theological agenda in Barth's eyes, though he was not blind to the monstrous treatment of the Jews by the state.

It was to Barth's credit that he later saw that the fate of the church does indeed rest with its recognition of the command of God in terms of the neighbor who is deprived of basic humanity by systemic discrimination and persecution. The fate of the church cannot take precedence as an ethical criterion over the fate of the neighbor, with whom the church is bound up in human solidarity. This became an explicit theme of Barth's doctrine of the church in the world. The community that knows the world, said Barth, is necessarily the community that is committed to it. Not in a "cunning masquerade."

> but in an unmasking in which it makes itself known to others as akin to them, rejoicing with them that do rejoice and weeping with them that weep, not confirming and strengthening them in evil nor betraying and surrounding them for its own good; . . . by accepting the fact that it must be honestly and unreservedly among them and with them, on the same level and footing, in the same boat and with the same limits as any or all of them.[48]

The public character of the moral agenda that is concerned for the good of individuals does not surrender to a public consciousness or to a universal ethical principle the criterion for theological ethics. It simply means that when Christians act for the good of the neighbor as an ethical goal, the object of the ethical action is the same as for an ethical action that recognizes the same goal but from differing perspectives. This is one way of understanding the freedom of God. God's freedom is not itself an ethical criterion over and against what people know as the good, but it is the freedom to seek the good of human beings through the ambiguity of human moral attitudes and actions.

It should also be recognized that there may be good reasons why it is not prudent or sound practice to participate in actions that purport to be morally governed in any given situation when measured by other factors.

Acting out of blind and stubborn passion for what one holds to be right, without

---

[48]CD 4/3, pp. 774-75.

regard for consequences, is a form of moral self-indulgence. Authentic concern for the neighbor carries with it an assessment of what might be better, when the best cannot be done without destroying the structure of fellow humanity itself. But when these factors do not bind one to silence or inaction, one ought always to be free in accordance with theological ethics to take up a form of moral action for the sake of the neighbor with good conscience.

The "critical comprehensiveness" that Barth suggests always attends a theological ethic that enters into public discussion and moral action. It is not enough to say "neighbor." One must also say neighbor as Jesus Christ in need of our ministry and concern, as well as neighbor to whom we minister on behalf of Jesus Christ. The concept of neighbor is comprehensive—there is no human moral reason that adds further ethical imperative to that of neighbor as an ethical criterion. But it is Jesus Christ who commands the Christian conscience in its moral reflection and action, not merely the neighbor. This is because we cannot view the neighbor independently of Christ, nor Christ independently of the neighbor. Ultimately, Christ is the true neighbor.

Moral Parity Through Social Repentance

The criteria for moral discernment and action are set squarely within the structures of humanity itself, even though individuals apart from the renewing grace of God cannot consistently identify and carry out these actions. This means, as I have tried to show, that there is a public side to the moral agenda to which all persons have access and which takes precedence, ultimately, over all other commitments. I thus agree with Brunner that there is an openness of all human beings to the moral structure of the command of God. But I also wish to say, along with Barth, that with this openness of all persons to the moral structures of human life, there is not the readiness to discern and do what is right. Moral competence is not lodged in abstract moral reason alone but in a moral life renewed by grace.

Because the goodness of humanity is understood theologically to be a determination of God as experienced as fellow humanity, moral parity in the form of full participation in this good is assured as the basis for an ethics of reconciliation and creation. The God who is Reconciler and Redeemer is also God who is Creator. Again, we are not suggesting that fellow humanity as expressed in the concept of neighbor becomes the single criterion of theological ethics. Barth clearly will have none of that. But it is also fair to say that the concept of neighbor is a criterion of a theological ethic based on the theological foundation of God's election of persons to be covenant partners and upheld by the command of God.

The neighbor as ethical criterion thus comes under the cross of Jesus Christ, where a radical judgment is pronounced against all claims based on the differentiations of sexual identity, racial characteristics, kinship ties and religious forms of self-consciousness, as well as all religious and secular ideologies and institutions created out of these factors. While Barth explicitly made a distinction between the order of male and female and parent and child as over and against racial and national factors, he submitted both kinds of differentiation to the command of God to exist in fellowship, love and unity.

This has been fulfilled in Christ, suggests the apostle Paul, where there is "no longer Jew or Greek, there is no longer slave or free, there is no longer male or female; for all of you are one in Christ Jesus" (Gal 3:28). Abraham is elected as the covenant partner of God, and through him all of the families on the earth have their blessing. One way of understanding this blessing is to say that all people are determined by God to inherit the same promise and to enjoy the same parity of access to the goodness of humanity as a gift of God. While differentiations remain as part of this present world order, they are effectively relativized in Christ and cannot be made to serve as barriers to human relationships grounded in love of God and the neighbor.

God does not abandon humanity in its sheer contingence away from his grace. Instead he continually seeks to uphold the humanity of all persons, even in their state of sin and rebellion. In assuming human form God the Son brought all humanity under the judgment of the cross through his own vicarious human obedience and personal existence as the neighbor to God, as his father, and to each person as his and her brother.

But here we see that moral persuasion is not enough. Here we discover that a moral argument is insufficient to penetrate through to the stubborn core of the human heart, which is not ready to acknowledge what is already objectively the case.

The criterion for moral action cannot be the conscience alone, as the apostle Paul clearly saw. The conscience is the center of moral ambivalence, not moral authority. True, conscience does "bear witness," as Paul wrote, but it also is the center of "conflicting thoughts" that both "accuse and excuse" (Rom 2:15). That which conscience points to are the criteria for moral responsibility sunk deep into the structures of created human goodness experienced as fellow humanity.

When a natural theology is based on creation alone and on human nature as a bearer of moral reason that points to God, this theology masks the inveterate sin plaguing all human moral action and turns it into self-preservation at the expense of the other. There will be no real moral parity between the strong and the weak, between the oppressed and the oppressor.

The formation of moral authority without the transformation of moral power will leave the powerless weak and will strengthen the hand of the powerful. A natural theology that does not have at the center a cross sunk deep into human flesh will not find transforming love at the center of human moral action.

It is through the death and resurrection of Jesus Christ that the transformation of moral authority takes place. Here, as Paul clearly states, all of the old antitheses and the natural hostilities are brought to an end (Eph 2:16). No longer can sexual status, economic status or racial distinctives be used as criteria for relationship with God or for seeking advantage over others. The incarnation was not for the purpose of putting the humanity of God on the cross but for the purpose of sinking the cross deeply into human life. When God "dies" on the cross, what is put to death is all that is inhuman in humanity. As a result, the New Testament social ethic, says Leonhard Goppelt, is a Christian calling to life in existing historical structures, but not on the basis of a natural justice or social idealism. Rather the Christian is called to exercise a role of responsible witness to the new and true humanity that has been obtained through Jesus Christ.[49]

It is, finally, not enough to have an agenda for moral discussion that is public in nature and that gives every person access to the criteria for moral discernment and judgment. Moral discussions without moral authority to transform existing social and personal evils are themselves immoral discussions.

A moral theology not including "social repentance" as an evidence of the transformation of the moral authority by which one lives among others cannot be a truly evangelical theology, nor can it be an authentic natural theology. The atonement that the cross provides through the incarnate Christ as Reconciler and through the Holy Spirit as Redeemer can never be a legal or forensic construct in abstraction from the common humanity that Christ shares with all persons. To have experienced the grace of the cross and forgiveness of sins through the resurrection is to have received the grace of repentance as well.

Because God and the neighbor belong together, repentance toward God that does not include repentance toward the neighbor is not authentic. A cultus abstracted from action in social commitment, says Barth, "as often seems to be the case in the official religion of the temple in Israel, is no real cultus, no matter how strongly it expresses human humility before God."[50] Nor is repentance toward the neighbor inclusive of repentance toward God, as Barth also points out. Thus social repentance is not a moral agenda set by the world in its need to redress wrong but is God's own agenda by which he summons the world into relation with himself and consequently also into relation with the neighbor.

If there is a divine humility, which Barth also attributes to the eternal condescen-

---

[49]Leonhard Goppelt, *Theology of the New Testament,* ed. Jurgen Roloff, trans. John Alsup (Grand Rapids, Mich.: Eerdmans, 1982), 2:146, 157.

[50]Barth, *Ethics,* p. 420.

sion of God, there may also be said to be a divine social repentance. That is to say, through the incarnation God took up the cause of the estranged and sinful neighbor as his own cause, and through his death and resurrection provided a basis within his own actions for the humanization and social renewal of the sinner into a new community.

By social repentance, then, we mean (1) the nonviolent claim on the other as neighbor and therefore a fellow human. This will involve confrontation, even conflict, but not a strategy of violence. There is an inevitable dehumanization of the other that must occur in order to justify violence as a strategy to secure what is right. In too quickly depicting the neighbor who appears to oppose what is right as demonic, we can dehumanize them and thereby give ourselves moral permission to destroy them. When the demonic was recognized in Jesus' ministry, it was never for the sake of destroying the human person but liberating the human person and restoring human life.

The social repentance that lays claim to the neighbor as human must be prepared for the conflict and confrontation with that which is evil and destructive but not as a strategy of violence against the person of the neighbor. There may be a form of violence as a strategy of social justice but not as a strategy of social repentance. The divine social repentance expressed through the solidarity of incarnation suffered violence but did not take up violence as a strategy.

This is not simply an argument against violence based on the style of confrontation chosen by Jesus. The incarnation itself is a strategy of "social repentance" on the part of God whereby he enters into the concrete situation of evil and violence, not to "do violence" but to overcome violence through the "suffering of violence." There is a sense in which one can say that the movement toward the cross forces violence into open conflict with the sheer goodness of God in human form. Jesus could have avoided the "violence" of the cross by not "loving his enemies" in such a way that he confronted them. Social repentance is not a strategy of "nonviolence" as a form of appeasement of evil but a strategy that confronts violence in such a way that its moral evil is made visible in order that forgiveness might also be extended to those who do violence.

Therefore, social repentance is (2) a public *disinvestment* in one's own moral rectitude as a form of creating moral parity with the neighbor. By this is meant a refusal to create a posture of moral superiority as a means of clarifying and differentiating moral issues. The church must make its own confession of complicity with the moral ambiguities and the immoral attitudes and actions of the society in which it participates. It does this not by reciting its own sins so as to gain a superior moral and spiritual standing with God but by a positive social repentance in which it stands with the neighbor, even the ones who have taken up violence, as their advocate before and to

God. Nonviolence is not a higher moral principle but a strategy of constructive engagement with corrupt and evil structures for the sake of the goodness of humanity as fellow humanity.

Social repentance is grounded in human solidarity and, therefore, (3) makes a positive sacrifice of self-interests for the sake of an investment in the promise and the future of relationships between those who are estranged. Consequently there is an eschatological perspective to social repentance as a form of moral action. This action is deeper and more prepared for a sustained involvement than the ethical enthusiasm that rises quickly to a high pitch and then diminishes just as quickly. The basis for this, of course, is love for God and for the neighbor as our selves.

In his early lectures on ethics Barth has a section on gratitude that, near the end of his life, will become the theme under which he begins his treatment of ethics as response to God. What he said in that context can help us to see both the command and the constraints of what I have called social repentance.

The moral depth of social repentance is prepared for and expects some form of liberation, or loosing *(Lösung)*, even if not in the present a redemption *(Erlösung)*, as Barth put it.[51] Redemption is a promise and a goal assured through God's own participation in the struggle for the renewal of humanity. The Christian who understands social repentance will not fanatically demand repentance of others as an immediate condition of positive and constructive engagement. Rather, social repentance seeks to move with others toward that goal of redemption through the stages of releasing humanity from its systematic oppression. There are penultimate achievements that have ethical validity, even though there is not yet ultimate redemption from all forms of evil.

The poor, the hungry, the dispossessed, the oppressed, as well as the oppressor, constitute the criteria for responsible moral action. Poverty is not itself the criterion, nor is oppression, for this would leave the rich and the oppressor without a criterion for moral self-reflection and repentance. The criteria are lodged within the *relation* of the one to the other.

As a result, the impoverishment of one is immediately a matter of moral concern to the other. In the same way, the act of oppression is of moral concern to the oppressed ones. It is not enough to be liberated from the oppressor. One must also seek reconciliation with the oppressor for the sake of the humanity of the oppressor. Being oppressed does not free one from the moral demand of fellow humanity. Nor does being hungry free one from the moral responsibility to seek the good of those who have plenty. One might only suggest here in passing that a "theology of liberation" cuts both ways. The theological basis for liberation is a theology of reconcilia-

---

[51]Ibid., p. 502.

tion. To harm the oppressor, to diminish or no longer to uphold his humanity, is also to destroy the basis for reconciliation.

Here we are again reminded that Christian ethics is grounded in Christopraxis. The criterion by which we measure what Barth calls the "ethical event" between humans is the incarnation, death and resurrection of Christ by which humanity is liberated from the inhumanity of sin and restored and morally empowered through grace. Christopraxis is a form of moral empowerment rather than merely moral judgment. Moral transformation is not an ethical achievement apart from the release of human structures as well as human existence from the dehumanizing consequences of sin.

Moral actions grounded in repentance, which seek the true reconciliation of neighbor with neighbor, can and must be a transformation of moral authority into a gospel of liberation from inhumanity and for humanity. This, finally, is the contribution that the gospel of Jesus Christ can make to human goodness as a source of ethical concern.

10

SOCIOCULTURAL
IMPLICATIONS OF A
CHRISTIAN PERCEPTION
OF HUMANITY

Hidden within every culture lies an implicit social paradigm of humanity. Human beings are defined by the social structures of their behavior as well as by the ritual forms of their culture. This implicit social paradigm is the precritical mass out of which social theories are developed and with which cultural anthropologists and philosophers work. If this assertion is accepted, then it means that all theories as to the nature of "man" in the generic sense of human being are culturally relative. Yet if it is also accepted that a social paradigm of humanity lies behind each particular culture, then it is possible that the social structure of humanity contains elements of a common denominator, or essential core, that is recognizable to some extent in every culture, race and ethnic community.

It is the thesis of this chapter that there is such a social paradigm of humanity, and it is the task of a critical philosophy or theology to define that essential core. The task of defining this essential core leads further to the task of developing crosscultural and multiethnic concepts and structures that have as a goal the disclosure of the essential goodness and unity of humanity, with the differentiations fully present and concretely affirmed.

This critical task of definition and disclosure is scientific in its methodology and comprehensive in its epistemology. That is to say, the concrete social structure of humanity as a "precritical" mass is the objective reality that controls, by its very nature, the methodology by which it is known. Cultural anthropologies, or theories about the nature of human beings, must be submitted to the scientific rigor of examination in light of the concrete core of humanity itself as a social structure. These anthropologies, or theories, are thus relative by their very nature, the same as any scientific theory. But they are not relative only to the cultural matrix of experience and thought out of which they are conceived. If this were so, they would be viewed in an absolutist sense within that particular culture or worldview. The relativity of theory is to the objective reality of human beings as such. And it is the thesis of this chapter that humans exist essentially in concrete social relationships or what I have called a social paradigm. This also means that there must be a comprehensive and open epistemological approach to the task of defining and explicating the implications of the social paradigm. No theory of knowledge that is culturally relative can be permitted to conceal or deny the nature of humanity as it confronts us in the sheer objectivity of social relations. We know humanity in the concrete form of its being humanity; this is discovered in the core social paradigm.

Having said this, it must now also be admitted that the perspective of this chapter is that of a particular culture and worldview that is predominantly European and Western rather than Asian and Eastern. In addition it must be admitted and, begging the consent of my readers, allowed that the conceptual framework that determines the assumptions and direction of this inquiry is that of a Christian theological anthropology. My objective is to set forth first of all the basic assumptions that underlie a Christian anthropology and then to draw forth implications from the social paradigm itself for the Christian's approach to the goal of seeking the goodness and unity of humanity. This task is a theological task. The chapter is thus addressed first of all to Christians, particularly Asian Christians, but also in a spirit of openness and humility to those who do not share the same assumptions.

The fact that this task is now being addressed in the context of questions that Asian theologians and philosophers are asking concerning the nature of the human is all the more significant in light of the Swiss theologian Karl Barth's "Letter to Southeast Asian Christians," published in *Southeast Asia Journal of Theology* in autumn 1969. In that letter, Barth asked two questions: "Can the theology presented by me be understandable and interesting to you—and how? And can you continue in the direction in which I believed I had to go, and at the place where I had to set a period—and to what extent?"[1]

---

[1]Karl Barth, "Letter to Southeast Asian Christians," *Southeast Asia Journal of Theology,* autumn 1969, p. 3.

Addressing Asian theologians in particular, Barth continued:

> Now it is your task to be Christian theologians in your new, different and special situa-
> tion. You truly do not need to become "European, Western men," not to mention "Bar-
> thians," in order to be good Christians and theologians. You may feel free to be South
> East Asian Christians. In my life I have spoken many words. But now they are spoken.
> Now it is your turn.[2]

Barth's words should be heard as an encouragement to continue developing a
theological anthropology relevant to the Asian context and culture. But his words
must also be understood in the form of a caveat, for I write as one who lives and
thinks as a Western man, and to some extent, at least, one who is an extension of the
European tradition.[3]

My attempt is to present neither a Western nor an Eastern perspective concerning
the nature of the human but a Christian perspective. This Christian perspective is not
intended to be identical with either Western or Eastern modes of perception of reality.
Yet it must also be said that every theological perspective is also a contextual one. The
appropriate mode of doing theology is therefore one of dialogue in a crosscultural
and crosscontextual setting.

The core assertion of a Christian theology is that the controlling social paradigm
by which humanity is defined sets squarely within the objective relations that exist

---

[2]Ibid., pp. 4-5.

[3]In contemporary Christian theology, it was the Swiss Reformed theologian Karl Barth who developed
most fully a theological anthropology grounded upon the concept of the "humanity of God." Barth
took as his starting point not the "humanity of man" in general but the humanity of Jesus Christ.
Barth's concern was for the inherent goodness of "real man" as God created them, not human beings
as subjects of their own self-determination. There can be no knowledge humans have of themselves,
said Barth, "from which the idea of God is excluded" (*CD* 3/2, pp. 197, 72). Barth reiterates what John
Calvin asserted at the beginning of his *Institutes of the Christian Religion:* knowledge of God and
knowledge of man are mutually intertwined and conditioned in such a way that the knowledge of
God must precede the knowledge of man. Yet Barth suggests that Calvin's exposition is not entirely
satisfactory because he does not tell us on what grounds all of this is affirmed. Calvin does not make
explicit what must be said. It is only the concrete humanity of the man Jesus of whom it can be said
that humanity is explicable in God, and whose humanity is real because it exists in relation to God
(ibid., p. 73). Only from this christological perspective, says Barth, can there be an understanding of
"real man" and therefore of the goodness of humankind as determined by God. For Barth, a radical
solidarity exists between the humanity of the first human being—Adam—and the humanity of Jesus
as the incarnation of God. In God's self-emptying through becoming human (kenosis), the real
humanity of all humans becomes the specific humanity of God, without God becoming less than he
is. For a discussion of kenosis as it relates to the assumption of the humanity of Adam as an
intratrinitarian act, see *CD* 4/1, pp. 187-90. I have discussed the implications of kenosis with respect
to the solidarity between the humanity of Christ and all human individuals in Ray S. Anderson,
Historical Transcendence and the Reality of God: A Christological Critique (Grand Rapids, Mich.:
Eerdmans, 1975), pp. 177-78.

between God and humans, through the humanity of Jesus Christ as divine Son of God. This actuality of real humanity lies at the core of the witness of the Christian tradition concerning the person of Jesus of Nazareth, who was called the Christ, thus identifying him as the one who represented the fulfillment of the social reality of Israel as a people of God. The nation Israel is not first of all a political or national entity, but it is a social paradigm of humanity through which the reality of God is disclosed and by which the nature and destiny of human beings are defined.

For Christian theology the event of the incarnation of God in Jesus Christ is understood as a social paradigm that defines and determines human nature and destiny. A Christian anthropology does not begin with the "humanity of man" in seeking to find relationship with God. Rather a Christian anthropology begins with the "humanity of God," as observed in the historical person, Jesus Christ, and with the social structure of the new human community within which he himself is known. This is what was meant earlier by a comprehensive epistemology, a way of knowing that is open to the social reality of the humanity of God as a definition of authentic humanity. This approach does not deny the empirical form of humanity as we know it in our own experience but makes possible the perception of humanity within its own social and cultural setting without confusing the social and cultural form of humanity with the core social paradigm itself. At the same time, this allows the particular form of humanity in its cultural setting to retain its distinctive.

It is my task, then, to enter into dialogue with those who seek a Christian perception of human beings from within the Asian context. The basic assumption that makes such a dialogue possible is that a Christian perception is conditioned by what is revealed about the nature and destiny of humans through the biblical witness to God's determination to create and sustain them as covenant partners. This does not deny that there are other perceptions of human beings, both religious and nonreligious. What is affirmed here is that a Christian perception of the nature and destiny of humans provides a critical and constructive perspective from which to understand individuals in their social and cultural context.

My procedure in seeking this perspective will be to set forth, first of all, several theses about the nature of humans as determined by an examination of the biblical tradition. Following that, the social and cultural implications of these theses will be drawn out with a view to the concrete situation of persons in a pluralistic and changing world. My partners in this dialogue can determine better than I whether and how these implications can be related to the Asian culture and context.

A Christian Perspective on What It Is to Be Human

To be human is to be the creature who is free to hear and respond to God. It is from the perspective of this "election" to be a covenant partner with God that the story of creation is itself written. The opening chapters of Genesis can be understood as a polemic against prevailing theories of the nature of the human as under the "spell" of nature as a mute and blind force. Even as the divine word has created a history of covenant relation between God and Israel, by which all other "histories" are brought under critical judgment, so this same word is understood to have placed the original man and woman in a history of response and relation to God. In the same way, this account can be seen as a polemic against prevailing views of human nature as intrinsically evil due to the phenomenon of evil as a constant factor in human experience. The nature of that which is good is not defined over and against evil but as that created and determined by God, such as humans are. The human is good as God determined humanity to be, good in creaturely form, good as taken from the earth, and good in the freedom to hear and respond to God as covenant partner.

The author of the first account of creation in Genesis makes it clear that the distinction between the human and the nonhuman is "from above," and not "from below." That which marks the human off from all else in creation is the fact that the human is addressed, not merely called into being, by the divine word. "And God said to them . . ." is the event that constitutes these creatures to be human and, therefore, to bear his own image and likeness (Gen 1:28).

Having established this qualitative distinction between the human and nonhuman as a structural openness of being to the divine Other, the story immediately sets forth a theological critique against the assumption that this divine image and likeness can be contained in a solitary individual. "It is not good that the man should be alone." This is the divine verdict, not merely a complaint of the man (Gen 2:18). Not only is this a polemic against the confinement of the human to the solitary individual, but it is a judgment against the theory that the natural world, even under the command of the solitary man, could produce of itself the "helper" or counterpart to the man. After the task of naming the animals, with its implied quest for an answer to the man's own being, the divine verdict again is heard: "But for the man there was not found a helper as his partner." (Gen 2:20). An ex nihilo is introduced that separates the man as creature of nature from his creaturely humanity. The man is put to sleep and when awakening discovers the partner to be "bone of my bones and flesh of my flesh." This is understood to be the result of an unmediated act of God. By this is taught the truth that real humanity is fellow humanity and that the divine image is not manifested primarily by the superiority of the man over nature but by the complementary reality of cohumanity. Indeed, it is cohumanity in the form of male and female that integrates biological sexual differentiation into the essential differentiation of the meeting and communion of persons.

Here too, then, is found the source for a theological understanding of human sexuality, marriage and the family.

To be human is to be the creature who is free to hear and to respond to God. This was the first thesis. But the second immediately follows as was shown above: *To be human is to be the one who is free to respond to the other person as the counterpart to one's own personhood.*

A third thesis can now be suggested with respect to a biblical perspective on humanity. *To be human is to find and fulfill one's nature and destiny in a symbiotic relation with the created world and its environment.* Having established the uniqueness of humanity as structural openness to God and the fellow human, the biblical author is free to place humans within the flow of creaturely reality where the human *bios* and the nonhuman *bios* share a common world. A speculative anthropology that originates within the human subject invariably seeks to elevate the human *bios* above the creaturely *bios,* through some principle of rationality or religion. All nontheological anthropologies, thus, tend to be dualistic in nature, unable to preserve the fundamental uniqueness of the human within the solidarity and continuity of creaturely existence.

At the same time, I do not intend by the concept of symbiosis to suggest that the uniqueness and particularity of humanity is dissolved into an undifferentiated whole. The essential uniqueness and differentiation has already been established by the first two theses. What is asserted here is that there is a cooperative and mutually dependent relation between the human and the nonhuman at the level of *bios.* Humans remain structurally open, even in this symbiotic relation with creation itself. It is the symbiotic relation between the human and the created world that overcomes the dualism often found in philosophical anthropologies.

The biblical perspective is quite free from this anthropological dualism. The relation of the human to the creaturely realm and the natural world is ambiguous only when viewed from the perspective of the human as subject. This ambiguity lends itself to both naturalistic and idealistic views of human nature as attempts to resolve human life into mere *bios* on the one hand or sheer mind on the other.

A Christian perspective, based on the biblical account, overcomes this ambiguity through a view of humans as persons who are objects of a divine determination by which the natural and the personal, the creaturely and the human are experienced simultaneously as a reality of life. This reality of life, or *zoē,* includes the *bios* of creaturely existence as a positive structure of humanity. The New Testament clearly marks off this distinctive by viewing the life that issues from God and that is constitutive of human life in its fullness as *zoē* and not mere *bios.* This is a theme of the Gospel of John, as well as the Synoptics and Paul's writings. *Zoē* refers to a person's life made abundantly full, and this life is inseparable from Jesus Christ as the source of life (Jn 10:10;

1 Tim 6:11-12, 19).[4] Human life is necessarily grounded in biological existence as a fellow creature with the nonhuman forms of life. Yet the life (*zoē*) of human beings is structurally open to God and the other in such a way that personhood occurs as the mystery and reality of that life. That which diminishes human life as *bios* also affects the quality of personal life, for the human cannot be considered in abstraction from its concrete form as biological life. In the same way, that which seeks the good of human beings as persons must seek the welfare of the total person, body as well as soul.

Understood in this way, human life integrates the duality of soul and body, personal and impersonal, subjective and objective, spiritual and material, as a positive relation established by the determination of divine will and love. Humans are determined to be both "of the dust" of the ground and "inbreathed" by the divine Spirit. Only when human subjectivity seeks to understand itself autonomously, as unconditioned by the divine word, does this duality break apart and become a desperate dualism.

There is thus given to humanity an essential order that permits the creaturely level to be considered in its own right with its own "natural laws" and physical structures that determine to some extent the nature and quality of human life. Yet this natural order is a contingent order and not an order that follows blindly and ruthlessly the order of nature itself. Because "human nature" is fully part of nature but is only *human* nature because it is under the divine determination that constitutes the human as distinguished from the nonhuman, it is expressed as a contingent nature. The contingent reality of human nature in its symbiotic relation to all of creatureliness, preserves both the physical and the personal reality of humanity. When humanity is viewed noncontingently, the human is under the determination of natural, social and empirical forces; this is the "spell of nature" from which the human is liberated by the power of the creative word.[5]

A fourth thesis can now be formulated from the perspective of human experience within the structures of creaturely and temporal life. *To be human is to be concretely "this person" belonging to "these people," while at the same time open to and responsible for the good of all people.*

Here we must recall my earlier insistence that real humanity cannot be established at the level of general humanity. It is the particular, concrete humanity of Jesus of Nazareth that is real humanity. It is the humanity of this man, this circumcised Jew,

---

[4]This distinction between *zoē* and *bios* has been developed by J. Robert Nelson, *Human Life: A Biblical Perspective for Bioethics* (Philadelphia: Westminster Press, 1984), pp. 107-8. Nelson argues that ethical decisions related to human life under marginal conditions, such as in embryonic situations and in terminal illness, are better determined by an understanding of human life as *zoē* and not mere *bios*.

[5]I have discussed in greater detail the contingent relation between the human and the creaturely in *On Being Human* (Grand Rapids, Mich.: Eerdmans, 1982), pp. 24-26. See also Thomas F. Torrance, *Divine and Contingent Order* (Oxford: Oxford University Press, 1981).

this member of a particular family and particular culture, who exists as the real form of humanity. Yet it was also this man who recognized and affirmed the humanity of the non-Jew, the uncircumcised, the despised Samaritan, the lowly slave, the "invisible" women, and the "foreigner" with his Greek language and culture, and even the hated Roman soldier, who represented the oppressive power of the quasi-divine claim of Caesar. Jesus penetrated through these social and cultural forms of humanity and addressed the true humanity of each person, and so revealed his own humanity as the touchstone of divine grace.

Through Jesus Christ we see that real humanity occurs as a particular form of humanity, never as abstract and ideal humanity. The "flesh" that the divine Logos assumes (Jn 1:14) was Jewish flesh, stamped with both the promise and judgment of the divine word. Yet the particular form of Jewish flesh was intended to be a sign that all flesh, every human race, is under the sign of that same judgment and promise. The death and resurrection of Jesus put an end to all claims that racial, sexual, social or cultural identity and status have a claim on the grace and righteousness of God. Now it is revealed that the Spirit of God is poured out on "all flesh," as Joel prophesied (Acts 2). Racial, sexual and cultural distinctives are not obliterated. Instead real humanity is now to be experienced in and through these distinctives.

The effects of sin are not overcome through a more rigorous form of spirituality but through a renewed structure of sociality. Love is defined as living peaceably in a domestic setting, as clothing the naked and feeding the hungry, and as loving the neighbor as oneself

In drawing persons around him, Jesus re-created humanity in the form of a community of shared life and common identity. Even this narrower circle, defined by the specific calling of the twelve, was structurally open to the unclean leper, the tormented demoniac, the self-righteous Pharisee, and the women of ambiguous reputation. In contact with Jesus, humanity was liberated from the blind and capricious powers of nature and disease, as well as from the cruel and inhuman practices of the social and religious tyranny of the strong over the weak. In the real humanity of Jesus we see the humanization as well as the socialization of humanity.

In his person and his actions Jesus embodied both grace and truth (Jn 1:17). His moral presence was both convicting and empowering. He drew to his side the fugitive from the law as well as the furtive Pharisee, without shaming either.

He ignored the categories established within his own society. For him the despised Samaritan was a woman who could give *him* a drink, the self-righteous Pharisee a man who wanted to talk, the leper a person who needed to be touched. While people came to him in bunches, needs came with a name. A congregation was not a mob to be sent home to eat but individuals to be fed with bread broken with his own hands. In a crowd he was never simply pushed by people but touched by someone who hurt. Within the shouting sounds of a multitude he heard the cry of the blind man, the sigh of a sinner, the murmur of a skeptic. He let people be like who they were and offered to help them become who they could be. He had no uniforms for his disciples and no masks for his friends. He did not ask for conformity but for commitment. His style was love, his pattern devotion.

In the person of Jesus there was a spiritual integrity that revitalized the spirit of human persons amidst the dead weight of tradition and legalism; where Jesus was, there was life. In the life of Jesus was a moral integrity that brought an absolute sense of right to specific human situations; where Jesus was there was truth. In the truth of Jesus there was a personal integrity that spoke with authority against the enslaving influences of religious formalism and demonic delusion; where Jesus was, there was freedom.

In the midst of a religious culture that prized appearance and cultivated form, he appeared among us clothed simply in grace and truth. He refused to recognize as spiritual that which was artificial and affected. He valued the truth of being and doing over the righteousness of words and prayers. He told it like it was—both in the street and in the temple. He had one language for both the saint and the sinner. He stated divine realities in terms of human experience. His lifestyle was that of a human person living among humans. Because he *was* the truth, he had no fear of exposure, nothing to defend. Because he was *human,* he had no fear of humanness, in himself or others.

Because he understood and accepted his own humanity, he never condemned another for being human. He demonstrated that a holy purpose can only be completed when the spirit and the flesh become one. He was in every sense a mature person. His feelings ran deep, but they had a bottom; his love flowed freely and yet within boundaries; he was sensitive to pain but not easily hurt; he had a dream, but consecrated his life in duty.

He came as a Son and introduced God as the Father. Out of this relationship he coined new words to explain human problems and possibilities: prodigal, enemy, reconciliation, friend, brother and sister, flock. He defined spiritual values in terms of human relationships: God forgives us as we forgive one another; to hate our brother is to hate God; to give of ourselves to another is to love Christ. He gave himself as the new basis for the community of persons. Those who love Christ become his body, with a common life and one heart.

He liberated the spirit from the law and created children of God out of slaves. He lifted the burden of the law by fulfilling it, not by breaking it, and pointed beyond it to a higher fulfillment. Those who become his slaves find their freedom. In his own life he brought both body and soul into balance.

He brought a new degree of tolerance to the sharp edge of divine justice. He held back the law long enough for people to discover *why* they were lawbreakers and to receive mercy. He brought a new spirit of liberality into the uptightness of a religiously structured society. He taught that the sabbath was made for humans, not humans for the sabbath; everything doesn't have to be perfect to please God, and pleasing God is more important than pleasing others. He brought a new dimension of practicality to the word *love*. Love from God can be worn on the back, put on the table and set down beside you; it is human as well as divine, tangible as well as spiritual. It is Jesus.

If there is a culture that belongs to the kingdom of God and transcends all other cultures, it is a culture of true humanity as the gracious power and presence of Christ in a structure of human social and personal relations. This culture of the kingdom of God has no other language and no other custom other than that of the particular people and society who become its manifestation. Yet these existing social and cultural forms are relativized to the real humanity of Jesus Christ as expressed through the embodiment of the gospel in the lives of Christians. One culture is not relativized to another culture, as has so often happened in the missionary expansion of the church. Rather, every culture is related to the critical construct of real humanity through the power of the gospel. And to that extent every culture can bear in its own social structures the reality of the kingdom of God and make manifest the humanity of the kingdom through its own forms.

We now need to restate the four theses in preparing to add some comments as to possible implications of a Christian perception of humanity for a society and culture that is in a process of change and where pluralism will certainly occur.

1. To be human is to be the creature who is free to hear and to respond to God.

2. To be human is to be the one who is free to respond to the other person as the counterpart to one's own personhood.

3. To be human is to find and fulfill one's nature and destiny in a symbiotic relationship with the created world and its environment.

4. To be human is to be concretely "this person" belonging to "these people," while at the same time open to and responsible for the good of all people.

Social and Cultural Implications

It is beyond the scope of this chapter to attempt an exposition and critical analysis of the factors that have produced a concept of humanity particular to an Asian culture and worldview. Whether or not there can be said to be a prototypical "Eastern" view of humanity in general as compared to a "Western" view is something that cannot be decided here.[6] The tone of this will continue to reflect a theological perspective. This

---

[6]For a helpful discussion of some of these issues see Emerito P. Nakpil and Douglas J. Elwood, eds.,

is not for the purpose of advancing this perspective as the only one but is done so that a constructive interaction and dialogue between a theological and nontheological approach can take place.

We can assume, I believe, that the factors of social transition, modernization and cultural pluralism will present challenges to an Asian perception and theology of human life even as they have in Western society. Not the least of these challenges will be the apparent loss of norms and values that are rooted in traditional practices and concepts. These are concerns for a Christian perspective on the nature of humanity as well as for non-Christian concerns.

The implications drawn from the theses stated above are thus directed toward this phenomenon of transition and change rather than toward specific concepts in an Asian perspective on the nature of the human. It is hoped, of course, that through the dialogue, there will emerge some specific interaction with those perspectives particular to the Asian context.

Three areas of concern can be identified with respect to a Christian perception of the human through a process of social change and cultural pluralism.

□ The first is for a continuity of content with regard to what defines the nature of real humanity; this can be said to be an epistemological concern.

□ The second is for a consistency of meaning with regard to what defines the nature of the good in terms of human values and decisions; this can be said to be an ethical concern.

□ The third is for a conservation of the essential order and stability of the foundational structure of human life; this can be said to be an ecclesiological concern.

These areas of concern are not exclusive of others nor exhaustive. However, they each are found to be concerns that emerged during the early assimilation of the gospel into the various social and cultural milieu's of the early church through the expansion of the mission of the church beyond Palestine into Asia Minor and southern Europe. Here we turn more directly to sources found primarily in the Christian tradition.

One only has to read Paul's letter to the church in Ephesus to see that he addresses these concerns as the core of his epistle. The question of what constitutes true knowledge of humanity, argues Paul, does not come from following the "passions of our flesh, following the desires of body and mind." Rather it is the "flesh" of Christ Jesus, who was put to death and raised again, that discloses true humanity (Eph 2:3, 15). Neither the traditions of the Gentiles nor the law of commandments and ordinances peculiar to

The Human and the Holy: Asian Perspectives in Christian Theology (Quezon City, Philippines: New Day, 1978). This volume contains the addresses, workshop reports and papers of the Consultation on Theological Education for Christian Ministry in Asia held in Makati, Metro-Manila, Philippines, in March 1977.

the Jews define true humanity. The humanity of Christ, brought to an end on the cross and raised again as the original and final determination of humanity, produces for Paul a critical epistemological criterion for both Gentile and Jewish humanity.

All human self-perception is culturally conditioned because all self-perception is socially determined. The effect of sin on self-perception is not primarily cultural but social. It is in the structure of core social relations of human life that false self-perceptions arise. Therefore, no true knowledge of oneself or of one's own humanity can occur apart from a true knowledge of the other with whom one is bound in social relationship. The Jews as well as the Gentiles were "darkened in their self-understanding" with respect to the knowledge of true humanity in their social relationships. One only has to read the Old Testament prophets Amos and Micah to hear this indictment. It is made explicit by Paul in Romans 3 where both Jew and Gentile are brought under the same judgment—there is no distinction; all have sinned and fall short of the glory of God. The continuity of real humanity by definition then cannot be grounded in human self-perception but must be discovered through repentance toward both God and the neighbor.[7]

Authentic repentance seeks the restoration of right relationships. This is both a spiritual and social healing of human subjectivity that has collapsed in on itself and thereby become isolated and defensive. The core identity of true humanity is thus bound up with this shifting of the criterion for self-perception to the other person. This shows that the single commandment of love—to love God and to love the neighbor as oneself—is grounded in social humanity, not merely in individual humanity. But we cannot *know* this love fully apart from the gracious love of God addressed to us in Jesus Christ. Thus our knowing of true humanity is also a revealing of true humanity through the gospel of Christ. For any attempt to define humanity on our own terms incorporates the fallacy of self-perception into our anthropological constructs. As a result, social revolution alone cannot lead to the discovery and form of true humanity. The constant factor through social and cultural changes in human

---

[7]The relation to the neighbor, argued Barth, becomes the concrete basis for repentance toward God. There can be no Christian humility "which exhausts itself in repentance before God and will not become ministry to the neighbor as well." While the two forms of repentance are not identical and repentance before God has a fundamental priority, there would be no real content in repentance toward God without genuine love of and service to the neighbor. The neighbor is the "brother whom God has set there for me" (Karl Barth, *Ethics*, ed. Dietrich Braun, trans. Geoffrey W. Bromiley [New York: Seabury, 1981], pp. 419, 421). Barth also makes clear the fact that the concept of the neighbor as the epistemological criterion for true knowledge of humanity as ethical responsibility crosses social and cultural boundaries of kin and people. "Is the human bond in which we stand any less a given factor because it is that of a broader circle than that of kin and people? And if the latter is a criterion of our conduct, why should not this, as a longer extension of the same line, but no less urgently on that account, be a criterion too? . . . The true concern even in blood relationship is humanity" (p. 195).

self-perception is the structure of humanity as a social reality of love experienced as a reciprocity of relations in which Jesus Christ is present as the objective reality of grace, freedom and responsibility.[8]

In his letter to the Ephesians Paul also addresses the ethical question. In the face of the abolishing of the law of commandments and ordinances, as well as the tearing down of the racial, social and cultural boundaries between Jew and Gentile (Eph 2:14-15), the norm for determining what is the good is consistent with the "humanization of humanity" through Christ. No longer are human beings under the power and spell of their natural passions and natural religion. No longer are they "strangers and aliens" one to another. No longer are they "tossed to and fro and blown about by every wind of doctrine" (Eph 4:14). No longer are they subjected to the inhumanity of personal egos bent on destructive and malicious behavior; no longer are they caught in the humiliat-

---

[8]No finer exposition of the structure of human personhood has been developed than that offered by Dietrich Bonhoeffer in his classic work *Sanctorum Communio* (London: Collins, 1967). For Bonhoeffer "person" means the socioethical, historical person whose existence is realized and comprehended in the I-Thou confrontation of wills. This "social construct" of personhood as a theme of Bonhoeffer has been explicated helpfully by Clifford Green in his doctoral dissertation, *The Sociality of Christ and Humanity* (Ann Arbor, Mich.: University Microfilms International, 1972). Green shows that the essential epistemological paradigm for Bonhoeffer is not *cogito ergo sum* but "I relate ethically to others, *ergo sum*" (*Society of Christ,* pp. 98-99). The encounter of wills through relationship, argues Bonhoeffer, is a social-ethical encounter that calls forth responsibility. In this encounter the historicity of the person is established, for the person must act "responsibly toward the other" in the existential moment of encounter, in a manner that upholds the "other's" humanity, the "other's" personal being; and thus the I upholds its own humanity by affirming this structure of cohumanity. The objective ground for this reality of cohumanity as an ethical relation is the "communityness" of relation between the Father and the Son, whose image was created to exist on the creaturely level in persons as cohumanity. Jesus Christ as objective humanity, and thus real humanity, is not immanent in the human I-Thou relation but is "objectively present" in the relation. Bonhoeffer seeks to explain this objective reality of Christ present as community through the concepts of "objective spirit" and "collective person." Two types of collective person are presented by Bonhoeffer: association (*Gesellschaft*) and community (*Gemeinschaft*). Association is a form of collective person in which the one wills to be in relation to the other as a means to an end. Community is a form of collective person where one wills to be with the other as an end in itself (*Sanctorum Communio,* pp. 55-56). Because the incarnation of God in Christ binds humanity to God, human beings are bound to each other in actuality, not mere factuality. The factual relation may involve estrangement and conflict. Through the presence of Christ in the human community as a sociological reality, the actuality of communityness as an expression of the objective relation between God and humanity in Christ is the basis for a new community. New social relations have been established that seek identity with all humanity in a structural unity, as important to one's own grounding in the reality of Christ (*Sanctorum Communio,* pp. 116-20). In the same way that the original tree of the knowledge of good and evil stood as a concrete barrier and limit to the original human couple, the social reality of the other constitutes this barrier and limit. But there is also a true knowledge of the self that results from the experiencing of the other as limit (cf. Dietrich Bonhoeffer, *Creation and Fall* [London: SCM Press, 1959]; and *CD* 3/1, pp. 256; *CD* 3/2, pp. 291-93). True self-perception is thus conditioned by accurate perception of the other in a structure of social-ethical encounter.

ing and demeaning roles that are defined by economic, sexual or political status.

The single criterion for what is good is that which upholds the dignity, integrity and essential value of the other person in the concreteness of every social relation (Eph 4—5). The ethical criterion is exhausted by the command of love, as Paul makes clear in his letter to the Roman church: "Owe no one anything, except to love one another; for the one who loves another has fulfilled the law . . . Love does no wrong to a neighbor; therefore, love is the fulfilling of the law" (Rom 13:8, 10).

Ethical norms remain constant when grounded in the true humanity of the other person rather than in culturally conditioned self-perceptions of individuals or the collective cultural mass. When understood in this way, the meaning of that which is good is not first of all an abstract principle mediated through one's own perception of the good, but it is first of all an "ethical event" that takes place between persons as the command of God. In writing to the Ephesian Christians, Paul does not ground his ethical appeal in the Jewish laws and ordinances, nor does he attempt to find some cultural principle in their own society as a "dynamic equivalent" to the law of God. Rather he reminds them that having "learned Christ" (Eph 4:20), they are to "speak the truth to our neighbor," not let anger carry over into grudges and grievances against the other, and not to steal from one another, but rather do "work honestly with their own hands" so that one may be able to give to those in need (Eph 4:25-28).

Concepts of human rights, justice and of concern for the unborn and the aged are not ethical self-perceptions subject to cultural modification but are constraints on individual and collective actions that would violate the very structure of humanity itself. When Jesus healed on the sabbath, ate with publicans and sinners, and asked a Samaritan women to minister to his thirst, he penetrated through all racial, sexual, social and cultural barriers to restore true humanity to others. Indeed, his own humanity could hardly have been the true humanity that it was if he had drawn back from the real humanity of others. Nor did Jesus institute some new ethical concept of the good as a kind of "Christian ethic." He merely reinstated the criterion of goodness that belongs to true humanity as the ethical foundation for all of the laws and commandments. This same criterion was quite clear to the prophet Micah: "He has told you, O mortal, what is good; and what does the LORD require of you but to do justice, and to love kindness, and to walk humbly with your God?" (Mic 6:8).

In the same way, our third concern for the conservation of the essential order and stability of foundational human structures is dealt with by Paul. With the breakdown of traditional orders and with the secularizing of sacred myths and concepts that were used to provide stability for the Gentile world, Paul provides a criterion of Christian community grounded in the identification of Christ himself with those in whom his Holy Spirit dwells. Here too both Jew and Gentile must learn to shift their obedience and loyalty from traditional concepts of authority, by which they sought stability and order, to the structure of social life as regulated by the community as the body of Christ (Eph 2:11-22). The foundational social structures of family, marriage, parents and children, as well as the existing political and economic structures are basically affirmed as good and necessary. Yet all of these structures are radically qualified by the "humanization of humanity" that occurred through Jesus Christ (Eph 5—6).

One of the most devastating effects of the so-called phenomenon of modernization is the breakdown of existing structures within any culture that are assumed to provide social stability and moral authority. Being human, as we have earlier asserted, means living as this specific person belonging to these particular people who speak the same language and participate in the same rituals of community life. All human self-perception is thus culturally conditioned and socially approved. Not to have the social approval of one's own people is to suffer estrangement, if not derangement. Jesus himself experienced this powerful social judgment when he was thought to have an "unclean spirit" by the standard of the self-perception of the Pharisees (Mk 3:30). Even his mother, brothers and sisters sought to intercept his ministry and remove him from public exposure because they concluded that he had "gone out of his mind" (Mk 3:21).

The gospel of the kingdom was itself thought to contribute to the breakdown of these essential social constructs of marriage, family, parental obedience and even economic and political structures. The radical demands of the kingdom were indeed couched in terms that challenged these structures as having a prior claim on men and women. Yet when we observe the actual practice of Jesus, we see that he affirmed the validity of these very structures, even though they were relativized to the demands of the kingdom of God. What is questioned in the sayings of Jesus concerning the radical demands of the kingdom is one's captivity to these domestic and social relationships, not their role in upholding human life. The coming of the kingdom of God means the end of the absolute hold, the "spell" that the natural order has over the person who is first of all determined by God to be free to love him and also to love the neighbor. The kingdom of God values love as the core of discipleship.[9] There is a gospel of the family as well as a gospel of the kingdom.

In his letter to the Ephesian Christians, Paul drew out the implications of the gospel of Christ in such a way that the basic structures of that society were to be "humanized" through the activation of the Spirit and law of Christ. Paul did not seek to replace their culture with a concept of "Christian culture." Rather he called for the liberation of authentic human life within the culture as a freedom from the "magical" as well as from the mythical.

---

[9]I have discussed the relation of the demands of the kingdom of God to the human family and social life more fully in Ray S. Anderson and Dennis B. Guernsey, *On Being Family* (Grand Rapids, Mich.: Eerdmans, 1986), pp. 140-44.

In Ephesus Paul created an uproar when those who practiced the magical arts discovered that their profitable business was threatened by their conversion to Christ (Acts 19). The power struggle is not between the gospel and culture but between the gospel and the "powers" within any culture that dehumanize and enslave persons. Paul views the human mind as well as the human spirit to be enslaved and in need of conversion. Therefore he appeals to the Ephesian Christians to abandon the futility of the mind that is darkened, even in its intelligence, and to be "renewed in the spirit of [their] minds" as well as in their emotions and passions (Eph 4:17-24). Paul sought the renewal of the social structures and the humanization of culture, not the replacing of these structures and culture with a kind of freedom that destroys them. The continuity of order and stability through social change and cultural pluralism is thus grounded in the nature of the human itself as that which produces and lives by culture. In this respect, only when culture is open to change is it able to remain in continuity with the development of true humanity and those social structures that uphold humanity.[10]

The encounter of the gospel in an Asian culture and context is thus basically an encounter of the gospel with humanity. Several specific implications of this might be suggested as contributing to further dialogue. Here again it should be noted that these implications are directed first of all to Christians. I do not presume to propound theories or to offer criticisms beyond the boundaries of my own competence or constituency. I speak as a theologian, and I speak from within the Christian church as one who seeks to understand what the church is saying and doing when it lives and

---

[10]Jürgen Moltmann makes this point very well: " 'Every culture is a way of the soul to itself' (Georg Simmel), and all cultures can be understood as fragments of and routes to that human humanity which still lies hidden in the bosom of the future. In every culture man makes a form for himself and acquires an image of himself. But all historical forms and images which he has given or now gives himself, are transitory and open to change. This permits the conclusion that it is only the bare fact that from out of his inner amorphousness man always expresses himself in cultural forms that are lastingly and everywhere basically human. Man as he appears in different cultures (*homo hominatus*) is an historical figure, but the creative germ-cell in man (*homo hominans*) is eternal. In this sense man learns to know himself through historical encounter and historical understanding of other men and of other cultures. This presupposes that man by the very nature of his being stands in a cultural process, which arises out of his inner biological incompleteness and openness to the world. He attempts constantly to complete himself and to close the inner empty space which is embedded in his existence" (*Man: Christian Anthropology in the Conflicts of the Present*, trans. John Sturdy [Philadelphia: Fortress, 1974], p. 11). This latter point made by Moltmann is developed at greater length by Wolfhart Pannenberg as a fundamental "incompleteness" in the human as a biological creature, which is also then the source of sociality and thus humanity (Wolfhart Pannenberg, *Anthropology in Theological Perspective*, trans. Matthew J. O'Connell [Philadelphia: Fortress, 1985], pp. 157-59). While Moltmann's concept of the development of humanity as necessarily cultural is helpful, one can hardly agree with his assertion that there is a "germ-cell" in human beings that is eternal.

ministers within a particular society and culture.

1. In evangelism, the presentation of the good news that Jesus Christ is Savior of humanity might better address the core social structures rather than attempting to alter the individual's self-perception through the mind alone. A theology of evangelism must be developed that is indigenous to the social and cultural context in terms of the social structures that the gospel seeks to address. Strategies for evangelism might better be developed out of social and cultural analysis rather than through culturally blind apologetics or socially driven marketing techniques.

2. In seeking the conversion of persons to a life of faith and discipleship to Jesus Christ, the evidences of the reality of Christ might better be interpreted in terms of existing cultural and social patterns of life than to impose standards and criteria that are strange to the people. This, of course, can only be done where these patterns permit the full expression of human dignity and value measured in terms of freedom from powers that are alien to that true humanity. A theology of conversion must be developed that confronts the cultural self-perception of the collective society at the core of its inhumanity and thus presents a fundamental orientation to Christ in terms of true humanity. There is often a form of "Christian conversion" that is not unlike the proselytizing activity of the Pharisees whom Jesus denounced. This is conversion to a self-perception of Christ or of Christianity rather than to an authentic human life related to Christ.[11]

3. For the church, as a core social paradigm offering healing, hope and salvation to humans, the life of community in Jesus Christ might better be shaped by the structure of social community that enhances the participation and belonging of each person, rather than by a so-called "New Testament model" of the church. A theology of the church must be developed that embodies an authentic "human culture" in terms of the existing culture and social structures. The church must develop strategies of "humanizing" culture where it takes place as the body of Christ rather than strategies that exploit the weaknesses and insecurities of individuals. The unity of the church will be found in the diversity of the gifts of the Spirit that seek to uphold and upbuild the humanity of the church as the body of Christ in each particular culture.

The incarnation of God through Jesus Christ continues to be the mandate for the affirmation of the goodness and dignity of human beings as God intended them to be, as Christ made them to be, and as the Holy Spirit empowers them to be. My attempt has been to suggest that there is a core social paradigm that Christian anthropology finds both in the gospel of Jesus Christ as well as in the created structures of human personhood. It is hoped that this provides a basis for constructive dialogue and a strengthening of our common humanity for the sake of all humanity.

---

[11]For a discussion of conversion from psychological, cultural and theological perspectives, see Eddie Gibbs, "Integrator," *Theology, News and Notes* (special issue), June 1986.

11

THE HUMANITY OF GOD & THE SOUL OF THE CITY
Where Is the Church?

The humanity of God in the person of Jesus Christ seeks incarnation in the soul of the city before taking up residence in the sanctuary of religion. The "soul of a city" has become a metaphor that speaks of the humanity of a people who share a common destiny and whose lives impinge on one another in a struggle for survival and sustenance. In biblical times Moses established "cities of refuge" for those who sought protection from violence and as a haven for the homeless (Num 35:9-15). These cities constituted the "soul of the people" and the guarantee of human and civil rights.

Viewed from this perspective our nation appears to have lost its soul. Our urban societies have become national disposal centers for the homeless and chemical dispensing outlets for the drug traffic. Social anonymity without communal identity breeds autonomy and finally anarchy. The badge of belonging for the unemployed and disenfranchised youth comes with gang colors, graphic graffiti and spilled blood. Ethnic diversity without an infrastructure of social humanity produces ethnic rage. Economic materialism without an underlying core of spiritual humanism creates cultural hedonism. Perhaps this is what Jesus prophetically saw when he paused before entering Jerusalem and wept over it, saying, "If you, even you, had only recognized on this day the things that make for peace! But now they are hidden from your eyes" (Lk 19:41-42).

Where Is the Church?

In the riots that turned the inner city of Los Angeles into a flaming inferno in April of 1992, there was an outbreak of ethnic and racial anger as well as an outcry against economic and legal perceptions of injustice. This was an outbreak of a "charismatic spirit" quite different than the Pentecost event, and a phenomena for which the churches, evangelical and Pentecostal alike, were largely unprepared to understand and with which they were certainly ill-equipped to deal.

For the Korean American, Asian American, Mexican American and African American, the connecting tissue is not "American" but human. When one's ethnic identity only serves as the adjective and not the noun, there is already a loss of personhood at the human level. When the noun defining our identity is the impersonal and imperious ideal of a state or nation, demagoguery fuels political rhetoric to the fever point. Such ideology is the disease, not the cure. In the parable of the good Samaritan the Samaritan remains a Samaritan in becoming good. His goodness was in his perception of the other and in being a neighbor to him (Lk 10).

The church's flight from the cities is a retreat from the struggle for the soul of a society. Not every church has abandoned the city, it is true. But by and large the church has failed when it has tried, and it has fled when it has found greener pastures. The disciples of Christ may have to give ground, wrote Dietrich Bonhoeffer, "provided they do so with the Word, provided their weakness is the weakness of the Word, and provided they do not leave the Word in the lurch in their flight."[1] In the abandonment of the city the church may well be leaving Jesus "in the lurch." Christians cannot turn away from any form of inhumanity without separating themselves from the humanity of God.

Most Christians would be scandalized to be told that abandoning the homeless, overlooking the deep injustice of poverty and systematically excluding the socially unacceptable is the moral and spiritual equivalent of apartheid. But it is so. In an attack on the practice of apartheid in South Africa, Johannes Verkuyl speaks to the various forms of separation of peoples practiced in our own society. His words are highly relevant for the church in every society:

> It is far easier to believe in a god who is less than love and who does not require a discipleship of love. But if God is love, separation is the ultimately opposite force to God. The will to be separate is the most complete refusal of the truth. Apartheid is a view of life and a view of man which insists that we find our identity in dissociation from each other. A policy of separate development which is based on this concept therefore involves a rejection of the central beliefs of the Christian Gospel. It reinforces divisions which the

---

[1]Dietrich Bonhoeffer, *The Cost of Discipleship*, trans. R. H. Fuller et al. (New York: Macmillan, 1963), p. 207.

Holy Spirit is calling the people of God to overcome. This policy is therefore a form of resistance to the Holy Spirit.[2]

The church finds its true humanity in the relation between Jesus Christ and all humanity. The church finds its true ministry in the upholding, healing and transformation of the humanity of others as already grasped and reconciled to God through the incarnation, atoning life, death and resurrection of Jesus Christ. This is the authentic praxis of Christ's ministry through his humanity—this is Christopraxis. The church cannot be truly human when it denies and dehumanizes the humanity of others.[3]

A Call to Repentance and Responsibility

I often tell my students, "Only the church that is willing to repent of being the church can truly be the church of Jesus Christ." They always want me to say more!

First of all I must explain that repentance is itself a positive and creative turning toward the source of life and renewal in God. As such, repentance is not a "once and for all" act of renouncing the world but a continuing act of transformation of a worldly mind. The transformed mind seeks to be conformed to the mind of Christ. One of the New Testament words used for this process is *metanoia*, which means having a new or different mind. John warns those who came out to be baptized by him, "Bear fruits worthy of repentance" (Lk 3:8). Jesus used the example of the people of Ninevah who repented at the preaching of Jonah as a witness against his own generation. In this case an entire city was spared destruction through corporate repentance and spiritual renewal (Lk 11:32).

"Do not to be conformed to this world," wrote Paul, "but be transformed by the renewing of your minds" (Rom 12:2). To the Philippian church, Paul wrote, "Let the same mind be in you that was in Christ Jesus, who, though he was in the form of God, did not regard equality with God as something to be exploited, but emptied himself, taking the form of a slave, being born in human likeness. . . . He humbled himself and became obedient to the point of death—even death on a cross" (Phil 2:5-8).

---

[2]Johannes Verkuyl, *Break Down the Walls: A Cry for Racial Justice,* ed. and trans. Lewis Smedes (Grand Rapids, Mich.: Eerdmans, 1973), p. 144.

[3]Adrio König, a member of the Dutch Reformed Church in South Africa and professor of systematic theology and ethics at the University of South Africa, writes, "What makes the separation of apartheid so bad is that it is enforced, and that it benefits one group and harms the other group. It is actually not separation, but a marginalization of the blacks away from the center of the country. Thus apartheid is essentially the exploitation, humiliation, and oppression of certain people over against the inclusion and advantage of the other group, who knowing or unknowingly plays the role of the oppressor" ("Covenant and Image: Theological Anthropology, Human Interrelatedness and Apartheid," in *Incarnational Ministry: The Presence of Christ in Church, Society and Family*, ed. Christian D. Kettler and Todd H. Speidell [Colorado Springs, Colo.: Helmers & Howard, 1990], p. 163).

Repentance is the spiritual gift of having the "mind of Christ." This mind runs contrary to the mind of the world, which is set on self-preservation and self-justification. Christ assumed the form of humanity in its rebellion against God and bent that mind back into conformity and obedience to God through the empowerment of the love of the Son for the Father and the Father for the Son. The mind of Christ is thus a mind that has already been "transformed" from death to life and from self-serving to self-giving through his own positive obedience.

"But why should the church need to repent of being the church?" my students persist. I explain further.

The church exists in the world and for the world, though it does not "belong to the world" (Jn 17:16). At the same time, Jesus prayed that the Father might send the church into the world "as you have sent me into the world" (Jn 17:18). The church, as the body of Christ, can only exist in the world by means of worldly forms, even as Jesus ate the same food, used the same boats and followed the same customs of his day. The church must be in the world, says Karl Barth, "on the same level and footing, in the same boat and with the same limits as any or all of them." This must be done, Barth added, "willingly and with a good conscience."[4]

But the church will also have the same temptation as other organizations and institutions in the world. The church will always have the temptation to make a name for itself and build its towers to reach up to the heavens. This is why the church must repent of being the church in order truly to be the church of Christ.

The sin of the people who built the tower at Babel was not their common life and language but their technological presumption to "make a name for" themselves and to reach up into the very heavens (Gen 11). The Holy Spirit, given at Pentecost, releases the Spirit of Christ into the world, reversing the confusion and division of humanity at Babel, enacting the ecclesial reality of liberation and reconciliation accomplished through the life, death and resurrection of Jesus.

The early church experienced a form of repentance in the breakdown of ethnic,

---

[4]"Solidarity with the world means full commitment to it, unreserved participation in its situation, in the promise given it by creation, in its responsibility for the arrogance, sloth and falsehood which reign within it, in its suffering under the resultant distress, but primarily and supremely in the free grace of God demonstrated and addressed to it in Jesus Christ, and therefore in its hope. . . . Solidarity with the world means that those who are genuinely pious approach the children of the world as such, that those who are genuinely righteous are not ashamed to sit down with the unrighteous as friends, that those who are genuinely wise do not hesitate to seem to be fools among fools, and that those who are genuinely holy are not too good or irreproachable to go down into 'hell' in a very secular fashion. . . . Since Jesus Christ is the Savior of the world, [the church] can exist in worldly fashion, not unwillingly nor with a bad conscience, but willingly and with a good conscience. It consists in the recognition that its members also bear in themselves and in some way actualise all human possibilities" (*CD* 4/3, pp. 773-74).

religious and language barriers. There were conflicts and struggle, to be sure, as evidenced in the controversy between the Greek-speaking and Jewish widows (Acts 6). But the apostles insisted on the full assimilation of each group into the life of the community. Where the Spirit of Christ prevails, there can no longer be discrimination based on race, gender or economic status (Gal 3:28). There can be no "acts of favoritism," writes James, where the "royal law of liberty" prevails through Christ. To show partiality is to commit sin. (Jas 2:1-9). The ministry of God as Redeemer in the particular work of the Holy Spirit commands and enables us to restore the true humanity of every person through the praxis of Pentecost.

Through the resurrection of Jesus Christ and the coming of the Holy Spirit at Pentecost, the very structures of human social and political existence are opened up for redemption. Where there is emphasis on individual repentance alone, there is a tendency to concentrate on the means by which persons enter the church through personal repentance and faith. This is important, to be sure, but such an individualistic understanding of repentance can fail to call the church and social structures into repentance for the sake of healing, liberation and hope. Both individual repentance and social repentance reveal a praxis of empowerment and the reality of the kingdom of God as the eschatological and transforming power of the Holy Spirit.

Christopraxis begins by calling the church itself into a radical conformity with the Spirit of Christ as the formative reality of new humanity. Christopraxis becomes the hermeneutical criterion and spiritual conscience of the life and mission of the church.

"But *how* does a church repent?" my students ask.

"Theologically, spiritually and socially," I respond.

Theological repentance is demanded of the church when it offers flavored water to those who come expecting the new wine and stale bread to those expecting a nourishing meal. The church repents through engaging in theological reflection on the work of God's Spirit under the mandate of God's Word. Theological repentance begins with the confession that the church has exchanged its theological birthright for the fast food of cultural relevance. When the church confesses with the church at Laodicea that its theology is "wretched, pitiable, poor, blind, and naked," the Christ who stands at the door knocking will find a welcome. "Who do you say that I am?" asks this Christ. When the church has answered that question fully and forthrightly, it will have rediscovered its theological heritage.

Spiritual repentance is demanded of the church when it is found opposing the mission of God for the sake of preserving its own institutional and traditional forms. The church repents when it brings out new wineskins of worship and weaves new patterns of communal life out of the "unshrunk" cloth of the next generation.

After several years of ministry as the pastor of a church, I stood before the congregation and announced, "It is my intention to take this church away from you and give it to your children!" When the members concluded that this was more than a state-ment intended to shock, it brought a mixture of reactions. Some were delighted, while others were offended and defensive. Spiritual repentance for the church involves the labor pains of giving birth and the joyful welcome of unexpected twins! The wind of the Spirit "blows where it chooses," said Jesus (Jn 3:8). When the church opens its windows to the world and feels the fresh breeze of the Holy Spirit blowing in its face from across the street, it has begun the process of repentance. "Do not quench the Spirit," urges Paul (1 Thess 5:19). But we have! And we repent of it.

Social repentance is demanded of the church when its institutional life demands a privileged space in the world for God's grace without expressed concern for those without benefit of food, shelter and justice. Christological repentance is demanded of the church when it binds Christ solely to its rituals at the altar, abandoning the naked and imprisoned Christ.

As the mediator who stands with humanity as advocate, healer and transformer, Jesus Christ is not primarily a principle by which ministry is defined but, as James Torrance has reminded us, is present with and among us as the ministering one:

> Christ does not heal us by standing over against us, diagnosing our sickness, prescribing medicine for us to take, and then going away, to leave us to get better by obeying his instructions—as an ordinary doctor might. No, He becomes the patient! He assumes that very humanity which is in need of redemption, and by being anointed by the Spirit in our humanity, by a life of perfect obedience, by dying and rising again, for us, our humanity is healed *in him*. We are not just healed "through Christ" because of the work of Christ but "in and through Christ."[5]

The authentic praxis of Christ's ministry through his humanity is objectively com-pleted through his own vicarious life in solidarity with all humanity, *eschatologically confirmed* through his resurrection to be a living and faithful paraclete ever-present alongside of and on behalf of all humanity, and *historically manifested* as a healing and transforming presence in the life and ministry of the church. If the church is found resisting to the praxis of Christ, it must search out a contemporary mission theology that renews the vision of Pentecost and traces out the contours of Christ's ministry in the midst of and on behalf of the peoples of the world.

A Call to Celebration and Renewal

From Pentecost the church views its origins in the crucified and risen Messiah of Israel and envisions its destiny as the "holy city, the new Jerusalem, coming down out

---

[5]James B. Torrance, "The Vicarious Humanity of Christ," in *The Incarnation: Ecumenical Studies in the Nicene-Constantinopolitan Creed, A.D. 381,* ed. Thomas F. Torrance (Edinburgh: Handsel, 1981), p. 141.

of heaven from God, prepared as a bride adorned for her husband" (Rev 21:2). The city over which Jesus stands weeping is a metaphor that gathers up the tragedy of human pain and suffering. The city John sees descending from heaven is one with foundations, whose architect and builder is God (Heb 11:10).

The one city will pass away, along with the heavens and the earth. "Death will be no more; mourning and crying and pain will be no more, for the first things have passed away" (Rev 21:4). The holy city, the new Jerusalem, is the dwelling place of God: "He will dwell with them as their God; they will be his peoples, and God himself will be with them; he will wipe every tear from their eyes" (Rev 21:3-4).

The church in the world not only stands with the weeping Jesus over the city, it celebrates the victorious and glorious Jesus as the coming one whose manifestation breaks through the broken clouds like the bright rays of the dawning sun. The church is not only called to repentance and responsibility, it is called to celebration and renewal of this vision of Christ.

The church not only points to the future, it is the advent of the glorious kingdom of God that is even now coming. These two concepts of the future are represented by the Latin words *futurum* and *adventus*. Our English word *future* is derived from the Latin *futurum,* which means what will be or what may be. The *futurum* arises out of the present and has its possibilities in what does not yet exist.

In contrast, the English word *advent,* derived from *adventus,* points to that which is coming into the present and that which already is manifest in the present. The New Testament concept of the future in terms of the advent of the day of the Lord at Christ's coming is quite different from that of the ancient Greeks. Hesiod described the eternal being of Zeus by saying, "Zeus was and Zeus is and Zeus will be." John, in the prologue to his vision of the new Jerusalem writes, "Peace from him who is and who was and who is to come" (Rev 1:4). Instead of using the future tense of the verb *einai,* "to be," for the third phrase, John uses the future tense of *erchesthai,* "to come." God's future is not in "what comes to be," but in him "who comes."[6]

When John baptized Jesus, he announced, "Here is the Lamb of God who takes away the sin of the world" (Jn 1:29). John did not point away from his own ministry toward an invisible personage. He pointed to the one already present and announced his mission. The baptism of John was a call to both repentance and celebration of the one who "baptizes with the Holy Spirit."

In the same way the church of Jesus Christ experienced the baptism of the Spirit at Pentecost and through repentance and renewal celebrates the advent of the risen and

---

[6]For this discussion of *adventus* and *futurum* I am indebted to Jürgen Moltmann, "Theological Perspectives on the Future" (a colloquium paper presented at a meeting of the Lutheran Brotherhood, Houston, Texas, January 29, 1979).

coming Christ. In becoming the church through repentance and renewal, the church makes visible its reality as the dwelling place of God's Spirit on earth. Where the Spirit of Christ is there will be celebration of life.

The vision of John was not that of an ideal church that will never be. Rather the vision is that of the real church that has its provisional and partial manifestation in its temporal and institutional form.

I meet far too many Christians who say that they are disillusioned by the institutional church and want no part of it. Jesus, yes; the church, no! is their credo. I understand their frustration and even cynicism concerning the church. At the same time, I question their alternative. One does not baptize oneself into Christ.

The reality of Christ in the world is his body, the community of believers indwelt by the Holy Spirit. Christ seeks to gather Christians into fellowship and communion. It is the world that isolates persons and then gathers them into anonymous crowds, only to exploit them for its own gain. It is Christ who personalizes and humanizes persons, creating new families of fellowship where each one is a brother and sister to the other.

The praxis of Pentecost does not seek to replace the church with private and individual experiences of Christ. The Christ of Pentecost is not a lone ranger, riding into town with silver bullets and leaving without a forwarding address. The Christ of Pentecost is not a rancher, branding his sheep and then turning them loose without a name. He is the great shepherd; he knows his sheep by name, and, while he has other sheep, "they will listen to my voice. So there will be one flock, one shepherd" (Jn 10:16).

Pentecost occurs wherever and whenever the kingdom of God appears with the power of the Spirit manifesting the eschatological signs of healing, forgiveness of sins, and restoration to emotional and spiritual wholeness in community. Pentecost promises a paraclete to everyone who stumbles and falls, to everyone who is weak and powerless, to everyone who is tormented and torn by the demons of doubt, discouragement and despair. Jesus is the Christ of the wounded city.

Pentecost occurs wherever and whenever the church as the body of Christ celebrates the presence of the glory of Christ in its worship and life in community. Pentecost delivers the promise of the resurrected Christ to return and light up the lives of those who dwell in darkness. He is the bright and morning star already appearing in the new heavens and earth. Jesus is the Christ of the heavenly city descending to earth.

The presence and reality of Christ in the world must take place through our own presence and in our relationships with others. We have no alternative. If the church is to be the redemptive presence and power in the world that God intends, it will be where the Spirit of Christ crosses the boundary and breaks through the wall that sep-

arates us from each other, and where the world and the church live separate lives.
Even so, come Lord Jesus!

> It must be that Christ is involved if there is reality of change into the good. If, instead of
> the righteousness of Christ as a mental substitute for my own reality as a person, I
> acknowledge the existence of God in the inner movements of my own awareness, and
> this I claim with assurance in that Christ did send the Holy Spirit, his own Spirit into my
> life, so that the estrangement of myself from myself and from God could be bridged; if
> then I acknowledge the presence of God in my movements, those who become part of
> me through that perilous exchange of selves involved with genuine relationship, cannot
> escape being involved in the reality of God in a redemptive way.[7]

[7]Ray S. Anderson, "Soul Prints," unpublished journal notes, December 1, 1964.

Part 3

PRACTICAL PASTORAL THEOLOGY

12

PRACTICAL THEOLOGY AS PARACLESIS

Pastoral Implications

The relation between the risen Christ and the historical Jesus is established by promise and fulfillment and is a relation of election and grace. That is to say, the connection between the old covenant and the new covenant is a real one but also one that is eschatological in nature. The relation is not predicated on historical necessity but on covenant faithfulness on the part of God. The giving of the Holy Spirit through Pentecost is a testimony to God's faithfulness and the creation of continuity between the messianic community and the Messiah.

Following the reading of the messianic promise of the anointing of the Spirit from Isaiah (Is 61:1, 2; 58:6), Luke records Jesus as saying, "Today this scripture has been fulfilled in your hearing" (Lk 4:18-21). Mission theology operates in the eternal present so that with the coming of the Spirit to each contemporary day, the "today this is fulfilled" comes to pass. Because the Spirit is the Spirit of the resurrected Christ and also the Spirit that forms the life and ministry of the church, there is continuity with both past and future.

This is the breakthrough that Jürgen Moltmann has contributed with his book *The Church in the Power of the Spirit* when he suggests that the messianic mission of Jesus is not entirely completed in his death and resurrection. Through the coming of the Spirit, his history becomes the church's gospel for the world. The church participates in his mission, becoming the messianic church of the coming kingdom. There is, says Moltmann, a "conversion to the future" through which the church enters into the messianic proclamation of the coming of the kingdom.[1]

The mission and nature of the church have their common source in the mission of God through the incarnate Messiah continuing in the world through Pentecost. This thesis requires that nature and mission be considered as a unity of thought and experience. This Paul was careful to do in his formulation "one body . . . one Spirit . . . one Lord . . . one baptism" (Eph 4:4-5). Hence Paul made it clear that the ministry of the Holy Spirit is essential to a knowledge of Jesus as the incarnate Lord. "No one speaking by the Spirit of God ever says 'Let Jesus be cursed!' and no one can say 'Jesus is Lord' except by the Holy Spirit" (1 Cor 12:3). He also warns, "Anyone who does not have the Spirit of Christ does not belong to him" (Rom 8:9).

The Eschatological Nature of Apostolic Ministry

The nature of the early church as the "dwelling place of the Spirit" had already been established in the Pentecost experience and the subsequent manifestations of the Spirit through the early missionary work of Paul and others. Some within the New Testament church apparently attempted to take Paul's concept of the church as the "body of Christ" and ground its nature in some kind of historical or institutional continuity with the incarnation. The church at Jerusalem had strong tendencies toward this kind of historical, apostolic and institutional continuity.[2]

---

[1]Jürgen Moltmann, *The Church in the Power of the Spirit* (New York: Harper & Row, 1977), pp. 83, 80. Moltmann suggests that "the sending of the Spirit" can be viewed as "a sacrament of the Kingdom" (p. 199). "In so far as Jesus as the Messiah is the mystery of the rule of God, the signs of the messianic era are also part of his mystery. In so far as the crucified and risen Jesus manifests the salvation of the world determined on by God, proclamation and faith and the outpouring of the Holy Spirit on the Gentiles are also part of this salvation. . . . It also follows that a christological-ecclesiological rendering of the term—Christ and the church as the primal and fundamental sacrament of salvation—certainly touches on a further sphere covered by the New Testament but does not go far enough, especially if the church of Christ is only understood in its sacraments and not at the same time in the context of the eschatology of world history" (pp. 204-5).

[2]Emil Brunner has argued the thesis that the earlier Pauline ecclesiology, based on the ecclesial community under the direction of the Spirit, stands opposed in the New Testament to the Jerusalem form of "the church." He also argues that by the end of the New Testament period, the Pauline community had given way to the hierarchical and institutional form of the church: see his *The Christian Doctrine of the Church, Faith and the Consummation,* vol. 3 of *Dogmatics* (London: Lutterworth, 1962). This thesis was presented earlier in *The Misunderstanding of the Church* (London: Lutterworth, 1952). Karl Barth's response and criticism of Brunner's thesis is found in *CD* 4/2, pp. 683-87. Otto Weber, while not following Brunner's argument to its conclusion, also suggests that the New Testament "always conceives of the *Ekklesia* as the 'eschatological community of salvation,' " based on the fact that the coming Christ is the present Christ in the community (*Foundation of Dogmatics* [Grand Rapids, Mich.: Eerdmans, 1983], 2:514-15).

Paul argued vehemently against this position on the ground that his own apostolic commission had come from the risen Christ, though he had never belonged to the community of the historical Jesus. Paul first experienced Jesus Christ as the resurrected Lord who ministered to him and who called him to become a minister of the gospel. The nature of the church, argued Paul, could not rest only on a historical link with Jesus and the twelve disciples but on the Spirit of the resurrected Christ who has "broken down the dividing wall . . . the hostility" and created in himself "one new humanity in place of the two" (Eph 2:14-15). The critical phrase for Paul with regard to the nature of the church is "new creation." This is "from God, who reconciled us to himself through Christ, and has given us the ministry of reconciliation" (2 Cor 5:17-18).

When Paul was challenged as to the authority by which the Gentile churches were operating, he argued that with the death and resurrection of Jesus Christ a new age had broken into the old, so that these eras now overlapped. As David Ford puts it:

> The new is being realised now through the Holy Spirit, so the most urgent thing is to live according to the Spirit. It certainly involves present eschatological freedom, hope beyond death and the significance of the Church in history. . . . But as regards contemporary ecclesiology there are two implications that seem most important. The first is that the determinisms of history are broken by the gift of the Spirit as the downpayment of what is to come. If God is free to open history from the future then the future need not mirror the past. In the Church this combines with the message of the cross to allow for discontinuities and innovations. The criterion for something is no longer whether that is how the Church has done it in the past or even whether Jesus said it (cf. Paul on his means of subsistence) but whether it embodies the new creation and its vision of love. . . . For Paul the content of eschatology is christological and the final reality is face to face.[3]

While there was historical discontinuity between the community of Jesus Christ prior to his death and resurrection and the community of believers empowered at Pentecost, there was also a direct continuity through the identity of the Spirit given at Pentecost and the person of Jesus Christ. This was the distinctive reality of the early church and its source of empowerment. The continuity was one of the Spirit rather

---

[3]David F. Ford, "Faith in the Cities: Corinth and the Modern City," in *On Being the Church: Essays on the Christian Community*, ed. Colin E. Gunton and Daniel W. Hardy (Edinburgh: T & T Clark, 1989), p. 248. Because Paul's concept of authority was grounded in the eschatological as well as the historical Christ, Ford says, "Perhaps on no other area are Churches so subject to legalisms, bondage to the past, entanglement with distorting interests and idolatries than in that of authority. Paul's clarity about his ministry as helping to realise God's future and his refusal to absolutise past or present is a principle of liberation with wide relevance. At its heart is the great symbol of authority, the glory of God, enabling freedom and confidence, inspiring a whole community in energetic mutuality and glorifying of God, while recognising that the full transformation into the glory is to come (2 Cor 3). And incarnating the glory of God is the fact of Christ, the ultimate embodiment of a persuasive, vulnerable authority, freely distributed through his Spirit" (p. 253).

than the institutionalizing of historical precedence. The fact that this "pneumatologi-cal" constitution of the church's life and mission did not last, has been noted by Edward Schillebeeckx.

> The continuity between Jesus Christ and the church is fundamentally based on the Spirit. The ministry is a specific sign of this, and not the substance itself. Whereas in the early church ministry was seen rather in the sign of the Spirit that fills the church, later, people began to see the ministry in terms of the ecclesiology, which regards the church as the extension of the incarnation. People moved from a pneuma-christological view of ministry to a theology of ministry based directly on Christology.[4]

Colin Gunton makes the same point when he calls for a renewed consideration and emphasis on the constitution of the church by the Spirit rather than an overstress on its institution by direct continuity with the past.

> What is required, therefore, is a reconsideration of the relation of pneumatology and christology, with a consequent reduction of stress on the Church's institution by Christ and a greater emphasis on its constitution by the Spirit. In such a way we may create fewer self-justifying and historicising links with the past and give more stress to the necessity for the present particularities of our churchly arrangements to be constituted by the Spirit. . . . What is needed is, rather, a greater emphasis on the action of the Holy Spirit towards Jesus as the source of the *particularity* and so historicity of his humanity.[5]

The concept of apostolic authority as rooted in historical continuity with the twelve disciples and the first-century apostles, has tended to institutionalize and to paralyze the church's order of ministry. The church, as Paul was to declare, is "built upon the foundation of the apostles and prophets." But what he also saw clearly was that it is a foundation with "Christ Jesus himself as the cornerstone" (Eph 2:20). There is a strong tendency in the theology of the church to ground the nature and ministry of the church in historical continuity with the foundation, with the incarna-tion as the "cornerstone." Because the first-century apostles are no longer "living apostles," apostolic succession was instituted as the only link between the ruling bishop and the original apostles. While the Reformers rejected this "mechanical" suc-cession of apostolic authority through the office, they tended to substitute in place of the concept of apostolic succession, apostolic teaching, that is, the content of the gos-pel of Christ bound with the canon of holy Scripture.

---

[4]Edward Schillebeeckx, *The Church with a Human Face: A New and Expanded Theology of Ministry* (New York: Crossroad, 1985), p. 206.
[5]Colin Gunton, "The Church on Earth: The Roots of Community," in *On Being the Church: Essays on the Christian Community,* ed. Colin E. Gunton and Daniel W. Hardy (Edinburgh: T & T Clark, 1989), pp. 62-63.

In that Christ was the "cornerstone," as Paul suggested, and given the fact that this cornerstone is a "living stone," as Peter reminds us (1 Pet 2:4-5), the apostolic nature of the church is grounded in a "living apostle," who is Jesus Christ. The book of Hebrews identifies Jesus as the "apostle of our confession" (Heb 3:1). The chief apostle of the church is Jesus Christ, and his apostleship continues through the age of the church until the end of the age.

In describing the sequence of events that will occur in connection with the day of resurrection, Paul argues that Christ, having been raised from the dead, constitutes the "first fruits" of all who have died and who will be raised at his coming:

> But each in his own order: Christ the first fruits, then at his coming those who belong to Christ. Then comes the end, when he hands over the kingdom to God the Father, after he has destroyed every ruler and every authority and power. . . . When all things are subjected to him, then the Son himself will also be subjected to the one who put all things in subjection under him, so that God may be all in all (1 Cor 15:23-24, 28).

This describes clearly the apostolic nature of Jesus' own ministry. As the Son of God he was given the messianic task of inaugurating the kingdom of God to rule over all things. When this is completed, he will then be relieved of his apostolic mission and continue in the eternal relation he has with the Father as the Son. Until then Jesus continues to be the apostolic source of the church's life and mission in the world through his power and presence as Holy Spirit. Pentecost, therefore, is the eschatological manifestation of the apostolic nature of the church as the continuing praxis of Jesus' apostolic authority to the end of the age.

Wolfhart Pannenberg makes a significant contribution to this discussion when he suggests that the eschatological motif in the early church provides the criterion for an empowering concept of apostolicity that is centered on the resurrection of Christ and his coming to the world by the Holy Spirit. While continuing to hold to the apostolic foundation in the first century, Pannenberg suggests that an eschatological motif among these apostles lighted the way forward to the transforming power of the resurrection.

This is what I see: the apostolic nature of Christ's continuing ministry through the Spirit as a power that will increasingly transform the church itself into what it should be at the end. Pannenberg describes what this means in terms of the apostolic life of the church in this present age:

> Even as there was a "first century church," there will be a "last century church." It follows that the true *vita apostolica* is to be sought in the life of the church's leaders and in the life of individual Christians who let themselves be permeated by the final, all-encompassing, liberating, and transforming truth of Jesus. The *vita apostolica* does not mean copying the way of life of the apostolic age or what we think that way of life was, and it certainly can-

not be lived by borrowing this or that form of life from the regulations of the apostles. That which was apostolic then may be irrelevant today or may even be a hindrance to our apostolic tasks. This insight enables the church to be free to live in its own historicity as opposed to that of the apostolic age and still remain in continuity with the mission of the apostles.[6]

The church itself should seek to become the church that Christ desires to find when he comes, where distinctions of race, religion, ethnicity, economic and political status, and gender identity will no longer be found in the church and its apostolic life. This is what Paul clearly had in mind in writing to the Galatians, "There is no longer Jew or Greek, there is no longer slave or free, there is no longer male and female; for all of you are one in Christ Jesus" (Gal 3:28). This surely was not a description of the first-century church, but Paul believed that it should be a description of the "last-century" church if it continued to grow into its own true nature under the apostolic ministry of Christ through the Spirit.

Some in the church today may feel compelled to deny the office of pastoral ministry to women either on traditional grounds or scriptural grounds in order to be apostolic. In fact, they may be placing a hindrance on the apostolic ministry of Christ in the church today. If the Spirit of the resurrected Jesus is present in the contemporary church, anointing and calling women as well as men to the office of pastoral ministry, then this is surely an apostolic ministry as commissioned by Jesus as the living apostle.[7]

According to Paul the baptism of the Spirit by which persons become part of the body of Christ removes historical discrimination between Jew and Gentile, male and female (1 Cor 12:13; Gal 3:27-28). Through baptism into Christ both men and women share in Christ's praxis of ministry through the Spirit. Edward Schillebeeckx makes this point emphatic when he says,

> The baptism of the Spirit removes historical discriminations. In principle, Christian baptism completely removes all these social and historical oppositions within the community of believers. Of course this is a performative and not a descriptive statement;

---

[6]Wolfhart Pannenberg, *The Church* (Philadelphia: Westminster Press, 1983), p. 57. "In this age of historical consciousness, therefore, the church needs a new concept of apostolicity that will allow it to recognize without reservation the difference between the age of the apostles and its own day, without thereby losing its connection with the mission of the apostles. Attention to the eschatological motif in the early Christian apostolate can help us do this. The only criterion of apostolic teaching in this sense is whether and to what degree it is able to set forth the final truth and comprehensive universality of the person and work of Christ in the transforming and saving significance of his resurrection and the power that gives light to the world" (pp. 56-57).
[7]See Ray S. Anderson, "The Resurrection of Jesus as Hermeneutical Criterion: A Case for Sexual Parity in Pastoral Ministry," *TSF Bulletin,* March-April 1986; and Ray S. Anderson, *Ministry on the Fireline: A Practical Theology for an Empowered Church* (Downers Grove, Ill.: InterVarsity Press, 1993), pp. 92-98.

however, it is a statement which expresses the hope which needs to be realized now, already, as a model in the community. . . . According to Paul and the whole of the New Testament, at least within Christian communities of believers, relationship involving subjection are no longer to prevail. We find this principle throughout the New Testament, and it was also to determine strongly the new Testament view of ministry. This early-Christian egalitarian ecclesiology in no way excludes leadership and authority; but in that case authority must be one filled with the Spirit, from which no Christian, man or woman, is excluded in principle on the basis of the baptism of the Spirit.[8]

The church does not "push" the kingdom into the world through its own institutional and pragmatic strategies. Rather it is "pulled" into the world as it follows the praxis of the Spirit. The church is thus constantly being "re-created" through the mission of the Spirit. At the same time, it has historical and ecclesial continuity and universality through its participation in the person and mission of Christ Jesus through the Spirit.

All apostolic authority and witness is grounded in the living and coming Christ, not only in the first-century Christ. The ministry of the church is apostolic when it recognizes the eschatological praxis of the Spirit in the present age and interprets this in accordance with the Jesus Christ who is the same yesterday, today and forever (Heb 13:8). The author of Hebrews reveals the priestly nature of Jesus when he argues that Jesus is a priest after the order of Melchizedek and not Aaron (Heb 6—7). Melchizedek was "without genealogy, having neither beginning of days nor end of life" (Heb 7:3). Apostolic authority is eschatological, not merely genealogical.

The Empowering Ministry of Paraclesis

The Greek word translated as "advocate" is *paraclete*. It literally means "called to the side" and denotes a role of comforting, exhorting and encouraging. The ministry of serving as a paraclete is one that continues the ministry of Christ through the presence and power of the Holy Spirit. What is distinctive about the role of the paraclete is that it took place first of all through the "Word [that] became flesh" (Jn 1:14), the humanity of God in the form of Jesus Christ. The continuing paracletic ministry of the Spirit takes place through a human encounter by which the Word produces change and growth through the motive power of the Spirit. It is important to note that the motive power is not located in who performs the paracletic ministry nor in the one who receives it, but the new motive power for growth and change is actually mediated into the relation through the Spirit by the human person.

The church has tended to stress two forms of the ministry of the Word of God: kerygma, the Word proclaimed; and didache, the Word taught. This leaves paraclesis,

---

[8]Schillebeeckx, *Church with a Human Face,* pp. 38-39.

the ministry of encouragement or exhortation, to the Holy Spirit. This way of thinking separates the rational form of the Word from the relational. It tends toward a presentation of the gospel through preaching and teaching, as though the task is fully completed if one is faithful to the *content* of the Word. The human response to the Word of God is thus primarily a rational one, so that the emphasis is on what one understands as true and not how one lives truthfully and authentically. If the Holy Spirit is considered at all as part of the gospel, it is to enlighten the mind or bend the will rather than to complete the gospel of forgiveness through producing health and wholeness at the level of the emotional and relational self.

We can see the problem with this dichotomy between Word and Spirit in the pronouncement of absolution from sin, where the truth of forgiveness is upheld without regard for truthful forgiveness as measured in spiritual and psychological health and wholeness. Under this form of teaching and practice, Christians tend to have all sorts of emotional problems that are not dealt with as part of the praxis of the gospel of Christ. One can even go so far as to suggest that the proclamation of the gospel of Christ without regard to the affective, or feeling, level of those who hear and respond contributes to emotional disorder and dysfunction.

The priestly nature of Christ's ministry through the power of the Spirit means that he comes alongside the church as the missionary people of God to be the advocate, or paraclete, by which those called to give leadership are empowered to empower the people for ministry. The church of Jesus Christ called forth by the Holy Spirit is an "ordained" community, baptized into the ministry of Christ. The leadership of this community is a function of the community and is empowered by the community; it is not a status over and against it.[9]

Baptism into Jesus Christ can be considered to be an "ordination" into the ministry of Christ.[10] Thus all those baptized into Christ by the one baptism and the one Spirit (1 Cor 12:13) are summoned into the praxis of Christ's continuing ministry and are empowered for this ministry by the *paraclesis* of the Holy Spirit. This "bap-

[9]"Leadership is a function of the Christian community," says Werner Jeanrond, "and not a status over against it" ("Community and Authority," in *On Being the Church: Essays on the Christian Community*, ed. Colin E. Gunton and Daniel W. Hardy [Edinburgh: T & T Clark, 1989], p. 96). "That the Christian community needs some form of leadership nobody doubts. That the Christian community needs an ordained ministry, however, cannot be taken for granted, but needs to be discussed with reference to both the theological demands of the Christian faith and the organisational demands of a contemporary human association. Given these requirements it seems rather odd that in some Churches the particular understanding of the ordained ministry is still focused on the now obsolete metaphysical understanding of past times and on the organisational needs of medieval congregations. Most urgently needed is a reassessment of the relationship between the ordained minister and the ordained community" (p. 98).

[10]See Ray S. Anderson, "Christ's Ministry Through His Whole Church," in *Theological Foundations for Ministry*, ed. Ray S. Anderson (Grand Rapids, Mich.: Eerdmans, 1979).

tism into ministry" by the Spirit breaks the historical determinism of an order of ministry with its precedents of race, gender and status.[11]

"Paraclesis," says Jacob Firet, "is the consolation and admonition of God which reorient people toward salvation in the concreteness of their situation; for the [caregiver] this means that he knows the concreteness of the situation of those people by participation in it."[12]

We need to see paraclesis as critical to the praxis of the word of Christ as proclaimed, taught and experienced. Word and Spirit must not be separated as though the Word was primarily mental and objective while the Spirit is primarily existential and subjective. A better way of looking at the praxis of kerygma, didache and paraclesis would be as follows: were God to come to me only in the mode of kerygma, that could mean "God has come; be silent before him"—hence my realities and interests do not really matter. The reality of the kingdom takes precedence. Were God to come only in the mode of didache, that could mean "God has come: the road on which life has brought me no longer is important; he has another way for me." When God comes to me in the mode of paraclesis, it dawns on me: "God has come and he wants to live in my place and my situation." Thus God enters my situation in its concrete historical reality and appears in it for that very purpose. Through the paracletic presence of the Holy Spirit, Jesus himself takes up my cause as his own.[13]

Firet made a distinction between the "hermeneutic moment" as a moment of understanding and the "agogic moment" as the moment of change and growth. The hermeneutical moment occurs when the Word of God is proclaimed and taught in such a way that a new insight or new understanding comes into the mind. This is when we have the "aha" experience. "Now I see what you are getting at" is the

---

[11]"The baptism of the Spirit removes historical discriminations," says Edward Schillebeeckx. "In principle, Christian baptism completely removes all these social and historical oppositions within the community of believers. Of course this is a performative and not a descriptive statement; however, it is a statement which expresses the hope which needs to be realized now, already, as a model in the community. . . . According to Paul and the whole of the New Testament, at least within Christian communities of believers, relationships involving subjection are no longer to prevail. We find this principle throughout the New Testament, and it was also to determine strongly the new Testament view of ministry. This early-Christian egalitarian ecclesiology in no way excludes leadership and authority; but in that case authority must be one filled with the Spirit, from which no Christian, man or woman, is excluded in principle on the basis of the baptism of the Spirit" (*Church with a Human Face,* pp. 38-39).

[12]Jacob Firet, *Dynamics in Pastoring,* trans. John Vriend (Grand Rapids, Mich.: Eerdmans, 1986), pp. 99, 133. For a discussion of Firet's material see Ray S. Anderson, *Christians Who Counsel: The Vocation of Wholistic Therapy* (Grand Rapids, Mich.: Zondervan, 1990), p. 66-67. See also Ray S. Anderson, *Self Care: A Theology of Personal Empowerment and Spiritual Healing* (Grand Rapids, Mich.: Baker, 1995).

[13]I am indebted to Jacob Firet for the substance of this paragraph (see his *Dynamics in Pastoring,* p. 70).

response when this moment occurs.

Many times one can listen to the Word of God preached and taught and have the feeling "I understand that. It makes sense to me. I see what you mean and agree." Yet one can go away without changing a pattern of behavior that contradicts the wisdom and truth of what has been understood. Firet makes the important point that God's Word intends to effect change and growth, not merely to produce new information or new concepts in the mind. This is why the pastoral counselor must go beyond the hermeneutic moment and create the conditions for the agogic moment to occur.

While the word *pedagogy* is familiar to us, the word *agogy* is less familiar. Agogy, which basically means "guidance," describes a situation in which a person is not merely addressed or talked at but is actually encountered by the Word in such a way that there is guidance from one kind of action to another. Through the intermediary role of a counselor (paraclete), the "agogic moment" can occur, which results in transformation, growth and change. Firet says that it is a "motive force which activates the person on which it is focused, so that the person begins to change."[14]

This "agogic moment," or what I prefer to call a "growth process" is a human and personal encounter, whether ordinary or extraordinary, that releases a motive power that generates change. Firet describes three aspects of the agogic moment: (1) a motive power enters the situation in the form of a word or symbolic action—this is understood theologically as the Word and Spirit of God; (2) another person acts an intermediary for the release of this motive power; (3) an effect is produced resulting in change and growth.

A biblical example of this agogic moment can be found in Nathan's confrontation with David following his adultery with Bathsheba and the murder of her husband (2 Sam 12). Nathan acts as an intermediary, a motive power is release in David's heart resulting in change, and the effect is produced as indicated in Psalm 51.

The key element in the agogic situation is the humanity of the intermediary, encountering the other person with what Firet calls, "equi-human address":

> All action toward a human being with a view to his or her humanization has its starting point in dealing with a particular person as a human being. . . . The growth promoter who does not enter the relationship as equal, does not enter the relationship: he not only does not come close to the other; he cannot even maintain distance; he is simply not there.[15]

With the kerygmatic and didactic ministry of the Word of God, the preacher or teacher may assume a role that conceals his or her humanity for the most part. With

---

[14]Ibid., p. 101.
[15]Ibid., pp. 161, 165.

the paracletic form of ministry, however, there must be a perceived *parity* at the human level between the one ministering the Word of grace and the one receiving it. What Firet calls "being there" suggests a therapeutic relation in which both the speaker and hearer, both the counselor and the counselee, are mutually defined through the encounter at the core level of human selfhood. This is more than a therapeutic strategy to gain confidence. It is an essential component of the process that produces growth and change as a therapeutic outcome.

We are reminded here of the role of Jesus as advocate for those who were victims of social stigma, devastating disease, humiliating moral failure, and oppression, both demonic and economic. He accepted the hospitality of Zacchaeus, a despised collaborator with Rome (Lk 19). He affirmed the value of both the woman and her ministry to him when others complained that she was unworthy to touch his feet (Lk 7:37-50). He placed himself on the side of the woman caught in adultery when the law called for her execution (Jn 8). On the cross Jesus assured the criminal who confessed his guilt and asked to be remembered that the man would be with him in paradise (Lk 23:42-43).

It is this Jesus of whom the apostle John wrote when he remembered his words concerning the sending of the Holy Spirit. Jesus was the first advocate, and the Spirit will come to be another advocate. "And I will ask the Father, and he will give you another Advocate, to be with you forever" (Jn 14:16). The Holy Spirit will continue the role of advocate that Jesus began, and those who receive the Spirit as their advocate then become advocates for others (Jn 14:26; 15:26; 16:7).

Through this ministry of Christ in the power of the Holy Spirit, I am not simply addressed with the demands of the kingdom of God; I am grasped by the love of God as Father, upheld by the intercession of God as Son, and made to share in the inner life of Godself through the indwelling Holy Spirit. This paracletic ministry of Christ through the Spirit does not leave me as an individual but incorporates me into the fellowship of the body of Christ, the missionary people of God. As part of this body and mission, I too share in the apostolic life of Christ in being sent into the world.

From this we can see that the paracletic ministry of Jesus is grounded in the incarnation. Becoming truly human he became and is the advocate for all that is human, pledging his humanity on behalf of all others. This advocacy is more than an instrumental one, performed for the purpose of affecting legal atonement. Yes, he did die on the cross in full payment of the penalty of sin and so made atonement. But atonement without advocacy does not empower those for whom Christ died so as to recover their own humanity in full fellowship with God and each other. James Torrance put this point well when he wrote,

> Christ does not heal us by standing over against us, diagnosing our sickness, prescribing medicine for us to take, and then going away, to leave us to get better by obeying his

instructions—as an ordinary doctor might. No, He becomes the patient! He assumes that very humanity which is in need of redemption, and by being anointed by the Spirit in our humanity, by a life of perfect obedience, by dying and rising again, for us, our humanity is healed *in him*. We are not just healed "through Christ" because of the work of Christ but "in and through Christ."[16]

Todd Speidell reinforces this when he adds:

> Christ presents himself in the depths of human need—the hungry, the thirsty, the naked, the sick, the imprisoned (Mt. 25:31ff). The stranger among us, the homeless and psychologically debilitated, may be the place of Christ's presence among us. The Gospel of Matthew does not exhort us simply to be like Christ—ministering to the needy "as Jesus would" (which implies that he is not actively present but merely serves as a model for our social action)—but attests that Christ discloses himself through the stranger. We must be where Christ is, and act where he acts.[17]

The advocacy of Christ for humans is the pledge of his humanity as the continuing representation of human persons to God, and the basis for the mode of paraclesis carried out by the Holy Spirit. The resurrection of Christ affirms his humanity and also ours as having an objective possibility of reconciliation to God. Thus the Spirit has no incarnation of its own, nor does the Spirit become incarnate in the humanity of the church as the body of Christ. The church participates in the humanity of the risen Christ as the objective basis for its own fellowship with God. So also the continuing humanity of Christ as the paraclete takes place through the life and humanity of the church in its apostolic mission.

Thomas Smail reminds us that Christians who are inspired and empowered by the Holy Spirit not only have their roots in relationship to God but "express themselves horizontally and practically in such a way as to challenge the oppressive structures of society in which the church lives." Our concern, Smail continues, should be as much for the socially demonic in the form of oppressive structures as for the personally demonic.[18]

The incarnation of God in Jesus is the pledge of the humanity of Jesus Christ on behalf of all human persons. Thus Christ is the advocate of all persons, not only those who are "in Christ." "Through Christ" all persons have an advocate with the Father. This enables Paul to say, "All this is from God, who reconciled us to himself through

---

[16]James B. Torrance, "The Vicarious Humanity of Christ," in *The Incarnation: Ecumenical Studies in the Nicene-Constantinopolitan Creed, A.D. 381*, ed. Thomas F. Torrance (Edinburgh: Handsel, 1981), p. 141.

[17]Todd Speidell, "Incarnational Social Ethics," in *Incarnational Ministry: The Presence of Christ in Church, Society and Family* (Colorado Springs, Colo.: Helmers & Howard, 1990), p. 146.

[18]Thomas Smail, *The Forgotten Father* (Grand Rapids, Mich.: Eerdmans, 1980), p. 179.

Christ and has given us the ministry of reconciliation; that is, in Christ God was reconciling the world to himself, not counting their trespasses against them, and entrusting the message of reconciliation to us" (2 Cor 5:18-19). The apostle John holds the same view. Immediately after writing that "we have an advocate with the Father, Jesus Christ the righteous," he adds, "and he is the atoning sacrifice for our sins, and not for ours only but also for the sins of the whole world" (1 Jn 2:1-2).

Practical theology issues from the perspective of this paracletic ministry of the Spirit of Christ taking place in the world before it takes place in the church. That is to say, Christ is not first of all contained by the nature of the church, so that only when Christ is shared by the church does the world encounter him. Rather, as Thomas Torrance has put it, "Christ clothed with His gospel meets with Christ clothed with the desperate needs of men."[19]

This paracletic ministry of Jesus, of course, presupposes the *kerygma* as the announcement of this act of reconciliation. But even as the incarnation provides the basis for the *kerygma* in the humanity of Jesus Christ as the ground of reconciliation, so the continued humanity of Christ provides the ground for the paracletic ministry of the Holy Spirit and the kerygmatic message. Christ is present as the advocate of the people who have not yet heard the good news. The praxis of Christ is that of encouragement and support for those who need help and support in hearing and believing the gospel of forgiveness. The gospel of encouragement is the work of Christ through the power of the Holy Spirit, enabling and empowering persons to receive the gospel of forgiveness. Through the empowering of the Holy Spirit, released through Pentecost, the Spirit's ministry becomes "Christopraxis," the continued ministry of Christ for the reconciliation of the world to God.

The Gospel of Forgiveness—Empowering Reconciliation

The kerygmatic form of the gospel of forgiveness is that "all this is from God, who reconciled us to himself through Christ, and has given us the ministry of reconciliation; that is, in Christ God was reconciling the world to himself, not counting their trespasses against them, and entrusting the message of reconciliation to us" (2 Cor 5:18-19). This is the gospel of Christ's reconciliation accomplished through death and resurrection. This is the gospel that is proclaimed as completed and sealed as God's work of grace, to be received unconditionally and freely.

The paracletic form of this gospel of forgiveness is also described by Paul when he wrote to the Thessalonians, "Our message of the gospel came to you not in word only, but also in power and in the Holy Spirit and with full conviction. . . . We were gentle

---

[19]Thomas F. Torrance, "Service in Jesus Christ," in *Theological Foundations for Ministry*, ed. Ray S. Anderson (Grand Rapids, Mich.: Eerdmans, 1979), p. 724.

among you, like a nurse tenderly caring for her own children. . . . As you know, we dealt with each one of you like a father with his children, urging and encouraging you and pleading that you lead a life worthy of God, who calls you into his own kingdom and glory" (1 Thess 1:5; 2:7, 11).

Paul is not satisfied with proclamation of the gospel of forgiveness alone. He knows that forgiveness has already been accomplished from God's side and that God "does not count trespasses" against persons who are sinners. But forgiveness has not yet been accomplished until there is reconciliation from the human side toward God and toward one another. This is why Paul found such encouragement in remembering the transformation of the lives of those in Thessalonica who had received the gospel of Christ. "Our coming to you was not in vain," Paul writes to them, because "when you received the word of God that you heard from us, you accepted it not as a human word but as what it really is, God's word, *which is also at work in you believers*" (1 Thess 2:1, 13, emphasis added). This is a gospel of forgiveness that empowers ministry to those crushed, broken and burdened, and empowers persons to move toward wholeness.

The pronouncement of absolution from sin is not only a kerygmatic pronouncement; it is a paracletic process. To give assurance of pardon and forgiveness to persons based on God's reconciliation to the world through Christ is not wrong. But it is incomplete without the assurance that arises from within the lives of those who hear this word. The word of absolution from sin based on the work of Christ in salvation history is premature apart from the praxis of forgiveness as the work of Christ in the hearts and lives of people through the presence and power of the Holy Spirit.

Let me say it as clearly as I can: a vision of forgiveness and freedom comes from the burning light of Pentecost before it can be seen in the sunless shadows of the cross. This has enormous theological significance both for the proclamation of the gospel of Christ as well as for the spiritual formation of Christ in the lives of people. A theology that is not continually enlightened by the praxis of Christ at work in the transformation of human lives can become a toxic theology. A theology that does not begin and end with grace both from God's side as well as from the human side is a theology that binds "heavy burdens" (Mt 23:4) and sets a "yoke of slavery" (Gal 5:1) on those who look for freedom and forgiveness. A theology that produces such a spiritual piety poisons rather than purifies.

All too often people become less whole and less human under the influence of a theology that does not understand that "take up your cross" must be preceded by "the Spirit of life in Christ Jesus has set you free from the law of sin and death" (Rom 8:2). The litmus test of theology is not only what it says of God but what it does to persons when it is preached, taught and practiced. The theology of Pentecost humanizes and heals, for it is a theology of resurrection and life, not of death and despair.

Practical theology in the mode of *paraclesis* is a summons and invitation for humanity to become truly human; it is an exhortation to move out of the place of sorrow and humiliation into a community of reconciliation, peace and dignity. Christopraxis as a form of the real presence of Christ is a pledge of comfort and consolation to the oppressed and the broken. It may have to take the "worldly" form of the presence of Christ in many cases, or the "nonreligious" form of Christ's presence in the world, as Bonhoeffer came to see it.[20] The praxis of forgiveness must first of all be a praxis of reconciliation and restoration of humanity in the world before its authenticity can be affirmed in the liturgy of the church.

The paracletic ministry of Jesus is a pledge of his humanity to and for all human persons in the concrete historical, social and moral dilemma of their existence. As the advocate for humanity, the criterion for what is authentically human is his own humanity, not a general principle of humanity. In his paracletic ministry Jesus pledges his own humanity, which has already passed through judgment and the penalty of death for the humanity of all persons. Jesus' advocacy is not only for the best of humanity, leaving the rest to their own fate; rather he is the advocate for all of humanity, bringing every human person into the place where no human distinctive, whether racial, sexual or social, can serve as a criterion for relation with God or with one another.

For the church this means that actions involving advocacy for the full humanity of persons have a priority and authority grounded in the humanity and ministry of Christ himself. The strategy of paracletic ministry is nonnegotiable in terms of advocacy for persons who suffer from discrimination, oppression and human torment of any kind. This strategy is not derived from ideological concerns nor from moral law alone. The strategy of advocacy as a form of Christopraxis is God's own strategy, enacted in Jesus Christ and through Jesus Christ for the sake of the world.

To separate evangelism and social justice as two issues to be debated and then prioritized is to split humanity down the middle. Theologically, it is a denial of the incarnation of God. In assuming humanity in its condition of estrangement and brokenness, Jesus produced reconciliation in "his own body," so that no longer can we see humanity apart from its unity in Jesus Christ. To approach persons in the context of their social, physical and spiritual existence, and only offer healing and reconciliation for the spiritual is already a betrayal of the gospel as well as of humanity.[21]

---

[20]Dietrich Bonhoeffer, *Letters and Papers from Prison* (New York: Macmillan, 1971), pp. 300, 344, 362.

[21]The prevailing theology of the church growth movement tends to divide social responsibility from evangelism, giving priority to evangelism but also attempting to include social responsibility as indispensable to the mission of the church, though not a primary form of the church's mission. See, for example, George W. Peters, *A Theology of Church Growth* (Grand Rapids, Mich.: Zondervan,

Christopraxis as a form of the ministry of the church *expects* the eschatological presence of Christ to be released as a "charismatic" experience. In this is the peril of succumbing to the temptations of pietism, individualism and corporate inwardness as alternatives to genuine Christian experience. To the extent that this happens, there is no longer "danger" in the manifestation of the kingdom of God in the real presence of Christ. The authentic *charism* that empowers is Christ's power that redeems humanity from the social, political, and institutional forms of power that dehumanize.

The goal of *paraclesis* is not merely deliverance from evil nor emancipation from structures that bind but empowerment to be truly human under circumstances and situations not yet redeemed. Pentecost occurs wherever and whenever the kingdom of God appears with the power of the Spirit manifesting the eschatological signs of healing, forgiveness of sins and restoration to emotional and spiritual wholeness in community. Pentecost promises a paraclete to every one who stumbles and falls, to everyone who is weak and powerless, to everyone who is tormented and torn by the demons of doubt, discouragement and despair. Jesus himself is the first paraclete. The Holy Spirit continues this paracletic ministry as "another Advocate" (Jn 14:16), sent by the Father as the very presence of Jesus.

The presence and ministry of the Spirit are the presence and praxis of Christ. This is Christopraxis—not a doctrine for which life is sacrificed, but the very being and life of God given for the sake of preserving and upholding human life; not an ideology or strategy that fights inhumanity for the sake of becoming human, but the very humanity of God that seeks the transformation of all that is inhuman in humanity. This life of Christ is vicarious in the sense that he offered his own humanity as pledge for ours by offering up his own obedience to the Father as the faithful Son. The bond between our humanity and his is not a metaphysical or mystical connection but is a filial bond; we are bound to him by the "spirit of adoption" by which we have received his very own Spirit so that we too can cry, "Abba! Father!" (Rom 8:15-17).

1981). The apostles, Peters writes, "put spiritual ministries before social and material services, . . . combined prayer with preaching without allowing either to usurp the place of the other . . . [and] put evangelism before all other ministries" (p. 125).

13

THEOLOGICAL ETHICS
& PASTORAL CARE

Practical theology, as we have seen, is a continuing activity of the church as the ministry of Jesus Christ though the Holy Spirit. I have called this Christopraxis, with an emphasis on the continued activity of the risen Christ through the presence and power of the Spirit. The concrete human situation with its various levels of social constructs and relationships is always an "ethical event," as suggested by Karl Barth.[1] The command of God—the basis for theological ethics—has material reality before it is conceptualized as a formal and theoretical rule. When we turn to the specific ministry of pastoral care, the moral and ethical components of the core social paradigm that defines human existence come into play: what do we mean by "human values" and "moral responsibility"? In this chapter we will look at the crisis of moral values in relationship to theological beliefs, what is meant by "moral character," and how the command of God can be understood as the will of God in the labyrinth of human relationships and decisions. The chapter will conclude with a discussion of the pastoral caregiver's role as moral advocate.

The distinction between the ethical and the moral is subtle and formal rather than explicit and material. At the practical level, we usually mean the same thing when we say that something is "unethical" or "immoral." We mean that it is wrong as measured by accepted norms and standards. Underlying the norms and standards by which we say that something is unethical or immoral is the concept of value.

---

[1]Karl Barth, *Ethics*, ed. Dietrich Braun, trans. Geoffrey W. Bromiley (New York: Seabury, 1981), p. 354.

According to C. Marshall Lowe:

> Values, which are created by individuals, must be differentiated from morals, which are produced by the culture. Culture can be seen as a system of consensually validated social expectations deriving from the personal values of diverse individuals. Morals provide the social standard for differentiating between the good and the bad. . . . There is a delicate balance between allowing the individual the freedom to choose values which have personal meaning and at the same time providing him with the stability of a morality shared with others.[2]

In this definition, morals are relative to social and cultural expectations. Values are thought to be discerned by individuals and moral standards derived from them as social norms. This would appear to make public morality relative to the agreed-on social determination of what is good, while leaving individuals free to follow privately held values as the basis for personal moral actions. We are not told what the source of the individually held values might be, except that they have "personal meaning."

The Crisis of Moral Values

Common to many complaints about modern society is the feeling that we have experienced a loss of moral values or that values are no longer based on absolute and universal moral truth. One way of viewing this problem is to suggest that the values by which people live today have become totally subjective and disconnected from belief in objective moral principles.

There was a time when people could assume that personal moral values were closely aligned with objective moral truth. It was assumed that what a person stated as a personal value connected to what she or he believed to be an objective moral value. It was expected that a commitment to a set of moral values would determine how a person would act and make choices. That is to say, it could be assumed that the moral content of a person's character determined their decisions and actions. This no longer seems to be true.

In Western contemporary culture, personal values have become separated from beliefs. Values have become related more to existential needs and desires than to the intrinsic worth or merit of a belief. Values now reflect individuals' behavior and choices more than what they say when asked to define the moral truth of what they believe. For example, in North America, up to 90 percent of the population owns some kind of belief in God or a divine being to whom they look for guidance and help. Yet many of these same people can be observed spending their time and money on things that bring immediate gratification rather than long-term fulfillment. Simi-

---

[2]C. Marshall Lowe, *Value Orientation in Counseling and Psychotherapy,* 2nd ed. (Cranston, R.I.: Carroll, 1976), pp. 2-3.

larly, the majority of Americans believe that marriage should be a lifelong commitment, yet more than half of all U.S. marriages fail, due largely to a perceived loss of personal value in the relationship.

As a result, the basic moral structure of our social institutions of family and community appears to be falling apart. We look to the church and educational institutions for moral and spiritual teaching to reverse this trend. Unfortunately, this is not the answer. Those who seek to establish the moral values of society can no longer do that by merely restating the traditional belief system on which moral values were originally based. We cannot change values by speaking of what we ought to believe. We can only redirect the personal values of persons in our modern culture in such a way that they are reconnected with what is believed to be true.

What we assert about family values is what we believe ought to be the case. Personal values are what we spend money, time and energy to achieve or experience. In our culture, behavior reflects values more than beliefs. For example, North American family sociologists Lucy and Dennis Guernsey have suggested that marital compatibility may depend more on common values than on a common belief system.[3] In their research they have discovered that couples who share a religious and moral belief system but who express different values in the ways that each finds pleasure, meaning and fulfillment are basically incompatible and will experience conflict and difficulty in their marriage. Couples who do share personal values even if they have been brought up with different religious and moral belief systems are actually more compatible.

What should we conclude from this? Are the moral values that once were believed to be universal and objective now relative to each culture? Are personal/individual values no longer dependent on objective moral truth? Finally, what role does moral character have in determining individual and personal values?

Character Formation and Moral Development

The broad range of ethical theory and the critical areas of ethical discourse cannot be considered in this chapter. My concern is to lay the foundation for ethical reflection on issues and concerns that arise in pastoral care, particularly in crisis situations. While we cannot separate the question of moral character from the question of moral actions, or moral values from moral obligations, pastoral care has a narrower focus on the area of decision making and actions. Rather than focusing on the abstract and formal issues of ethics, our interest is with the concrete "moral event" that takes place through a variety of social relations and encounters.[4]

---

[3]Lucy Guernsey and Dennis Guernsey, *Real Life Marriage* (Waco, Tex.: Word, 1987), pp. 107-19.

[4]For a helpful discussion of the distinction between moral being and moral character, see Bruce C.

Helmut Thielicke reminds us that moral imperatives cannot be produced in persons by "training," as though we could impose a sense of loyalty or duty as the basis of ethical life by the molding of instincts or behavior. An animal may be trained so as to evidence traits roughly equivalent to ethical life, such as obedience and loyalty. However, the animal kingdom does not have the "ethos," says Thielicke, from which we gain our concept of ethics. The uniqueness of human beings as ethical agents can thus be said to be grounded in ethical freedom constituted by one's relationship to oneself, to others, to the world and to God.

Adam is addressed by God and related to himself as a person free to act and make choices. Only when the woman is created and brought into the context of this freedom, however, can Adam finally experience the concrete reality of a "thou." His personhood is defined and his freedom oriented in relation to the other as "bone of my bones and flesh of my flesh" (Gen 2:23). Any moral instincts Adam may have had prior to this encounter could only have led to a kind of moral autonomy—defined in his freedom over and against the world and in his freedom over and against God. The "not good" (Gen 2:18) of this orientation of Adam to his world and to God points to the essentially human and personal foundation for moral actions and ethical reflection.

It is no longer necessary for Adam to have moral autonomy now that his own personhood is bound up in the personal and historical existence of the other person. Moral autonomy means that one is free to arbitrate absolute moral values from one's own perspective. Such moral solipsism, while claiming to ground personal moral values in a transcendent moral dimension (God or absolute moral principle), can make no ultimate differentiation between a moral principle and a moral decision. One could argue that Adam could not have had moral autonomy because his own life was ultimately grounded in God as the source of his own moral being. True. But this is only a formal distinction between Adam and God at the moral level. In order to exercise moral freedom as a personal reality, Adam must set himself over and against God as an autonomous moral agent, claiming the right to make moral distinctions, of which God and the good are but one possible choice. This, of course, is precisely the nature of the original temptation—to be like God.

It is significant that the command not to eat of the fruit of the tree of the knowledge of good and evil came to Adam when he was still alone, before the woman was created (cf. Gen 2:15-17). It is also significant that this command was violated by individual acts by both the woman and the man (cf. Gen 3:6). The action by which each gained a kind of moral autonomy, knowing good and evil, caused a loss of moral

Birch and Larry L. Rasmussen, *Bible and Ethics in the Christian Life* (Minneapolis: Augsburg, 1976), p. 81.

freedom and a loss of moral concern for the other. When confronted by God with this act, the man refused to recognize the woman's moral claim upon him and said, "The woman whom you gave to be with me, she gave me fruit from the tree, and I ate" (Gen 3:12). The claim of moral autonomy caused a loss of moral freedom, with the very structure of humanity itself threatened. No longer is human personhood in the form of cohumanity the criterion for moral responsibility. Yet there is no other criterion by which God holds persons accountable for moral actions.

After Cain killed Abel, his brother, God's first question is a moral one framed in terms of cohumanity: "Where is your brother Abel?" And Cain's response points to his claim for moral autonomy: "I do not know; am I my brother's keeper?" (Gen 4:9).

A basis for a theological ethic in pastoral care can be found in the observation that God intervenes in the supposed moral right of Abel's family to exact vengeance on Cain. The "mark of Cain" is not a banishment from the human social order but a "moral mandate" by which he is to be permitted to live within the human community without fear of retaliation (Gen 4:13-16). God becomes the moral advocate of one who has himself broken the moral law by his act of fratricide. An immoral act does not disqualify one from the moral advocacy of God. Thus God's moral will can be the basis for moral law and at the same time operate with freedom to uphold the life of the one who has broken the law. God's moral will clearly has a pastoral or redemptive dimension, directing pastoral care in cases where an apparent moral dilemma appears based on the moral law alone.

So we are moral persons, with an inherent capacity for making moral judgments. How we make these judgments and what criteria we use in making moral decisions is the function we assign to ethics.

Theological ethics, as a particular function of Christian theology, is reflection on the moral nature and moral decisions of human beings from the perspective of God's revealed nature and purpose. Lewis Smedes puts it as plainly as can be said:

> We have a deep primitive sense that morality is woven into the fabric of our humanness. Morality is not a con game that makes losers out of those who play it seriously. It is not a false rumor planted in an insecure society to help the weak keep the powerful in check by playing on their conscience. Nor is morality just an impressive name for the strong feelings we have about some things, a word we use to add some clout to our complaints. Morality is a basic component of any human sort of life, a reality we feel surely even if we cannot define it clearly. We do have choices, and they are sometimes between real moral options. The choice we make can put us in the wrong with God and our ideal selves—or leave us in the right. And being in the right means being in harmony with God's design for our humanity.[5]

---

[5]Lewis Smedes, *Mere Morality: What God Expects from Ordinary People* (Grand Rapids, Mich.: Eerdmans, 1983), p. vii.

Ethics can be construed as the science of determining precisely the nature of those values that determine moral principles and behavior. Karl Barth says:

> The morality or goodness of human conduct which ethics investigates has to do with the validity of what is valid for all human action, the origin of all constancies, the worth of everything universal, the rightness of all rules. With such concepts as validity, origin, worth, and rightness we denote provisionally and generally that which transcends the inquiries of psychology, cultural history, and jurisprudence—the transcendent factor which in contrast is the theme of ethical inquiry.[6]

Theological ethics thus grounds values not in individual and personal preference but in the personal character and purpose of God as the transcendent content of all values.

A Theological Foundation for Moral Character

If our fundamental presupposition is that all reality is created by God and upheld and redeemed by the power of God, we gain some key insights.

First, God's character provides the moral basis for God's creation. As Creator, God is not impersonal power but a moral agent to whom all of creation is accountable for its meaning as well as its goodness. The biblical account of creation asserts the goodness of all that God has made: "God saw everything that he had made, and indeed, it was very good" (Gen 1:31). The moral character of the created world is defined by the character of God. "For you are not a God who delights in wickedness; evil will not sojourn with you" (Ps 5:4). The psalmist attributes moral character to God as One who is faithful, just, merciful and filled with compassion in deeds as well as words: "The Lord is faithful in all his words, and gracious in all his deeds. . . . The eyes of all look to you, and you give them their food in due season. You open your hand, satisfying the desire of every living thing" (Ps 145:13, 15-16). Instead of abstracting from the created world to find the moral absolute as a formal principle, the biblical tradition finds the moral absolute in God's word of creation and redemption.

Second, the moral character of creation is revealed through human beings as the image bearers of God. While the psalmist views creation as an expression of God's power and majesty, human beings are described as the bearers of God's moral character (Gen 1:26-27; Ps 8:1-4). To be made in God's image and likeness is to have a moral character like that of the divine. Humans are thus moral agents not because of adherence to abstract moral law but because they bear the very moral character of God. This is why violence against another human is an offense against God. When the first murder is recorded in the Bible, God confronts Cain: "What have you done?

---

[6]Barth, *Ethics,* p. 4.

Listen; your brother's blood is crying out to me from the ground!" (Gen 4:10). Later the Lord reiterates the moral connection between humans: he "will surely require a reckoning" for taking of human life, "for in his own image God made humankind" (Gen 9:5-6).

Third, human character is expressed through the moral quality of social relations as well as the moral responsibility of scientific endeavor. The intrinsic value of each person is an absolute moral reality, as each bears the human image of divine moral character. A theological version of reality is grounded in anthropology, not sociology or psychology. Cultural moral standards are, at best, only relative moral indicators of the intrinsic moral character of humans created in the divine image.

The failure of an existentialist version of reality is not because it values the moral quality of human existence over the impersonal and ideal moral principle. The failure of existentialism is due to its valuing of the individual over the social relation. Søren Kierkegaard's attempt to escape the abstract and impersonal spirit of Hegelian philosophy led him to force reality into the narrow confinement of the self existing on the threshold of dread. The only epitaph he desired for his own tombstone was "The Individual."

A theological version of moral reality overcomes this fatal plunge into personal despair by viewing humankind as intrinsically social. The biblical account of creation has already corrected the existentialist error: "It is not good that the man should be alone" (Gen 2:18). The "goodness" of human existence is not a solitary, existential reach for a transcendent reality but the mutual recognition of the divine image in another's presence. When the woman is created alongside the man, they simultaneously and mutually awaken to their human existence in the divine image: "This at last is bone of my bones and flesh of my flesh" (Gen 2:23).

The character that underlies moral decisions and actions is not the possession of individuals, then, but the moral quality of core human relationships. What the existentialist seeks in "authenticity" of individual existence, a theological version of moral reality finds in mutual respect and responsibility for the moral character of each person with whom one is related. The biblical emphasis on moral character is defined in terms of social relationships. Husbands and wives, parents and children, slaves and masters are all reminded by the apostle Paul that the spiritual reality of their faith is expressed in the moral quality of their social relation. "Be subject to one another out of reverence for Christ" is Paul's admonition, followed by instructions to married couples, parents and children, slaves and masters (Eph 5:21—6:9).

Fourth, the formation of character takes place where personal values are created out of moral experience. This discussion begins with the suggestion that personal values have become detached from beliefs in our contemporary culture. As a result, attempts at moral development and formation of character through the teaching of moral principles will have little effect. I have suggested that one must begin with values and move toward beliefs. Another way to express it is that moral character must be perceived as having personal value.

When the Bible presents the moral challenge to have faith and live in obedience to the Word of God, appeal to the personal value will be received as a benefit. When Moses attempted to bring the people of Israel out of Egypt, the discipline of obedience by which a former slave people could be formed into a community of character was presented as a journey to a land "flowing with milk and honey" (Ex 3:8). The images of what would be achieved and experienced were vivid and compelling. This was an appeal to values rather than merely to moral duty. When Jesus warned against laying up treasures here on earth where thieves and corruption could attack, he urged his followers to "store up for yourselves treasures in heaven . . . for where your treasure is, there your heart will be also" (Mt 6:19-21).

The formation of Christian character is not achieved by the teaching of Christian doctrine alone, nor by setting down rigid rules of moral discipline. Rules are necessary to set boundaries, but it is relationship rather than rules that forms character. When the Bible speaks of character, it does so in terms of core human moral and spiritual values rather than religious rituals and regulations. The critical moral experiences that contribute to the formation of character do not take place in church meetings but in the family, in the primary encounters of people's daily lives.

Determining God's Moral Will

The specific concern of a theological and pastoral ethic is how we understand the relation of God to human moral decisions and actions, raising questions like the following:

1. Is God's will or his command an arbitrary criterion for moral action over and against the moral discernment of humans?

2. Are human moral decisions without an absolute criterion or authority until God has revealed his will?

3. Does the right moral action depend on the consequences of the decision or act, or on the moral character of God as an a priori ethical principle or law?

4. After the Fall, and with the knowledge that all human persons are in a condition of moral defection (sin), can human personhood continue to be viewed as a criterion for moral actions?

5. Does what God determines as a moral action change with respect to the situations in which a moral predicament is experienced?

6. Or is an apparent moral predicament merely the result of sin and evil, while God's moral law and principles remain unchanged?

These questions point us in a certain direction. Theological ethics must make clear precisely how the moral character and will of God bear upon human moral decisions. Thielicke puts the issue squarely before us: "We shall then focus attention on the cardinal ethical problem of how in a fallen world there can be any obedience whatsoever to the commandments of God, indeed how any congruity between demand and fulfillment can even be theoretically conceived, and what right we thus have to speak of the freedom of the Christian man."[7]

The use of Scripture. As theological ethics attempts to address questions of human morality and the commandment of God, the role of Scripture is of central concern. Several alternatives present themselves, each of which has advocates in Christian moral theology.

1. The Bible is prescriptive, providing highly specific, binding moral instruction—moral law.

2. The Bible is instructive, providing an overarching set of values, ideals and principles—moral criteria.

3. The Bible is illustrative, providing a compendium of moral examples grounded in the life, teaching and power of Christ as a guide for Christian ethics—moral wisdom.

While each of these contributes something of value to the formation of a Christian ethical value system, each also falls short of providing a methodology by which good moral decisions can be made and actions taken in critical situations where there appear to be moral predicaments. James Gustafson says:

> The Bible is more important for helping Christian community to interpret the God whom it knows in its existential faith than it is for giving a revealed morality that is to be translated and applied in the contemporary world. . . . The Christian moral life, then, is not a response to moral imperatives, but to a Person, the living God. . . . What the Bible makes known, then, is not a morality but a *reality,* a living presence to whom man responds.[8]

If by "giving a revealed morality" Gustafson means using the Bible as a methodological tool in determining the will of God in a critical moral decision rather than for establishing a theology of Christian moral life, then I think we could agree.

The inadequacy of the three above-mentioned alternatives is fundamentally methodological, not theological. That is, the Bible cannot be used as a method of arriving at ethical principles or moral criteria abstractable from the participation of God himself in the moral situation of human life. Or to put it another way, the Bible cannot be

---

[7]Helmut Thielicke, *Theological Ethics;* trans. William H. Lazareth (Grand Rapids, Mich.: Eerdmans, 1979), 1:463.

[8]James Gustafson, "Christian Ethics," in *Religion,* ed. Paul Ramsey (Englewood Cliffs, N.J.: Prentice-Hall, 1965).

used as a substitute for moral freedom grounded in responsibility.

While the Bible clearly gives authoritative status to the will of God as a determining factor in theological ethics applied through pastoral care, the Bible cannot be seen primarily as an ethical textbook, whether prescriptively, instructively or illustratively. There is a wrong use of the Bible in attempts to discern God's will in critical pastoral situations, as well as a right use.

It is wrong to attempt to use biblical proof texts to find strategies or solutions to modern problems. The Pharisees had a "proof text" from the Old Testament when they confronted the woman caught in adultery and presented her to Jesus for judgment. Correct use of the Bible in such cases requires taking up the hermeneutical task of discerning the purpose of Scripture, how it guides us to uphold the true nature of humanity through responsible decisions and actions. In this way Scripture serves divine moral freedom to act redemptively and creatively. Scripture does not proof text moral law but authoritatively upholds the will of God in restoring the moral quality of human life.

It is wrong to attempt to find parallels between our own situation and that of the biblical writers. Where such parallels seem to exist (e.g., Rahab's friendly welcome to the spies, Heb 11:31), we cannot assume a direct correlation of ethical principle; it is faith that is the connecting reality, not moral principle. Besides, this approach would make the Bible largely irrelevant where parallels cannot be found. The correct use of the Bible involves reading its stories so as to find ourselves confronted by the same demand and command of God to act with faith and not disbelief (cf. Rom 14:22-23).

It is wrong to extrapolate from the Bible one primary ethical principle or norm, be it love, the imitation of Christ, the kingdom of God, or the gospel as over and against law. The Bible itself, as the Word of God, would then be forced to surrender its authority to a principle or norm that stands independent of it. This would be a return to autonomous morality: one individual, together with the Bible, possesses an absolute ethical criterion. It is right instead to heed the Bible's insistence that all human actions and decisions are inherently moral and therefore answerable to the living God, who will bring every decision and act into judgment based upon God's will and purpose for humanity (cf. Rom 14:10-12; 1 Cor 4:1-5; 2 Cor 10:18).

The Bible itself forces us to see that there is an eschatological dimension to moral actions. No ethical system or moral principle can serve as an absolute criterion in the face of this eschatological claim upon human moral life and actions. Theological ethics therefore must bring this eschatological perspective to bear on the critical moral issues of our day.

This section opened with the heading "Determining God's Moral Will." We have seen that using the Bible in pastoral care, to discern God's moral will when there are critical moral issues at stake, must be in accordance with the Scripture's own purpose and goal—to hold us accountable to the will of God as an eschatological goal and a present reality.

The moral good as eschatological reality. God's moral will upholds created structures of human life and society, including the moral law by which human moral values and principles are determined. Human moral instincts are thus given by God and are to be used to uphold the quality of life God has created. Jesus validated the use of these moral instincts when he argued that the same human instincts that served the welfare of animals on the sabbath day ought to be considered as the basis for permitting him to heal a woman on the sabbath day (Mt 12:9-13; Lk 13:15-16). When Jesus stated that it is "lawful to do good on the sabbath" (Mt 12:12), he pointed to God's purpose for human persons as an ultimate moral value. The determination of what is "good" cannot be made at the expense of the value of the human person. So too, in saying, "The sabbath was made for humankind, and not humankind for the sabbath" (Mk 2:27), Jesus expresses the moral will of God as interpreted by what is for the good of the human person. In this case, we see that observance of the sabbath, which was given to uphold a moral value, must be modified when necessary to accommodate the moral value of "doing good."

In a theological ethic God cannot be posited as the abstract lawgiver whose being remains static and fixed in the moral law as the primary absolute. This was the binding force of Kant's ethics. The God of Abraham, Isaac and Jacob, the God who is present to us in Jesus Christ, is a living God who has created the moral law as the order of human life and society. Creation, however, including the human structures of moral life, is subject to the moral freedom of God. This does not place God's moral will in contradiction to the moral law. The tension is not between two orders of morality but between a created order with temporal and provisional design and the eternal purpose of God, which stands as the eschatological goal of the created design.

A theological paradigm can help orient us to this biblical perspective. Let us say that God has a design, purpose and goal expressed through both creation and redemption. God himself is related to each as an absolute criterion. Presented schematically, it would look something like figure 13.1.

In this theological paradigm there is a flow of God's will through design, through purpose, to the goal. God stands in an absolute relation to each. At the critical juncture of design and purpose, purpose interprets God's will; thus the design can be modified by purpose where necessary. In fact, a failure to modify design will be a frustration to God's purpose.

In the same way, at the critical juncture of purpose and goal, God's will shapes purpose to the goal. God's will is actually present in design as well as stated purpose, but does not become institutionalized or reified as sheer design or expressed purpose. Design and expressed purpose are servants of the eschatological goal.

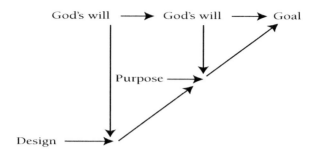

Figure 13.1. God's relationship to his design, purpose and goal

Jesus' presence among his contemporaries brought the eschatological goal into the already revealed design and purpose of God institutionalized in the religion of the Jews. At critical points, most of which were critical points of pastoral care, Jesus interpreted the moral will of God in terms of the goal toward which both design and purpose point. He did this in such a way that both design and stated purpose—as understood by the Jews in the sense of divine law—were modified to allow a moral decision to be made that upheld the goal as embodied in a whole and healed person.

This can be seen in the way Jesus related to the law of the sabbath (Lk 14; Jn 9), the law concerning adultery (Jn 8), and specific cultic laws and rituals prescribed in the Old Testament (Mk 7). The apostle Paul followed the same theological paradigm when he observed that circumcision as a sign of the covenant has now given way to a new spiritual life that fulfills its purpose (Gal 3). Where the former design had separated Jew and Gentile, slave and free, male and female, Paul saw that the purpose and goal of God for human beings is full equality and parity in the kingdom of God (Gal 3:28).

Some would argue that many of these instances are concerned with ceremonial and ritual law, not with moral law. But this is a fundamental misunderstanding of the intrinsic moral dimension of Old Testament laws. The ceremonial and ritual laws, including circumcision and the Ten Commandments, were oriented toward the health and wholeness of a people of God and thus were intrinsically moral in content.

Central to the theological-ethical paradigm presented here is the structure of a theological anthropology that views human beings as essentially bound to each other in a personal, spiritual and moral relationship. The design and the stated purpose for persons within God's design are clearly subject to God's goal for persons.

Theological ethics understands that God's design is the most easily modified in light of his purpose and goal. There can be no absolute or intrinsic ethical content to a design, even that designed by God. This of course does not mean that God's moral will is not discerned through design. But God's will can never be identified with design in any absolute or necessary way. This preserves the freedom of God's moral will to serve the redemptive purpose and goal for human beings. Moral law itself, while grounded in God's moral will, must be subject to the purpose and goal of God's will.

Does this mean that God's design for human life, such as marriage, family, sexual orientation or even the church, can be modified whenever it is convenient or mutually acceptable to the persons involved? Are there no permanent or fundamental designs, such as once were called "orders of creation"? The first question must receive an unequivocal no. Modification of God's design is not done for the sake of personal values. This would take us back to autonomous morality.

The answer to the second question is more difficult. If marriage, family or the state are assumed to be a created order and thus granted a moral status by virtue of natural order or natural necessity, then the moral law has its ground in natural law, which in turn is grounded in biology, sociology and culture. This would be the equivalent of saying that "humankind is made for marriage" rather than "marriage is made for humankind," to paraphrase the saying of Jesus.

In both questions we see a confusion of design, or order, with an absolute form of moral law. The Bible will not permit us to absolutize any design, even a design or order that has its roots in God's created world. It is God who remains free as the Creator. Thus Jesus highlights the priority of the kingdom of God over marital and family relations (Mt 10:34-39; Lk 14:26-27), and points out that he himself is "lord even of the sabbath" (Mk 2:28).

Marriage is not a design by which all persons are defined. The New Testament makes it quite clear that marriage is a temporal and provisional design, and in light of the eschaton it is already being treated as subject to modification. Nonmarried persons are not outside of the moral will of God. It is not the institution of marriage that provides the moral guideline for our sexuality but the intrinsic moral structure of cohumanity itself. The design of marriage and family may be modified in light of the approaching goal for persons in the kingdom of God. But the "good" of personal and social relations is rooted in the integrity and faithful commitment of the I-Thou relation, as upheld by the social structure (community/family) in which that relation is expressed. So human sexuality is subject to the moral order of humans existing in the image and likeness of God. The determination of this moral order continues to be of concern to theological ethics as a contemporary practice of pastoral care.

I agree with Smedes that there is a deep and primitive sense that morality is woven into the fabric of our humanness.[9] A theological ethic then is grounded in God's

---

[9]Smedes, *Mere Morality*, p. vii.

determination that the moral freedom of the human is an essential aspect of our cohumanity—of our being with and for the other person in the place where this encounter occurs. This is why moral freedom does not lead to moral autonomy and why personal moral values are intrinsically social and communal values. Because, as Barth has reminded us, every human relation and encounter is a "moral event," moral freedom can never be a matter of an individual's right to pursue a value or fulfill a need without regard to others.

Pastoral Care as Moral Advocacy

Earlier we briefly considered God's role as moral advocate where an apparent moral dilemma makes the human person vulnerable to the moral law itself. The moral will of God, then, is invested in a goal for human beings that often can be reached only through moral advocacy.

By "moral advocacy" I mean the extension of divine grace to persons who are guilty of breaking the moral law or who are suffering a loss of personhood through the existence of a structure mandated by moral law. The practice of moral advocacy places on the side of the marginal person the moral right for personal dignity, freedom from abusive relationships, and full parity in social and communal life.

By "pastoral care" I mean not only the broader responsibilities of clergy but the narrower role of the professional caregiver. This person may be a pastor who offers pastoral care through the church or may be a person trained to provide counsel, therapy and intervention in a private or public agency. Our focus here is caregiving provided at times of crisis, when life has become difficult, if not impossible, when relationships have been distorted, if not destructive, and when the tragic contravenes common sense, and even faith fails.

I have in view here such situations as the physical and emotional abuse of a spouse within a lawful marriage; the abuse of children within families and in social agencies; the breakdown of marriage and the trauma of divorce; the sudden death of a loved one or the lingering and ignominious delay of death where life no longer has dignity and value; the loss of personal freedom through the addictive power of substances or sex; and not least, the failure of will and nerve, the loss of meaning and purpose that strikes in midlife and plunges us into a tailspin that threatens the loss of every gain.

Because these life crises touch on the very heart of what it is to be human, they constitute moral dilemmas and require moral advocacy. One way or another, such breakdowns or failures constitute a threat to the value of human life or to faith in God as an ultimate value.

The crisis situations of life are borderline situations, with regard to the command of God, essentially ambiguous with regard to what God's will might be. Here "normal life" cannot be taken as providing the norms by which decisions can be made and a direction forward found. Too often caregivers make the mistake of using the normal as the paradigm for counsel and advice to those in abnormal situations.

Theological ethics, like medicine, faces the real problems when there is an absence of normality and health. In the face of what has become an inhuman situation, the caregiver must become the advocate of the person who has become marginal—not of the general principles of humanity.

Two aspects of caregiving as moral advocacy can help us find guidelines for approaching specific cases, a perspective that applies theological ethics to the task of giving pastoral care. I will discuss first the role of the caregiver as moral advocate and then the nature of pastoral care as it pertains to God's moral will for persons.

Again, the crises we face are borderline situations where the command of God is ambiguous. This ambiguity arises because the command and moral will of God is rooted in the freedom of God and consequently demands that there be freedom for the human being to discern and do the will of God.

If God's moral will were absolutely embodied in a commandment, such as "Thou shalt not bear false witness," we could conclude that in every case the telling of a lie is wrong. As we continually discover, however, a moral dilemma occurs in situations where telling the truth means betraying a person whose life depends on one's action. Ethicists have used situations like this to argue that one must choose the higher moral law, saving a life, over the lower moral law, telling the truth. This way of resolving the ambiguity involves playing off one moral law against another.

But God's moral will is not a higher principle or higher moral law. Rather, God's moral will is directed toward the goal of human life, and his moral laws are given so as to direct us toward that goal. If God himself were present in every case when it appears that moral laws collide, we would instinctively turn to him for assurance as to the best moral decision.

This appears to be the way Jesus functioned when confronted with a collision between human values and the moral law as stated in the Old Testament Scriptures. He assumed that his presence was the presence of the freedom of God's moral will to become the advocate for the human person. This advocacy clearly did not mean justifying the situation or the immoral actions (as in the case of the woman caught in adultery), but facilitating the restoration and liberation of the person to realize God's moral will.

The role of the caregiver who is a Christian and who seeks to provide pastoral care from the perspective of theological ethics is to be an advocate for God's moral will in a dual sense. First there is advocacy for God's own presence in the situation. The caregiver is present as the advocate of God's presence. This is possible because the risen

Christ has sent his own Spirit as the indwelling presence of God; we are the temple of the living God (2 Cor 6:16; cf. Jn 14:18-23; 1 Cor 6:19; Col 1:27). The one who provides pastoral care is thus one in whom the "real presence" of Christ is manifest as a form of advocacy to and on behalf of the one who is in a "borderline" situation.

Second, the caregiver provides advocacy for the person's own moral freedom to be a whole and functioning human being. The caregiver does not merely take up the counseling relationship as a moral authority, dispensing moral law or making moral decisions on behalf of the one who is caught in the dilemma. Rather, the caregiver is the advocate of the moral authority that belongs to the other by virtue of that person's status before God as one who bears the divine image and likeness in fellowship with other humans.

For example, a person who is suffering abuse in a marriage will often feel morally powerless due to the supposed obligation toward the marriage partner. This may even be reinforced by a feeling that she is being rightly punished for real or imagined failings. The one who intervenes with pastoral care needs to serve as an advocate for God's moral authority, intercepting the relentless sense of duty toward a "law of marriage." The advocate stands with the victim over and against any "legal" right of a marriage partner to inflict pain. Thus the caregiver is willing to place himself or herself where God's moral will is perceived to be.

At the same time, the caregiver will serve as an advocate of the moral authority that properly belongs to the victim who feels totally bereft of moral freedom. The caregiver does not possess moral authority by virtue of a role or professional skill. Rather, moral authority resides in the nature of personhood itself as determined by God to be free for the other in a healthy relationship.

It should be understood that a Christian perspective on caregiving does not introduce moral criteria that are not already present in the human situation. There is no "Christian ethic" that substitutes Christian morality for human morality. What the Christian can provide through caregiving is the advocacy of God himself as a power liberating the moral freedom belonging to persons by divine endowment.

Caregivers without such a theological ethic can provide therapeutic intervention and even moral wisdom in directing the client toward the good. Yet the caregiver may experience ambivalence about serving in an explicitly moral role without a specific theological orientation. The Christian is freed from this moral ambivalence and can help clarify the moral criteria involved in what is otherwise an ambiguous dilemma. What might be an "easy out" for a person who seeks a resolution of a moral dilemma on strictly self-centered terms will be intensified into a true moral issue by the one who brings theological ethics to bear.

Theological ethics does not solve problems, says Helmut Thielicke; it intensifies them by showing the point of any particular decision:

Its task is that of clarification. It does not seek to spell out precisely what must be done. It simply lays bare the full implications of that "what," so that the underlying issue of the particular decision is heard as a claim. Ethics in effect complicates matters by analyzing the contents of the decision. But there is a counterbalancing simplification for the one who then decides: When it comes to the point of actually taking concrete action his decision is simplified by the gift of the Holy Spirit.[10]

The Holy Spirit is called the "paraclete" in the New Testament (see Jn 14:16, 26; 15:26; 16:7). One translation of this word is "advocate," one called to the side of another. Jesus intimates that this is his own role when he says, "I will ask the Father, and he will give you another Advocate [paraclete], . . . the Spirit of truth. . . . He abides with you, and he will be in you" (Jn 14:16-17).

The gift of the Holy Spirit as the indwelling presence of God's moral will resolves the moral ambivalence otherwise present in the caregiver. This advocacy frees the situation from the moral autonomy that offers the "easy out"—my pain gives me a right to get even with the one who hurt me, or the injustice I have suffered gives me the right to break out of my commitment. At the same time, this advocacy that binds all persons, whether victims of their own immoral acts or of the acts of others, to the moral will of God also sets free those bound by the inhuman laws and practices of others. The person is also thus set free to forgive, which is a moral action related to his or her own goal of healing.

It should not be supposed, however, that the Holy Spirit is a moral criterion that counters other moral criteria. There is a form of moral autonomy that would claim the Holy Spirit as the content of one's own conscience. Rather, the Holy Spirit clarifies the content of God's moral will as intrinsic to human personhood as a gift and goal, as well as convinces us of the moral authority by which we act in accordance with these moral criteria. The Holy Spirit is not a "simplicity" on this side of complexity but the simplicity on the other side of complexity. Oliver Wendell Holmes is reported to have said, "I would not give a fig for the simplicity on this side of complexity; but for the simplicity on the other side of complexity, I would give my life."

When the moral options in a given situation have been surveyed from the perspective of the moral law by which human beings live, and when the moral implications of an action have been calculated, the decision that is finally made on the basis of theological ethics cannot ultimately be defended on moral criteria alone. If it were, it would always be subject to the moral ambivalence that is inherent in the complexity of life where good and evil are intermixed. The one who serves as a caregiver and moral advocate decides the moral issue on the basis of what one reckons God

---

[10]Helmut Thielicke, *Theological Ethics*, trans. William H. Lazareth (Grand Rapids, Mich.: Eerdmans, 1984), p. 621.

declares to be good. There is no shortcut to this decision as the good lies on the other side of moral complexity, not on this side of it.

When Abraham finally decides that it is "good" to offer his son Isaac as a sacrifice on Moriah, there is no way back to the moral criteria by which he made that decision. When Jesus decided that the cross and his incredible "obedience unto death" was a good, the simplicity of his decision lies on the other side of moral reason alone. There is no other way to practice moral advocacy. For one is not merely betting that the decision is the best one and that others using the same criteria would invariably come out on the same side. The issues ultimately link the divine moral will with the human moral decision, and the personal character of God with the character and quality of life advocated here on earth.

In the end, theological ethics insists that the moral outcome of therapeutic intervention be considered as bearing the weight of God's own moral will. Jesus provided for this when he said, "Whatever you bind on earth will be bound in heaven, and whatever you loose on earth will be loosed in heaven" (Mt 16:19; cf. Jn 20:22-23).

This is a costly kind of advocacy. The caregiver must be prepared to suffer the judgment of those who feel it necessary to uphold legal and formal structures. The presence of the liberating moral will of God will often appear ambiguous and even wrong to those who find security in "being good" as defined by legal morality. For this reason Dietrich Bonhoeffer insisted that the task of Christian ethics is not to be good but to do the will of Christ.

> What is of ultimate importance is now no longer that I should become good, or that the condition of the world should be made better by my action, but that the reality of God should show itself everywhere to be the ultimate reality. Where there is faith in God as the ultimate reality, all concern with ethics will have as its starting-point that God shows Himself to be good, even if this involves the risk that I myself and the world are not good but thoroughly bad.[11]

For Bonhoeffer this meant we must be prepared to be considered guilty in order to be responsible advocates for those who are victims of the established order.[12] But this can only be the kind of guilt that Christ himself bore, as the advocate of God and the advocate of the sinner in the same movement.

Finally, it must be said the role of the caregiver as moral advocate is an extension of the body of Christ. The pastoral care that provides this intervention and advocacy should be offered in such a way that the primary caregiver is not the sole advocate. A model of caregiving then would include the following guidelines.

1. The caregiver operates within a network of Christian community so that her or

---

[11]Dietrich Bonhoeffer, *Ethics* (New York: Macmillan, 1965), pp. 188-89.
[12]Ibid., p. 245.

his spiritual and personal life is nurtured and affirmed as belonging to Christ and indwelt by Christ's Spirit.

2. The Christian community that upholds the integrity and ministry of the caregiver is theologically informed regarding the nature of pastoral care as moral advocacy.

3. The Christian community makes explicit its commitment to the moral advocacy of the primary caregiver. This is done as a covenant between the community (or its representatives) and the caregiver prior to specific actions that involve moral advocacy.

4. The primary caregiver, while preserving the confidentiality of a counseling relationship, seeks the wisdom of the Spirit through the caregiving network in providing advocacy when moral criteria alone do not resolve the complexity—that is, where the "mind of Christ" is seen to be the determining factor and will be one's final appeal.

5. In making these guidelines operational, the caregiving network must be carefully selected and prepared to serve as a team that understands and provides moral advocacy for pastoral care.

Pastoral Care in Crisis Intervention

We come now to the second aspect of pastoral care as moral advocacy. Here we explore the theological dimensions of pastoral care in crisis intervention. The relation of theological ethics to pastoral care is, in effect, the relation of God's moral will expressed through his creative and redemptive grace to persons caught in a web of personal moral failure and general moral evil. The problem of sin and the problem of evil raise issues in pastoral care which theological ethics must address.

Pastoral care, by whatever means delivered, provides three forms of helping ministry by which persons can realize God's moral will: (1) an extension of God's grace, (2) a transfer of spiritual power and (3) the creation of a healing community.

An extension of God's grace: intervention. The concept of intervention has its roots in God's gracious interaction with human beings so they do not fall away from his determination that they bear his image and likeness and share his eternal life as their personal destiny. By nature, human beings are both creaturely and personal. The personal dimension of human life is contingent upon relation to God, who is the transcendent source of personal being.

The concept of intervention used in what follows includes God's gracious movement toward humans caught in the web of sin and its consequences, but it also includes human intervention as agents of God's grace. An example of direct divine intervention is God's appearance to Adam and Eve following their sin of disobedience and fall from grace (Gen 3). An example of human intervention is Nathan's confrontation with David following his sin of adultery with Bathsheba and the arranged murder of her husband (2 Sam 12).

Without God's intervention into the creaturely process, human personhood would not have come into being. God enters into covenant relation with human beings and, as covenant partner, aligns himself with them over and against nature. Sin is a moral and spiritual problem involving defection from the covenant relation. That is, sin is defined as defiance of God's gracious intervention which results in the separation of persons from the gracious life of God. The consequence of sin is the moral and spiritual disorientation that then afflicts the human person in this state of estrangement and alienation.

God's judgment against sin, from the standpoint of theological ethics, is itself a continued intervention of divine grace. For if the sinner were left to the consequences of moral and spiritual disorientation, human personhood would disappear beneath the sickness and turmoil of life. Sin is fatal to human personhood.

The consequences of sin are not then identical with God's judgment on sin, though they may sometimes be coincidental. God's judgment is itself an intervention between sin and its consequence, so that the sinner is now related once more to God rather than left to suffer the fate of sin's consequence—"in the day that you eat of it you shall die" (Gen 2:17). This death is not itself the divine judgment but the deadly consequence of sin. The divine judgment is the calling of Adam and Eve out of their fateful situation and back into relation with the living God.

The specific goal of divine grace as intervention is thus forgiveness—the renewal of a positive relation between humans and God. The content of forgiveness is restored relation, not merely the granting of an exception to a moral law. Thus the reality of forgiveness is the restoration of an authentic moral history as being in relation. Forgiveness is the ultimate moral good, which transcends the moral law but does not break it.

The moral law does not contain the possibility of forgiveness. Forgiveness is located in the moral good, which is necessarily personal. The moral good therefore must have its source in the divine intention—the same source for the moral law. Forgiveness offers a moral good without contradicting the moral law, for both have their origin in the same moral reality and intention of God. This is the content of a theological ethic with regard to forgiveness. Pastoral care recognizes the criteria of the moral law in determining what is right and provides moral advocacy through intervention in order to sustain the moral good as that which is right. But pastoral care also provides moral advocacy when one stands in the wrong through the consequences of sin and provides a moral basis for forgiveness through the extension of God's grace.

The consequence of sin may be perceived to be identical with a divine judgment, as in the case of a natural catastrophe, an act of aggression or even a fatal disease. In certain cases in the Old Testament, the judgment of God was considered to come in the form of a physical affliction, such as the leprosy that struck Miriam (Num 12:1-16) or the plague that struck the people of Israel when they forsook God and worshiped the golden calf (Ex 32:35). These cases are exceptional, however, and do not provide a case for separating God's judgment from his grace. For in each case, God himself intervenes and stands between the people and the consequence of their sin—even when the consequence is considered to be a divine judgment!

Those practicing pastoral care must be prepared to make a similar intervention, without being intimidated at the thought that a person's affliction or situation is the result of God's judgment against sin. The moral good of divine grace is manifested by God's intervention for the sake of restoring persons, even if the consequence of sin is viewed as divine judgment. God's judgment may be an expression of the consequences of violating a moral law, but his grace is an expression of God's moral will which has as its goal the moral good of forgiveness.

Quite often caregivers will be confronted with a situation in which a person may be considered, or consider himself or herself, to be suffering the consequences of an immoral or sinful action. The caregiver will struggle with moral ambivalence if she or he believes that the moral law and divine judgment exhaust God's moral will. There may be instincts to offer release from the moral judgment, but one may be unsure that it is right to do so.

Some who provide pastoral care to persons who have acquired the deadly disease AIDS (acquired immune deficiency syndrome) harbor the thought that this disease may be a punishment of God if it is contracted, as in most cases, through sexual contact, particularly homosexual relations. If homosexuality is viewed as sinful, and if AIDS is a disease contracted primarily by homosexuals, then the one who has contracted the disease may be experiencing God's judgment against sin, according to this way of thinking.

Those who give care to persons with AIDS may have theological or moral convictions that prevent them from intervening if they believe that God's judgment has fallen upon the person. Yet there are no theological grounds for assuming that disease and sin are connected in this kind of cause-and-effect relation. God has shown himself to be the covenant partner of human beings and is aligned with persons, not with nature (which includes diseases) against persons. In the few cases in the Old Testament where God appears to have brought judgment through a plague or a disease, there is often a gracious divine intervention that frees the person from the consequence of sin through forgiveness, even though some, like David's son (2 Sam 12) and those who perished in the plague (Ex 32), lose their lives. The New Testament cites virtually no case of a disease being given by God as a judgment against sin (though some experienced sickness and even death through disorder at the Lord's Table [1 Cor 11:29-30] and some were struck dead, like Ananias and Sapphira [Acts 5]). Jesus, on the contrary, acts to dispel the notion that sin causes disease (cf. Jn 9), and he acts in every case to make an intervention between the disease and the person.

A theological ethic of moral advocacy as an extension of God's grace and forgiveness calls for intervention in every case, even if one should suppose that a disease or other condition is a consequence of sin. The offer of grace need not be dependent on a determination of whether the person is experiencing the consequence of sin. Grace is itself God's moral intervention between the person and the consequence of sin, *even if* that consequence is viewed as divine judgment.

If intervention is considered an extension of God's grace so that forgiveness is realized as the moral good, we can have courage to offer forgiveness on God's own terms and not merely out of human instincts of pity or compassion.

But, some would respond, forgiveness cannot rightly be offered until there is repentance and restitution on the part of the one who has wronged God. This kind of thinking runs contrary to the moral quality of forgiveness itself. For if forgiveness were offered only upon the performance of an act of contrition, the God's grace would be contingent on a human moral act. Actually divine forgiveness is itself the ultimate moral act that enables the human act of repentance and restitution to take place. Forgiveness as an extension of God's grace does not depend on some prior form of meeting the demands of the moral law; it is the source of the moral good that produces faith and repentance. The judgment of God thus takes place in the context of God's forgiveness. For his forgiveness is his intervention by which he risks his own moral good again for the sake of restoring humans to their moral and spiritual good.

Why do I say that this form of pastoral care is a form of absolution? Absolution is the certification of the moral good that forgiveness provides. The moral law cannot provide absolution, for it cannot provide forgiveness. Only God can provide absolution, for he provides forgiveness as the moral good that upholds humans in the very moment in which they are without a moral good or moral freedom of their own. The caregiver then serves as a moral agent in binding the moral good of forgiveness to the life of the person through intervention.

Absolution offered without intervention is impotent and inoperative. Intervention that does not intend to grant absolution is ultimately a betrayal of the moral good that forgiveness is meant to create.

Transfer of spiritual power: advocacy. As we turn to the second way pastoral care can be viewed as a helping ministry, we must look at the dynamics by which moral advocacy serves to empower the one who is morally powerless.

In suggesting that pastoral care is a transfer of spiritual power, I must immediately make a qualification. Here *transfer* does not mean a literal transfer of power inherent in the one who provides care to the one who receives it. I have already said that the caregiver does not possess moral authority or power by virtue of his or her role. Yet the caregiver must be connected to the source of spiritual and moral power, the basis of all healing and personal empowerment. An incident in the ministry of Jesus can serve as an example.

As Jesus was passing through a crowd, Mark tells us, a woman who had an incurable physical ailment reached out in desperation to touch him, thinking, "If I but touch his clothes, I will be made well." She was healed immediately. At the same time Jesus felt that "power had gone forth from him," and he turned to seek her out of the crowd. Upon her disclosure that it was indeed she who touched him, he said, "Daughter, your faith has made you well; go in peace, and be healed of your disease" (Mk 5:28-34).

There was, in effect, a transfer of spiritual power. The woman was in a powerless position. Perhaps she had concluded that her inability to be healed by the physicians with whom she had consulted was a sign of God's judgment upon her. The way Jesus had previously offered intervention as liberation from demonic possession and disease had encouraged her that there was an available source of power by which she could be healed. She saw Jesus as a contact with that power and felt that she only had to make the most tentative touch in order to have this power.

This transfer of power was a form of moral advocacy in that health is a moral good that issues from God, while disease is a moral evil that renders one powerless. Yet Jesus did not credit his power with effecting her healing, but her faith! His concern was not merely to exercise power to liberate her from her illness but to empower her by summoning from within her the spiritual power of faith.

This woman would certainly face other illnesses and other forms of evil before her life on earth was over. Liberation from disease or demons is not an end in itself. Rather, the true end of liberation is the empowerment of the person to stand against prevailing evil with a spiritual and moral assurance that she or he is not cut off from God's moral and spiritual good.

How does such a transfer of spiritual power actually take place through pastoral care? First of all, the caregiver brings into the desperate situation the moral and spiritual authority that resides in God's person and presence. The caregiver fills the void left by the devastation of evil, in whatever form, with a moral and spiritual presence that sends a signal to the powerless that there is a good that will prevail. This is done primarily through presence but also, as appropriate, with words and even touch.

Second, the transfer of spiritual power, which is the empowering of the other to have faith in the moral good that is available from God, takes place through a sharing of the pain and agony that the devastation has left in its wake. It was in taking upon himself human suffering, pain and distress that Jesus brought the powerless into contact with moral and spiritual power. We must understand very clearly the logic at work here. *It is the suffering of God that brings those who suffer into contact with his divine power and goodness.* It is in sharing in the sufferings of God that we are able to receive the power of God and become empowered to survive the onslaughts of evil.

The caregiver reveals the suffering God through identification with the pain of human suffering, and releases the power of God by bringing God into contact with human weakness and distress. This is an incarnational kind of caregiving; the presence and power of God are not necessarily expressed in religious words or symbols but are present, active and evident through actions and advocacy that combine intervention skills with interactional dynamics—psychological, sociological and spiritual. Certainly prayer, worship and religious symbols can be part of this process. But pastoral care as intervention and liberation effects the transfer of spiritual power ordinarily through nonreligious means.

This form of pastoral care is a kind of exorcism. Theological ethics provides pastoral care with a perspective on evil that takes mental illness seriously as a pathological form of human existence but that also leads the caregiver to become the moral advocate of the person suffering mental and emotional distress—over and against evil as an invading force.

Behind the accounts of the New Testament and the ministry of Jesus which depict evil as demonic and satanic oppression, and healing in some cases as a form of exorcism of the demonic, lies the positive truth that moral goodness does not only heal, it liberates. God's grace does not only medicate sickness, it sets up a shield against invading forces and powers that seek to destroy the moral, spiritual life of persons.

The development of the human self involves critical vulnerability to forces that have great power to affect the personality. Without this vulnerability, the person would not be open to the personal and spiritual empowerment of goodness. This vulnerability also means people can become subject to confusion and misdirection, yielding to the "spirits" that promise to alleviate or satisfy their needs, desires and intentions. One way of viewing exorcism is as a transfer of spiritual power by which the self is enabled to "cast off" alien power and be opened up again to the formative power of moral and spiritual goodness. Without the positive and continual reinforcement of the good that constitutes a healthy spiritual environment for the life of the self, we would all become deranged, subject to conflicting forces that are present all around us.

What appears as an extraordinary event of exorcism, with Jesus as the personal embodiment of the moral and spiritual goodness of God, points us toward the ordinary and "routine" forms of exorcism as means for an effective transfer of spiritual power and liberation of the person from conflicting and competing forces. These forces by their very nature defy categorization as either "from without" or "from within." The borderline between mental illness and demonic possession is ambiguous and indefinable.

A pastoral care perspective that reduces all emotional and mental distress to psychosomatic disorder casts persons hopelessly back upon themselves as ultimately responsible for their own sickness and healing. On the other hand, interpreting everything from a headache to psychotic behavior as demonic possession voids the person of moral and spiritual identity—and also leaves him or her in an absolutely powerless condition.

Theological ethics respects the ambiguity that conceals the borderline between sin and sickness, between mental illness and the powers of evil. Moral advocacy is quite prepared both to treat and to rebuke disease. Treatment comes under the category of intervention that applies medicinal and therapeutic technique and practices to restoring health and the power of the self to live with faith and hope. Rebuke comes under the category of intervention that places the afflicted person under the shield of divine grace, so that a *no* is expressed to certain forces and powers and a *yes* to the powers of health and moral goodness.

Jesus apparently did not practice an overt form of exorcism with any of his immediate disciples. Yet he did confront the forces of evil that sought to torment and confuse them. This is one way of understanding his saying "If any of you put a stumbling block before one of these little ones who believe in me, it would be better for you if a great millstone were fastened around your neck and you were drowned in the depth of the sea" (Mt 18:6). Many scholars believe that these "little ones" were not in fact the little children Jesus used as an example but were his disciples. This is a form of moral advocacy practiced by Jesus in pastoral care. He is rebuking whoever and whatever would seek to destroy their relation to him and warning that there are appropriate uses for millstones for such evil powers! Perhaps each of us ought to have a millstone hanging on the wall of the counseling office to remind us of this warning against the power of evil.

Speaking to the disciples, Jesus rebuked even some of their own ideas as having no source and no place within their love for God and for him: "Get behind me, Satan!" Jesus said to Peter in response to the suggestion that it was wrong for him to go up to Jerusalem where he would meet almost certain death (Mt 16:23). Swiftly Jesus exorcised himself from such a thought, which he viewed as contrary to God's moral will, and exorcised his disciples from allowing such thinking to find a place in their minds and hearts.

Those who undertake the ministry of pastoral care must have the discernment and moral sense to create an environment where there is a clear distinction between the kind of power that is evil and destructive and the power that is good and constructive. From the perspective of theological ethics, it is not necessary to draw this boundary at the line between demons and illness. What is important is that evil from any source, and by any name, is placed outside the horizon of moral goodness that positively defines the person who is the object of God's care.

The creation of a healing community: affirmation. A third way pastoral care functions as moral advocacy is in the creating of a healing community. God's grace is extended in the Christian community, the body of Christ.

The effect of sin is to produce estrangement and alienation from the human community. The immediate consequence of Adam's sin was an estrangement between God and human beings, as well as estrangement and alienation between the humans. The proper differentiation of the I-Thou relation has now become division. No longer is the other affirmed as "bone of my bones and flesh of my flesh"; instead "the woman whom you gave to be with me, she gave me fruit from the tree, and I ate" (Gen 3:12). No longer is Adam prepared to provide moral advocacy for the woman as he would for his own life. Instead when he is threatened he betrays her, placing her in the position of being the cause of his moral predicament. Even God is put on trial, so to speak, by Adam's moral autonomy—it is "the woman *whom you gave* to be with me"!

The test of true moral advocacy as a dimension of pastoral care is willingness to give affirmation to the person who otherwise would be vulnerable to the demands of the moral law and powerless in the face of God's judgment on sin. The one who provides caregiving must be ready to stand with the one who lacks status and to affirm that person as necessary to one's own good. Effective liberation, the goal of moral advocacy, is accomplished with the binding of the one who is estranged to the community of those who rest in God's moral good of forgiveness and community.

Moses' theological instincts led him to make precisely this kind of move when the people with whom God had established his covenant rebelled and worshiped the golden calf as an idol. Aaron, Moses' brother, disclaimed his own advocacy for the people when he claimed a kind of moral autonomy for his self-justification: "I threw [the gold] into the fire, and out came this calf!" (Ex 32:24). In contrast, Moses ascended the mountain to intervene between the sin of the people and the dreadful consequences that had befallen them.

In dialogue with God, who threatens to abandon his people and make a new beginning with Moses, Moses argues as the moral advocate of the people: "Alas, this people has sinned a great sin; they have made for themselves gods of gold. But now, if you will only forgive their sin—but if not, blot me out of the book that you have written" (Ex 32:31-32).

Moses interpreted God's stated intention to abandon his people because of their sin as a test of his knowledge of God's moral advocacy, which had its roots in God's covenant election and partnership. In arguing against God's stated intention to bring a final and fatal judgment upon the people, Moses knew that he was arguing out of the moral goodness of God, whose ultimate intention is forgiveness and affirmation rather than judgment and reprobation.

The content of affirmation is threefold. There is first of all the affirmation that intercepts the consequences of sin and lays claim to the person who otherwise would be alienated from all hope of moral goodness. In making intercession for his people, Moses placed his own relation with God on the side of the people who had sinned (Ex 32:32). Here there is also an interception of the demand of the moral law, so that the law does not end by destroying the image of God in persons; instead the moral law is redirected away from the lawbreaker to the lawgiver—to God, the creative source of moral goodness.

The one who offers pastoral care is a moral agent of such creative redirecting of the moral law so that the consequences of sin are not fatal and final. In doing this, that person represents God's own moral goodness, affirming the person as having extreme value to God.

The second aspect of affirmation is creative ritual effecting reentry into the community. When a plague falls on the people as a direct consequence of their sin, and God states that he will not reveal his presence to them as he has in the past, Moses entreats God, "Yet you have said, 'I know you by name, and you have also found favor in my sight.' . . . Consider too that this nation is your people." And God responded, "My presence will go with you, and I will give you rest" (Ex 33:12-14).

A ritual of reentry was created into fellowship with God, enacted by the renewing of the covenant between God and the people (Ex 34:10), followed by an offering of gifts for the tent of meeting: "And they came, everyone whose heart was stirred, and everyone whose spirit was willing, and brought the LORD's offering to be used for the tent of meeting" (Ex 35:21).

The third aspect of affirmation is the moral renewal that occurs in the offering up of thanksgiving. In the expression of thanksgiving the circle of moral advocacy is completed. Moses leads the people in a celebration of their affirmation by God: a renewal of the covenant and a liturgy of sabbath rest (Ex 35). What began as a movement toward those who are without moral status and without goodness as defined by the moral law is now completed as a movement of moral goodness expressed as thanksgiving to God as the source of healing and hope.

In the psalms of David, who is a paradigm of pastoral care from the perspective of the one who has experienced God's moral advocacy, we hear a repeated refrain of thanksgiving as the positive content of affirmation.

Let me hear joy and gladness;
    let the bones that you have crushed rejoice. . . .
Create in me a clean heart, O God,
    and put a new and right spirit within me. . . .
Restore to me the joy of your salvation,
    and sustain in me a willing spirit. . . .
O Lord, open my lips,
    and my mouth will declare your praise. (Ps 51:8, 10, 12, 15)

In this sense we can speak of the theological dynamic of pastoral care as a kind of Eucharist. Jesus added to his words of affirmation—"I have called you friends" (Jn 15:15)—the ritual of giving thanks through the Last Supper with his disciples.

Here pastoral care breaks out of the narrow confines of the therapeutic and clinical and enters into the creative and healing community that has at its center the eucharistic celebration of peace, God's shalom. Not only is pastoral care an extension of the healing community that provides the spiritual and moral resources for moral advocacy, but it leads back into the very center of the community, where a "new and right spirit" finds expression in eucharistic celebration.

This is no argument for a particular form of ecclesiastical ritual; it is an argument for the theological necessity of a eucharistic experience as the substantive content of each person's affirmation of being of extreme value to God. No person can see directly the moral goodness of God, as Moses learned when he requested such an experience (Ex 33:18). There is, however, an indirect yet powerful experience of God's moral goodness.

The final and therefore continual act of pastoral care is the creative experience of God's moral goodness as constitutive of one's own personal value and of one's own share in God's glory. As the apostle Paul exults, we are not like Moses, who had to veil his face so that the people would not see the fading away of the glory of God on his face. For we are ministers of the new covenant in the Spirit. "And all of us, with unveiled faces, seeing the glory of the Lord, . . . are being transformed into the same image from one degree of glory to another; for this comes from the Lord, the Spirit" (2 Cor 3:18).

It is the privilege of those who give pastoral care to see indirectly the very glory of the moral goodness of God in the faces and lives of those for whom we are moral advocates.

14

THE KINGDOM OF GOD AS THERAPEUTIC CONTEXT

T he concept of the kingdom of God is central to the Judeo-Christian tradition.[1] The kingdom is a social reality over which and through which God exercises his power and presence, rather than merely a realm over which he reigns. God promised Jacob's descendants a land, but he established a people before he gave them a land.

The kingdom of God is a culture that takes form in world culture. That is to say, there is a culture unique to a society and people whose personal, social and religious life is oriented to this particular God who makes a covenant with them. But this kingdom culture exists only as a particular form of "world culture." The cultural matrix of the Semitic people, descended from Shem, a son of Noah, became the world culture in which the kingdom culture took form. However, no essential language, race, sexual role, ethnic origin or worldview belongs to the culture of the kingdom of God. This was not made clear in the Old Testament, although it was implicit in the original covenant promise to Abraham—"in you all the families of the earth shall be blessed" (Gen 12:3)—and quite explicit in the prophecy of Joel: "I will pour out my spirit on all flesh; your sons and your daughters shall prophesy" (Joel 2:28).

The relativity of all world cultures became clear through the incarnation, death

---

[1] An earlier version of this chapter was printed in Ray S. Anderson, *Christians Who Counsel: The Vocation of Wholistic Therapy* (Grand Rapids, Mich.: Zondervan, 1990), pp. 81-102.

and resurrection of Jesus of Nazareth. Though Jesus was born a male Jew and was socialized into the Palestinian culture of the first century, his resurrection and the sending of his Spirit fulfilled the prophecy of Joel and broke down the wall of cultural particularity as a criterion of the kingdom of God (cf. Gal 3:26-29; Eph 2:14-22).

Thus again the kingdom of God is a culture with its own social and religious life that takes form in existing world cultures. The culture of the kingdom uses existing cultural forms and corrects and adapts these forms to the content and reality of the kingdom of God. The kingdom of God understood in this way has a therapeutic aim that seeks the health and wholeness of individuals in the context of the community that provides their core identity. God enters into the personal, social and historical life of people in order to release a motive power for wholeness (shalom), righteousness, faith, and love of God and neighbors.

Therapeutic Context
Understanding the therapeutic task in the context of the kingdom of God is critical for Christian therapists and pastoral counselors. It means that the context of each person's life is not alien to the culture of the kingdom of God. People can be accepted in the social context in which they live. Christian counselors can authentically relate to non-Christians at this level. The kingdom of God does not discriminate between those who believe in God and those who do not, but treats each person as someone created in the divine image and as an object of God's love and care.

This also means, however, that the kingdom of God works from within the existing social and cultural matrix of each person to bring liberation and healing, especially from the forms inflicted by that person's own social setting. The kingdom of God is not primarily a religious culture but a power that liberates and frees persons within their existing culture to experience the "human" culture that belongs by right of God's creation to each person.

No longer are individuals oppressed by impersonal and tyrannical world powers; they are liberated (as in the exodus) to become a new people whose social relationships become the source of personal identity, and power is transformed into covenant love.

No longer are people subject to the blind and capricious powers of nature; they are aligned with the power of a creator God who intervenes in natural forces and sustains the fragile life of his own people.

No longer are people possessed by powers and spirits that defile and destroy; they are filled and directed by the good and holy Spirit of God.

No longer do moral failure, outbreaks of cruelty and breakdown of family leave hopeless victims and unmediated guilt; the same God who demands holiness in life and action provides atonement, healing and restoration through rituals of forgiveness and renewal.

With the person and ministry of God incarnated through Jesus of Nazareth, the culture of the kingdom became a living power and presence. Through the calling of the twelve disciples, Jesus reconstituted the kingdom community and culture. He delivered the ethical mandate of the kingdom as the Sermon on the Mount and invited everyone, without discrimination, to enter the kingdom. Conflict arose between the culture of the kingdom and the prevailing culture of religious Judaism, where the concerns for justice, forgiveness, righteousness and healing had been forgotten.

Jesus did not specialize in individual therapy as a clinical procedure—though he did not turn away from offering such help. His concern was for the personal health and well-being that belong to persons created in the divine image. He called for the integration of the entire self and pointed to the healing and purifying power of the inner life directed outward toward others and toward God. He demanded the integration of religious truth with social concern. He sought the integration of prayer with feeding the hungry and healing the sick. He enacted the integration of social unity over the barriers of racial, sexual and religious discrimination.

Jesus left no person standing in the spot where they were healed; he either sent them back to be reintegrated with their own people, as a sign of the kingdom of God, or called them as followers into the new community of the kingdom.

Ecological Dynamics in the Therapeutic Process

As we turn our focus to spiritual dynamics in counseling, we need to clarify the ecological factors of human existence that bear on therapeutic interventions made by Christian therapists and pastoral counselors. The *ecological* dimension to the self involves relationship to others as well as to God. This necessarily entails a social and cultural context in which healing takes place.

Figure 14.1 represents the three spheres that make up the ecological construct of persons: physical, spiritual and social. The "ego-self" is present in each of the three spheres, but each sphere also touches on the others, affecting the behavior of the person.[2]

---

[2]The concept of ecological relationships was first developed in biology (1869) and then brought into the sphere of social science in 1944 by Kurt Lewin and later by Roger Barker, *Ecological Psychology: Concepts and Methods for Studying the Environment of Human Behavior* (Stanford, Calif.: Stanford University Press, 1968). The concept of ecological psychology was then developed by the "Kansas School," with emphasis on how the environment restricts and affects the range of human personality and behavior. Urie Bronfenbrenner applied ecological systems to human development in *The Ecology of Human Development: Experiments by Nature and Design* (Cambridge, Mass.: Harvard University Press, 1979).

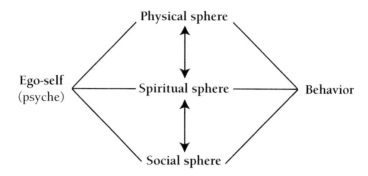

Figure 14.1. Three spheres making up the ecological construct of persons

S. L. Halleck writes in *The Politics of Therapy,* "There is no way in which the psychiatrist can deal with behavior that is partly generated by a social system without either strengthening or altering that system. Every encounter with a psychiatrist, therefore, has political implications."[3] This was certainly true for Jesus! The religious authorities condemned his healing of the man blind from birth (Jn 9) because it occurred on the sabbath. Jesus' healing challenged a social and religious system that tolerated people's sickness and deformities to preserve its institutional life. On one occasion, when confronted with a man having a paralyzed arm, Jesus challenged the authorities with a question: "Is it lawful to do good or to do harm on the sabbath?" (Mk 3:4). When they did not reply, he immediately healed the man. This healing directly challenged the prevailing ethical and religious culture of Jesus' society. Often he explicitly commanded those healed from mental illness to return to their homes and communities and there testify of their healing as a sign that the kingdom of God had manifested its power (Mk 5:19).

Therapeutic gains do not occur in a cultural or social vacuum. Christian caregivers are keenly aware of this—too keenly aware, in many cases, for their own comfort. They realize that they cannot intervene therapeutically without a conscious or unconscious intention to help the client adapt to his or her cultural context. The very fact that a person seeks therapy or is urged by others to seek help indicates some degree of cultural and social maladaptation. "Implicit in every therapy is a theory of culture," suggests Alvin Dueck.[4]

From a Christian perspective, the issue of a cultural theory with regard to thera-

---

[3]Seymour L. Halleck, *The Politics of Therapy* (New York: Harper & Row, 1971), p. 36.
[4]Alvin Dueck, "Righteousness," *Pastoral Psychology* 35, no. 4 (1987): 249. I am greatly indebted to Dr. Dueck for his contribution to my thinking about the kingdom of God as a context and resource for therapy as well as for the overall emphasis and some of the specific themes of this chapter.

peutic goals becomes critical. The counselor's attempts to extend therapeutic gain to include growth toward specific personal and religious values and goals could be viewed as inappropriate or even "unethical" from the perspective of secular culture.

The social and cultural context that the client brings to the growth process will affect the process in at least two ways. First, any growth or change in the client will require integration back into her or his culture and context. This often involves therapeutically redefining one's identity and relationship to that culture. Failure to make this integrative movement will leave the client alienated from the only culture he or she knows.

Second, the culture that the therapist brings to the situation will affect the growth process in some way. The long-range therapeutic goals negotiated between the therapist and client may require modifying the culture of either one. When the culture of the Christian counselor includes values and goals assumed to be essential to human health and wholeness as theologically defined, there may be a confrontation of cultures in working out the therapeutic goals. The counselor will have to determine how far these growth goals can be made part of the therapeutic goals without occasioning a confrontation that is disruptive and nontherapeutic. Even Jesus could not do more for some people than provide mental and physical healing. Beyond that he urged the transformation of the culture itself to provide a context for growth (as seen in the Sermon on the Mount, Mt 5—7).

When a Christian counselor has a client who is suffering mental and emotional abuse in marriage and the other partner will not respond to therapeutic intervention, a separation or even divorce may result. Counseling an alcoholic to sobriety will greatly affect the client's marital or family relationships. If a codependent is involved, that person, unable to sustain a relationship with a recovering alcoholic, may leave. The counselor's own values and cultural framework will be influenced as well. Therapeutic gains are social and cultural realities that affect both counselor and counselee.

For Christians who counsel, the biblical theme of the kingdom of God provides a therapeutic context in which to consider these factors.

The Praxis of Kingdom Therapy

This understanding of the context of therapy provides an approach to therapy from a Christian perspective. The kingdom of God is a therapeutic context that offers, as Jesus claimed, "the way, and the truth, and the life" (Jn 14:6).

☐ This way is the way of wisdom, which leads to the good and fulfilled life.

☐ This truth is the truth of righteousness, which gives moral worth and value to life.

☐ This life relates the individual to the community of faith and hope, a community extending beyond, yet including, this present existence with its suffering and sorrow.

These "ways," constituting the heart of the Christian life and grounded in Jesus himself, give us a threefold paradigm to explore further the culture of the kingdom of God as a context for therapy and pastoral counseling.

The way of wisdom: a discerning praxis. If people who seek help from counselors could express in one word what they would like, beyond relief from pain or depression, it probably would be wisdom. They would be quick to point out that wisdom does not mean knowledge, though knowledge helps. You may need knowledge to know how to take the first step, but before you take that first step you need wisdom to know how to take the second!

In the Old Testament, wisdom means discovering and living the kind of life that brings health, happiness and fulfillment. The book of Proverbs extols wisdom as fruitfulness, meaningful work, moral sensibility, and security for body and soul.

The kingdom of God provides a context for discerning and practicing wisdom. The wisdom of the kingdom is not abstract and theoretical; it is practical and within reach of each person through the right actions. Wisdom, says Samuel Southard:

> is reflection upon human possibilities and limitations in the light of God's revelation. It is guided both by realistic observations of ourselves and explanations of our attitudes and behaviors that are drawn from revealed knowledge of God's original intentions for his creation. The context for the wisdom of God is the power of his love shown in understanding of the self and others—both friends and strangers.[5]

Those who seek counseling often lament their inability to act and behave in ways that result in happiness and well-being. They know better than most philosophers that wisdom is discovered in the living of life, not in reflecting on it. This discovery of the way of living is called praxis. Wisdom is a discerning praxis, and as such it is one important aspect of the culture of the kingdom of God.

The concept of praxis originated with Aristotle, who distinguished between two kinds of action. The first he called *poiesis,* the act of making something that results in a product. The *telos,* the final value or character, of this activity is not included in the product. The second kind of action Aristotle called praxis. Here the *telos* is intentionally incorporated in the action as an outcome and also as a criterion for the quality of

---

[5]Samuel Southard, *Theology and Therapy: The Wisdom of God in a Context of Friendship* (Dallas: Word, 1989), p. ix. Southard also says, "And this is why some theologies are defective in wisdom. They do not prepare counselors for realistic testing of mind and heart. They do not deal with the question, how do we receive and respond to God's revelation? This misses a consistent theme of wisdom, that human claims of righteousness may conceal as well as reveal the self" (p. 2). C. Stephen Evans makes a distinction between wisdom and shrewdness. A shrewd person knows how to manipulate situations so as to gain the most and lose the least. True wisdom, says Evans, means understanding "one's own life, an understanding which may be painful. But the fact that wisdom cannot be guaranteed by a technique does not imply that nothing can be done to encourage the development of wisdom" (*Wisdom and Humanness in Psychology: Prospects for a Christian Approach* [Grand Rapids, Mich.: Baker, 1989], p. 71).

the action. In praxis, one not only is guided by the intention of realizing the *telos* but also discovers the telos through the action itself.[6]

The distinction can be illustrated in the construction of a house. We measure the competence of the builder by the technical specifications and quality of the house as a product of professional craftsmanship. The end use of the house, in terms of the character of the people who will inhabit it (its telos), is not a factor in its making. The builder would presumably devote the same skill and diligence to constructing a brothel or a church. The one who merely builds the house is not liable for its final use or purpose (telos). The way of wisdom is discovered through an authentic praxis in which God's purpose is more and more realized in the living of life.

Praxis is not merely a "practice" involving the making of a product or application of theoretical knowledge; it means discerning the truth as a final outcome of one's action. The action itself contains its own good end, and if the end is not "good," the action cannot be the right one. For example, when Jesus healed on the sabbath, he was acting in accordance with the telos of the sabbath—that is, God's purpose for the sabbath, reconciliation and restoration of life to its God-intended value. This was praxis. The religious authorities who challenged Jesus "practiced" the keeping of the law like a blueprint, ignoring the telos of the law of the sabbath. This was *pōiesis,* as Aristotle would say. Such blind keeping of the law concealed from the self-righteous Pharisees the true purpose of the law. Even more serious, their action failed to yield wisdom to see Jesus as the One in whom the work of God was actually present.

The Old Testament emphasizes that God in his actions intends good for his people. Likewise, the good life in word and deed will lead people to the goal of shalom— peace and prosperity as a divine gift.

Jesus reiterated this concept of wisdom embodied in praxis when he said, "You will know them by their fruits" (Mt 7:16), and "Why do you call me 'Lord, Lord,' and do not do what I tell you?" (Lk 6:46). He used the analogy of the good and the bad tree to make his point: "No good tree bears bad fruit, nor again does a bad tree bear good fruit; for each tree is known by its own fruit" (Lk 6:43-44).

The kingdom of God is revealed through a praxis that embodies the telos, or maturity, of a life through its actions. The New Testament Greek word *teleios* (mature, perfect) was used by those who translated the Old Testament into Greek (the Septuagint) to render the Hebrew word *salem* (shalom), which means "sound, complete, whole." The stress is on being whole, perfect or intact. The word is used of the heart

---

[6]Aristotle *Nichomachean Ethics* 9.6.5. For a more extended discussion of the concept of praxis as applied to the development of competence for ministry, see Ray S. Anderson, "Christopraxis: Competence as a Criterion for Theological Education," *Theological Students Fellowship Bulletin,* January-February 1984, pp. 10-13.

that is wholly turned toward God (1 Kings 8:61; 11:4) and of the person who is wholly bound to God (Gen 6:9; Deut 18:13).

Teleios is often used in the New Testament to mean "mature, adult, fully developed" (1 Cor 2:6; 14:20; Phil 3:15). Paul uses the word to say that he has not yet become fully "perfect" (Phil 3:12). But then he adds, "Let those of us then who are mature *[teleios]* be of the same mind" (Phil 3:15).

There is both an anthropological and an eschatological concept of maturity or perfection. From the anthropological perspective, maturity is not a process of ethical perfection realized by degrees. Rather, maturity is the undivided wholeness of a person in his or her behavior (cf. Mt 19:21; Jas 1:4). When applied to individuals, *teleios* does not denote the qualitative endpoint of human endeavor but anticipates eschatological wholeness in actual living.

For example, a baby is "perfect" if it is healthy and growing, even though it has not yet reached its "perfect" or "complete" maturity. Through the praxis of living, the child not only will grow but will discern and discover a way of living. No person's wisdom can be given to another; each must discover it through the praxis of living.

Jesus encouraged his disciples to "be perfect" even as the heavenly Father is perfect (Mt 5:48). In his high priestly prayer Jesus asked that his followers be perfected in unity so that the world might recognize the presence of Christ in their lives (Jn 17:21). Maturity therefore not only must relate to an eschatological goal but also must be a christological reality given in the present time through the gift of the Holy Spirit. The gift of the Holy Spirit is then confirmed through a praxis of living: the fruit of the Spirit—love, joy, peace, gentleness, goodness and so on—is experienced as part of what I have called growth goals.[7]

The "wisdom" discerned through praxis is not a maturity arising from age or experience alone. It is a gift of discernment by which one's life is secured and upheld from an ultimate source—God's love and grace. In a praxis of faith one's attitudes, emotions and actions become ordered and integrated through appropriation of this reality. This is to "know the truth" (Jn 8:32). It is to "walk in newness of life" (Rom 6:4), to "live by the Spirit" (Gal 5:16), to "live in love" (Eph 5:2) and to "walk during the day" rather than in darkness (Jn 11:9).

The metaphor of walking pictures praxis as the discernment of wisdom. To "take up one's bed and walk" (see Jn 5:8) is not merely for the exercise but to be integrated back into life, to gain the maturity of those who are fully functioning personally and socially. The physical healing that enabled the paralyzed man to walk also reintroduced him to

---

[7]For additional information on the concept of maturity or perfection see Colin Brown, "Telos," in *New International Dictionary of New Testament Theology*, ed. Colin Brown (Grand Rapids, Mich.: Zondervan, 1976), 2:59-66.

his society and culture; he could no longer carry about with him the old culture of being a cripple. In carrying his own bed he now has a praxis of life to discern the wisdom of life as his personal goal and purpose within his social and communal life.

Paul's exhortation to those who steal calls for the praxis of wisdom: "Thieves must give up stealing; rather let them labor and work honestly with their own hands, so as to have something to share with the needy" (Eph 4:28). It is not enough to cease committing a crime. The one who formerly stole must now become productive so as to contribute to the life of others.

The apostle Paul suffered an apparently incurable physical problem that he called his "thorn in the flesh." After praying three times for it to be removed, he came to the understanding that it was to be a means of grace: "My grace is sufficient for you." Therefore, concluded Paul, "[God's] power is made perfect in weakness" (2 Cor 12:9). By this way of wisdom one can gain inner strength and coherence of life to cope with what cannot be removed or changed.

Now then, how does the kingdom of God serve as a context for therapy? We must see that therapy offers more than psychological restoration. The goals of therapy go beyond removing physical or emotional dysfunction. Integrating self with self, with others and with God is a praxis that discerns meaning and purpose. The way of wisdom is the *telos* that reaches into the actions (praxis) of therapy to enable the client to establish a coherent meaning to life. This itself can be transforming, even when not every situation can be transformed. There are losses that can only be grieved: a failed marriage, the loss of a child through abortion, damage done to others through one's carelessness.

The moral law supports moral judgments in such cases. But the moral law does not itself contain wisdom's freedom to provide healing and restoration. The kingdom of God brings moral wisdom, not merely a relentless application of the moral law.

The church is often tempted to think its primary responsibility is to uphold the moral law of God—and thus those without moral virtue or standing are left exposed as victims or failures. But if the church as the sign of the kingdom of God in the world is to embody the moral wisdom of the kingdom, it will need to offer restoration and renewal to those who have no moral standing.

To say that God hates divorce (see Mal 2:16) does not give the Christian community the right to deny God's grace to those who have experienced the tragic failure of marriage vows. The moral wisdom of God receives greater emphasis in the Old Testament than God's moral outrage! The story of Hosea contains a powerful message of mercy and grace extended to a people who have "committed adultery" with God as their marriage partner, yet are the objects of God's love and renewal in grace. The restoration of a person who has shattered a marriage, aborted a fetus or damaged another person's life has high priority with God, for it is the restoration of his image in humanity. The tension between upholding the divine order in its perfection and upholding the divine intention in restoring humanity is a praxis of moral wisdom. Christian caregivers are agents of redemption when they function in this way.

Therapists who wish to bring a Christian perspective to bear in the therapeutic process need to have the "maturity" or wisdom that comes through praxis before they set themselves up in "practice." So too the criteria for assessing and measuring effective therapy will consider the client's growth goals in terms of the wisdom that belongs to those who experience the kingdom of God.

The Gospels tell of a demon-possessed man who lived naked among the tombs and bore the broken chains with which his former neighbors had tried to control him. After Jesus healed the man, he was found "sitting at the feet of Jesus, clothed and in his right mind" (Lk 8:35). We marvel at the healing of this man's emotional and mental condition. But who provided the clothes? The man's clothing symbolizes his reentry into the community, his acceptance with trust and loving care, and his newly discovered praxis of community. In the end this healing, marked by his clothing and acceptance into the community, is as great a marvel as the healing of his tortured mind.

In a sense this case is a parable of the culture of the kingdom of God as therapeutic context. Jesus could not have done the healing alone. The man was not "made perfect" until he was clothed and restored to community.

The wisdom and the healing praxis by which one's life is made whole are marks of the culture of the kingdom of God. This is the way Jesus offers as the discernment of wisdom for life.

The way of righteousness: a coherent moral vision. The biblical concept of truth is lodged in the larger concept of righteousness. The righteousness of God is his acting "rightly" so as to bring forth the truth. We cannot be "in the truth" unless we are rightly related to God and to our neighbor. The opposite of truth is unrighteousness, a life devoted to deception and deviousness. This is a basic theme in Paul's letter to the Romans (especially chaps. 3-6).

A life congruent with the truth of God's purpose has a moral vision that is shared with one's community and culture. In the Christian community and culture, moral vision and moral discourse permeate all structures and relationships. Stanley Hauerwas makes this point:

> The church as a community of moral discourse gives meaning to its ethical terms. To use such terms as freedom and equality as values that are Christian and hence appropriate in a theory of government or therapy neglects the fact that these terms have material content in Jesus' definition of the Kingdom and as they are incarnated in His life and death. Ethical terms are not self interpreting but require a tradition to give them content.[8]

---

[8]Stanley Hauerwas, *A Community of Character: Toward a Constructive Christian Social Ethic* (Notre Dame, Ind.: University of Notre Dame Press, 1981), p. 134.

In the environment of the kingdom of God, personal goals are thus subject to kingdom goals; at the same time, kingdom righteousness is exemplified in the integrity of social relationships. While the kingdom is concerned with the inner righteousness life of the individual person, it is even more concerned with justice for the oppressed, fairness in trade and commerce, regard for the poor and the "stranger within the gate," and genuineness in approach to God through the worship and rituals of community life.

The kingdom of God imposes a coherent moral vision on existing cultural and social structures, stressing righteousness as an ethical link between persons and a religious connection between the people and God. In the culture of the kingdom of God, the moral and spiritual apostasy of one person affects the righteousness of the community. This is seen when Achan stole and hid some of the things taken from the enemies in the Israelites' victory over Jericho. His single action caused Joshua's defeat in the next military campaign, and the writer says that in this situation the people of Israel broke faith (Josh 7). In many other incidents, the actions of a few resulted in the loss of righteousness for the entire people.

A coherent moral vision, then, is not an abstract set of moral principles. It is a vision of the social structure of community in which individual lives are bound up in a coherent and interconnected whole.

The righteousness of a single person is derived from the righteousness of a people as a whole. However, this righteousness is not the result of the perfecting of individual moral lives. The righteousness of the people solely depends on the grace of God, who constitutes them as a people. The covenant, as the binding metaphor of this relation between the Lord and the people, is the basis for the moral vision of a people who "belong to Yahweh" and are a holy people because he who called and constituted them as a people is holy.

This can be seen from another perspective as well. The individual partakes of the righteousness of the community as a privilege and gift. Circumcision sanctified a person symbolically both by cutting away the flesh of natural origin and by creating a new identity as a covenant person. The community, not the individual act, was the source for renewal of faith and the renewal of moral and spiritual integrity.

The community functioned both as administrator of justice and as mediator of mercy between God and the individual. No private contrition or familial bond could sufficiently dissolve the ethical relation of the individual to the community. Achan repented of his wrongdoing, but the community nonetheless stoned him to death for his sin. Parents might excuse their children's rebellious acts, but they still had to hand them over to the elders of the community for discipline (Deut 21:18-21).

Yet the community was also commanded to provide cities of refuge for the "manslayer" to find protection against the avenger (Num 35). Righteousness is not only retribution for wrongdoing to satisfy a sense of moral justice; it is an act of restoring lost personhood. The community, as the source of a person's moral dignity, provides that moral worth through concrete actions of social inclusion.

In dealing with "outsiders" and those without any claim to righteousness, Jesus himself provided a circle of refuge for the sinner. To self-righteous critics who accused him of indiscretion, he said, "The tax collectors and the prostitutes are going into the kingdom of God ahead of you" (Mt 21:31; see also Lk 7:29-30).

The one who mediates between the individual and the community performs a priestly service, both as an advocate of the individual who approaches the community for healing and restoration, and as representative of the community, an agent of righteousness. This priestly service is closely linked to the growth process, releasing a motive power to experience change and growth. As an intermediary, the one who performs priestly service shares a common humanity and mediates the righteousness of grace and healing:

> Every high priest chosen from among mortals is put in charge of things pertaining to God on their behalf, to offer gifts and sacrifices for sins. He is able to deal gently with the ignorant and wayward, since he himself is subject to weakness; and because of this he must offer sacrifice for his own sins as well as for those of the people. And one does not presume to take this honor, but takes it only when called by God, just as Aaron was. (Heb 5:1-4)

This person embodies the moral horizon that constitutes the community of the kingdom of God. But the person does not function primarily as an *ethical* agent, bound to ethical codes of professional practice alone. This person is an agent of *righteousness*. It can be a therapeutic gain to remove psychological guilt, but to establish the person in righteousness places the person in truth. The gift of forgiveness and peace is affirmed by one's belonging to and participating in the kingdom of God. Such forgiveness goes beyond even contrition and confession, which themselves are not sufficient to establish righteousness. The righteousness of the kingdom of God is a social and communal reality mediated through and by the one who performs priestly service.

Therapists and pastoral counselors can represent this culture of the kingdom of God. They need to think of righteousness in terms of a life that is given a moral horizon as a growth goal in addition to the growth goals of the process of therapy. The wisdom that people seek when they come for counseling will often be hidden from them, and perhaps from the counselor as well. A skill even more important than clinical intuition is the discerning praxis of wisdom that orients the client to a trajectory of health and growth beyond specific therapeutic gains.

Didn't Jesus suggest that, with his authority and presence, every Christian could act as an agent of righteousness (cf. Jn 20:21-23; Acts 1:8)? The early church seemed to think so. "You are a chosen race, a royal priesthood, a holy nation, God's own people, in order that you may proclaim the mighty acts of him who called you out of darkness into his marvelous light. Once you were not a people, but now you are God's people; once you had not received mercy, but now you have received mercy" (1 Pet 2:9-10).

Christian counselors should represent the coherent moral vision embodied in a community that offers righteousness beyond therapeutic gain. Such counselors provide the growth goal of righteousness through authentic forgiveness and affirmation by a community representing the kingdom of God.

Does this mean that a Christian therapist must in every case provide therapy through the institutional form of the Christian community—say a local church setting? Not necessarily. In the parable of the good Samaritan, it was the Samaritan who became the agent of righteousness, not the priest or the Levite, both of whom represented the institutionalized religious community.

It does mean, however, that the concept of "private practice" will be radically qualified for the Christian therapist, because the mediation of righteousness requires a living community as a context in which the therapist lives and to which the therapist is accountable. It also means that to lead the client past therapeutic gain, the counselor must establish on the trajectory of growth the goal of righteousness as embodied affirmation of belonging.

There can be no definitive model for the way a Christian therapist serves in a professional capacity. Many work at mental health or psychological clinics where services are offered without a context of community or church support. In these cases, therapists will have to think out for themselves what it means to provide this service as a Christian, establishing growth goals beyond mere therapeutic gain.

Kirk Farnsworth, who offers a concept of "embodied integration" based on an incarnational model, suggests that one of the best strategies for bringing our counseling practice under the lordship of Christ is to establish a group of believers to whom we are professionally accountable. This provides a Christian forum for discussion, prayer and shared concerns and also places the counselor in a context and culture that extends the Christian community.[9] But what about the growth goals of the client? The counselor may try to provide this linkage for the client if it does not already exist. Who will "clothe" the client when therapy comes to an end? And just as important, what community will provide the moral horizon of health (righteousness) for the client during therapy?

---

[9]Kirk E. Farnsworth, *Wholehearted Integration: Harmonizing Psychology and Christianity Through Word and Deed* (Grand Rapids, Mich.: Baker, 1985), p. 90.

These questions have no easy answers. The Christian who counsels, however, cannot define therapy so narrowly as to ignore the culture of the kingdom of God as a context for therapy. The concept of "private practice" will need to be reexamined from this perspective. If we use the adjective *Christian,* we must recognize it as a verb of action that includes a praxis of community life.

The implications of what we are saying here also apply to the church. A Christian community that is not providing this "priestly" service of therapy "on the streets," so to speak, is failing to be neighbor to those in need. In the culture of the kingdom of God, the community cannot itself sustain righteousness without being also the "good Samaritan."

We are tracing out the implications of the kingdom of God as a culture that provides a context for therapy from a Christian perspective. Using the formula statement of Jesus—"I am the way, and the truth, and the life"—we are developing a context for therapy that includes wisdom, righteousness and now community. The community of the kingdom fulfills the individual's quest for identity, meaning and hope.

The way of the community: an embodied identity. The emergence of "identity" psychologies in the early and middle part of the twentieth century was as much a response to the growing emphasis on the individual self and the thirst for experience as to a weariness with earlier naturalistic and biological attempts to explain human behavior. Behavior no longer preoccupied therapists, but rather the phenomenon of the person as an experiencing self.[10] Humanist and existential psychologists found a ready market for a variety of new therapies in contemporary Western society, where older, traditional ties of community identity were broken or rejected outright. The quest for "reality" even led to "reality therapy" (William Glasser).

Alvin Dueck suggests that naming reality is the central task of any healer. When the search for reality at the experiential level moves the self inward rather than outward, the person loses reality. In the ecological model of personhood presented above, I suggested that people operate in a three-sphere matrix: the physical, the social and the spiritual. The self (psyche/soul) is totally present in each of the three spheres, but the reality of the self is experienced as a praxis of intentionality, belonging and identity that includes all three. This is what "embodied identity" means.

---

[10]In late-nineteenth-century Germany, Wilhelm Dilthey (1833-1911) was outspoken in urging the need for a psychology that would appreciate individuals as living entities capable of personal integration. In the early part of the twentieth century, other German psychotherapists continued an emphasis on the whole person, including Wilhelm Stem, Kurt Goldstein and Edward Spranger. Other psychiatrists and psychologists developed humanistic psychologies in this direction, including Alfred Adler, Karen Horney, Erich Fromm, Kurt Lewin, Gordon Allport and Carl Rogers. For an excellent survey of some of these psychologies see Roger Hurding, *The Tree of Healing* (Grand Rapids, Mich.: Zondervan, 1988), chaps. 6-7.

Embodiment is not only in one's physical body but in the "body" of the community, a corporate identity from which self-identity is derived and on which it is always somewhat dependent.

The identity of Abraham, Isaac and Jacob—founders of the new family and community of the kingdom of God—was given embodiment through the covenant promise of God. The ritual of circumcision was one form of creating a new identity. The new identity, of course, was actually the naming of reality: the individual was integrated into the tradition of the community in continuity with Abraham, Isaac and Jacob. Interestingly, this ritual affected the identity of the self (psyche/soul) at three levels. Identity was literally (1) cut into the flesh through circumcision, which was both (2) a ritual of incorporation into the family and community and (3) a sign and seal of the spiritual reality of covenant promise by which one became a member of the kingdom of God. Circumcision, like the Christian ritual of baptism, is not performed on oneself; it is performed by significant others who represent the community or "body" that gives the person primary identity.

The community that represents the culture of the kingdom of God names this reality through story, in which the tradition is carried forward through its living members. Personal identity is thus derived from the community identity of a people who have as their essential being a history of community with God. This identity is firmly grounded in a particular history of a people of God. This is one reason the concept of history is so important for the Hebrew people.

Losing this community identity and participation in a living history will result in a sense of anomie or disassociation for the individual. The person may move from finding his or her reality in community to finding it in the reality of the inner life. Brooks Holifield suggests that this tendency appears in the development of a distinct emphasis in pastoral counseling over the past several centuries in North America: "The story proceeds from an ideal of self-denial to one of self-love to self-culture, from self-culture to self-mastery, from self-mastery to self-realization within a trustworthy culture, and finally to a later form of self-realization counterpoised against cultural mores and social institutions."[11] Holifield also suggests that the contemporary preoccupation with psychology may be traced to the influence of experiential piety in religion.

German theologian Wolfhart Pannenberg has analyzed the effect of "penitential piety" as related to the loss of a sense of community identity in Western society. He points out that the Protestant tradition has emphasized attaining an individualistic spirituality based on a sense of deep personal guilt over sin and suggests that a better model for spirituality would be celebration of one's life in community. This he calls

---

[11]E. Brooks Holifield, *A History of Pastoral Care in America: From Salvation to Self-Realization* (Nashville: Abingdon, 1983), p. 12.

"eucharistic piety."[12] It is indeed possible that modern culture's tendency toward self-realization owes something to a religious inwardness that has become separated from the righteousness of the kingdom of God. The culture of the kingdom demands a righteous concern for the "fatherless," that is, those whose identity as members of the community is threatened. This righteousness integrates marginal persons into the mature life of the community; it does not segregate them through discriminatory practices or institutional dormitories.

"Our believing is conditioned at its source by our belonging," writes Michael Polanyi.[13] Therapeutic gains that do not establish or reinforce a trajectory of growth through participating in community life as a culture of the kingdom of God fall short of the growth goals essential to the maturity of the self. It is not enough to give a name or create an identity for an individual. The naming of reality by which personal identity is formed and sustained is a function of community, not the client or the therapist. The character of this community will determine the significance of the identity and reality by which the members are named.

In the early church, baptism was sometimes enacted as a household or family ritual (cf. Acts 16:33). But even if performed on an individual, it was always with the intent of baptizing the person into the community, and it was always an act on behalf of the community. For many people entering the culture of the kingdom of God represented a break with previous family and kinship ties. This necessitated a praxis by which a new sense of family and kinship became a concrete reality.

The church has never fully developed its function as a "therapeutic bridge" for individuals who lack a strong sense of identity and belonging in modern society. In fact, many of the church's evangelistic methods may actually contribute to the breakdown of persons' social identity. The remarkable proliferation of clients from within the Christian church who are seeking therapeutic relief from personal and emotional stress may be one indication of this.

While this phenomenon assures a ready market for Christian therapists, one has to question the root cause of the failure of psychological health among church members. This book aims to present a case for a Christian approach to therapy that will address the structures of Christian community itself, both as a contributing cause to lack of emotional health among its members and as a resource for providing a context where growth goals can be realized beyond mere therapeutic gain.

For all its concentration on the concrete present and the history in which one's present is grounded, the kingdom of God embodies a strong sense of the future. This

---

[12]Wolfhart Pannenberg, *Christian Spirituality and Sacramental Community* (London: Dartman, Longman & Todd, 1983).

[13]Michael Polanyi, *Personal Knowledge* (London: Routledge & Kegan Paul, 1958), p. 322.

future does not merely extend the present into some ideal state of existence beyond today, although that expectation exists. The future in the culture of the kingdom is a reality that is coming into the present.

The kingdom of God presents the future as advent, as a reality that is coming into the present. It is given as promise and carries signs in the present of its coming to us. For Christians, this advent has occurred in the coming of Jesus Christ as the incarnation of God himself and, therefore, as embodiment of the future that belongs to all who are in the kingdom. The physical and psychical healings by Jesus can be understood as dramatic signs of ultimate wholeness and healing.

Promise, then, does not mean escaping the present but using the future as a basis for belief and as a growth goal by which the self can experience integration and wholeness. Promise enables and empowers us to grasp with hope the present and all its imperfections and uncertainties. The maturity of faith integrates hope into a realistic and creative approach to life.

How can people experience now this hope that provides wholeness and faith? Through forgiveness of sin, for one thing. Absolution is not merely a formal pronouncement, because it liberates us from the consequences of our actions and from psychological and spiritual anguish. It assures us that our hope for forgiveness and freedom from sin will not in the end be betrayed.

Beyond the therapeutic gain that comes from dealing with the inner dynamics of guilt through confession, absolution as an act of the community is a growth goal. Here too the therapist must mediate between the client and the community, which uses the therapist to embody its culture as a people of God.

Hope can also be experienced now in the promise that life itself is a value and good that cannot be lost through one's feelings of insignificance or the threat of suffering or even death. The kingdom of God does not make suffering a good, but it affirms the one who overcomes suffering through patience and steadfast hope.

Does my small life count? Does what I do, despite my failures and even deliberate digressions from the good, really mean something in the end? I should hope it does! The gift of God's Spirit, the community upholding my baptism, and the reality of belonging that holds me even when I suffer confusion, disorder, or sickness—all these compel me to hope and empower me to live.

15

THE CHURCH'S MISSION TO THE FAMILY IN A POSTMODERN CULTURE

The structure of the family in any society is a reflection of the cultural ethos and traditions of that society. In the face of what appeared to be relativism and pluralism, Christians in the modern era have tended to appeal to a version of the family thought to transcend cultural and social forms. Biblical texts were chosen which lent support to definitions of family based on a Western/European, often bourgeois view of the family. The ideal family was narrowly construed as the nuclear unit of husband, wife and one or more children, living together and separate from extended family members.

Armed with what was considered to be a "biblical" and therefore morally correct concept of the family, missionaries moved aggressively into other cultures, often deploring their forms of family life as unbiblical and therefore immoral. Where polygamous marriage traditions existed, for example, missionaries refused to baptize males until they abandoned all of their wives except one, regardless of the social and moral consequences for the abandoned wives.

A student newly arrived on our campus from Africa was asked by a colleague of mine whether his family had come with him. The student replied, "Oh no, they had to remain back in Africa."

"I'm so sorry," my colleague responded; "it must be difficult to be here for such a long time without your family."

"Not really," he replied, "my wife and children are here with me!"

Somewhat chagrined, my colleague realized that he was speaking a different cultural language when it came to family, though the conversation took place in English.

The Emergence of a Postmodern View of Reality

Only recently have some theologians awakened to the fact that their construct of a biblical version of the family was essentially a reflection of what has now become known as the "modern" period of Western intellectual and ethical thought, baptized as the Christian norm.[1] In brief, the modern mindset was optimistic, always looking for progress as knowledge increased—for knowledge was good. The modern mindset valued objective certainty, based on rational—rather than religious or mystical—means of attaining truth. The modern mindset looked for totality and unity in all knowledge, believing that all rational minds operating independently would come to similar conclusions about what is universally true and good.

In contrast, a postmodern worldview celebrates diversity, which can result in moral relativism and a demand for tolerance. Claims of universal truth and norms are now considered by some postmodernists as arrogant and imperialistic, with a "secretly terroristic function."[2]

From a Christian perspective we can agree that claims of universal truth objectively held by the human mind cannot certify the truth of divine revelation. A modern view of reality based solely on objective human thought is not Christian, and we should be prepared to make this concession.

Second, Christians can agree with postmoderns in acknowledging the importance of communities in our perception of truth. None of us is an autonomous individual, cut off from the influences of social traditions. We belong to communities that help shape our perception of reality. The distrust of reason as the sole basis for truth leads to the conviction that truth must be experienced to be believed. It is in the church as the community of believers that the truth of the gospel is experienced and lived out.

Third, postmodernism rightly emphasizes the significance of narrative and story. Though there is skepticism and even hostility toward metanarratives in our postmodern world, that condition cannot last. Human beings cannot live without the meaning and purpose that such stories give. In deconstructing the false stories of modernism,

---

[1] Bill Kynes, "Postmodernism: A Primer for Pastors," *The Ministerial Forum* (National Evangelical Free Church Ministerial Association) 8, no. 1 (1997).

[2] J. Richard Middleton and Brian J. Walsh, *Truth Is Stranger Than It Used to Be: Biblical Faith in a Postmodern Age* (Downers Grove, Ill.: InterVarsity Press, 1995), p. 71.

postmodernism plays a useful function, "pulling the smiling mask of arrogance from the face of naturalism."[3] But it has no answers of its own for the future.[4]

What effect this shift to a postmodern view of reality will have on the church and its ministry to families remains to be seen. We must look again at the Bible as God's revelation of divinely created purpose for persons who exist primarily and essentially in social structures, including the family.

Revisiting a Biblical Perspective on the Family

Biblical theologians now realize that the Bible does not give us a definition of family intended for all cultures and societies. The quintessence of family from a biblical perspective is covenant love, expressed in a variety of social and familial forms.[5] The Bible does not describe one cultural form of family intended to serve as an ideal, nor does the Bible focus on the family as the primary form of the kingdom of God. Swiss theologian Karl Barth says:

> In the more limited sense particularly the idea of the family is of no interest at all for Christian theology. . . . When the New Testament speaks of a "house," it means the *familia* in the comprehensive sense of a household fellowship which can become the centre of the message heard and reproduced in the wider life of the community. . . . Parents and children are still emphasised, like men and women, masters and servants, but as persons and for the sake of their personal connections and duties. The family collective as such plays no further part at all.[6]

The gospel of the kingdom and the gospel of the family. The first-century Christian community came into existence amid social and political orders that were largely determinative of family life. The traditional Jewish social structure bound family life to the rigid requirements of the law as interpreted by the scribes and enforced by the religious authorities. In the Gentile world, the sacred myths and concepts were secularized to provide stability and continuity. In the face of these structures which demanded rigid conformity, Jesus spoke of a kingdom that challenged the priority of older structures and appeared to set aside family relations as dispensable. "Everyone who has left houses or brothers or sisters or father or mother or children or fields, for my name's sake, will receive a hundredfold, and will inherit eternal life" (Mt 19:29; see also Mk 10:29-30; Lk 14:26).

The gospel of the kingdom was thought to contribute to the breakdown of essential social constructs of marriage, family, obedience of parents, even economic and

---

[3]James Sire, *The Universe Next Door: A Basic Worldview Catalog*, 3rd ed. (Downers Grove, Ill.: InterVarsity Press, 1997), p. 189.

[4]Kynes, "Postmodernism."

[5]Ray S. Anderson and Dennis B. Guernsey, *On Being Family: A Social Theology of the Family* (Grand Rapids, Mich.: Eerdmans, 1985), p. 14.

[6]*CD* 3/4, pp. 241-42.

political structures. The radical demands of the kingdom were indeed couched in terms that challenged these structures as having a prior claim upon men and women. Yet the actual practice of Jesus affirmed the validity of familial structures, even though they were relativized to the demands of the kingdom of God. What the sayings of Jesus concerning the radical demands of the kingdom challenge is one's captivity to domestic and social relationships, not their role in upholding human life. The coming of the kingdom of God means the end of the absolute hold, the "spell," that the social and natural order has over the person—for first of all God has determined us to be free to love him and also to love our neighbor. The kingdom of God values love as the core of discipleship. A gospel of the family is included in a gospel of the kingdom.

In his letter to the Ephesian Christians, the apostle Paul draws out the implications of the gospel of Christ: the basic structures of a society are to be humanized through the activation of the Spirit and law of Christ. Paul did not seek to replace the Ephesians' culture with a "Christian culture." Rather, he called for the liberation of authentic human life within the culture as a freedom from the magical and mythical.

Paul provides a criterion of Christian community that is grounded in Christ's identification with those in whom his Holy Spirit dwells. Both Jew and Gentile must learn to shift their obedience and loyalty from traditional authority by which they sought stability and order to the structure of social life regulated by the community as the body of Christ (Eph 2:11-22). The foundational social structures of family, marriage, parents and children, as well as existing political and economic structures, are basically affirmed as good and necessary. Yet all of them are radically qualified by the "humanization of humanity" that comes through Jesus Christ (Eph 5—6).

In drawing persons around him, Jesus re-created humanity in a community of shared life and common identity. Even the narrower circle, defined by the specific calling of the Twelve, was structurally open to the "unclean leper," the tormented demoniac, the self-righteous Pharisee, the woman of ambiguous reputation. In contact with Jesus, humanity was liberated from the blind and capricious powers of nature and disease, as well as from the cruel social and religious tyranny of the powerful over the weak. In the real humanity of Jesus we see the humanization as well as the socialization of humanity.

The incarnation and the humanizing of social structures. In Christian theology, the event of God's incarnation in Jesus Christ is understood as a social paradigm by which human nature and destiny are defined and determined. A Christian anthropology does not begin with the "humanity of humankind" seeking relationship with God. Rather, a Christian anthropology begins with the "humanity of God" as observed in the historical person Jesus Christ and with the social structure of the new human community within which he is known.

This approach does not deny the empirical form of humanity that we experience.

It makes possible the perception of humanity within a particular social and cultural setting without confusing this sociocultural form with the core social structure of humanity itself. At the same time, this allows particular forms of humanity in their cultural settings to retain their distinctives.

If there is a culture that belongs to the kingdom of God and transcends all other cultures, it is a culture of true humanity as the gracious power and presence of Christ in a structure of human social and personal relations. This culture of the kingdom of God has no other language and no other custom than that of the particular people and society who become its manifestation. Yet existing social and cultural forms are relativized to the real humanity of Jesus Christ, expressed through the embodiment of the gospel in the lives of Christians. One culture is not relativized to another culture, as has often tragically happened in the missionary expansion of the church. Rather, every culture is related to the critical construct of real humanity through the power of the gospel. In this way every culture can bear in its own social structures the reality of the kingdom of God and can make manifest the humanity of the kingdom through its own forms.

One of the most devastating effects of social chaos is the breakdown of structures that are assumed to provide social stability and moral authority. Being human means living as this specific person belonging to these particular people who speak the same language and participate in the same rituals of community life. All human self-perception is thus culturally conditioned and socially approved. Not to have the social approval of one's own people is to suffer estrangement, if not derangement. Jesus himself experienced this powerful social judgment when he was thought to have an "unclean spirit" by the standard of the self-perception of the Pharisees (Mk 3:30). Even his mother, brothers and sisters sought to intercept his ministry and remove him from public exposure because they concluded, "He has gone out of his mind" (Mk 3:21).

The effects of sin and the Fall, as recorded in the third chapter of Genesis, were the breakdown and confusion of the core social structure that bound the first humans to each other and, together, to God. From that point on, social and cultural patterns of human life reflected various degrees of distortion, alienation and conflict. The moral and spiritual integrity of human life is bound up in the social structures particular to a society and culture. Humans cannot exist apart from some social structure, even those that are less than perfect or are actually corrupt.

The kingdom of God exposes sin and seeks to overcome its effects through the liberation of humans from sinful structures that stand as an authority over them, as well as from inner motives of pride and self-seeking which tend to undermine all authority. The effects of sin are overcome not through a more rigorous form of spirituality but through a renewed structure of sociality. Love is defined as living peaceably in a domestic setting, as clothing the naked and feeding the hungry, and as loving the neighbor as oneself.

Concepts of human rights, of justice, of concern for the unborn and the aged are not ethical perceptions subject to cultural modification but constraints on individual and collective actions that violate the very structure of humanity. When Jesus healed on the sabbath, ate with tax collectors and sinners, and asked a Samaritan women to minister to his thirst, he penetrated through racial, sexual, social and cultural barriers to restore true humanity to others. Indeed, his own nature could hardly have been true humanity if he had drawn back from the real humanity of others.

Jesus did not institute some new ethical concept of the good as a "Christian ethic." He merely reinstated the criterion of goodness that belongs to true humanity as the ethical foundation for all of the laws and commandments. This same criterion was quite clear to the prophet Micah: "He has told you, O mortal, what is good; and what does the LORD require of you but to do justice, and to love kindness, and to walk humbly with your God?" (Mic 6:8).

The Core Social Paradigm and Family Formation

Human beings are defined by the social structures of their behavior as well as by the ritual forms of their culture. Hidden within every culture lies an implicit social paradigm of humanity. This implicit social paradigm is the precritical mass out of which social theories are developed and with which cultural anthropologists and philosophers work.

All humans exist essentially in concrete social relationships or a core social paradigm, as Herbert Anderson helpfully points out:

> A theology of the family is shaped by two similarly contradictory principles. First, the family is a necessary component of creation. Despite wide diversity of form and function throughout human history, the family has fulfilled God's intent to provide a context for creation and care in order to insure the continuity of the human species. . . . There is no known human community without family in some form.[7]

Experience of family is indispensable to the development of personhood; it is the "world" of the child, as Brigitte and Peter Berger put it:

> Children need a *world* to grow into. [This world is not merely a physical environment, but a social environment in which socialization occurs.] Socialization is impossible without a strong sense of belonging existing between the child and one or more "significant" adults. Minimally, therefore, every human society must provide community in the social locale where children are raised.[8]

In this sense family can be said to be the "locale" or "world" where primary social-

---

[7]Herbert Anderson, *The Family and Pastoral Care* (Philadelphia: Fortress, 1984), p. 31.
[8]Brigitte Berger and Peter Berger, *The War over the Family* (Garden City, N.Y.: Doubleday/Anchor, 1983), p. 146.

ization takes place. No cultural form of the family can completely conceal or deny the nature of humanity as it confronts us in the sheer objectivity of core social relations. We know humanity in its concrete form; this is discovered in the core social paradigm.

All theories regarding the nature of human beings are culturally relative. If a social paradigm of humanity lies behind each particular culture, however, then it is possible that the social structure of humanity contains elements of a common denominator, or essential core, that is recognizable to some extent in every culture, race and ethnic community.

The core social paradigm that is the basis for all human life regardless of cultural context has at least three components. These can be drawn from the creation story in Genesis 1—2. Humans are related to the concrete world (taken from the dust), to each other (bone of my bones, flesh of my flesh) and to a transcendent spiritual reality (made in the image of God).

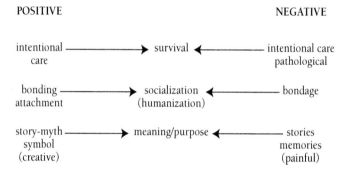

POSITIVE   **NEGATIVE**

Figure 15.1. The core social paradigm

First, having been created originally out of the dust of the ground, we are creaturely beings, dependent for our basic needs on our earthly environment. Second, our personal existence and identity are grounded in the life we experience with others in community. And third, we are spiritual beings; our quality of life is grounded in the ultimate reality that gives hope and meaning in the face of frustrations, failures and the finality of death.

The core social paradigm is subcultural, existing within every human culture and society as the "hermeneutical criterion" for evaluating family roles and relationships. A depiction of this core paradigm (figure 15.1) parallels to some degree Abraham Maslow's hierarchy of needs but is meant to be more developmental than hierarchical.

The core social paradigm in this model begins with the basic human need of survival—food, drink and shelter as well as other "creature comforts." Humans are born "premature," as it were; each infant is totally dependent on others for the intentional care that is necessary for survival. Every human society, regardless of its cultural patterns, must provide this intentional care in order to survive. It is on this basis that social customs and cultural patterns must be judged as either leading to healthy human development or pathological.

Second, the core social paradigm includes some form of socialization, which becomes the formative process of human development. A culture's bonding or attachment rituals and practices perform this task, in either a positive or negative fashion. The need for bonding in development can lead to a form of bondage that cripples and deforms the spirit. Every culture is thus accountable for the moral development of its members by holding in check and exposing the tendency for traditional and culturally approved rituals and practice to become bondage.

Third, the core social paradigm depicted in figure 15.1 involves provision of meaning and purpose to those under the authority and influence of those responsible for developing and maintaining the community's life. The stories, myths and symbols used by a culture—and all cultures have them—fulfill this function, often mediated by priests, elders, teachers and parents. Where these stories and symbols enhance and liberate the spirit by inspiring sacrificial love, abiding faith and sustaining hope, they are creative and enriching. Where the stories and symbols produce negative effects, they are painful and destructive.

More important than who fulfills the role and provides the function at each level is that it is done effectively. Cultures have ways of identifying and mentoring persons who are charged with the responsibility of filling these roles. But there is a danger. Those who carry the role responsibility can wrongly assume, or be expected to believe, that it is their role that gives them moral and spiritual authority. When this occurs, authority can become authoritarian and tyrannical, if not abusive.

Not all experiences of family are positive. Theodore Roszak points this out dramatically:

> The violation of personhood begins in the cradle, if not in the womb. . . . We are born into other people's intentions. We learn our names and our natures at their hands, and they cannot teach us more truth than they know or will freely tell. Can there be families whose love is not treason against our natural vocation? . . . We know that every ideal that supports the family has been used to tell a lie.[9]

This is reminiscent of a statement by Hauerwas: "No one rules more tyrannously than those who claim not to rule at all because they only want to love us."[10]

---

[9]Theodore Roszak, *Person/Planet* (Garden City, N.Y.: Doubleday/Anchor, 1979), pp. 139, 142.
[10]Stanley Hauerwas, *A Community of Character: Toward a Constructive Christian Social Ethic* (Notre Dame, Ind.: University of Notre Dame Press, 1981), p. 172.

There is no single cultural form of family that carries the moral authority by which all others can be judged. When abuse occurs, or the kind of violation of which Roszak speaks, we must look deeper than cultural forms of family and hold up the core social paradigm as the basic moral basis for accountability. I have argued that the core social paradigm is rooted in a biblical account of the creation. A biblical theology of the family must build on this model and take into account God's redemptive purpose in relation to family. This must be done in the context of the social and cultural patterns and practices that determine the forms of family structure and relations in a fallen and sinful world.

Recovering a Biblical Theology of Family

Looking again at the Bible, we see that while certain cultural role patterns are viewed as means by which the core paradigm is carried out, it is the actual function and result that God values and expects, not who it is that performs the role. The people of God in the Old Testament were basically a patriarchal society, with some forms of polygamy accepted as common practice. The twelve sons of Jacob who became the founders of the twelve tribes were born to four women. Yet this same tradition, as later expounded by Moses, clearly taught a monogamous form of marriage as reflective of the divine image (Gen 2:23-24). Working from within the cultural form of the "family" as it existed at the choosing of Abraham, God revealed a deeper core of human dignity and integrity that showed polygamy to be inherently degrading and inhuman.

Thus we fail to find in the Bible a single, unambiguous *form* of family that we can with certainty call the "Christian family." At the same time, the *content* of the word *family* is unambiguous and carefully contoured with moral and spiritual authority when grounded in the core social paradigm. Herbert Anderson expresses it well:

> A theology for the family begins by identifying themes from the whole of the Christian tradition that are of particular significance for understanding the family. Such an approach seeks to avoid absolutizing either the family or the theological tradition. It allows for the possibility of a lively interaction between Christian texts/traditions and common human experience. A theology for the family begins by exploring general theological principles—order, change, uniqueness, mutuality, justice, forgiveness, diversity—in order to understand first of all what it means to be live in a family. The pastoral theologian's agenda is not to identify a "Christian family" but to help people find ways of being Christian in families.[11]

My former colleague Dennis Guernsey used to say, "We should speak of 'familying'

---

[11]Herbert Anderson, *The Family and Pastoral Care* (Philadelphia: Fortress, 1984), pp. 15-16.

rather than of 'family.' Family is a verb before it is a noun." Being family is grounded in the core social paradigm rather than in any particular cultural pattern and practice.

All things being equal, certain social forms relating to marriage and family serve more effectively and efficiently to fulfill the mandate of the core social paradigm. Monogamy rather than polygamy has already been mentioned. Yet there are many monogamous marriages that are abusive, destructive and close to being demonic. For this reason we cannot lodge moral law and biblical authority with the form of marriage alone.

Given the confusion and uncertainty in our present culture, even among Christians, we need to clarify and give fuller expression to a biblical theology of the family in our postmodern world. Based on the argument developed thus far, I offer these suggestions as a tentative step toward such a task.

The family as image of God. Contemporary attempts to define a biblical theology of the family come to grief when they begin with role relationships within marriage and family rather than with the quality of life that persons experience within these roles and cultural patterns. Because the Bible does not present a single, unambiguous model of marriage and family structure, one form or another of a contemporary cultural form is assumed with Scripture texts chosen to make it a "biblical" model.

When we look at the biblical account of creation we can discern the contours of family life revealed in the core social being of human life. "It is not good that the man should be alone" (Gen 2:18) precedes "Therefore a man leaves his father and his mother and clings to his wife, and they become one flesh" (Gen 2:24). The latter statement is often taken as a reference to the first marriage, and thus discussion of family is based on the social institution of marriage rather than on the essential core of human social existence. Marriage, as it becomes clear in the New Testament, is a possibility, not a necessity, for persons to find fulfillment as created in the divine image. Social being, however, is a necessity, as the Genesis 2:18 text makes clear.

The first human was not deficient because he lacked a wife but because he lacked a human counterpart necessary to his existence. The divine image is not grounded in a social or cultural pattern but in a core social relation. Biblical theologian Phyllis Trible draws out of this story the exegetical point that this first "man" prior to the creation of the woman was not described as a male but merely as *adam*, the Hebrew equivalent of "earth creature," a term closely related to the Hebrew word for "earth" (*ha-adama*). Trible therefore concludes that the creation of human persons as "male and female" (*ish* and *isha*) occurs only after both are present simultaneously, not sequentially.[12]

---

[12]Phyllis Trible, *God and the Rhetoric of Sexuality* (Philadelphia: Fortress, 1978), pp. 80, 99.

The mutual existence of the first humans constitutes the essential core of what the Bible means by family—mutual care—where development in self-identity, personal maturity, acquiring of moral values and spiritual formation take place. Because our reproduction takes place through sexual relations, marriage is needed as a social institution that binds parents to another prior to their bonding to offspring. Yet it is not marriage that constitutes the essence of the image of God but mutual, creative and spiritually enriching social existence.

The family as a social context for identity formation. "In every hour the human race begins," wrote Martin Buber.[13] Biologically this may be true. All creatures begin anew with the perpetuation of their own species through the reproduction of their individual components. But more is needed than biological reproduction to be human persons. Personhood is certainly a mystery—not only the question of why there should be persons at all, but the fundamental mystery in the experience of one's own personhood. Without the mystery of personhood, love and relationship would be little more than instinct and drive. Biological creatureliness is a necessary but insufficient condition for human existence. Personal existence with a sense of self-identity derives from existence in relation to other humans.

Social scientist Clara Mayo says that human "dependence of offspring is much longer than in animals and is guided by more than the biological heritage. Only sustained social contact enables the child to develop a sense of self and a capacity to cope with the tasks that the environment presents."[14] The development of self-identity therefore is based not only in being created as persons in the divine image but in becoming persons through the socializing process—experiencing bonding and attachment to other persons.[15]

The failure of care and love as a social context for formation of self-identity is a deprivation of personhood, not merely an ethical fault. Ordinarily it is assumed that the biological parents will provide this essential matrix of social relation, but often others—extended family members or foster or adoptive parents—assume this responsibility. Again, a biblical theology is not so concerned with who provides the context of care but that it is provided. Whatever definition we give the word *family,* it is the context of primary social relations that, for better or for worse, contribute to the formation of self-identity and moral character.

The family as a moral context for character formation. The shift from the modern to postmodern view of reality has raised the question of the status of values with regard to marriage and family. If moral values are no longer held to be universal principles

---

[13]Martin Buber, *Between Man and Man* (London: Collins/Fontana, 1961), p. 109.
[14]Clara Mayo, "Man: Not Only an Individual, but a Member," *Zygon* 3 (1968): 21.
[15]Anderson and Guernsey, *On Being Family,* pp. 55-56.

binding on all persons regardless of their social institutions and cultural patterns, then where do we look for moral guidance in a multicultural society? If cultural diversity and moral ambiguity have replaced uniformity and certainty in our postmodern world, does each community determine its own moral standards? And what does this mean with regard to a biblical view of moral character?

The moral foundation on which commandments are given in the Bible is not abstract principles but the core social bond of love. Jesus' two great commandments—love of God and love of neighbor—are both based on love (Mt 22:37-39; cf. Deut 6:5; Lev 19:18). The apostle Paul wrote that all of the commandments of God are grounded in the law of love.

> Owe no one anything, except to love one another; for the one who loves another has fulfilled the law. The commandments, "You shall not commit adultery; You shall not murder; You shall not steal; You shall not covet"; and any other commandment, are summed up in this word, "Love your neighbor as yourself." Love does no wrong to a neighbor; therefore, love is the fulfilling of the law. (Rom 13:8-10)

Family is the context of primary relations responsible for the care and development of persons in the image of God. This is an intrinsic moral responsibility, with moral character determined by quality of life grounded in the core social paradigm. All moral principles and all commandments, as Paul has indicated, are ultimately grounded in the moral structure of life lived in mutual care and common commitment to the development of the human potential of each person.

Because parents are considered to be the primary caregivers, the Bible places responsibility for the development and formation of moral character on mothers and fathers. "Hear, my child, your father's instruction, and do not reject your mother's teaching; for they are a fair garland for your head, and pendants for your neck" (Prov 1:8-9).

At the same time, parents do have not have ultimate authority, even over their own children, for parents are accountable to the larger community in their responsibility to develop their children's moral character. In Hebrew culture, failure at this level required judgment and discipline by the elders in the community. Parents could not shield their delinquent and disobedient children from the community's ultimate responsibility to discipline (Deut 21:18-21).

Thus moral development and character formation are delegated to the primary unit of family, but ultimately belong to the community itself. Yet the community is not free to base its standards on cultural patterns from its own tradition and ethos, but is to derive its moral criteria from the core social paradigm that lies behind all cultures and social institutions. In this way the core social paradigm places the responsibility for moral character formation within the community. Moral values are acquired within each core social unit of family, not relative to each community's moral culture.

Postmodern thinking tends to emphasize each community's own narrative of its moral perception of reality. In this perspective it is hard to avoid the charge of moral relativism. The core social paradigm overcomes this problem by lodging moral values and character in that which is essential to the full expression of human life in faithfulness to the biblical mandate. This means that the core family unit is the critical context for moral values and character formation. This grounds the criteria for moral character in the social core that underlies all cultures. Abuse of children, for example, is a moral transgression cutting across all cultural attitudes and patterns.

The temptation to impose moral imperatives in the hope of engendering spiritual conformity to biblical principles is hard for pastors and therapists to resist. Some, in a zeal to justify their role as a Christian counselor and avoid the appearance of offering only secular psychology, find it necessary to speak of moral values and imperatives.[16] Others who are anxious about their own spiritual life may feel morally compromised by clients who exhibit immoral behavior or attitudes. They then impose moral imperatives on others as a way of reducing their moral anxiety. The effect is the same. To offer moral imperatives to one in need of empowering grace is to give a stone when one asks for bread.

What is normative in biblical teaching is not a certain structure or form of family, but acting and living in ways that create, nurture and support persons within their social structures, including marriage and family. This is why "familying" is a verb. Being family is a process of spiritual formation, even as living in the power of the Spirit redeems and restores family.

Spiritual formation is a process of spiritual empowering more than a program of moral development. The contemporaries of Jesus were scandalized by his apparent tolerance of the lack of conformity to the moral law among those to whom he brought the good news of the kingdom of God. What concerned Jesus were the personal and social disorders and derangements that marginalized people and minimized their significance. "I came not to judge the world, but to save the world," he said (Jn 12:47).

Spiritual formation, as one aspect of family therapy, cannot afford to use moral judgments as qualifying standards attached to healing presence. God's moral freedom is the basis for God's moral law. Unconditional grace mediated through the spiritual power of forgiveness is itself a moral quality of love. Moral imperatives without spiritual empowerment only cripple and condemn. To moralize under the guise of Chris-

---

[16]Ray S. Anderson, *Christians Who Counsel: The Vocation of Wholistic Therapy* (Grand Rapids, Mich.: Zondervan, 1990).

tian counseling is a form of spiritual abuse.

The family as the domestic context of spiritual formation. Not only are human beings intrinsically social, but spirituality is located at the essential core of social being. Spiritual formation is thus an essential component of self-identity and competence in social relationships. A theology of the family that fails to recognize spiritual formation as the essential core of each person's growth toward maturity is reductive, partializing and lacking in therapeutic insight.

In his doctoral dissertation completed at the University of Berlin, Dietrich Bonhoeffer wrote that the general spirituality of persons is woven into the net of sociality: "It will appear that all Christian and moral content, as well as the entire spirituality of [persons], is possible and real only in sociality. . . . Here we have to show that [a person's] entire so-called spirituality . . . is so constituted that it can only be seen as possible in sociality."[17]

The social structure of personhood is intrinsically spiritual. Social spirituality thus reflects the divine image and likeness constitutive of the human person, not a religious feeling, instinct or practice. The individual person exists as structurally open to the spirit of another person as well as to the Spirit of God. German theologian Jürgen Moltmann reminds us, "The Spirit of God does not constitute something alongside of, or merely inside of a person as an individual. Rather, the Spirit of God joins the human spirit at the core of its social reality. Human spirituality is the core of the self as it becomes a self through social relation with others."[18]

Social spirituality is not only the source of authentic relation with God, it is the first casualty of sin and in need of redemption. What the apostle Paul calls the "works of the flesh" as contrasted with the "fruit of the Spirit" are symptomatic of negative and pathological social spirituality—enmities, strife, jealousy, anger, quarrels, dissension, factions (Gal 5:20). These are some of the diagnostic categories by which the Bible identifies sin—not first of all violations of an abstract moral law, but breakdown of the social spirituality that is necessary for healthy marriage and family life, as well as other social relations.

The therapeutic effects of spiritual formation through the indwelling of the Holy Spirit are likewise described in terms of healthy social spirituality—love, joy, peace, patience, kindness, generosity, faithfulness, gentleness, self-control (Gal 5:22-23). Authentic spiritual life is learned in the context of primary relationships; it is a domestic skill.[19]

---

[17]Dietrich Bonhoeffer, *Sanctorum Communio* (London: Collins, 1967), pp. 44-45.
[18]Jürgen Moltmann, *God in Creation: A New Theology of Creation and the Spirit of God* (San Francisco: Harper & Row, 1985), p. 263.
[19]Anderson and Guernsey, *On Being Family*, pp. 115-28.

Every person speaks two languages when expressing the deeper pain of the soul. Clients speak their pain with both a psychological and a spiritual voice. The counselor who does not have "bilingual" competence will tend to reduce symptoms to either psychological treatment or spiritual instruction.[20] An integrative approach to counseling draws on multilevel competence in recognizing and dealing with persons as physical, social, psychological and spiritual beings.

We are reminded again of the man who not only was possessed of demons but who had become a maniac, running naked and wild among the tombs, mutilating himself. After the demons were cast out, he was found "sitting at the feet of Jesus, clothed and in his right mind" (Lk 8:35). The casting out of demons was relatively easy. And self-destructive behavior was stopped. But the ministry of Jesus went beyond modifying behavior. The man, clothed, sane and open to the kingdom of God, offered by Jesus images what all Christian ministry should have as its aim. In this case the result was systemic, hygienic, ecological and integrative. The clothes did not come with the casting out of demons. Someone in the community—his family we hope—reached out to him and reclaimed him.

We may be attracted by dramatic exorcisms, but they are no shortcut to spiritual formation. We do not always know what demonic powers lie hidden in the pathology of mental illness. Nor should we attempt to develop a diagnostic category of demonic disorder as a therapeutic technique. But in removing the effects of demonic disorder, we have, in effect, practiced a kind of exorcism without naming the devil. Spiritual formation restores and rebuilds the life of persons from the inside out.[21]

This chapter has examined the shift from a modern to a postmodern view of reality and its effect on a biblical theology of the family. With certain qualifications, we can accept the postmodern emphasis on family as closer to a biblical perspective as represented by the core social paradigm that underlies all cultural forms and practices. Cultural diversity can be allowed as expressive of the essential components of the core social paradigm. At the same time I have argued that the moral and spiritual values that determine authentic family life are not relative to any particular culture but are intrinsic to the quality of human life that God intended. The church's mission to families thus seeks to bring the good news of the kingdom of God as a redemptive and healing ministry to all people within their own cultural and ethnic identity. Cultural sensitivity begins with respect of persons. The culture of the kingdom of God

---

[20]See Deborah van Deusen Hunsinger, *Theology and Pastoral Counseling: A New Interdisciplinary Approach* (Grand Rapids, Mich.: Eerdmans, 1995).
[21]Ray S. Anderson, *Self Care: A Theology of Personal Empowerment and Spiritual Healing* (Grand Rapids, Mich.: Baker, 1995).

restores the moral and spiritual character of persons in the context of their primary social relations—the family. In this way culture too is redeemed and brought into conformity to authentic human life as created by God.

16

HOMOSEXUALITY
Theological & Pastoral Considerations

How should the church respond to some of its members who openly acknowledge homosexual orientation and practice, particularly with regard to the office of teaching and pastoral ministry? My purpose in this chapter is not to promote further polarization and division within the church. Rather, I would like to contribute to an ongoing discussion in which compassion and clarity, along with a sense of the tragic, provide a context for the church to acknowledge both fallibility and faithfulness in attempting to be the body of Christ under the authority of Scripture and the guidance of the Holy Spirit.

The ancient world had no word for or concept of "homosexuality" as it is currently used today. The word *homosexual* was not coined until 1869, when a Hungarian physician writing in German used it with reference to males and females who from birth are erotically oriented toward their own sex. The word first appeared in English in 1912, according to the *Oxford English Dictionary,* and its earliest use in an English Bible was in 1946, in the first edition of the Revised Standard Version rendering of 1 Corinthians 6:9.[1]

The Biblical Data
Examination of the biblical texts must therefore take note of the problem of transla-

---

[1]See Victor Paul Furnish, "The Bible and Homosexuality: Reading the Texts in Context," in *Homosexuality in the Church: Both Sides of the Debate*, ed. Jeffrey S. Siker (Louisville, Ky.: Westminster John Knox, 1994), pp. 18-35.

tion into English of the original Hebrew and Greek terms. Theological reflection on homosexuality within the Judeo-Christian tradition begins with an examination of the biblical data. Unfortunately, the question "What does the Bible say about homosexuality?" has not led to answers on which all can agree. Some have even argued that an appeal to Scripture cannot settle the issue at all, as this is basically a moral and not a theological concern.[2] Same-sex relations are mentioned in the Bible, however, and so the biblical data must be taken into account in consideration of homosexuality as it relates to Christian faith and practice.

There is no biblical passage referring to homosexuality as a "condition" or "orientation." The word *sodomite* appears nowhere in the Hebrew text of the Old Testament, not even to designate a person living in ancient Sodom. The Hebrew term translated as "sodomite" (*qadesh*) in the King James Version refers to a male temple prostitute (Deut 23:17-18; 1 Kings 14:22-24; 15:12; 22:46; 2 Kings 23:7; Joel 3:3). Though the English word *sodomite* is used twice in the New Revised Standard Version (1 Cor 6:9; 1 Tim 1:10), it is an incorrect translation of the Greek words *malakoi* and *arsenokoitai*.

The story of the incident at Sodom (Gen 19:1-25), which can be read as an attempt to rape Lot's two male visitors by a mob of other males, is not often cited in subsequent Scripture as a sin of a homosexual nature. In Ezekiel 16 the sin of Sodom is named as greed and indifference to those in need. In Matthew 10:12-15 and the parallel passage in Luke 10:10-12, Sodom's sin is described as inhospitality in general. In Matthew 11:23-24 the city's destruction is recalled as a reminder of what happens to those who rebel against God.[3] The book of Jude, however, identifies the sin of Sodom as sexual immorality: they "pursued unnatural lust" or, as the Greek puts it, "went after other flesh" (*sarkos heteros*; Jude 7). Much more was wrong with the citizens of Sodom than the sexual intent described in the story. But as David Wright points out, this consideration should not be allowed to eliminate the sexual element from the text and the moral judgment implied.[4]

Based on Leviticus (Lev 18:22; 20:13) and New Testament texts (1 Rom 1:26-27; 1 Cor 6:9; 1 Tim 1:10), some have argued that homosexuality is an "unnatural affection" contrary to God's will. This interpretation reflects an assumption that a male's having sex with another male is forbidden in the holiness code of Leviticus 18 and thus homosexual practices of all kinds are forbidden, including contempo-

---

[2]Pim Pronk, *Against Nature? Types of Moral Argumentation Regarding Homosexuality* (Grand Rapids, Mich.: Eerdmans, 1993).

[3]Furnish, "Bible and Homosexuality."

[4]David F. Wright, "Homosexuality: The Relevance of the Bible," *The Evangelical Quarterly* 61 (1989): 291-300.

rary homosexual relations between committed homosexual partners.[5]

The context of the Leviticus prohibition indicates that an act by two males where one takes the part of the female is a violation of the maleness of both; the Hebrew text literally says one partner is required to "lie the lying of a woman."[6] The Hebrews did not appear to make a distinction between same-sex practices and a same-sex orientation or condition. Rather, the emphasis was on an objective act that violated the holiness code separating "clean" from "unclean" actions and objects as a representation of Israel's separation to the holiness of God.

There is no record in the Gospel traditions of Jesus making any comments about same-sex relations, though he did offer clear teaching concerning fornication, adultery and remarriage (Mk 10:6-9; cf. Mt 19:4-6). Jesus' silence on this point, however, does not necessarily constitute approval. It would be unlikely that the practices the Pauline texts forbid within the Hellenistic Jewish community would have been unknown during Jesus' time. It is more likely that the immediate context of Jesus' ministry amidst the Hebrew-speaking Jews did not present situations demanding his response. Romans, 1 Corinthians and the Pauline text in 1 Timothy make specific references to same-sex relations, each with a negative connotation.

> Do you not know that wrongdoers will not inherit the kingdom of God? Do not be deceived! Fornicators, idolaters, adulterers, male prostitutes, sodomites . . . (1 Cor 6:9)

> For this reason God gave them up to degrading passions. Their women exchanged natural intercourse for unnatural, and in the same way also the men, giving up natural intercourse with women, were consumed with passion for one another. Men committed shameless acts with men and received in their own persons the due penalty for their error. (Rom 1:26-27)

> This means understanding that the law is laid down not for the innocent but for the lawless and disobedient, for the godless and sinful, for the unholy and profane, for those who kill their father or mother, for murderers, fornicators, sodomites, slave traders, liars, perjurers, and whatever else is contrary to the sound teaching. (1 Tim 1:9-10)

What is at dispute is the exact meaning of the terms used in these texts. *Malakoi,* translated "male prostitutes," literally means "soft ones." From this some have concluded that the word denoted the passive partner in a same-sex relation—thus "effeminate."[7] The second word used by Paul is *arsenokoitai* (1 Cor 6:9; cf. 1 Tim 1:10), which the NRSV translates "sodomite." The word is actually a compound word

---

[5]George Grant, *Unnatural Affection: The Impuritan Ethic of Homosexuality in the Modern Church* (Franklin, Tenn.: Legacy Communication, 1991).
[6]Furnish, "Bible and Homosexuality," p. 20.
[7]Ibid.

including the words for "male" and "bed." Victor Furnish suggests that the word was coined by Paul and refers to a male who has intercourse with another male.[8] Other sources suggest that *arsenokoitai* was in use in at least a limited sense prior to Paul.[9]

Paul's statement in Romans is explicit regarding same-sex relations and is descriptive in nature rather than prescriptive. In this text Paul does not state what Christians should or should not do; rather, he describes the consequences of rebelling against God and turning to one's own passions as an object of desire and even worship (Rom 1:25). At the same time, from Paul's statement here it is difficult to conclude otherwise than that Paul would say that those who are "righteous" would not or ought not do these things. The word *unnatural* (Rom 1:26) translates the Greek phrase *para physin*, which is standard terminology in other ancient texts for homoerotic acts.[10] From this it can be argued that Paul clearly identifies homosexual relations as sinful and contrary to God's purpose for men and women.[11]

The biblical concept of sin is not restricted to specific acts but addresses the fundamental structure of all that is human, including sexuality. This is the context of Paul's statement concerning homosexual relations. "The wrath of God is revealed from heaven against all ungodliness," Paul writes. Therefore none is better than another, for all are "under the power of sin" (Rom 1:18; 3:9).

At no point does Paul elaborate on his reasons for his negative view of same-sex relations. From other contemporary sources, however, scholars have discovered that homoerotic acts were viewed as "willful" disregard for one's natural relations with the opposite sex and "lustful" excess of sexual desire extending beyond what was "natural" within the marriage relationship.[12] According to some theologians, the context of the biblical texts that appear to condemn same-sex relation is culturally determined. They suggest that what is forbidden is not consenting, committed same-sex relations grounded in love, but rather the use of same-sex relations in idolatrous worship or the sexual use of a boy by an adult male, a threat to what was considered to be "natural" sexual relations between men and women. Consequently, some conclude that the Bible is silent regarding contemporary same-sex

---

[8] Ibid., pp. 18-35.

[9] James H. Moulton and George Milligan, *The Vocabulary of the Greek Testament* (London: Hodder & Stoughton, 1972).

[10] Richard B. Hays, "Awaiting the Redemption of Our Bodies: The Witness of Scripture Concerning Homosexuality," in *Homosexuality in the Church—Both Sides of the Debate*, ed. Jeffrey S. Siker (Louisville, Ky.: Westminster John Knox, 1994), pp. 3-17.

[11] Cardinal Joseph Ratzinger, "Letter to the Bishops of the Catholic Church on the Pastoral Care of Homosexual Persons" (1986), in *Homosexuality in the Church: Both Sides of the Debate*, ed. Jeffrey S. Siker (Louisville, Ky.: Westminster John Knox, 1994), pp. 39-48; Andy Comiskey, *Pursuing Sexual Wholeness* (Santa Monica, Calif.: Desert Streams Ministries, 1988); Grant, *Unnatural Affection*.

[12] Furnish, "Bible and Homosexuality."

relations grounded in love and fidelity.[13]

While the purpose of this chapter is not to resolve the debate on purely exegetical grounds, one can hardly dismiss all of these texts as irrelevant. Robert Johnston has reminded us that the context of Paul's statements in Romans 1 goes beyond human lust and disorder within one's nature. Homosexuality, while not the worst sin, is nonetheless listed by Paul among sins that are regarded as distortions of God's intended order.[14]

Those who argue that the "Bible is silent" with respect to homosexual relations that are grounded in personal love, fidelity and mutual openness will dismiss the Leviticus texts as well as Paul's statement in Romans 1 as irrelevant. But for those who say that the silence is broken by the Genesis 1:26-27 text, the Romans 1 and Jude 7 texts confirm the view that same-sex genital relations are contrary to God's intended purpose for humans created as male and female in the divine image. In response to the question about grounds for divorce, Jesus responded, "From the beginning of creation, 'God made them male and female' " (Mk 10:6; cf. Mt 19:4). Here Jesus reminds us that we must go back to the beginning and search out the contours of human sexuality as originally designed by God as the theological context in which to discuss any issues of sexuality—including homosexuality.

The purpose of this chapter is to present critical theological reflection on the issues concerning homosexuality as both an orientation and a practice within the contemporary Christian community. Here, then, is a summary of my conclusions drawn from the above discussion. These points serve also to introduce the next and major concern of the chapter.

First, it is admitted by all that the biblical literature includes no positive statements regarding same-sex relations, regardless of what the context may be. At best, those who argue that same-sex relations between committed and loving partners are within God's purpose must argue from silence.

Second, the argument from silence would require that one dismiss the unique and original appeal to nature in Paul's statement in Romans 1. The allusions to nature in Romans 1:20, 25 suggest that Paul held to a divinely created order with regard to

---

[13]See, for example, James B. Nelson, "Sources for Body Theology: Homosexuality as a Test Case," in *Homosexuality in the Church: Both Sides of the Debate,* ed. Jeffrey S. Siker (Louisville, Ky.: Westminster John Knox, 1994), pp. 76-90; Jeffrey S. Siker, "Homosexual Christians, the Bible and Gentile Inclusion: Confessions of a Repenting Heterosexist," in *Homosexuality in the Church,* pp. 178-94; Robin Scroggs. *The New Testament and Homosexuality* (Philadelphia: Fortress, 1984); George R. Edwards, *Gay/Lesbian Liberation: A Biblical Perspective* (New York: Pilgrim, 1984); John Boswell, *Christianity and Social Tolerance: Gay People in Western Europe from the Beginning of the Christian Era to the Fourteenth Century* (Chicago: University of Chicago Press, 1980).
[14]Robert Johnston, "Homosexuality and the Evangelical: The Influence of Contemporary Culture," in *Evangelicals at an Impasse* (Atlanta: John Knox Press, 1979), pp. 113-45.

human sexuality. Other statements in the Pauline literature regarding the significance of the one-flesh heterosexual relation (1 Cor 6:16; 7:1-9; cf. Eph 5:31-33) make it inconceivable that Paul would contravene that order by allowing for same-sex genital relationships.[15]

Third, the distinction between homosexual orientation and homosexual acts, as understood today, appears to have been unknown or at least of little concern to the Hebrew people. Indeed, the concept of a psychological or biological predisposition to homoerotic relations appears to be a modern one quite foreign to a biblical worldview.[16]

Fourth, the moral issues relating to homosexuality are not determined solely by whether homosexuality is an orientation or a practice but by the way one's sexuality is related to the intrinsic nature of human personhood in the image of God. This leads us to the deeper issue of the nature and purpose of human sexuality itself as taught by Scripture.

Fifth, a theological and pastoral approach to the issue of homosexuality within the church must take into account a wider spectrum of biblical teaching than the few texts that condemn specific homosexual acts. The theological predispositions, I will argue, are more significant than discussion based solely on homosexual references in the biblical text.

Theological Assumptions

If the biblical texts that mention homosexual acts are read in such a way that author's intent is disregarded in favor of a reading bearing on only the cultural context of their own time, this deconstructs the text in such a way that no certain meaning can be gained that speaks to our present situation. If the biblical texts are judged to have no relevance for contemporary questions of homosexual orientation and practice, the use of such texts will only lead to a standoff—an impasse that makes serious discussion of the moral, theological and pastoral issues impossible.

Serious discussion will not remove differences, to be sure. But what is important is that these differences be grounded in the basic assumptions concerning the nature of human sexuality related to the image of God. The purpose of this chapter is not to resolve the impasse created by scholars who argue the fine points of linguistic exegesis, though that work remains to be done. What I attempt here is what might be called a theological exegesis of the biblical teaching concerning human sexuality, both in the original intention of creation and in its fallen and often tragic state.

Theologically, we see perfection only through the grace of God experienced

---

[15]Wright, "Homosexuality."
[16]Hays, "Awaiting the Redemption."

through imperfection. We are not first of all concerned, then, with homosexuality but with human sexuality—or with personhood as bound to human biology.

The biblical teaching regarding human sexuality is linked with the statement that humans are created in the image and likeness of God, male and female.

> Then God said, "Let us make humankind in our image, according to our likeness; and let them have dominion over the fish of the sea, and over the birds of the air, and over the cattle, and over all the wild animals of the earth, and over every creeping thing that creeps upon the earth."

> So God created humankind in his image,
>   in the image of God he created them;
>   male and female he created them. (Gen 1:26-27)

Two modern theologians, Emil Brunner and Karl Barth, represent two approaches to the theological question of the relation of human sexuality to the image of God. Brunner separates the statement concerning the divine image from the statement concerning male and female. This interpretation allows for the divine image constitutive of human personhood to be located primarily in the person as a spiritual and moral being without regard to biological sexual differentiation. Barth, on the other hand, links human sexual differentiation at the biological level with the divine image including both.

These two ways of relating sexuality to the image of God will account for differing views regarding the relation of homosexuality to personhood. Those who hold that sexual differentiation is not an essential aspect of the divine image will tend to view the moral issue of homosexuality as grounded solely in the quality of the personal encounter. Others, who hold that sexual differentiation is an essential aspect of the divine image, believe that sexual orientation as well as sexual practice is part of the intrinsic order of human personhood. Let us consider each in turn.

Human sexual differentiation not included in the divine image. Figure 16.1 diagrams a contemporary approach to personal and sexual relations based on the premise that they are not grounded in created sexual/biological differentiation. In this view, the sexual identity of persons created in the image of God does not include biological sexual differentiation as determinative of human sexual relations. Same-sex relations are considered to be natural and normal in the same way that heterosexual relations are. The biological and the personal do not overlap (see figure 16.1).

In this model the personal I-Thou sphere is linked with the male-female biological sphere only by cultural and ethical structures of society. This understanding leads to the claim that sexual orientation and behavior are matters of human and civil rights (ideological) in the same way that racial and ethnic aspects of humans are based on "rights" rather than "nature." In this view, to judge same-sex orientation and relations as inappropriate or wrong is to discriminate against the basic rights of individuals to express their personal sexual orientation freely and with the same social acceptance and affirmation as those of differing skin color or ethnic origin.

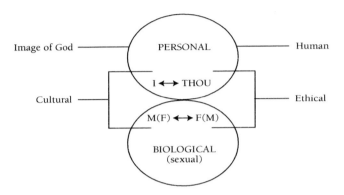

Figure 16.1. The personal and biological spheres

Brunner held that the erotic sexual impulse is an "unbridled biological instinct" that can be only consecrated through marriage or the ethical demand of abstinence.[17] While Brunner did not develop his view to the point of stating that homosexual relations are appropriate, his only argument against them was an ethical one, grounded in culture and the use of the biblical texts as applying to contemporary same-sex relations. As we have seen, if his ethical position depends primarily on these texts, his argument against homosexuality would carry little weight with those who see the texts as quite unrelated to the kind and quality of homosexual relations under consideration in our contemporary culture.

When human sexuality is considered as primarily biological and in the same category as race and ethnic origin, issues of discrimination, equal rights and justice become the criteria for deciding the question. There is ample biblical witness in support of full rights and equal justice if homosexual orientation and practice are considered solely from the grounds of human relationships with no biological aspect involved.

Human sexual differentiation as an essential aspect of the divine image. Karl Barth argued that human sexuality is a manifestation of the image of God as corelation (cohumanity) and that the mark of the human is this same corelation grounded in sexual differentiation as male and female, male or female.[18] The only differentiation at the

---

[17]Emil Brunner, *Love and Marriage* (London: Collins/Fontana, 1970).
[18]*CD* 3/1.

personal and social level with ontological (created being) status is thus human sexuality. The creation of Eve was more than a replication of humanity by numerical multiplication, suggests Barth. The solitariness of Adam would not have been overcome by another male, for such a one could not confront him as "another"; he would only recognize himself in that one. Consequently Barth condemned homosexuality as "humanity without the fellow man."[19]

Barth's view leads to what one might call an "ordered ontology": sexual differentiation as male and female is grounded in the personal being of humanity. By "ordered ontology" I mean that every human has an essential created structure that is sexually and personally differentiated, as male and female, male or female. In this view, sexual differentiation at both the personal and the biological level is one aspect of the structured being (ordered ontology) of human life, while skin color and ethnic distinctives are related solely to the biological and cultural.

Figure 16.2 is a schematic diagram of such an approach, which grounds the personal and biological differentiation of male and female, male or female, in the image of God as created and intended by God and determinative of essential humanity. In this model the personal sphere overlaps with the biological sphere, so that the image of God as constitutive of humanity includes biological sexual differentiation.

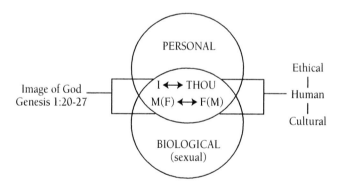

Figure 16.2. Sexual differentiation and the image of God

If one takes Genesis 1:26-27 as the foundational text for understanding human sexuality as rooted in the divine image, sexual orientation may be considered a personal and biological differentiation expressed through the "ordered ontology" of male and female, male or female. A theological perspective on homosexuality thus does

---

[19]*CD* 3/4, p. 166.

not rest alone on biblical texts that speak against homosexuality, but also on the foundational biblical texts that set forth human sexuality as an "ordered ontology" of personal and biological differentiation.

It can be argued, as Barth does, that there is an implicit semantic parallelism between the statement about the divine image and male and female sexuality, not only a formal parallelism. Barth protests that dividing the sentence in the text so as to separate the statement about the image from the statement about sexual differentiation is arbitrary and unwarranted:

> Is it not astonishing that again and again expositors have ignored the definitive explanation given by the text itself [Gen 1:26-27)]? . . . Could anything be more obvious than to conclude from this clear indication that the image and likeness of the being created by God signifies existence in confrontation, i.e., in this confrontation, in the juxtaposition and conjunction of man and man which is that of male and female, and then go on to ask against this background in what the original and prototype of the divine existence of the Creator consists?[20]

Phyllis Trible calls the differentiation alluded to in the Genesis 1:27 text "sexual dimorphism" and suggests that this can be used as a basis to establish male and female gender equality as part of the divine image.[21] Judith Gundry-Volf argues otherwise, suggesting that the statement concerning male and female relates to the command that follows, "Be fruitful and multiply" (Gen 1:28), rather than to the preceding statement "in the image of God he created them." Gundry-Volf, following more recent higher critical theories of authorship of the Genesis account, argues against an interpretation of the "male and female" differentiation as a basis for asserting an egalitarian relation between the sexes.[22]

Yet one need not accept Trible's attempt to read gender equality into the Genesis 1:26-27 text in order to appreciate her exegetical point regarding the simultaneous emergence of human being as male (*ish*) and female (*isha*) as constitutive of the divine image. In the Genesis 2 account, she points out, the specific terms for male and female (*ish* and *isha*) are used only after the creation of woman. Prior to the emergence of the female, the *adam* is not a particular person differentiated from other persons, but rather the creature from the earth (*ha-adama,* the earth creature). More important, this creature is not identified sexually.[23]

---

[20]*CD* 3/1, p. 195.

[21]Trible, *God and the Rhetoric of Sexuality.*

[22]Judy M. Gundry-Volf, "Male and Female in Creation and New Creation: Interpretations of Galatians 3:28c in 1 Corinthians 7," in *To Tell the Mystery: Essays on New Testament Eschatology in Honor of Robert H. Gundry,* ed. Thomas E. Schmidt and Moisés Silva (Sheffield, U.K.: Sheffield Academic, 1994).

[23]Trible, *God and the Rhetoric of Sexuality,* p. 80.

It follows then that Gundry-Volf's criticism of an egalitarian exegesis of Genesis 1:26-27 does not relate directly to Barth's thesis for the following reasons. First, Barth argues that the text's statement on sexual differentiation has ontological content, not only procreative implications. Barth would allow for the implication of the text with regard to the command to be fruitful and multiply. However, he insists that the obvious syntactical connection between the statement on the divine image and the one immediately following on sexual differentiation is evidence of the ontological relation between personal and sexual being.

Second, Barth's interpretation does not address the issue of sexual egalitarianism but of sexual differentiation as constitutive of humanity created in the image of God. In fact some who argue for sexual equality based on the Genesis 1:26-27 text do not accept Barth's thesis, showing that sexual egalitarianism and sexual differentiation are two different issues.[24] If we allow for Gundry-Volf's reading of Genesis 1:26-27 as the basis for the command to be fruitful and multiply, this does not rule out the further conclusion that sexual differentiation is also grounded intrinsically in the image of God.

It is this basic theological assumption that led Barth to conclude that same-sex genital relations are prone to confusion and distortion of the divine image. In the remainder of this chapter I intend to trace out the implications of Barth's view of human sexuality as grounded in the image of God with respect to issues arising concerning homosexuality.

I realize that this view presents difficulties; some recent research, for example, suggests that at least some homosexual orientation may be caused by genetic factors[25] or by psychopathological factors outside of the individual's control.[26] In the discussion that follows I will attempt to deal with some of these problems and develop the thesis that human sexuality is grounded essentially in the image of God and is a "created order" represented by differentiation as male and female, male or female. Pastoral implications for dealing with the issue of homosexuality and the church will conclude the chapter.

Discussion: Moral and Theological Issues

I have attempted in this chapter to show that underlying the biblical texts that view

---

[24]Cf. Letha Scanzoni and Virginia R. Mollenkott, *Is the Homosexual My Neighbor? A Positive Christian Response,* rev. ed. (San Francisco: HarperSanFrancisco, 1994); Paul K. Jewett, *Man as Male and Female* (Grand Rapids, Mich.: Eerdmans, 1975).

[25]Chandler Burr, "Homosexuality and Biology," in *Homosexuality in the Church: Both Sides of the Debate,* ed. Jeffrey S. Siker (Louisville, Ky.: Westminster John Knox, 1994), pp. 116-34.

[26]Stan L. Jones, and Donald E. Workman, "Homosexuality: The Behavioral Sciences and the Church," in *Homosexuality in the Church: Both Sides of the Debate,* ed. Jeffrey S. Siker (Louisville, Ky.: Westminster John Knox, 1994), pp. 93-115.

same-sex relations negatively is a positive affirmation of human sexuality based on an essential differentiation grounded in a biblical doctrine of creation. If we accept Barth's thesis that personal sexual differentiation is expressed through biological differentiation as male and female, male or female, same-sex genital relations would constitute a violation of this divinely created order of human sexuality. In this case, same-sex genital relations can be said to be sinful—a moral judgment based on a theological assumption regarding our created human nature.

The moral issue. A moral argument based on nature is what Pim Pronk calls a "naturalistic fallacy." The concept of "unnatural" in the sense of "against nature," argues Pronk, cannot denote a moral defect, because nature in the sense of biological determinism has no intrinsic moral quality. Pronk charges Barth with committing this fallacy by inferring a moral order out of biology.[27]

Pronk argues that the moral objections to homosexuality based on one's "nature" have no merit. Therefore, theology in search of moral guidelines cannot appeal to either biology or revelation concerning biological nature. The moral criteria for judging all sexual behavior, including homosexual, argues Pronk, derive from the moral instincts of the community as a whole.

Is Barth guilty of this "naturalistic fallacy" in his judgment against homosexuality? I do not believe so. Pronk has failed to grasp Barth's central thesis concerning human sexuality and the image of God. While Barth does link human sexual differentiation with creaturely nature, this is not a relation determined by "biology" but by the command of God. The moral basis for human sexuality is not inferred out of biology, as Pronk charges, but out of the command of God that summons humans to live out the divine image under the conditions of their creaturely nature and existence. The essential order of differentiation that constitutes the divine image is not determined by biological sexual characteristics but is "expressed" through one's biological nature.[28]

I agree with Pronk that biology alone cannot determine morality. At the same time, as Barth rightly argues, biological nature is a necessary though insufficient condition for living as human persons created in the image of God. Even as it is morally wrong to injure the physical being of another person, the expression of one's personal being through a physical action constitutes a moral action.

Pronk, it would appear, can be said to follow the basic assumption depicted in figure 16.1 (above), which separates personal humanity from biological humanity, leaving culture and ethics to mediate the moral aspects of human sexuality. Thus Pronk concludes one should only go to Scripture to reinforce the position one has found convincing based on other moral grounds.

---

[27]Pronk, *Against Nature?*
[28]*CD* 3/4.

Lisa Cahill warns against making moral judgments against persons who express same-sex orientation, as though such persons were morally inferior beings.[29] While a heterosexual context may be the "normative ideal" for sexual practice for Christians, she allows that, especially for persons with a strongly "homosexual identity," same-sex relations may be "objectively justifiable" as exceptional. Cahill ends up closer to Pronk in locating the moral basis for her judgment in the complex situation of human life, though she has more appreciation for biblical revelation as the source for moral criteria.

Following Barth, I suggest that theological criteria derived from biblical revelation concerning sexuality is the basis for moral guidelines, and not the reverse. If the theological assumption is held that sexual differentiation is part of an essential order rooted in the divine image and expressed through each person's biological nature, it follows that homosexual relations cannot be affirmed as belonging to that order in the same way as heterosexual relations. As I will show below under pastoral considerations, the context of human sexuality under the conditions of fallen humanity is always less than ideal, and moral judgments concerning people's sexual life must be conditioned by compassion.

The genetic issue. Some have claimed that recent research shows that at least some homosexual orientation is caused by genetic factors or by psychopathological factors outside of the individual's control, though conclusions drawn remain somewhat inconclusive. Chandler Burr cites Evelyn Hooker's attempt to correlate homosexual orientation to responses to the Rorschach test.[30] Three eminent psychologists interpreted the results and concluded that no such correlation could be found. Her study, along with many others, led to the 1973 decision of the American Psychiatric Association to remove homosexuality from its *Diagnostic and Statistical Manual.* By and large, psychologists today do not recognize homosexuality to be pathological and thus most do not attempt to change sexual orientation.

Research into possible hormonal and biological predisposition to homosexual orientation has been both promising and puzzling. Burr suggests that evidence of hormonal factors as a predisposition toward sexual orientation remains inconclusive and fails to answer the question, if hormones influence sexual orientation, what influences the hormones?[31]

The quest for genetic markers correlated with sexual orientation has led to findings that appear to be more compelling, though surrounded by a host of unanswered

---

[29]Lisa Sowle Cahill, "Homosexuality: A Case Study in Moral Argument," in *Homosexuality in the Church: Both Sides of the Debate*, ed. Jeffrey S. Siker (Louisville, Ky.: Westminster John Knox, 1994), pp. 61-75.

[30]Burr, "Homosexuality and Biology," p. 119; Jones and Workman, "Homosexuality," pp. 93-115; Pronk, *Against Nature?*

[31]Burr, "Homosexuality and Biology."

questions as to the implications. The final irony, says Burr, is that if sexual orientation, like left- or right-handedness, can be shown to be genetically determined, the conclusion will be morally irrelevant. If God made some persons gay, Burr argues, then the only thing that hurts them is hatred and ignorance.

It is not within the scope of this chapter to assess the validity of such scientific claims. At the same time, the moral issue remains, particularly for theologians and pastors who are now confronted with persons who argue that sexual orientation is not a matter of "choice" but is rooted to some degree in genetic predisposition. If sexual orientation is not a matter of individual choice in every instance, then how can one pass moral judgment on the sexual practice of homosexuals whose only "sexual preference" can be toward members of the same sex?

For those whose theological assumption corresponds to figure 16.1, the argument that condemnation of homosexuality is unfair, discriminatory and a violation of human rights is quite compelling. Same-sex relations, many theologians assert, can have the same moral content and be as expressive of the divine image as heterosexual ones. Heterosexual relations may also fail to express the image of God where the personal aspect is absent or diminished. This has been argued from the Roman Catholic[32] as well as the Protestant perspective.[33]

The situation is quite different, however, if one argues that biblical teaching upholds heterosexual relations as God's designed and preferred order for human sexual orientation as well as practice, as figure 16.2 depicts. Is it unfair and a violation of human rights to expect all persons to conform to this ideal, especially when some claim that their sexual orientation was determined by factors over which they had no control?

The answer depends on how we have determined what is "right" and "fair." In a broken world, moral issues are often laden with such complexity and tinged with personal pain that application of abstract moral criteria can offend concrete moral sensibilities. No one has a choice with regard to being born, and certainly not with regard to the physical, emotional and social conditions and context in which one is expected to enter life. Some regard life itself as unfair and reject it.

Pastoral Considerations

There is, as Cahill has said, an element of the tragic in the sexual arena of life, where persons struggle to find meaning and value in contexts that are less than ideal and fall

---

[32]John J. McNeill, *The Church and the Homosexual* (Kansas City, Mo.: Sheed & Ward, 1976); John J. McNeill, "Homosexuality: Challenging the Church to Grow," in *Homosexuality in the Church: Both Sides of the Debate,* ed. Jeffrey S. Siker (Louisville, Ky.: Westminster John Knox, 1994), pp. 49-58.

[33]Nelson, "Sources for Body Theology"; Boswell, *Christianity and Social Tolerance;* Scanzoni and Mollenkott, *Is the Homosexual My Neighbor?*

outside of what society considers normative.[34] Theological assumptions concerning human sexuality, grounded in biblical revelation, must include an acknowledgment of the brokenness and tragic aspects of the human sexual experience as well as of the divine intention regarding it.

Running right through the center of human sexuality is the element of the tragic. When the beauty and promise of human love and intimacy are linked with the capacity for sexual desire and fulfillment, no experience will prove completely adequate and completely fulfilling. Whatever one's sexual orientation and practice, be it homosexual or heterosexual, the element of the tragic will always be present. The tragic can involve as little as the temporary frustration of sexual desire when there is no partner available or willing to share it. It can also mean the choice to live in a relationship where sexual relations are impossible for physiological, psychological or moral reasons. Redemption from the tragic does not guarantee perfect fulfillment of every capacity or desire. It does offer grace to bear with what must be borne and to sublimate self-gratification in one area to self-fulfillment in another. Every human being is a sexual being and will experience some degree of the tragic in this area.

If a person considers himself or herself to have been born with a same-sex orientation, does that mean moral freedom to practice same-sex relations? Many would answer yes. But if morality (and sin) is not determined by the freedom of individual choice but by conformity to God's revealed design and purpose for humanity, then a different answer must be given. The choice for abstinence where sexual practice would violate the moral structure of life as created and commanded by God is tinged by the tragic, regardless of one's sexual preference—but it can be a "good" choice. Genetic or hormonal predisposition toward sexual orientation, like other factors one inherits from one's parents and psychosocial environment, determine certain options in our lives but do not remove from us the responsibility to make good choices in living under these conditions.

Richard Hays quotes a letter from his friend Gary, a Christian homosexual who chose abstinence out of obedience to Scripture prior to his death in 1990: "Are homosexuals to be excluded from the community of faith? Certainly not. But anyone who joins such a community should know that it is a place of transformation, of discipline, of learning and not merely a place to be comforted or indulged."[35]

So how may the church respond to persons with homosexual orientation who seek to belong and live within a community of faith?

There is ample scriptural authority for establishing both God's preference for human relationships and God's presence with persons struggling to fulfill God's pur-

---

[34]Cahill, "Homosexuality."
[35]Hays, "Awaiting the Redemption," pp. 14-15.

pose for them through a labyrinth of confusion, failure and brokenness. The Old Testament is replete with God's expressed preferences for his people but also contains a multitude of examples of God's presence as One who graciously forgives, restores and empowers within the limits and constraints of consequences and conventions.

In using the word *preference* I intend to suggest not that God merely "chooses" for us what is good in an arbitrary way, but that his preference is designed into the very structure of our existence as personal beings. This is what some would call the ideal or perfect will of God for our lives. Failing to achieve this ideal in one's life does not rule out God's gracious presence. Persons with homosexual orientation can receive the Spirit of Christ and become part of Christ's body through forgiveness and mercy the same as those with heterosexual orientation.

The church as the body of Jesus Christ expresses both divine preference and divine presence in the lives of its members. All members of the body of Christ fall short of God's preference, including Christians who are homosexuals. The church must be as inclusive as Christ's outreach into human society and as clear-headed as Christ's vision of the created purpose for humans who bear the image of God.

It would be a source of great confusion and grave error for the church to make God's presence the only means of grace and to argue that God's preference was a law that died with Christ. Both preference and presence are grounded in the grace of God, and both alike must be upheld in the teaching and practice of the church's ministry. The presence of Christ in the lives of Christians, both heterosexual and homosexual, does not condone behavior and actions that confuse and contradict God's preference, though such actions might satisfy deeply felt needs and desires. The church ought to be the place where such struggles and tensions can be experienced with the healing power of hope and love.

It must also be said that membership in the body of Christ by virtue of having been received by Christ into fellowship does not entail the right to serve in the teaching office of the church. The criteria for membership in the church are much broader than the criteria for being set apart within the church for leadership, teaching and pastoral ministry. It is therefore no contradiction for the church to trace the pattern of divine preference in its teaching and, at the same time, to follow the contours of divine presence in receiving and affirming the lives of all who seek the kingdom of God, not on the basis of natural rights but on the basis of divine grace.

Inclusion on the basis of God's presence does not grant anyone in the body of Christ the right to ordination. Whether or not a person with homosexual orientation should be excluded from consideration for ordination is a matter for the church to decide.

While Paul addresses the members of the church at Corinth as "saints" (*hagiois*, 1 Cor 2:2), he says that it is God who appoints in the church those who serve as teachers, leaders and apostles (1 Cor 13:28). Furthermore, those who are set apart for these ministries are to consider themselves "stewards of God's mysteries" and accountable to Christ for what is taught and practiced (1 Cor 4:1-5).

The later Pastoral Epistles set forth specific qualifications for those who hold offices of bishop, elder and deacon (1 Tim 3:1-13; Tit 1:5-9). The inference one can draw from these passages is that those set apart for ministry have no claim on the office by virtue of membership in the body. Instead they are recognized as gifted and called by the Spirit of God to the office for the purpose of upholding sound doctrine and exemplifying spiritual maturity, self-discipline, marital integrity, domestic peace and a good reputation among those who are "outsiders."

Discerning who should be set aside for the teaching office entails both wisdom and discernment on the part of the church, taking into account many criteria, including maturity, domestic stability, personal integrity and spiritual giftedness. Might not these criteria include sexual orientation as well as sexual practice measured by the responsibility to uphold both divine preference as well as divine presence?

Where the church has determined on biblical grounds that homosexual practice is inconsistent with God's preference for human sexual relations, church members with a homosexual orientation may be required to abstain from such practice as a condition for ordination. Such a church cannot do otherwise and retain its integrity.

Some have argued that to ordain women to pastoral ministry while denying ordination to those who practice homosexuality is discriminatory and a violation of human rights. Yet there are biblical antecedents for the role of women in ministry, in both the Old Testament and the New Testament. In certain cases God has clearly expressed what I have called "preference" by anointing and setting apart women for ministry. Huldah was recognized as a prophet (2 Kings 22:14), as were Deborah (Judg 4:4) and Noadiah (Neh 6:14). Despite Paul's restriction on the role of women in certain cases, he affirmed Phoebe as a deacon and Junia as among the apostles (Rom 16:1, 7).

Though these cases are exceptional, they nonetheless constitute biblical antecedents for the contemporary practice of ordaining women as led by the Spirit. There appears to be no biblical antecedent for approving or affirming practicing homosexuals as teachers, leaders or pastors. While the Holy Spirit liberates and empowers persons for ministry, one should always seek a biblical antecedent for the work of the Spirit in the contemporary church. On this basis, the ordination of women does not constitute an open door to the ordination of practicing homosexuals.

While the church is a fallible institution, often in its practice and sometimes in its teaching, God's gracious presence is not withheld from its members. Recognizing its fallibility, the church orders its life with both humility and a sense of the tragic. Fallibility is not an excuse for conceding to human frailty, nor is it an argument for abandoning the search for authentic biblical teaching. With humility, the church seeks the mind of Christ through the unity of the Spirit.

Tragic as it is to live with unfulfilled sexual desires and with unrealized vocational aspirations, even more tragic would be the rending of the body of Christ over a matter of who should occupy the chairs at the head of the table when Jesus gave priority to those who serve.

The community of faith can be a community of transformation and discipline for both those with homosexual orientation and those with heterosexual orientation. The testimony of many is that empowerment to move toward the discovery of sexual wholeness as male or female can be found through the grace and power of Christ's presence in such a healing community.[36] When homosexuality becomes a divisive issue within the church, it raises the danger of shifting human sexuality from a possibility to a necessity under the banner of human rights.[37] This attempt to escape the tragic by trading what is partial for the whole will, in the end, prove to be a greater tragedy for us all.

---

[36]Comiskey, *Pursuing Sexual Wholeness.*
[37]Jack Rogers, "Sex, Philosophy and Politics: How and What the Church Must Decide in the Debate over Ordination of Homosexuals," in *Homosexuality in the Church: Both Sides of the Debate,* ed. Jeffrey S. Siker (Louisville, Ky.: Westminster John Knox, 1994), pp. 161-77.

17

CLERGY BURNOUT
AS A SYMPTOM OF
THEOLOGICAL ANEMIA

A clergyman walks in. He's a big man, 240 pounds. He strikes the desk with his fist and says, 'Look, there's nothing more boring than walking around the block. If I have to eat differently than the rest of the family I'm not going to. Besides, if God takes me then he takes me. Then I'll be traveling without any baggage.'"[1]

Dr. Taylor, a physician concerned about clergy morale, paused, as if peering into the mental picture he had created for some clue, and then continued. "Professor Anderson, here is someone who believes that if he gives himself to the work of God, God will look after him. Even if he burns himself out for God, his future is secure. What is this person really saying?"

Now it was my turn to pause. I was being asked to respond as a theologian, but I experienced an instantaneous flashback through eleven years of pastoral ministry. Quite without thinking, I replied, "The man is experiencing a kind of quiet despair that can subtly creep into one's ministry, and he may even be experiencing an unconscious death wish."

Dr. Taylor was intrigued, and I must admit I myself was not a little surprised at the intensity with which I had responded. Was I diagnosing the blustering, overweight

---

[1] A version of this essay was first printed in Fuller Theological Seminary's *Theology News and Notes,* March 1984, pp. 11-21.

clergyman or delving into my own pastoral psyche? I suspect it was the latter. I remember a series of sermons I once preached from Job, and the strange sense of identity I had with him when he cried out:

> Let me have silence, and I will speak,
>   and let come on me what may.
> I will take my flesh in my teeth,
>   and put my life in my hand.
> Behold, he will slay me; I have no hope;
>   yet I will defend my ways to his face.
> This will be my salvation,
>   that a godless man shall not come before him.
> (Job 13:13-16 RSV)

Let's face it, this is suicidal!

I see Job as feeling caught in an inescapable bind. He is convinced that his life is given over to God, and yet God has become his adversary. There is only one way out: risk himself to the very edge of destruction, and then God himself must be his vindication and his salvation.

This is the "Job syndrome": "My ministry is slowly killing me, so I will 'take my flesh in my teeth' and kill myself through my ministry. Then we shall see what God will say!" Many a minister has preached his own eulogy as a healing balm to his ulcerous soul.

Personal Inadequacy

Coupled with despair over never being able to satisfy the demands is the minister's personal sense of inadequacy—including spiritual inadequacy—for the task. Left to herself, the minister can only seek to atone for spiritual failure by throwing herself even more into the work of the ministry.

It becomes a vicious circle. The demands of the ministry produce a sense of inadequacy. Inadequacy carries the overtone of spiritual weakness. You turn to God in desperation, seeking some relief, escape, if not renewal. Failing here too, you find nothing to do but throw yourself more deeply into the work of the ministry. And the cycle repeats itself.

Personal Needs

Periodically someone intervenes with a commonsense question: "Shouldn't you be concerned about your physical health?" or "You need a day off once in a while; what do you do to relax?"

Caught in the undertow of this "divine madness" that has seized you in the name of ministry, how do you explain that the risk of a physical, or even emotional, break-down is almost incidental compared to the high stakes for which you are playing in the deadly game of ministry? Can we now understand what the pastor means by "God will look after me"?

Of course ministers know when they are neglecting their own physical and emotional well-being, the same as they know when they are precariously close to nervous exhaustion or dangerously close to the point of throwing in the towel and taking the emotional and spiritual equivalent of Chapter 11 in the bankruptcy clause—it's burn-out time! This is why being told, or even warned, is not an effective deterrent. The well-meaning appeal to common sense actually can compound the problem and accelerate the vicious circle. "We are driven" is not only an effective advertising slogan for automobiles but a shrill echo of the divine call sunk deep in the psyche of a minister who seeks salvation through ministry.

Factors Causing Burnout

Lest this become overly melodramatic, let's reflect a bit on the factors that might cause the typical symptoms of stress fatigue or burnout to assume the unique proportions of "clergy burnout."

A root problem may lie in how one perceives being "called of God" for the ministry, or the "calling of the ministry." Those who enter into pastoral ministry are encouraged to pursue this occupation as a divine calling. "If you can avoid becoming a minister with a clear conscience before God," we are often told, "then you do not have the calling." The implication is that the call is unavoidable and thus inevitable; it marks one for life, becomes one's fate. "Woe to me if I do not proclaim the gospel!" (1 Cor 9:16)

Whatever existential assurance this sense of calling gives, it soon takes a pragmatic turn in being understood as a calling "to the ministry." Note the subtle shift from the emphasis on the One who calls to the work of the ministry as a calling. It is one thing to experience God as one's fate, and quite another thing for the work of the ministry to determine one's fate. When this happens, the calling to ministry comes close to being fatal.

Here, I believe, is the source of the "quiet despair" that can seep into our celebration of the sacred task and turn it into a joyless marathon of sheer endurance. We all know what the ministry is:

☐ It is the torment of the artist who must fashion creative and inspired sermons to be thrown into the insatiable craw of hungry hordes who appear at least once a week for the "word of God."

☐ It is the weariness of the long-suffering doctor who hides her own illness from the patients who extract her vital energy in scheduled and unscheduled counseling sessions.

☐ It is the exasperation of the executive whose goals and plans are sabotaged by an army of volunteers, each of whom is serving a different master.

☐ It is the loneliness of the shepherd whose faithful pursuit of the lost sheep leaves his own humanity starved for affection and comfort.

☐ It is the dilemma of the priest who dispenses forgiveness freely to sinners in human words and gives assurance of God's presence through a community of loving persons, and yet is told to seek the solace and strength he needs from God alone in his private place.

This is the work of the ministry—an insatiable and unrelenting master we serve in the name of Christ.

Have I been overly dramatic? I suppose so. But to paraphrase Jesus, "I am speaking not to those who are at ease but to those in dis-ease." I speak out of the battle, not offering good advice from the sidelines. But I speak as a survivor, not as a victim. And I tell of hope and freedom, not retreat or escape.

I firmly believe that what we need in times of stress is intervention, not merely information. Others more capable than I can describe modes of intervention that address emotional, physical and social causes of distress and suggest forms of therapy that lead to greater well-being of body and soul. But a theological intervention may be helpful as well. Much of what I have described above is as much due to bad theology, in my opinion, as to an unhealthy psyche.

Jesus' Theology of Ministry

Jesus had a better theology than his critics, not to mention his disciples. When he reached the point of exhaustion from teaching and healing, he had the freedom to stop and to spend time alone or with his disciples. His instincts told him that his freedom from the claims on him was upheld by the same gracious Father who gave him the freedom and power to teach and heal. When told that his dear friend Lazarus was sick to the point of death, Jesus remained three days where he was. He felt sure that his Father loved Lazarus as much as he did, and that he could go whenever the Father sent him (Jn 11).

It is bad theology to have to love the world more than God, and to confuse our service to God with our being sent into the world. It is bad theology to interpret the calling of God in terms of the needs of the world, rather than in our being sent to the world to do God's work and reveal his glory.

A theology that cripples and destroys the self-esteem and sense of worth of a minister is not made better by "success" in ministry. A theology allowing no "sabbath rest" for the one who does the work of ministry is a theology of the curse, not a theology of the cross. A healthy theology contains healing for the healer and freedom for the fighter of God's battles. A healthy theology, of course, is a theology of a loving God who knows that to be God is to be responsible, even for our faltering and fallible efforts.

Perhaps the turning point began the night I spent hours counseling a woman who had spoken to her teenage children of suicide. It was the children who had called me to minister to their mother. This was not the first time. There had been professional psychotherapy. There had been interminable hours of pastoral counseling recalling the promises and grace of God. But now, well after midnight, the end of my resources had come.

Quietly, I stood up and said, "I'm going home and going to sleep. I am not God and I am not anyone's savior. In the morning, if you are alive, call me and we will talk again."

I went home with the knowledge that I might well have to prepare for a funeral. But I also knew with a deep sense of assurance that I could do that if I had to. For I sensed that God was now my advocate and not my adversary. Yes, I was betting on my judgment that the woman would survive—and she did. But it was a turning point for me. I understood more of the grace of God than I had ever before. I understood the grace of God because I was in a position to receive the grace of God.

Through the realization of my inadequacy when only the grace of God could suffice, I experienced in a new way the reality of God as the source and sustaining power of my "call" to be a minister. My ministry no longer could be equivalent to my salvation or destruction.

It was the beginning of a theological renewal that led to liberation and a deep sense of goodness within myself. This sounds strange, even as I write it. For I had been taught that "nothing good" dwelt within me and that a feeling of well-being and satisfaction was dangerously close to pride. But this goodness was not like "being good" or thinking of myself as better than others. It was the echo within me of "God is good," and therefore what I do, even with its limitations, is part of the goodness that God is. I felt called to be an agent and instrument of that good. I felt good about myself because I felt forgiven and loved. No longer was I living on the edge of that terrible marginality in ministry, where the abyss always looms threateningly over and against every action. Driven back by obstacles, confronted with failure and frustration, attacked by symptoms of overstress, I experienced the healing of God's goodness from within.

Jesus had a good theology of the sabbath. Not only did he understand the sabbath as contributing to the good of persons, but he realized in his own person the healing effects of God's sabbath rest. As the Lord of the sabbath, he not only interpreted the sabbath in terms of God's purposes but fulfilled the sabbath rest in his weak human flesh. He brought the sabbath out from the casuistry of the legalist mind, where immobilized persons had been impaled on the bed of self-incrimination. He remembered that for the Jews there was at least one liberating moment each week when they could stand with their backs straight against God's gracious goodness and say to the six days of work and travail, "You have no power over me, for we live out of God's shalom, and we are a people of peace and wholeness."

We who are called of God for Christian ministry are called first of all into the sabbath rest that Christ himself completed through the offering up of his own humanity in obedient, faithful service to God. With our backs straight up against the rock of his healed humanity, we reach out to meet human needs, do battle with evil and take the Word of God on our lips to proclaim his salvation. No temptation has ever overtaken us, says the Scripture, that has not already been experienced and healed in Jesus (Heb 4:15). I venture to say that no injury can ever be sustained in the work of God's ministry for which there is not already healing waiting at home.

Help for Pilgrims

Dare I suggest some practical helps for those who are looking for the way to inner healing, without appearing to resort at the end to merely "good advice"? The following thoughts come out of my own pilgrimage.

First, turn to the source of all good theology-contemplation of Jesus as the paradigm for ministry. In his priestly prayer, Jesus said to the Father, "As you have sent me into the world, so I have sent them into the world" (Jn 17:18). I once wrote "AS HE WAS SENT" on one side of a page and "SO I HAVE BEEN SENT" across from it on the other side. In an exercise that took me through all four Gospel accounts of Jesus' life and ministry, I listed all I could discover of how Jesus had been sent to this world. Then I began to list in the facing column the ways I was sent to minister, in a way that precisely corresponded with how he had been sent. This was absolutely revolutionary for me, and my theology began to be healed. By the way, the exercise also provided me with months of sermon material!

Second, explore the inner correlation between ministry and theology. A ministry that produces dissonance and distress in the minister is theologically impoverished. Theology is the interpretation of God through his Word and Spirit in the arena of the gospel's struggle for the reconciliation of the world. Jesus knew what he was doing when he healed on the sabbath, when he forgave sin in the streets, when he drove the moneychangers out of the temple. He was saying, This is what it means to know and experience the living God. Methods can show us how to do ministry. The purpose of theological reflection is to give us the courage to know and to say that our ministry is Christ's ministry.

It may sound strange, and there will be disbelievers, but I maintain that renewing one's theology through rediscovery of Christ's presence and power in ministry will reduce debilitating stress and restore joy and hope in ministry. A daily journal for theological reflection on the evidences of Christ's ministry in one's own work of ministry will become a diary of spiritual and personal renewal. It is true!

Third, consent to be one of the sheep as well as being the shepherd. When the sheep we are attempting to feed appear to be ravenous wolves, we are the ones in distortion. When I began to feel that there was goodness within me because I was forgiven and loved, the circle of my life opened up, and I could allow other people to love me and affirm that goodness. Frankly, I found that professional ministerial groups only reinforced inadequacy by making me feel like a competitor. Perhaps that was only my problem, but Scripture does not give evidence that there is much healing and feeding when shepherds get together! Jesus, the great shepherd, loves and cares for the sheep. In permitting ourselves to be part of the sheep, even if only in informal and intimate social gatherings, we experience absolution for our sins of being the minister and the affirmation we need to continue to minister. Such relationships restore the soul, for we experience his shepherding together (Ps 23).

A healthy practical theology of clergy vocation and practice rests on the foundation of all ministry as God's ministry through Christ. Christopraxis means that Christ's continued ministry to the world in the power of the Holy Spirit is a ministry that empowers as well as equips.

When I am in distress and anxious about approaching the threshold of burnout, it makes sense to avail myself of all the resources at hand for intervention at the psychological and physical levels. But it makes no sense to neglect the single most important resource: theological intervention through a new view of my life in Christ. We do well to begin this even before we feel desperate need—for it is good to have the goodness inside and not just in God.

18

A PRACTICAL THEOLOGY OF FORGIVENESS

A Journey Toward Reconciliation & Healing

To err is human, to forgive is divine. The aphorism is partially correct. The Judeo-Christian tradition at its very core is anchored in the mercy and forgiveness of God, while humans are notoriously corrupt. Though Abraham knew Sodom was a wicked place, because of his nephew and family he sought the Lord's mercy for the city. "And the Lord said, 'If I find at Sodom fifty righteous in the city, I will forgive the whole place for their sake' " (Gen 18:26). In the end, Abraham negotiated from fifty down to ten (Gen 18:32)! The failure to find even ten righteous persons in the city was, I am sure, a source of consternation to Abraham, who then witnessed its destruction. One wonders what would have happened if Abraham had not stopped at ten but had continued to plead for God's forgiveness based solely on his mercy and compassion.

In the New Testament, Jesus set aside the demands of the law for the sake of offering forgiveness, even for the thief on the cross. Paul, himself the recipient of divine forgiveness, never forgot the grace and mercy of the Lord toward him and urged fellow Christians to offer the grace of forgiveness in their mutual relations. "Be kind to one another, tenderhearted, forgiving one another, as God in Christ has forgiven you" (Eph 4:32). Being Christian means not merely being forgiven but being a forgiving person. Forgiveness is not only a spiritual grace but a human virtue, to be experienced and expressed as a mark of graceful living.

There are many myths and some misconceptions concerning forgiveness. Before developing a theology of forgiveness, we will do well to look at some of these popular assumptions.

Popular Assumptions About Forgiveness

Forgiveness is good for you. Popular self-help books often stress the psychological benefits of forgiveness. There is even a biblical text that might be interpreted as supporting this assumption: "Forgive, and you will be forgiven; give, and it will be given to you. A good measure, pressed down, shaken together, running over, will be put into your lap; for the measure you give will be the measure you get back" (Lk 6:37-38). A therapeutic reading of this text stresses the subjective benefits of forgiveness. To express forgiveness, we are told, is to purge the self of anger and bitterness and thus to attain greater mental and emotional health. "It is immutable mental and spiritual law," writes one author, "that when there is a health problem, there is a forgiveness problem. You must forgive if you want to be permanently healed. . . . Health cannot be accepted by a body that is filled with the poisons generated by unforgiveness."[1]

Psychologist Beverly Flanigan offers a more sophisticated version of this same assumption. Forgiveness is good for you because

> people who forgive sever themselves from the past and look to the future. In the emergence of a new self, the person who has gone through major conversions in his beliefs about very central things in his life (like other travelers) ends his journey, unpacks his figurative bags, and gets life back to normal. Whatever he chooses to do, it will be a time when his new beliefs gathered along the journey to forgiveness are consolidated and tested. . . . If nothing can ever be the same, this time around it can be even better. . . . The gift of forgiving, then, is the relaxation of vigilance. The new self becomes more relaxed, less defensive and brittle. Forgivers know they can be wounded and have learned to take the idea in as part of their working perceptions of reality. They have experienced the worst of pain. Everything ahead should be much easier.[2]

From a cognitive behavioral approach, this therapeutic suggestion offers a way to overcome the cognitive dissonance caused by an injury to the self. The perception of inadequate self-worth, Flanigan believes, can be removed through interjection of a new belief about the self. By the "gift of forgiveness" the old self is forgotten and a new life of the self begins. What this therapeutic bromide lacks, as we shall see, is the

---

[1] Quoted by John Patton in *Is Human Forgiveness Possible? A Pastoral Care Perspective* (Nashville: Abingdon, 1985), p. 123.
[2] Beverly Flanigan, *Forgiving the Unforgivable: Overcoming the Bitter Legacy of Intimate Wounds* (New York: Macmillan, 1992), pp. 162, 168.

spiritual and moral dimensions of forgiveness.

Forgiveness is demanded of you. A second popular assumption stresses the moral duty of forgiveness. If we seek to do our duty to God, we simply do not have the option of unforgiveness. Sermons and spiritual instruction tell us it is quite "un-Christian" to withhold forgiveness.

Here again, certain biblical texts can be read so as to demand forgiveness as a moral and spiritual duty. Jesus admonished his disciples: "Be on your guard! If another disciple sins, you must rebuke the offender, and if there is repentance, you must forgive" (Lk 17:3). Paul adds his own imperative of forgiveness: "Bear with one another and, if anyone has a complaint against another, forgive each other; just as the Lord has forgiven you, so you also must forgive" (Col 3:13).

Unable to muster up a spirit of forgiveness toward someone who has violated sacred trust or injured us in body and soul, we often feel guilty for not being able to forgive. But as we shall see, the command to forgive as a moral and spiritual duty, when imposed on a victim, may itself be an act that needs to be forgiven!

Divine forgiveness is conditional upon human forgiveness. A third assumption follows closely on the concept of forgiveness as a moral duty. In this case, forgiveness becomes a legalistic requirement.

"Forgive us our debts as we forgive our debtors." Even this petition in the Lord's Prayer may be read from a legalistic viewpoint. Scottish biblical scholar William Barclay urges this view on us:

> Jesus says in the plainest possible language that if we forgive others, God will forgive us; but if we refuse to forgive others, God will refuse to forgive us. . . . If we say, "I will never forget what so-and-so did to me," and then go and take this petition on our lips, we are quite deliberately asking God not to forgive us. . . .
>
> No one is fit to pray the Lord's prayer so long as the unforgiving spirit holds sway within his heart.[3]

Who of us, if we are honest, can truly say that we are free of an unforgiving spirit? So ought we avoid praying the Lord's Prayer? Is the forgiveness of God conditioned on our forgiveness of others? Does God then withhold mercy and grace until we merit it? I suppose some would even read Jesus' words in a legalistic way: "When you are offering your gift at the altar, if you remember that your brother or sister has something against you, leave your gift there before the altar and go; first be reconciled to your brother or sister, and then come and offer your gift" (Mt 5:23-24).

Lewis Smedes suggests something similar when he says that God's forgiveness is conditional, based on our prior repentance. "A person who wrongs God should not

---

[3]William Barclay, *The Gospel of Matthew,* Daily Study Bible (Philadelphia: Westminster Press, 1959), 1:223-24.

expect God to forgive her unless she is sorry for the wrong she did. So much for that. . . . The same goes for us mortals. Nobody can expect to be forgiven and reunited with the person he wounded unless he repents of what he did to hurt her in the first place."[4] Perhaps Smedes only means one should not expect God's forgiveness without genuine repentance, but that God may graciously extend forgiveness anyway, as a way of initiating and empowering repentance. I hope that is what he means.

It is not that repentance is irrelevant to forgiveness; surely reconciliation can come only through genuine sorrow for wrongs done. My own view is that God's grace of forgiveness is offered unconditionally through Jesus Christ and that this is the motive power of genuine repentance. To withhold God's grace and forgiveness on the condition that humans first express the grace of forgiveness to others is close to spiritual abuse. As we shall see, forgiveness is a systemic grace that intends to create reciprocity between humans and God in their social and spiritual lives. But this gracious reciprocity of divine forgiveness can never be reduced to a legalistic requirement.

Forgiveness is a shortcut to reconciliation. Another popular assumption is that forgiveness is a quick fix for ruptured and broken relationships.

"I worry about fast forgivers," writes Smedes. "They tend to forgive quickly in order to avoid their pain. Or they forgive fast in order to get an advantage over the people they forgive. And their instant forgiving only makes things worse."[5]

Norm (not his real name), a family man and regular church attender, was arrested for indecent exposure. As part of his probation, he was required to seek counseling from his pastor. As the pastor met with Norm and his wife, he found them composed and outwardly cordial to each other. After a few minutes of casual conversation, the pastor asked, "Have you talked about the incident when Norm was arrested for indecent exposure?"

"That's between him and God," Ella quickly responded. "He said that he confessed his sin to God and that he had been forgiven. So I have forgiven him too."

The pastor waited a few moments before speaking. He noted that Norm and Ella were sitting close together holding hands, but they did not look at each other. He asked quietly, "How do you feel about Norm now?"

Letting go of Norm's hand, Ella began to weep. "I feel humiliated and angry at what he put our family through. But I know that I'm not supposed to feel that way. I have told him that I forgive him, but he doesn't believe me."

When the pastor met with Norm and Ella for the next session, Norm spoke up first. "I can't believe how foolish my behavior was. It was really stupid of me to dis-

---

[4]Lewis B. Smedes, *The Art of Forgiving: When You Need to Forgive and Don't Know How* (New York: Ballantine, 1996), pp. 92-93.
[5]Ibid., p. 137.

play myself in public. I'll never understand what came over me, but believe me, I have really learned my lesson. I know better than to do something like that again."

Ella appeared more at peace, and nodded. "I think that getting caught may be the best thing that happened to Norm," she said. "It was painful for all of us, but he has promised not do anything like that again, and I believe him."

Several weeks later Norm and Ella returned. Despite Norm's attempt to take responsibility for his actions by admitting that they were "stupid" and stating his intention never to do it again, he confessed that he had not found inward peace. Nor was Ella able to sustain her confidence in him. "I don't really think he will ever change," she confided to the pastor. "He has withdrawn more into himself than ever."

The pastor continued to explore Norm's feelings about himself. "I think God has forgiven me," Norm said, "but I cannot forgive myself. I really hate myself for having sexual desires and thoughts that I cannot control."

Forgiveness had been claimed by Norm as a mercy of God and granted by his wife as her spiritual duty. When the pastor probed deeper into Ella's feelings for Norm, it became clear that while she had given assurance of forgiveness, the relationship had not yet come into healing and hope. As for Norm, confession of sin to God had given him immediate assurance of forgiveness but left untouched and unhealed his deep inner shame and self-hatred.

Forgiveness as a quick fix for a bruised self and a broken relationship fails at both levels. Forgiveness that fails to lead to personal and social renewal at the human level has also failed to reach God at the spiritual level, according to Dietrich Bonhoeffer.

In confession a man breaks through to certainty. Why is it that it is often easier for us to confess our sins to God than to a brother? God is holy and sinless, He is a just judge of evil and the enemy of all disobedience. But a brother is sinful as we are. He knows from his own experience the dark night of secret sin. Why should we not find it easier to go to a brother than to the holy God? But if we do, we must ask ourselves whether we have not often been deceiving ourselves with our confession of sin to God, whether we have not rather been confessing our sins to ourselves and also granting ourselves absolution. And is not the reason perhaps for our countless relapses and the feebleness of our Christian obedience to be found precisely in the fact that we are living on self-forgiveness and not on real forgiveness? . . . Our brother breaks the circle of self-deception. A man who confesses his sins in the presence of a brother knows that he is no longer alone with himself; he experiences the presence of God in the reality of the other person. . . . Mutual, brotherly confession is given to us by God in order that we may be sure of divine forgiveness.[6]

There is no shortcut to forgiveness, but it is a journey that we must take if we are to

[6]Dietrich Bonhoeffer, *Life Together* (London: SCM Press, 1970), pp. 115-16.

push through the self-deception that blinds us and experience personal healing and reconciliation with others.

Theological and Practical Aspects of Forgiveness

The announcement of the kingdom of God was central to the message and ministry of Jesus. His ministry of deliverance and healing was a sign of the presence and power of the kingdom. "But if it is by the Spirit of God that I cast out demons, then the kingdom of God has come to you" (Mt 12:28). As the beatitudes suggest, the kingdom of God is a state in which the values of the world are reversed and the values of God established. The poor become rich, mourners are comforted, the meek inherit the earth (Mt 5).

In the messianic banquet described by Jesus, reconciliation between those outside Israel and those who are descendants of Abraham takes place in table fellowship. "I tell you, many will come from east and west and will eat with Abraham and Isaac and Jacob in the kingdom of heaven" (Mt 8:11). In the prayer taught by Jesus, the petition about the kingdom of God precedes the petition about forgiveness.[7] Biblical scholar Norman Perrin says:

> God is to be experienced as king in the provision of "daily bread," in the experienced reality of the forgiveness of sins, and in support in the face of "temptation." It is very evident that the symbol Kingdom of God evokes the expectation of the activity of God on behalf of the petitioner, and that the symbol is by no means exhausted in any one manifestation of that which it evokes.[8]

David Augsburger, quoting Hannah Arendt, says, "Forgiveness is the 'remedy against the irreversibility and unpredictability of human actions,' . . . and it is an act that can correct previous actions or release persons from the consequence of those actions."[9] Actions and events are irreversible; we cannot rewrite history so as to change the facts. What forgiveness does, as a spiritual dynamic, is release us from the consequence of those actions.

The context of forgiveness is thus not a courtroom but a social structure of human relations, such as friendship, marriage and being neighbors. In the core social relationships that bind persons to one another, the culture of the kingdom of God constitutes a significant reversal of human values rooted in self-preservation and self-justification. To express forgiveness is contrary to the instincts of retaliation and vengeance. To actually forgive in such a way that relationships are restored and a new culture of mutual care and regard comes into existence requires restora-

---

[7]See Patton, *Is Human Forgiveness Possible?* p. 150.
[8]Norman Perrin, *Jesus and the Language of the Kingdom* (Philadelphia: Fortress, 1976), p. 47.
[9]David Augsburger, *Helping People Forgive* (Louisville, Ky.: Westminster John Knox, 1996), p. 9.

tion of the moral structure of relationships.

The moral dynamics of forgiveness. Any injury to the self produces an instinctive moral judgment, usually in the form of an accusation against the one who caused the injury. Until this moral judgment is resolved it is not possible to talk of forgiveness. Along with the moral judgment there is the desire to inflict punishment on the offender.

A distinction between judgment and punishment is essential if we are to understand the role of forgiveness in self-recovery. A judgment is something like a verdict rendered in a court of law: one is pronounced guilty or innocent. Punishment is like the sentence imposed by the court. In a determination of punishment, extenuating circumstances can be taken into consideration; thus not all who are judged guilty experience the same punishment.

Ethel (not her real name) is the wife of a pastor. She had suffered sexual abuse from her brother at an early age and only recently had disclosed this to her husband. Her brother denied the abuse ever took place. Her husband refused to take sides and told her this was something that only she could resolve through forgiveness and spiritual healing.

Despite more than a year of therapy with a Christian psychologist, she was unable to let go of her anger and was troubled by her inability to forgive. At a pastor's conference where I spoke on the subject of abuse, she approached me and told her story. When I asked whether a verdict had ever been rendered concerning the offense, she shook her head: "No one will take sides against my brother. Even my husband feels that he is in no position to make a judgment, as he was not part of the family at the time."

I explained again the difference between verdict and punishment and told her that I accepted her account as true. "The verdict is 'guilty as charged,'" I told her. "Now you can think about the punishment your brother deserves. Forgiveness does not nullify a verdict; it only releases the offender from punishment."

After pondering this for a few minutes, Ethel replied, "I think that he has suffered enough, even though he would never admit that he abused me. I have no need of punishing him now."

In cases of domestic violence or child abuse, a deep moral offense has been committed. The victim will need to be supported and affirmed in making a judgment against the offense as well as against the offender, addressing the moral issue in the abuse hidden within the pain. Once this judgment has been rightfully directed against the offender, the victim no longer is caught in self-blame. The feelings of outrage have now been dealt with. The feelings of anger can be processed as emotion.

Outrage is grounded in a moral sense, while anger is primarily an emotion that is capable of cognitive reframing. Bringing forth a judgment against an offender draws outrage to a conclusion. To continue to express condemnation once judgment has been rendered is not necessary to satisfy the moral instinct. Judgment and punishment can sometimes become blurred in the feelings of a victim. Moral outrage and anger are not clearly distinguished at the emotional level.

Judgment and punishment are actually part of a two-step process. To judge one who has abused you as morally wrong is to satisfy the moral instinct of the self. To inflict punishment is a step beyond judgment. Punishing an offender for a wrong done may be beyond the power or competence of the victim. The Bible does not prohibit us from passing judgment against moral wrong. At the same time, it warns us about exacting vengeance. "Beloved, never avenge yourselves," writes the apostle Paul, "but leave room for the wrath of God; for it is written, 'Vengeance is mine, I will repay, says the Lord'" (Rom 12:19; see Deut 32:35).

Once judgment has been rendered, the moral issue has been resolved and the basis for outrage removed. Anger, of course, continues, as does the feeling that the offender should suffer for the wrong done. Forgiveness does not excuse wrongdoing or bypass judgment. Forgiveness is possible only when moral judgment has been rendered and supported. Forgiveness is itself a moral and spiritual achievement when it can be exercised. It is an acknowledgment that justice has been rendered through moral judgment and moves the self toward recovery through the building of positive self-esteem.

Forgiveness is not an end run around the moral bar of justice in search of a less costly route to reconciliation. Genuine forgiveness involves more than an adjustment of the psyche under the skilled hands of a therapist—emotional surgery by which anger is transformed into acceptance and old injuries are removed. No, forgiving does not mean forgetting, nor is it a moral victory for the offended. "It is not a self serving mercy that controls, obligates, or morally judges the offender; rather it transforms the relationship."[10] Forgiving is the costly grace of releasing one who is truly guilty from the consequences of the offense, all for the sake of and with the hope of reconciliation. Because it is grace, even though costly, it is essentially a spiritual dynamic rather than a psychological process.

The spiritual dynamics of forgiveness. To say that forgiveness is a spiritual dynamic rather than merely a psychological process is not to suggest it is a religious rather than human act. In his perceptive work on the nature of human personhood and the church, Bonhoeffer says that spirit is necessarily created in community and the general spirituality of persons is woven into the net of sociality:

It will appear that all Christian and moral content, as well as the entire spirituality of [per-

---

[10]See ibid., p. 166.

sons], is possible and real only in sociality. . . . [A person's] entire so-called spirituality, which is presupposed by the Christian concept of person and has its unifying point in self-consciousness . . . is so constituted that it can only be seen as possible in sociality.[11]

Personal being and social being, says Bonhoeffer, are intrinsically bound together in a structure of human spirituality.

Injury and wrong done by one person to another is not only a moral fault demanding justice but an offense against the spirit that binds us together as personal beings. If a wrong were only a moral fault, punishment of the offender would satisfy moral justice. But this would leave the spiritual bond between persons broken and unhealed.

When Paul sent the slave Onesimus back to his owner, he wrote a letter to Philemon urging him to forgive whatever wrong he had done. But he also asked Philemon to receive him back "forever, no longer as a slave but more than a slave, a beloved brother—especially to me but how much more to you, both in the flesh and in the Lord" (Philem 15-16). The kind of forgiveness Paul sought from Philemon was more than "wiping the slate clean" so as to start the master-slave relation over again. Paul viewed forgiveness as a spiritual dynamic that had the possibility of altering the former relationship and creating a new one based on reconciliation and mutual trust.

The spiritual reality of "being in Christ," for Paul, meant a new creation, not only a new start within the old one:

> So if anyone is in Christ, there is a new creation: everything old has passed away; see, everything has become new! All this is from God, who reconciled us to himself through Christ, and has given us the ministry of reconciliation; that is, in Christ God was reconciling the world to himself, not counting their trespasses against them, and entrusting the message of reconciliation to us. So we are ambassadors for Christ, since God is making his appeal through us; we entreat you on behalf of Christ, be reconciled to God. (2 Cor 5:17-20)

Forgiveness in the New Testament is more synonymous with *reconciliation* than with *love*.[12] Paul is not satisfied with proclamation of the gospel of forgiveness alone. He knows that forgiveness has already been accomplished from God's side and that God does not "count trespasses" against persons who are sinners. But forgiveness has not yet been accomplished until there is reconciliation of human beings with God and one another. This is why Paul found great encouragement in remembering the transformation of the lives of those in Thessalonica who had received the gospel of Christ. "Our coming to you was not in vain," Paul writes to them, because "when you

---

[11]Dietrich Bonhoeffer, *Communion of Saints* (New York: Harper & Row, 1963), pp. 43-44.
[12]David W. Augsburger, *The Freedom of Forgiveness* (Chicago: Moody Press, 1988), p. 25.

received the word of God that you heard from us, you accepted it not as a human word but as what it really is, God's word, which is also at work in you believers" (1 Thess 2:1, 13). This is a gospel of forgiveness that empowers ministry to those crushed, broken and burdened, and empowers persons to move toward wholeness.

This gives a new slant to the saying of Jesus: "When you are offering your gift at the altar, if you remember that your brother or sister has something against you, leave your gift there before the altar and go; first be reconciled to your brother or sister, and then come and offer your gift" (Mt 5:23-24). Reconciliation of human relationships, though not always within our power to achieve, must be within our vision of God.

The social dynamics of forgiveness flow directly out of the spiritual dynamics. Here we come up against the most difficult and painful aspect of forgiveness.

The social dynamics of forgiveness. Robert Bellah says that when a community of memory tells painful stories of "shared suffering as well as shared love; it will remember not only stories of suffering received but of suffering inflicted—dangerous memories, for they call the community to alter ancient evils."[13]

How does one "alter ancient evils"? Suppose an abuser denies the offense, as typically happens. When an offender does not acknowledge the wrong done through abuse, it is difficult, if not impossible, for forgiveness to be expressed. This is because forgiveness demands a moral threshold on which to stand, ordinarily established when a judgment has been rendered.

James Leehan reminds us that it may be inappropriate to expect the moral behavior of "forgiveness" from a victim of abuse. The moral virtue of forgiveness offered to an offender requires a reciprocity of relation as a moral context, which is not always present. In the case of child abuse, for example, victims may be expected to express forgiveness as a moral or religious virtue. "To expect forgiveness to be their initial response to abusive parents is to deny the reality of what was done to them. They need to deal with that reality in order to heal the scars which mar their lives. To berate them for their behavior may well convince them that they are not able to live up to the moral expectations or religious beliefs of any church or synagogue."[14] The point is this: We cannot lay the burden of forgiveness on the victim of abuse as a moral or spiritual obligation apart from a context where there is healing and hope of recovery through an experience of God's grace. In some cases, forgiveness in a formal sense simply may not be possible.

When Simon Wiesenthal was in a Polish concentration camp, a nurse took him to

---

[13]Robert Bellah et al., *Habits of the Heart: Individualism and Commitment in American Life* (San Francisco: Harper & Row, 1985), p. 153.

[14]James Leehan, *Pastoral Care for Survivors of Family Abuse* (Louisville, Ky.: Westminster John Knox, 1989), p. 90.

the bed of a dying SS Nazi, twenty-two years old. The soldier, whose name was Karl, said he had to speak to a Jew to confess his crime of murdering innocent women and children. He begged Wiesenthal, as a Jew, to forgive him so that he could die in peace.

"I stood up and looked in his direction, at his folded hands. At last I made up my mind and without a word I left the room." The German went to God unforgiven by a fellow human being.

Later a fellow prisoner wrote, "You would have had no right to forgive him in the name of people who had not authorized you to do so. What people have done to you, yourself, you can, if you like, forgive and forget. That is your affair. But it would have been a terrible sin to burden your conscience with other people's suffering."[15]

Smedes is not entirely comfortable with the idea that some evil may not be able to be forgiven, at least humanly speaking. In a commentary on Wiesenthal's story, he writes:

> Forgiving does not reduce evil. Forgiving great evil does not shave a millimeter from its monstrous size. There is no real forgiving unless there is first relentless exposure and honest judgment. When we forgive evil we do not excuse it, we do not tolerate it, we do not smother it. We look the evil full in the face, call it what it is, let is horror shock and stun and enrage us, and only then do we forgive it. . . . When we declare an evil person to be beyond the pale of forgiveness, we create a monster who does not even need to be forgiven—a monster is excused from judgment by the fact that he or she is beyond humanity. This is the paradox of making any human being *absolutely* evil.[16]

I suspect that what Smedes calls forgiveness is really mercy. Forgiveness is not always a possibility, but mercy is. There are people who may be beyond forgiveness on human terms, but as persons who have done evil, even they are not to be excluded from mercy. For in becoming merciless, we also become inhuman.

In the end, we must resist making a moral law or even a spiritual virtue out of forgiveness. We should always remember that even where there is forgiveness, punishment as a consequence for actions against another is still appropriate. Some have forgiven those who murdered a child or other family member, but the offenders still remain in prison. Compassion as an expression of mercy is quite different from forgiveness and is expected even where forgiveness is not possible.

Compassion is only a feeling until it becomes an act of mercy. In showing mercy one seeks to alleviate pain, temper justice and restore relationships. While mercy is prompted by compassion, it has its source in the moral virtue of upholding the value

---

[15]Quoted by Lewis B. Smedes, *Forgive and Forget: Healing the Hurts We Don't Deserve* (San Francisco: Harper & Row, 1984), p. 127.

[16]Ibid., pp. 79-80.

of a human life when it least deserves it or cannot bear it. We applaud acts of mercy because we recognize the moral goodness of such actions that go beyond the demands of the law.

While some people show no mercy because they have no compassion, others who have deep feelings of compassion are reluctant to extend mercy in fear of undermining justice. For some, punishment for violation of a natural, civil or divine law contains the moral content of the law itself. To release a person from the consequences of breaking the law is considered by some to be a violation of the moral law.

The moral value of mercy, on the other hand, is grounded in the moral being of God and of humans created in the divine image. Forgiveness has to do with release from punishment, not exemption from the law. Mercy is shown to those who have no power or right to establish their own righteousness and human well-being. Mercy is a moral demand, while forgiveness is not. We cannot hold persons accountable to forgive when they have been sinned against, but we can expect them to show mercy where it is appropriate. Where forgiveness is offered, mercy has preceded it and constitutes the moral basis for forgiving.

Some might argue that in extending mercy one has already made a commitment to forgive. Not necessarily. As I have said earlier, forgiveness has to do with releasing an offender from further punishment. Those who have committed crimes should receive mercy but should also suffer the consequences, such as imprisonment if so ordered by the justice system. At the personal level, where no crime is involved, if one forgives an offender, one cannot then continue to exact punishment or seek revenge. Mercy is not the same as forgiveness, though forgiveness is an act of mercy. Mercy begins with compassion and recognizes that even an offender is a human person. When mercy is extended to one guilty of a crime, punishment is carried out in a merciful way. In this case, the offender receives mercy but is not forgiven by the state. When mercy is extended to one who has offended us but has not committed a crime, it may also lead to forgiveness. In this case, no further punishment is exacted in the hope that reconciliation might occur.

Reconciliation is the ultimate goal. Obstacles to reconciliation might be the offender's lack of repentance, irreparable damage to a relationship, the death of an offender. For a woman who as a child was sexually abused by a parent, reconciliation may be a possibility as long as the parent is alive. With the parent's death, if there was no repentance or acknowledgement of wrong, reconciliation on earth is impossible. At this point forgiveness is no longer directed toward the goal of reconciliation but toward personal healing. In the end, reconciliation as well as forgiveness is a divine gift of grace that we receive bit by bit and grow into.

Forgiveness that seeks reconciliation is a social and spiritual reality that must be pursued for the sake of our own healing and recovery. "If another member of the church sins against you," said Jesus, "go and point out the fault when the two of you are alone. If the member listens to you, you have regained that one" (Mt 18:15). Mennonite theologian Norman Kraus argues that reconciliation between humans and God through Christ is a social act as well as a forensic one:

> The intention of forgiveness is to nullify shame and guilt so that reconciliation and a new beginning become possible. The shamed person must find new identity and personal worth. And the guilty person must find expiation. Both objective alienation and hostility which have been institutionalized in our social and legal systems and the subjective remorse and blame that so inhibit personal fulfillment in human relationships must be overcome. . . . Only a forgiveness which covers the past and a genuine restoration of relationship can banish shame. What is needed is a restoration of communication. The rage which isolates and insulates must be overcome. Reconciliation and restoration of mutual intimate relationship through a loving open exchange is the only way to heal resentment and restore lost self-esteem.[17]

Forgiveness must not be content with "forgetting the past," but must acknowledge and transform our memory of the past. Augsburger comments that for many who appear to have forgotten the past, their "memory just became fatigued—which is not true forgiveness!"[18]

Those who have been victims of abusive behavior need an advocate to enter in and empower them to render a moral judgment against the offender, whether the offender acknowledges wrong or not. This intervention serves to authenticate the outrage done to the self and to render a moral judgment against the offender and on behalf of the victim. This does make forgiveness possible in the sense of giving over to God the punishment (vengeance) and freeing the self to be healed of the hurt and anger.

Behind all injuries to the self, regardless of the cause, there is a moral need for justice to be done. This can take the form of expressing a moral judgment on behalf of the injured person, even if the offender will not acknowledge responsibility. Those who are moral if not literal descendants of the people who created a new nation on the backs of slaves brought from Africa and on the land taken from American Indians must enter a journey of forgiveness and reconciliation alongside of the descendants of people whose rights and basic humanity were violated. To say that we are "Americans" is to acknowledge our inheritance as much as to proclaim our freedom.

We cannot deny the fact of ancient evils, but we can alter our memory of them through the creation of a new story of reconciliation and peace. Indeed, failure to do

---

[17]C. Norman Kraus, *Jesus Christ Our Lord: Christology from a Disciple's Perspective* (Scottsdale, Penn.: Herald, 1987), pp. 207, 211.

[18]Augsburger, *Freedom of Forgiveness*, p. 48.

so leaves us perpetual victims, salting unhealed wounds with tears of bitterness.

"Forgiveness," suggests John Patton, "involves a letting go not only of the negative energy connected with an injury, but also of the meanings which were learned as a result of that and similar injuries throughout one's life. Next is the repairing of relationships from the past that have been found to be recapitulated in the present."[19]

The repairing of relationships that contain "ancient evils" is a journey that begins with a bias toward reconciliation; we begin as equal partners in the task of repairing and restoring.[20]

The Journey Toward Forgiveness and Reconciliation

David Augsburger reminds us that

> forgiveness is not an act—it is a process. It is not a single transaction—it is a series of steps. Beware of any view of instant, complete, once-for-all forgiveness. Instant solutions tend to be the ways of escape, of avoidance, or of denial, not of forgiveness. Forgiveness takes time—time to be aware of one's feelings, alert to one's pain and anger, open to understand the other's perspective, willing to resolve the pain and reopen the future.[21]

Forgiveness is a journey, sometimes a lifelong journey. We have no control over the end; some relationships will never be mended this side of heaven. Some offenses are so grievous that it is not within our power to forgive. And yet the journey must begin, for it is a journey toward our own freedom and peace.

In 1993 Amy Biehl, a twenty-six-year-old Fulbright scholar, was murdered by four blacks in South Africa while attempting to end apartheid by registering voters for the nation's first free election. Her murderers were apprehended and imprisoned. Her parents, Peter and Linda Biehl, went to Cape Town to establish a foundation in their daughter's name aimed at violence prevention and have continued to maintain a presence there as a continuation of Amy's commitment to peace. Under the Truth and Reconciliation Commission, established to grant amnesty to persons who confess political crimes and give the whole truth about their actions, the four men who murdered Amy were given full pardon and release from prison on July 29, 1998.

Commenting on this result, which they supported, Amy's parents said, "It is this vision of forgiveness and reconciliation that we have honored." They believed this

---

[19]Patton, *Is Human Forgiveness Possible?* p. 163.

[20]David Augsburger argues that reconciliation is not only one of several outcomes to a dispute or conflict but should be the "bias" or prior intention of those who undertake the move toward forgiveness. Citing Jesus, Augsburger says, "His expressed concern is not about the inner peace of the person who forgives to find release from private feelings of guilt; his goal is the reestablishing of relationship, the restoring of harmony, the regaining of community" (*Helping People Forgive*, p. 148).

[21]Augsburger, *Freedom of Forgiveness*, p. 42.

was what their daughter would have wanted. Peter Biehl added, "We're not dispensing forgiveness. We're not God. But we support the decision." Releasing the men from further punishment in no way mitigated their crime, to which they confessed. Forgiveness in the form of amnesty, however, was an act of mercy that the Biehls saw as an important step in the journey toward peace and reconciliation.[22]

In Arthur Miller's classic play *After the Fall,* the character Quentin struggles to find a clue to the hatred, prejudice and violence that led to the Holocaust with its breakdown of the most fundamental structures of love, trust and friendship between people. An attorney in the McCarthy era, he is accused of communist sympathies because he is defending his friend Lou, who published a book interpreted as favorable to Russia. Watching his marriage disintegrate because of mistrust, Quentin cries out in desperation to his wife, "We are killing one another with abstractions. I'm defending Lou because I love him, yet the society transforms that love into a kind of treason, what they call an issue, and I end up suspect and hated. Why can't we speak with a voice that speaks below the 'issues'—with our real uncertainty?"[23]

Finding a voice that "speaks below the issues" seems to me to be the beginning of a dialogue, the launching of the journey toward reconciliation through forgiveness. As a tentative movement toward such a conversation, let me suggest some voices with which we might speak.

The voice of pain rather than the voice of complaint. All injury begins with a betrayal of trust, a violation of our common humanity as well as of our most intimate relations. Trust is the fabric that binds the inner self to the outer world. When this fabric is torn, the self is cast into a dilemma. The openness to others that brought pleasure and expanded dimensions has now become an instrument of pain and violation. The betrayer cannot be isolated as merely an untrustworthy person, as one would pick a rotten apple out of a sack and throw it away. Betrayal ruptures the sack itself so that all the apples spill out. The self perceives that it is not just the one apple but the sack itself that is dangerous. For in allowing oneself to be "gathered up" in the lives of others, one has become vulnerable to all.

The voice of complaint focuses on issues. "I was treated unfairly. I was innocent but still charged with a crime. You never listen to what I say. You had no right to treat me that way."

The voice of pain speaks below the issues. "I am not sure that I can ever feel safe again. I did not know that you felt that way. I have no excuse or explanation for what happened, I only know that it hurts to think about it."

Each of us suffers pain, whether it be chronic physical pain, the emotional pain of

---

[22]Reported in *The Orange County* (California) *Register,* July 29, 1998, pp. 1, 16.
[23]Arthur Miller, *After the Fall* (New York: Viking, 1964), pp. 55-56.

unhealed grief or the pain of unfulfilled desires and dreams. Whatever the cause of pain, the voice of pain is the same. We cannot really hear the pain of others until we can speak with a voice that pain recognizes, or that recognizes pain.

We begin to trust only a person who can share our pain. The sympathy of those who recognize our hurt and wish to help is not sufficient. Those who are vulnerable at the level of their own pain create access to our pain, and thus to the very core of our being, without requiring a commitment or a promise. Without the experience of shared pain, those who have had trust shattered cannot find a point of beginning.

This is the point where Christopraxis as the shared experience of Christ who suffered our pain enters in. The Holy Spirit, the Spirit of the historical as well as the resurrected Jesus, comes to us fully "clothed" with the character of Christ. Suffering with another is more than a human therapeutic skill and deeper than human compassion. It is the praxis of Christ's own consolation, as Paul puts it:

> Blessed be the God and Father of our Lord Jesus Christ, the Father of mercies and the God of all consolation, who consoles us in all our affliction, so that we may be able to console those who are in any affliction with the consolation with which we ourselves are consoled by God. For just as the sufferings of Christ are abundant for us, so also our consolation is abundant through Christ. (2 Cor 1:3-5)

Second, the reality of shared pain creates an implicit bond that requires explicit recognition and affirmation. Once we have experienced bonding through shared pain, a further step becomes possible. The implicit bond of companionship and shared life has now taken the place of the distrust that served as a protective mechanism against risking further hurt. While there is not yet a capacity to make promises that require trust, there is "ground under one's feet," so to speak. The ones who provided unconditional acceptance through their shared pain now stand with us and for us. There is less risk involved in saying yes to a bond already established than in trying to create a new one out of nothing.

Third, shared life in a common bond creates a new basis for trust. The yes to shared life creates implicit trust. The undeniable reality of this trust provides a basis for belief. Belief is the content of hope based on experienced trust, and reaches out through faith to expand the horizon of life beyond shared pain to shared promise.

Fourth, entry into community with others is a shared promise as an expression of love. One has recovered the capacity to trust and love when one can risk betrayal again! As Craig Dykstra has said, "It is not the failure to keep promises, in and of itself, that destroys family. Such failure happens in every family and can be expected. Family can remain family in the midst of unfulfilled promises. What destroys family is the collapse of promise-making. It is when the very making of promises is no longer believed and believed in that families die."[24] The mutual journey of reconciliation begins when we are able to make promises again and enter into a promise-making community.

Wounds wear many faces, but pain speaks with a single voice. Learning to speak and listen with the voice of pain rather than complaint can be the beginning of a dialogue about forgiveness and reconciliation.

The voice of compassion rather than the voice of criticism. Words of sympathy can sound cruel when not spoken with the voice of compassion. "I am sorry that your son was killed, but I'm sure that the Lord has a purpose in all things." The person who said that meant well, but the words lack compassion for the devastating loss and the pain that remains. Platitudes spoken without compassion can indirectly be heard as critical of one's continued grief.

Compassion has to do with how we perceive others as much as it does with our own feelings. Augsburger credits Robert Schreiter with seven ways in which we can perceive others:

> We can *demonize* the other as an evil to be eliminated. We can *romanticize* the other as a superior to be emulated. We can *colonize* the other as an inferior to be pitied and used. We can *generalize* the other as nonindividual and generic. We can *trivialize* the other by stereotyping and ignoring. We can *homogenize* the other by denying and assimilating. We can *vaporize* the other by blinding ourselves to the other's existence, by making the oppressed invisible.

Or, says Augsburger, we can recognize and empathize.[25]

When God speaks, it is with a voice of empathy and compassion. God does not only see our pain but feels and experiences it. As James Torrance has eloquently said,

> Christ does not heal us by standing over against us, diagnosing our sickness, prescribing medicine for us to take, and then going away, to leave us to get better by obeying his instructions—as an ordinary doctor might. No, he becomes the patient! He assumes that very humanity which is in need of redemption, and by being anointed by the Spirit in our humanity, by a life of perfect obedience for us, by dying and rising again, our humanity is healed *in him.*[26]

When we speak with the accent of Jesus, we communicate compassion rather than criticism. Voices of criticism were constantly raised against Jesus. "He eats with

---

[24]Craig Dykstra, "Family Promises: Faith and Families in the Context of the Church," in *Faith in Families,* ed. Lindell Sawyers (Philadelphia: Geneva Press, 1986), p. 143.

[25]Augsburger, *Helping People Forgive,* p. 156. See Robert Schreiter, *Reconciliation* (Maryknoll, N.Y.: Orbis, 1992), pp. 32-33.

[26]James Torrance, "The Vicarious Humanity of Christ," in *The Incarnation: Ecumenical Studies in the Nicene-Constantinopolitan Creed, A.D. 381,* ed. Thomas F. Torrance (Edinburgh: Handsel, 1981), p. 141.

unwashed hands." "If he had known what sort of woman this was, he would not have allowed her to touch him." "He eats with tax collectors and sinners." Even the disciples were critical of Jesus when he suggested that they feed the multitudes who flocked to hear his teaching. But Jesus said, "I have compassion for the crowd, because they have been with me now for three days and have nothing to eat" (Mt 15:32).

The praxis of Christ is released through compassion by which one may say to another, "It must be hard to face the rejection of others who criticize and judge you." Or, "It must be difficult to bear this loss that you did not deserve and that God did not seem to prevent." Such statements allow the other to express pain, grief and even anger. For it is indeed hard to be on the wrong side when others seem always to be on the right.

The Samaritan woman sought to engage Jesus in discussion over the issue of the Jews' hatred of Samaritans, but Jesus spoke with a voice below the issues when he said, "Give me a drink." Still she sought to bring up the issue of the proper place to worship God, and Jesus said, "True worshipers will worship the Father in spirit and truth, for the Father seeks such as these to worship him" (Jn 4:1-26).

Learning to speak with a voice below the issues requires that we set aside the issues that prompt criticism for the sake of sharing a common human need and perspective. Having compassion is not unlike being a companion on the same journey. Whether we know it or not, the issues that divide us onto separate pathways are illusions that blind us to our common destiny, from the earth, on the earth and finally to the earth.

Perhaps the voice with which we speak to our own souls is the most strident and unforgiving. Learning to speak with oneself "below the issues" is the best preparation for being a companion on the road to reconciliation. Let us look for and listen to this voice.

The voice of the psalmist rather than the voice of the historian. When King David slept with the wife of another man and then had her husband murdered to cover up the crime, he was confronted by Nathan the prophet and confessed his sin. The child conceived as a result of that relationship subsequently died. When Bathsheba conceived again, a second son was born to David. David gave him the name Solomon. Nathan brought a message from God, indicating that this child was "beloved of the Lord." Therefore David gave him an additional name, Jedidiah, which literally embodied the promise of God's love and grace (2 Sam 12:25).

The intervention was of divine origin, as I suspect all creative beginnings are. Having the consequences of his actions explained to him by the prophet, and accepting those consequences as facts, David no longer felt it necessary to continue his negative feelings about himself. But where should he now invest his feelings? Again the prophet brought a divine word. The child is "loved by the Lord." This gave David a new birth of hope, which he consecrated by blessing the child and giving him a name signifying this new beginning.

In our emotional dilemmas we make hundreds of new beginnings and a thousand promises to ourselves as well as to others. But these all are swept away by the undertow of negative emotions flowing back out to the empty sea of our past. The historian who wrote 1 and 2 Samuel recites these facts in David's life with relentless honesty and accuracy. But David had the voice of a psalmist. And in composing his psalms of confession and restoration, he "altered the ancient evil" by viewing it through the lens of God's grace and forgiveness.

Some of us may have a historian self that has been carefully trained by parents and teachers to take note of discrepancies and to mark the red-letter days in our lives. It often seems that the former occur with greater frequency than the latter! Our past is preserved, if you can picture it, by an efficient but faceless librarian who has never misfiled or lost a date or document that causes us pain, but who disappears into the stacks when we are on a search for the elusive fragment of personal esteem. How could we have trained such devilish efficiency with such devastating results?

Is there also a psalmist in us who receives little recognition and less reward? David, I assume, did not become a psalmist as preparation for becoming a king. It was in his early life as a shepherd that he sang his feelings into song. Sheep are a passive but also permissive audience. Shepherding is a lonely but exquisitely lovely commune with the self. His psalms are the unbounded expression of his self-journey with God, sometimes painful but always hopeful.

The Scriptures of the Hebrew people contained not only a book of Chronicles but a book of Psalms. They kept the histories to remind them of their origin and pilgrimage with God. But they sang the psalms to consecrate their lives with feelings of gratitude and praise to God.

Our journey of forgiveness and reconciliation has not begun until we have written our psalm—and published it. The breakthrough to certainty of forgiveness for David did not occur only through confession but also through the communication of his feelings. We compose our psalm for the purpose of bringing the psalmist in us, like Cinderella, out of the kitchen into the living area to sit, with our treasured and trusted friends, at the head of the table. This place, ordinarily reserved for the historian self, may feel uncomfortable and uneasy for the psalmist self. This is due to our neglect, not the intrinsic inadequacy of the psalmist.

Learning to speak with the voice of the psalmist rather than the historian begins when we have received the gift and grace of divine forgiveness. The prophetic words of Hosea are drenched with the healing power of God's love in an invitation to return and be reconciled: "Return, O Israel, to the LORD your God. . . . Take words with you and return to the Lord" (Hos 14:1-2). Take words with you—what an intriguing thought. Learning to speak with the voice of the psalmist means finding words of hope with which to take hold of wordless pain and sing a new song of thanksgiving and praise to the Lord (Is 42:10). We are moving toward forgiveness and healing when we compose our own psalm and share it with those who have shown that they can hear our voice.

As an exercise, read a psalm of David each day for a month before attempting to write your own psalm. We need to become familiar with the art of using past events as a framework for painting word pictures with feeling. Remember, the psalm should contain some elements of the emotional audit, the confession in the context of unconditional love, and the consecration of a new birth of hope.

The psalm is published when it is shared with a trusted person, like Nathan the prophet, to do as he or she pleases with it. It cannot be taken back or protected by any "right of privacy." Do it!

19

THE LITTLE MAN ON THE CROSS
Where Is God When We Suffer?

Two brothers, with enmity between them, found themselves in a confrontation.[1] Cain rose up against his brother Abel and killed him. Hearing the sound, God came and asked, "Where is your brother Abel?"

Cain said to no one in particular, "I do not know; am I my brother's keeper?" (Gen 4:8-9).

Some have wondered why Cain's question did not seem to warrant an answer, but what is surprising is not that the question went unanswered but that the answer came so patiently, so thoroughly, so conclusively. Only after a hundred thousand generations of human experiences of love and hate, only after nations had risen up against nations, only after the Word of God had been taken captive in Israel, only after that same Word of God had become flesh, and only after that flesh had been nailed to a cross did God turn and face Cain and say, "There, there it is. There is the answer! No, you are not your brother's keeper, you are your brother's brother."

The Principle of Cohumanity
Social justice is not an abstract principle, nor is it an ideal to be pursued. Social justice is the core of human experience. It is bread and water; it is blood and bones; it is brothers and sisters who unlearn the knowledge of how to hurt and how to kill and

---

[1]This chapter first appeared as an article in *The Reformed Journal*, November 1982, pp. 14-17.

who learn to live in the power, the freedom and the hope with which God intended that we should live.

If there is any theological basis for social justice, it lies between us, within our humanity; it is anthropological. Social justice is a divinely ordained order of human existence. Humanity is essentially cohumanity. "It is not good that the man should be alone" was God's judgment upon the solitary person (Gen 2:18). God then provided an answer through his own power, a provision not capable of being taken out of the earth itself. The provision of the one for the other was a divine order. And so Adam cried out, "This at last is bone of my bones and flesh of my flesh!" (Gen 2:23). What is good and right, and therefore just, is that the one should exist with and for the other. No social or psychological theory can account for this. It is divinely ordained; it is theological knowledge. It is not a truth of nature, though it is experienced as a natural order. It is God's determination of the structure of human existence, and in this structure, the one for the other, the one with the other, is essential humanity. This is the basis for social justice.

Social justice is a divinely endowed gift of human freedom. Freedom for the other is a divine gift, a calling to be human. It is the imago Dei, the image and likeness of God. The "ought" of social justice is anchored not in an individual and natural right but in the divine word: "Let us make humankind in our image." Human rights and social justice argued on the basis of the individual, natural right to live will ultimately be impersonal, tyrannical and destructive. I will eventually fight you for my natural right to live. Being with and for the other is the core of being human. It is an expression of a freedom to be human, accepting the responsibility of being human. Recognizing one's self in another is an affirmation of the divine gift of freedom. Where there is not that freedom, there will not be social justice.

Social justice is a divinely enabled power of community. John MacMurray, the Scottish philosopher, writes, "The inherent ideal of the personal is a universal community of persons in which each cares for all the others and no one cares for himself." The apostle John tells us, "We love because he first loved us" (1 Jn 4:19). Love is the very structure of social justice, the enabling power of cohumanity. It is not merely an ethical obligation added to being human. It is being human.

The Voice of Your Brother's Blood

"We know love by this," says John, "that he laid down his life for us—and we ought to lay down our lives for one another. How does God's love abide in anyone who has the world's goods and sees a brother or sister in need and yet refuses help?" (1 Jn 3:16-17). Cohumanity, essential humanity, divinely ordained of God, given as freedom to be with and for the other, experienced as the enabling power of human community—this is social justice. But the rhetorical question hangs over John's statement.

If I close my heart against the sister or brother, if I act against that fundamental core of humanity, how does the love of God dwell in me? The answer is that it does not. Hearts are closed. The power is gone, and in its place has come law and duty. Freedom is gone, and in its place is license on the one hand and slavery on the other. The divine order is gone, and in its place are chaos, terrorism and fear.

Now we can see more clearly the anatomy of social injustice; now we know what injustice is—not a violation of some Platonic principle or ideal but a fundamental act against humanity. Social injustice is a human, not merely an ethical, problem. It is a human disorder; it is a breakdown of the essential structure of humanity. It is not totally an impersonal, inhuman, evil force. It is not essentially demonic, though it can become so. It is our problem, because it is a human problem. It is my problem, because it is not good for one to be alone. It is a problem of sin, not merely a problem of evil.

This is the deeper issue in the social and ethical problem of injustice. "Your brother's blood is crying out to me from the ground!" said God to Cain (Gen 4:10). God hears the cry of the oppressed; God help the oppressor! Here is also the hopeful aspect of social injustice. No impersonal evil stares out at us through the unblinking eye of fate. Injustice can be engaged and thwarted, because it is a structure of human order in which God himself participates. God's own dignity is at stake in ours, for we are in his image. Injustice is therefore a problem that can be solved. And the means for the solution are at hand. Through Jesus Christ, the brother has come. What the blood of Abel could not do the blood of this man could and has done.

Social justice flows not from the justice of God as an abstract principle but from his humanity as a historical and continuing power of reconciliation. It is not God's justice but his humanity that is our hope.

We will kill each other out of the abstract principle of justice. Cain could have argued that he was just in defending himself against his brother. His brother had taken away his rights. His brother had secured by some means the favor of God. "No one has the right to take the favor of God away from me; that is unjust!"

Incarnation and Social Justice

No, the key to social justice is not the justice of God but his humanity. And therefore we are inescapably brought to the incarnation. The humanity of God is the theological basis for the recovery of social justice. In the humanity of God through Jesus Christ we know the solidarity of God with us. The vicarious humanity of Christ binds both the victim and the oppressor to God. But even more, the continuing humanity of God in Christ binds God to the cause of social justice from the side of those who suffer injustice. The incarnation, in the words of James Torrance, is the ministry of Jesus Christ who comes from God to be the True Priest, bone of our bone, flesh of our flesh, in solidarity with all men, all races, all colours, bearing on his divine heart the names, the needs, the sorrows, the injustices of all nations, to offer that worship, that obedience, that life of love to the Father we cannot offer.[2]

The author of Hebrews reminds us, "The one who sanctifies and those who are sanctified all have one Father. For this reason Jesus is not ashamed to call them brothers and sisters" (Heb 2:11). And Jesus himself, near the end of his life, taught, "Truly I tell you, just as you [performed acts of care] to one of the least of these who are members of my family, you did it to me" (Mt 25:40).

The brothers and the sisters of Jesus are not only those who know his name but those whose names he knows. The excluded ones are not unknown to him. And he is not ashamed to call them his brothers and his sisters. This is the solidarity God has established through his own humanity, a solidarity that is the basis for the recovery of humanity and therefore of social justice. In the incarnation, God bears the contradiction of sin in his own human body. The love and obedience of Jesus establish a new order, a new humanity. Through Jesus' suffering love and solidarity with a humanity that has become disordered, the structure of sin and social injustice is taken within the humanity of God and overcome. The apostle Paul writes:

> For he is our peace; in his flesh he has made both groups into one and has broken down the dividing wall, that is, the hostility between us. He has abolished the law with its commandments and ordinances, that he might create in himself one new humanity in place of the two, thus making peace, and might reconcile both groups to God in one body through the cross, thus putting to death that hostility through it. (Eph 2:14-16)

The theological basis for social justice is cohumanity. And this in turn helps us understand social injustice—it is humanity turned against itself destructively. Through the humanity of God, through the incarnation, this contradiction, this disorder that is against humanity, has been taken hold of at the extreme, at the borders where the pain is. The nameless ones have been named; the blind have been led to see; the oppressed have been given the kingdom of God—then and now.

The Church as the Place of Justice

We must then ask, where is this humanity of God? One of the metaphors used in the New Testament for the church is *body*. The church, as the body of Christ, seeks and serves the humanity of God. The church as an agent of social justice is not the continuation of the incarnation. Nor is it another incarnation. But the church is the place and

---

[2]James Torrance, "The Vicarious Humanity of Christ," in *The Incarnation: Ecumenical Studies in the Nicene-Constantinopolitan Creed, A.D. 381,* ed. Thomas F. Torrance (Edinburgh: Handsel, 1981), p. 141.

the presence and the power of the incarnate One who through his Spirit inhabits our humanity and leads us to meet his humanity in the world. Thus the church restores, through its witness to Jesus Christ, the new order of humanity in the midst of the old. This of course is the original order of cohumanity, but it is also the new humanity of God. The church is not Christ, but it is the means by which Christ reconciles the world.

Thomas Torrance has so well said:

> The Church cannot be in Christ without being in Him as He has proclaimed to men in their need and with being in Him as He encounters us in and behind the existence of every man in his need. Nor can the Church be recognized as His except in that meeting of Christ with Himself in the depth of human misery, where Christ clothed with His gospel meets Christ clothed with the desperate need and plight of men.[3]

The church risks its own survival for the sake of those who would not otherwise survive. The apostle Paul says, "I am now rejoicing in my sufferings for your sake, and in my flesh I am completing what is lacking in Christ's afflictions for the sake of his body, that is, the church" (Col 1:24).

Recently I read of an astounding plan developed by the director of the "Noah's Ark Project," for evacuation of Los Angeles in the event of an impending nuclear attack. The strategy involves evacuating people from the Los Angeles basin in order of their supposed value. The first to be taken out will be the trained specialists—doctors and nurses. Next will be craftspeople indispensable to rebuilding a new society. The next will be the young, who are the hope of the future. And left behind: the elderly and the infirm; they are dispensable.

I wonder, would Jesus be on the list? Perhaps as a carpenter, but not as the Messiah! The church may need to risk its own survival. If the church is truly the body of Christ, it ought to covenant with those who will not be evacuated that it will stay and minister in solidarity with them. The church represents the power not only of the cross but of the crucified God, to use Jürgen Moltmann's term. The cross has power as a symbol, but the greatest power of the cross is the power of the crucified One—the crucified humanity of God in solidarity with all humanity.

Some time ago I heard of a woman who had been brought up Roman Catholic, but who in later days had left the church and had come upon bad times. No longer connected to the church, she happened upon a Christian bookstore and went in to browse. The salesperson came over and said, "May I help you?"

The woman said, "Yes, I'm looking for a cross, but do you have one with the little man on it?"

---

[3]Thomas F. Torrance, "Service in Jesus Christ," in *Theological Foundations for Ministry*, ed. Ray S. Anderson (Grand Rapids, Mich.: Eerdmans, 1979), p. 724.

Where is the little man on the cross? The cross in our churches is empty, stripped of flesh, disincarnate, hung on invisible wires designed by architects, suspended by engineers, in total ambivalence, ascending or descending somewhere between heaven and earth.

Where are the little people on the cross? Go into the laundromat on any urban street corner after 8:00 some evening and note the mothers who are the sole support of their families there to do their washing with their little children by their side. Contemplate hospital beds on which people toss and turn and cry out in the night and become disoriented. Take a good look at the federally funded housing projects that are an embarrassment to the city but the only haven for the hopeless.

There are neon crosses, "old rugged crosses," crosses on gold chains—but they are all empty. And a cross without its humanity is a cross without its power of reconciliation. "I want a cross with the little man on it," said the woman.

But the truth of the gospel is not that humanity has been put on the cross; it is rather that the cross has been sunk deep into humanity. The incarnation has the cross on it before the incarnate One hangs on the cross. More stupendous than the thought of a crucified God is the self-giving and suffering love of the humanity of God. More powerful and more effective than an instrument of death is the instrumental means of reconciliation through incarnational presence in life. More significant than the cross as a religious symbol is the power released through the bearing of the cross under the already inspired witness of resurrection and healing.

Too often, I fear, we have torn the cross out of the flesh and made it the symbol and servant of our highest religious aspirations. When Jesus commands us to take up the cross and follow him, we cannot do it by tearing it out of the flesh of his brothers and sisters. We must take them with us if we are to have the cross.

Or to put it in an even better way, we must stay with them in order to be where the cross is. To be with our brothers and sisters into whose flesh and bones the cross has been sunk is to be part of the meeting of Christ with himself, where Christ clothed with his gospel meets Christ clothed with the needs and the hurts of his brothers and sisters.

This is no bondage of the spirit of the resurrected One, nor is it an eclipse of a theology of glory. This is a true theology of liberation, where humanity is released from the self-destructing and self-defeating instinct for preservation and protection of the soul and opened up to the life-sustaining order of community and the life-renewing discipline of love.

20

MEMO TO THEOLOGICAL EDUCATORS
A Proposal

I am well known by my own theological faculty and administrators for writing provocative and, I am afraid, sometimes pretentious memos![1] I do not claim either the honest perception or the naive courage of the boy who cried out, "But the emperor has no clothes!" On the other hand, I have sometimes been known to say out loud what others have been thinking. Because I think this may be one of those times, I write this memo with the hope that it will be read with some degree of seriousness by those to whom it is directed, and that all others may look over my shoulder as I write.

To My Colleagues in Theological Education for Ministry
Do you sometimes feel, as I do, that we serve two masters? On the one hand, our academic and professional status as members of theological faculties is rigorously defined and reviewed by criteria that carry the threat "publish or perish." At the same time, we are held accountable to the mission statements of our schools, which set high standards and goals having to do with spiritual formation, personal mentoring

---

[1]An earlier version of this chapter appeared in Ray S. Anderson, *Ministry on the Fireline: A Practical Theology for an Empowered Church* (Downers Grove, Ill.: InterVarsity Press, 1993), pp. 197-209.

of students and building of community.[2]

As academicians we are fitted for the iron collar of scholarship forged in the dungeons of the universities and led through the promotional ranks with the whips and goads of scholarly footnotes and literary fetishes. At the same time, we are reminded that we are accountable to the church to provide men and women who are spiritually mature, biblically astute and skilled practitioners of a dozen crafts needed for successful ministry.

The captivity of the church's theological agenda by the guild of so-called professional scholars in academic theological education is a charge often raised by pastors as they look back on their theological education. Some have likened it to the alliance Israel created with Assyria for the sake of gaining political power and to compensate for its own weakness. I am afraid I must agree.

The church as an institutional structure has too often become an accomplice in the seduction and captivity of its theological nerve center by the professional academic academy. Intimidated by the claims of biblical scholars and theologians whose own professional careers are evaluated and affirmed by other scholars, the church acquiesces, surrendering its role in determining its own theological agenda. Seldom permitted access to the halls of scholarship or to the helm of theological education, the church receives its theology through a "trickle-down" process. The filter, unfortunately, is so constructed that most theology as well as the tools of critical biblical study is thrown out with the "coffee grounds" when the students return to take up their posts on the frontline of ministry. There, under pressure to be successful leaders of the organizational church, they are easily attracted to pragmatic strategies for church growth, conflict management and pastoral counseling.

Institution Versus Pentecost

This is not a new problem. There are historical antecedents going back to the first century.

I see two traditions directing the task of theological education, emerging out of the New Testament period itself. One is based on a theology of the nature of the church as an institutional embodiment of Christ, and the other follows the trajectory of Pentecost as a paradigm for the mission and ministry of the church.

We can see the antecedents of these two traditions in the formulation of the first-century church. Peter, James and John were the "pillars" in the Jerusalem church to

---

[2]For a discussion of the contemporary situation with regard to theological education, see Barbara G. Wheeler and Edward Farley, eds., *Shifting Boundaries: Contextual Approaches to the Structure of Theological Education* (Louisville, Ky.: Westminster John Knox, 1991); Robert Banks, *Reenvisioning Theological Education: Exploring a Missional Alternative to Current Models* (Grand Rapids, Mich.: Eerdmans, 1999).

whom Paul refers in his sarcastic aside when writing to the Galatians (Gal 2:9). Peter, though he thought of himself as God's choice to preach the gospel to the Gentiles (Acts 15:7), and though he defended Paul at the Jerusalem Council, never seemed to get very far away from Jerusalem. During these early decades there is no indication that Peter ever planted a Gentile church, nor did he contribute any substantive theology to this movement, even taking into consideration the two epistles that bear his name. Peter had a profound eschatological vision of salvation through Jesus Christ which provided both a source of confidence through suffering and encouragement for witness to the world (1 Pet 1—2, 4). But there is little hint of Pentecost in his appeal for steadfastness and in his mission strategy.

James, the brother of Jesus and apparently titular head of the Jerusalem church due to this relationship, was viewed by Paul as the source of a good deal of the trouble that the Judaizers contributed to his own efforts. Paul charges Peter with being intimidated by this tradition. "Until certain people came from James, he used to eat with the Gentiles. But after they came, he drew back" (Gal 2:12). James contributed an apparently early and very practical epistle, but again it contains no evidence of a substantive theological contribution regarding the identity of the church and its mission and ministry. The Jerusalem church may have been influenced more by a "traditional-hierarchical" leadership model in its organization than an "entrepreneurial-situational" leadership style, as we would put it today.

My point is that the Jerusalem community sought to extend its own life as the church of Jesus Christ through continuity with the historical transmission of authority in the "tradition of the Twelve" rather than through the new event of Pentecost. This approach tended to subordinate the charismatic order of the church to the traditional order, represented by those who had historical continuity with Jesus and the disciples. This is what I mean by an institutional embodiment of Christ as contrasted with a charismatic and Pentecostal presence of Christ through the Spirit.

Paul's theology and mission were directed more by the Pentecost event, which unleashed the Spirit of Christ through apostolic witness rather than apostolic office. The praxis of Pentecost became for Paul the "school" for theological reflection. In Paul's theology, the nature of the church is revealed through a theology of its mission and ministry in relation to Pentecost. From Pentecost as a praxis of the Spirit, Paul reflected back on the resurrection and beyond to the historical significance of Jesus Christ as the incarnation of God, the Messiah promised to Israel. Indeed, one might argue that this was the way the theology of the church took initial shape and form.

At the same time, we must agree with Emil Brunner: the Pauline vision of the community of Christ as the charismatic fellowship (*ekklēsia*) gave way to institutional and sacramental structure by the end of the first century.[3] Though Brunner may have overstated his case, a strong argument can be made that, very quickly, the early church moved toward a centralized and highly organized concept of its teaching and sacramental authority. Within this tradition, Paul's mission theology became subordinate to an official "ecclesial theology," with the result that the praxis of the Spirit became subordinate to the ecclesial office and teaching.

I do not despise the contributions made to our present theological task by an understanding of history and appreciation of tradition. It is not as though tradition itself is to be cast aside and ignored. All theology is practiced within a context of tradition, which gives it continuity with past theological reflection and enables it to enter into dialogue with others who share theological and ecclesial roots. But a tradition can become closed and turned in on itself. Christian tradition is misunderstood and misused if it becomes institutionalized and loses its cumulative and liberating function within the praxis of the Spirit.[4]

Theology is in danger of losing contact with its object of study when it is no longer open to the critical interaction of spiritual praxis and revealed truth. A mission theology is not neglectful of tradition but practices theological reflection in the context of mission. Mission theology begins with Pentecost as the formative event of the church in its relation to the incarnate Son of God on the one hand and the world as the object of God's mission on the other hand.

The development of an official ecclesial theology along the lines of continuity with the incarnation led gradually to the theological and institutional marginalization of a Pentecostal experience where the ministry of the Holy Spirit appeared in supernatural phenomena of ecstatic utterance, miracles of healing and dramatic "power encounters" with demonic spirits. Left without a strong theological tradition of its own, Pentecostal experience tended to develop its own criteria for the ordering and empowering of ministry. "Evidences" of the Spirit's manifestation were given the status of authority and even infallibility with regard to what is personally real, as opposed to what is only formally true.

When the mainstream theological tradition set out to define its task primarily as abstract reflection on the nature of God, Christ and the church, the Pentecostal expe-

---

[3]Emil Brunner, *The Misunderstanding of the Church* (London: Lutterworth, 1952).

[4]Writing from the context of the South African theological tradition, John de Gruchy says, "Theological reflection within the community of faith has, then, the task of being critical of the tradition in which it stands. . . . The practical theologian, at that moment of theological reflection in the pastoral-hermeneutical circle, draws on the insights and symbols of the tradition in order to help the community of faith finds its way. In particular, the practical theologian reappropriates those symbols in the tradition which communicate the liberating and transforming power of the gospel of the Kingdom of God in Jesus Christ" (*Theology and Ministry in Context and Crisis: A South African Perspective* [Grand Rapids, Mich.: Eerdmans, 1987], pp. 153-54).

rience saw little value in theological dogmatics of this nature. First, Pentecostal experience itself was not susceptible to this kind of theological examination because the Spirit was not considered capable of definition in the abstract categories theologians tended to use. Second, for many Pentecostals most such theological works were at best uninteresting and at worst deadly. The charge that the Pentecostal experience lacked "theological integrity" was taken by many Pentecostals as assurance that their experience and movement had spiritual vitality!

With the marginalization of Pentecost as a phenomenon of experience, the incarnational theology of the church took up issues having more to do with its own origin and nature than with its mission. Pentecost as a praxis of the Spirit and a means of access to theological reflection on the incarnational mission of the church lost its place in the theological curriculum.

The triumph of orthodoxy over orthopraxis in the church left mission theology without a christological center. The mission of God was left without theological content; missiology replaced mission theology, with cultural anthropology as its core curriculum. Some schools have even gone so far in this direction as to separate theology from missions altogether, with missionaries teaching missions and academic theologians teaching future pastors for the church! The school of missions was considered adjunctive to the central task of the seminary. The school of theology was placed at the center, making it accountable to the theological academy rather than to the mission of God and to the church.

The theological task, which properly belongs to the church as a means of determining its own origin, nature and mission, was handed over to scholars, so that church theology became academic theology. While the church continues to ordain its ministers, the theological academy, usually in the context of the university, prepares its theologians. These theologians then train students in their respective disciplines of study for the church to ordain to ministry. Even the free-standing theological seminaries, while serving the church in the main, look to professional academic accrediting associations for certification of their degrees. This means that faculty members are, for the most part, university trained with little or no experience and expertise in leading the mission of the church.[5]

Despite the monumental efforts of Karl Barth to recover an authentic theology of the church, the theological momentum tends to remain with the academy. Barth's own christological instincts led him toward a theology of the

---

[5]Edward Farley has made a trenchant and provocative critique of this trend in *Theologia: The Fragmentation and Unity of Theological Education* (Philadelphia: Fortress, 1983). "Theology as a personal quality continues (though not usually under the term *theology*), not as a salvation-disposed wisdom, but as the practical know-how necessary to ministerial work. Theology as a discipline continues, not as the unitary enterprise of theological study, but as one technical and specialised

proclaimed Word, and thus the event of proclamation became for him the locus of evangelical theology. At the same time, however, Barth's theological agenda was dominated by the same issues that had preoccupied the older theological tradition: the origin and nature of the church's existence and confession. He rightly saw that the incarnation of God in Jesus Christ is the theological basis for the reconciliation of the world to God as an act of God's freedom and grace. From this perspective he critically reviewed all the loci of theology, grounding each doctrine in the completed ministry of God's reconciliation through Christ. In the end, his magnum opus stands "outside the camp" of the theological mainstream for his radical refusal to bind theology to the critical mind of the scholar/theologian. At the same time, however, his attempt to do a "theology of the Word" left him tantalizingly near but strangely remote from the context where the mission of the church is actually taking place.[6]

Academy Apart from Spirit

Let me now become more specific. By and large, the theological academies to which the church sends its members to be taught and equipped for ministry are staffed by faculties that tend to isolate biblical studies and theology from the Holy Spirit's minis-

---

scholarly undertaking among others; in other words, as systematic theology" (p. 39). Wolfhart Pannenberg argues for the unity of the theological disciplines from the perspective of the historical integrity of theology as a science, alongside the other disciplines in the university curriculum; see his *Theology and the Philosophy of Science* (Philadelphia: Westminster Press, 1976). For a critique of both Farley and Pannenberg, see Richard Muller, *The Study of Theology: From Biblical Interpretation to Contemporary Formulation* (Grand Rapids, Mich.: Zondervan, 1991), pp. 45-60. Muller's own approach leans closer to Pannenberg's search for objectivity through the discipline of historical methodology and, as such, is a textbook example of what I have called an "institutional church theology." One looks in vain for any mention of the Holy Spirit in his depiction of the theological task, either as part of the hermeneutical circle or as the praxis of Christ in the mission of the people of God.
[6]I would argue, though this is not the time or place, that Karl Barth offers more encouragement for the development of a mission theology than any other modern theologian. His fascination with the Blumhardts, who took Pentecost seriously and who saw manifestation of the "signs and wonders" of the kingdom of God, caused him to lean ever so slightly in the direction of a praxis of the Spirit as a theological hermeneutic. For a recent study of the life and thought of Johann Christoph Blumhardt (1805-1880) see Friedrich Zuendel, *The Awakening: One Man's Battle with Darkness* (Farmington, Penn.: Plough, 1999). Barth's emphasis on the present and historical reality of the Holy Spirit as the ontological connection with the inner relation of the Father and the Son provides a beginning point for a mission theology that is both incarnational and trinitarian. His emphasis on the nature of the church as "proclamation event" produced a dialectic that prevented nature from encapsulating grace. What remained elusive for him, however, was the dynamic of Pentecost as related to the formation of the church through the Spirit's ministry in the world *extra-ecclesia*. In the end, he retreated from the kingdom theology of the Blumhardts and produced a church theology with the world already encompassed by the eschatological reality of the incarnate Word of God. We can learn from Barth but must go beyond him for the sake of integrating Pentecost with incarnation and the mission of the church with the nature of the church.

try in the church's interface with the world. This is a generalization that allows for plenty of exceptions while still being true. The teachers in these theological schools often earn their doctoral degrees and receive their academic promotions by practicing research and scholarship centering primarily on the citation of each other's work in copious footnotes. One becomes a scholar when one's own thought is cited in the footnotes of other scholars! This is a form of scholarship appropriate to the mastery of knowledge in a particular discipline of study. As such it is a criterion of excellence in matters requiring disciplined thinking, writing and the guidance of others in such a process.

What I question here is not the striving for excellence in knowledge, but the omission of competence in discerning God's Spirit in the revealing of truth through God's ministry in the world. There is no need to denigrate the academic profession for its striving for excellence in things of the mind. Saul of Tarsus sat at the feet of the renowned scholar Gamaliel (Acts 22:1) and later says of himself, "I advanced in Judaism beyond many among my people of the same age" (Gal 1:14). Yet after his own private Pentecost on the Damascus Road where the Spirit of Christ encountered him, Paul counts all of these credentials as nothing for the sake of knowing Christ (Phil 3:7-8). The degree of knowledge one has is not a measurement of the degree of truth one possesses when it has to do with the things of God. Paul's interpretation and teaching of the Old Testament Scriptures changed radically after he had encountered Christ and experienced the manifestation of the Holy Spirit through his preaching of Christ.

In many theological seminaries, those who teach the art of biblical preaching are not ordinarily permitted to teach the Bible to those who are preparing to be preachers. Only those with earned doctoral degrees in the science of biblical and textual criticism are allowed to teach the Bible. Many of these professors of Bible have never subjected their own teaching to the critical test of effective preaching and teaching.

It seems to me that the truth of Scripture is discovered in its effect, that is, in the context of its effective preaching and teaching, as well as in its source. The prophet speaks for God when he says, "So shall my word be that goes forth from my mouth; it shall not return to me empty, but it shall accomplish that which I purpose, and succeed in the thing for which I sent it" (Is 55:11). Are there not truths of Scripture that can be known only through preaching and teaching the Word? It is not unusual for graduates from university divinity schools to move directly into teaching positions in theological seminaries without having demonstrated competence in the ministry of the gospel. Many become teachers of those who are preparing for ministry without themselves having served as ministry interns under supervision within a network of accountability.

A Modest Proposal

It would not be fair of me to raise such serious questions and make such radical criticisms without offering some suggestions for integrating mission theology with a theology of the church in the task of theological education.[7]

Introduce a praxis-based curriculum. In a praxis mode of theological education, the goal, or *telos,* is located beyond the issuing of the diploma in divinity. Those who complete the degree and enter into the ministry for which they have been prepared become critical points of validation of the curriculum in the context of their lives and ministry. One could say that in a praxis-based curriculum designed to prepare women and men for Christ's ministry, those who teach are accountable to the effectiveness of those who are taught rather than primarily to their academic colleagues. In a praxis-based curriculum, one teaches toward competence in ministry rather than merely toward a discipline of study.

Those who have earned doctoral degrees in theology write theological manuals and dissertations that are reviewed by other theologians. Seldom are they evaluated by pastors, missionaries or therapists who experience regularly in their work the power of God in the burning bush and tongues of fire. In my fifteen years of teaching in a theological seminary I have yet to experience a debriefing in which those who are attempting to carry out the teaching and strategy received in school return to discuss the effectiveness of this theology with their teachers.

Research into the cause and nature of fires and means of effective firefighting is often done in the field. Those who study the science of fires team up with those who fight fires, and manuals are revised based on a collaborative debriefing with firefighters and members of the command center. In theological academies it is usually quite the opposite. Research is done in the catacombs of the library, not among the smoldering embers of the latest firestorm. Even where the "tongues of fire" creep into the seminary constituency, such manifestations of the Spirit's presence are sometimes viewed with suspicion, if not alarm.

I propose the creation of some kind of feedback loop where those involved in the praxis of ministry provide critical insight into the assumptions and methods by which the theological curriculum is constructed and delivered by the schools. Without abandoning commitment to excellence in rigor of critical thought and study, a more rigorous demand on the curriculum needs to be made from the context of its outcome, as measured by the effectiveness of those who are doing the ministry of Christ in the world.

Establish parity between mission theology and academic theology. Too long have we

---

[7]For a very helpful discussion of curriculum changes aimed at the integration of practical theology into seminary education see Banks, *Reenvisioning Theological Education,* especially pages 232-62.

relegated mission theology to the back benches, away from the theological core of the curriculum. Systematic theology need no longer have exclusive franchise rights over the teaching of theology. This deprives those doing academic theology of a mission context and so diminishes and distorts theology itself. It also tends to allow the praxis of mission to avoid critical theological reflection on its methods and practices.

I suggest that the theological mandate to develop an authentic mission theology be placed on those who are experiencing the praxis of Pentecost. Like Paul, those who attribute to the work of the Spirit a revelation of the inner relation between Holy Spirit, Spirit of Jesus Christ and Spirit of God should be expected to practice theological reflection. This theological mandate begins with the praxis of mission and reflects back through the church, to the gospel.

We have no right to expect theological credibility of those who practice the theology of Pentecost without enabling them to occupy some of the chairs of theology in mainstream theological schools. In this way a creative and fruitful interchange could result between academic theology and mission theology.

The problem is as much a structural problem in the formation of a theological faculty as it is a problem between theology and mission. When the mission of the church becomes separated from the institutional theology of the church and takes up its task under the discipline of missiology, both suffer from the structural dichotomy. When theologians have no praxis context from which to do theological reflection, academic theology and mission theology find it difficult to coexist, much less have fruitful dialogue.

Restructure the academic units of the faculty around mission outcomes rather than disciplines of study. It is time to approach the problem creatively by suggesting a new configuration for theological training for the whole of God's missionary people throughout Christ's body. This includes ordained ministers, missionaries and laypersons.

The traditional separation of biblical studies, church history, theology and ministry (practical theology) into separate academic divisions follows too closely the modern university model. It tends to reinforce the separation of theological study from the task of ministry and lends support to the idea that ministry, or practical theology, is primarily a matter of acquiring pastoral, pedagogical, homiletical or liturgical skills and techniques. It further reinforces biblical study as a discipline involving matters of source criticism, problems of authorship and literary construction. This approach allows biblical studies to become a discipline or field of study alongside other academic disciplines, in which one can earn a doctoral degree by mastering the literature in the field and making a small contribution to that literature.

Without discounting the value of the scholarly work that has contributed much to our modern understanding of the Bible in its rich context and tradition along with the historical development of the church and its theology, we need to find more creative ways of structuring the faculty and curriculum. If mission theology as defined in this book be taken as a guide, we could first of all integrate more clearly the missiological and theological curricula and faculty. The various degrees granted by a theological seminary or college could each be defined in terms of ministry or vocational outcomes, drawing on a faculty rich in the interdisciplinary fields relating to the total mission of God in the world through his people.

Where the content of the Bible is taught, there should be faculty who are experts in teaching the Bible, preaching from the Bible, using the Bible in addressing social and spiritual needs of persons, as well as experts in the critical study of the text and its sources. Here there would be a creative dialogue within the faculty as well as a rich resource for students who come to study the Bible for purposes relevant to their own life and ministry in the church and the world.

In a similar way, where formal academic theology is taught, there should be faculty who are experts in evangelism and church growth, equipping members of the church for ministry, leading and managing the church organization, pastoral care and counseling, as well as experts in the history of the church's life and theology.

This proposal would lead to the displacing of systematic and historical theology as the theological core and the creating of a multiplex theological faculty with mission theology as the integrating force. For some schools this might require a "Jerusalem conference" like the one Paul experienced (Acts 15). There will be those who will remain at Jerusalem. But if Paul had not won his right to be the primary theologian of Pentecost, Christian theology might very well have become a subheading under Jewish theology!

This is a proposal for the recovery of an authentic mission theology alongside historical theology, both for the sake of preparing men and women for church ministry and for the ministry of the people of God in the world. This proposal calls into question the structure of the traditional theological curriculum, where biblical studies tend to be preoccupied with critical textual concerns and where theological reflection on the mission of the church in the world is dominated by critical historical theology.

The theological mandate can best be fulfilled from the perspective of those who are responsible to answer the question, how do you account for what you are doing in the name of Jesus Christ? This is not to say that systematic and historical theology is unimportant. Theological reflection as mission theology must be informed by historical theology. Those who are to take leadership in the mission of the gospel as well as in the church, however, must have a mission theology, not merely a foundation of systematic and historical theology.

A Call for Repentance and Renewal

The church as an organization finds its real continuity by always being open to theological repentance in order to manifest the power and presence of the kingdom of God. Theological repentance was at the very heart of Peter's sermon on that first Pentecost: "This man . . . you crucified and killed. . . . But God raised him up" (Acts 2:23-24). Mission theology places the church in its institutional life at the foot of the cross for the sake of its participation in the Pentecostal life given to it through the life of the resurrected Lord Jesus.

In social repentance the church confesses its sin of neglecting the humanity of the world as the object of God's loving grace while it is preoccupied with its own institutional life. In theological repentance the church submits its doctrinal formulations to the praxis of mission informed by theological reflection on the mission of God through Christ as an eschatological and apostolic form of its sending into the world.

This is also a call for institutional repentance: the educational institutions that serve the church in its mission can subject its teaching curriculum and faculty orientation to the critique of Christopraxis as competence in training of the members of the church for ministry.[8]

Educational institutions charged with the mandate of serving the church in its total mission will be called to repentance for separating mission theology from academic theology and bowing before the false gods of academic scholarship while sacrificing to the contemporary gods of pragmatism and secularism. The mandate of equipping and preparing the total people of God through the church will be the first step toward recovering an authentic mission theology and reformation of the theology of the church in its life and mission.

The theological mandate of Christopraxis will lead to the emancipation and liberation of the church from captivity to the philosophy and structures of its own creation. This calls for a renewal and reorientation of the church from the side of its mission of being sent into the world, as well as new theological reflection on the mission of God as delivered in the gospel of Christ through the empowerment of Pentecost.

All of this will mean a radical revisioning of the comfortable dichotomy between clergy and lay categories of ministerial service and preparation. Mission theology is first of all the task of the entire missionary people of God. As the people of God determine the various orders of ministry, persons can be set aside (ordained) and prepared to exercise this ministry in specific vocational forms. It is baptism into Christ, however, that constitutes the calling of every Christian into the ministry of Christ.

---

[8]See Ray S. Anderson, "Christopraxis: Competence as a Criterion for Theological Education," *Theological Students Fellowship (TSF) Bulletin,* January-February 1984.

Through the praxis of Pentecost, a revisioning of ministry can take place, with old wineskins giving way to new and creative forms of ministry.

My desire is to stimulate a new vision for a Christian mission theology that is biblically based and that is singed by the flames of a burning bush and touched by the tongues of fire lighted at Pentecost.

For the thousands of pastors and church leaders who are on the firelines of God's mission in the world, we need a theology that sings even as it stings, exciting the mind and stirring the heart. I want all to experience burning hearts within, hearing again the living Christ who is the theologian of the Emmaus Road (Lk 24). I appeal to every member of the body of Christ, because every member is a minister of Christ, to become a theologian in life and deed.

I hope to fan the fires of renewal already burning and light new ones among the underbrush of the church's institutional bureaucracy. I want the fire to burn back into the theological faculties and reinvigorate weary and disheartened academicians, opening windows and throwing open doors through which men and women of the Spirit can learn from each other. I want our theological manuals and mission strategies to be opened for audit by those who have stories to tell of God's power and presence and who themselves have been transformed, healed and empowered by the reality of Christ, who comes where two or three are gathered in his name.

We need to begin again with Pentecost; the waiting is over. The Jesus who ascended comes again through his Holy Spirit to lead us back into the mystery and miracle of God's mission, and forward into the glorious dawn of the reconciliation of the world.

Bibliography

Anderson, Herbert. *The Family and Pastoral Care*. Philadelphia, Penn.: Fortress, 1984.

Anderson, Ray S. *Christians Who Counsel: The Vocation of Wholistic Therapy*. Grand Rapids, Mich.: Zondervan, 1990.

—————. "Christopraxis: Competence as a Criterion for Education for Ministry," *Theological Student Fellowship Bulletin*, (January-February 1984).

—————. "Empowering Ministry: The Praxis of Pentecost." In *The Call to Serve: Essays on Ministry in Honour of Bishop Penny Jamieson*. Sheffield, U.K.: Sheffield Academic Press, 1996.

—————. *Historical Transcendence and the Reality of God*. Grand Rapids, Mich.: Eerdmans, 1975.

—————. "Karl Barth and New Directions in Natural Theology." In *Theology Beyond Christendom: Essays on the Centenary of the Birth of Karl Barth*. Edited by John Thompson. Alison Park, Pennsylvania: Pickwick, 1986.

—————. *Ministry on the Fireline: A Practical Theology for an Empowered Church*. Downers Grove, Ill.: InterVarsity Press, 1993.

—————. *On Being Human: Essays in Theological Anthropology*. Grand Rapids, Mich.: Eerdmans, 1982.

—————. "The Resurrection of Jesus as Hermeneutical Criterion: A Case for Sexual Parity in Pastoral Ministry." *Theological Students Fellowship Bulletin*, (March-April 1986).

—————. *Self-Care: A Theology of Personal Empowerment and Spiritual Healing*. Wheaton, Ill.: Victor, 1995.

—————. "Socio-Cultural Implications of a Christian Perception of Humanity," *Asia Journal of Theology* 2, no. 2 (1988): 500-515.

—————. *The Soul of Ministry: Forming Leader's for God's People*. Louisville, Ky.: Westminster John Knox Press, 1997.

—————. *Soul Prints: Personal Reflections on Faith, Hope, and Love*. Pasadena, Calif.: Fuller Seminary Press, 1996.

—————. "Toward a Post-Apartheid Theology in South Africa," *Journal of Theology for South Africa* (June 1988).

—————, ed. *Theological Foundations for Ministry*. 1979. Reprint, Grand Rapids, Mich.: Eerdmans, 1999.

Anderson, Ray S., and Dennis B. Guernsey. *On Being Family: A Social Theology of the Family.* Grand Rapids, Mich.: Eerdmans, 1985.

Aristotle. *The Nichomachean Ethics.* Translated by J. E. C. Weldon. New York: Promethian, 1987.

Asquith, Glenn H., Jr., ed. *Vision From a Littler Known Country: A Boisen Reader.* Decatur, Ga.: Journal of Pastoral Care Publications, 1991.

Augsburger, David. *The Freedom of Forgiveness.* 2nd ed. Chicago, Ill.: Moody Press, 1988.

————. *Helping People Forgive.* Louisville, Ky.: Westminster John Knox, 1996.

Ballard, Paul, and John Pritchard. *Practical Theology in Action: Christian Thinking in the Service of Church and Society.* London: SPCK, 1996.

Banks, Robert. *Reenvisioning Theological Education: Exploring a Missional Alternative to Current Models.* Grand Rapids, Mich.: Eerdmans, 1999.

Barclay, William. *Daily Study Bible: The Gospel of Matthew.* Philadelphia: Westminster Press, 1959.

Barker, Roger. *Ecological Psychology: Concepts and Methods for Studying the Environment of Human Behavior.* Stanford, Calif.: Stanford University Press, 1968.

Bartchy, Scott. "Jesus, Power, and Gender Roles." *Theological Students Fellowship Bulletin,* January-February 1984.

————. "Power, Submission, and Sexual Identity Among Early Christians." In *Essays on New Testament Christianity.* Edited by C. Robert Wetzel. Cincinnati: Standard, 1978.

Barth, Karl. *The Knowledge of God and the Service of God.* Translated by J. L. M. Haire and Ian Henderson. London: Hodder & Stoughton, 1938.

————. *Church Dogmatics.* Volumes 1/1—4/4. Translated by various scholars. Edited by Geoffrey Bromiley and Thomas F. Torrance. Edinburgh: T & T Clark, 1955-1961.

————. *Ethics.* Edited by Dietrich Braun. Translated by Geoffrey W. Bromiley. New York: Seabury, 1981.

Bellah, Robert et al. *Habits of the Heart.* San Francisco: Harper & Row, 1985.

Berger, Brigitte and Peter Berger. *The War Over the Family.* Garden City, N.Y.: Doubleday, Anchor, 1983.

Birch, Bruce C., and Larry L. Rasmussen. *Bible and Ethics in the Christian Life.* Minneapolis: Augsburg, 1976.

Bonhoeffer, Dietrich. *Cost of Discipleship.* New York: Macmillan, 1963.

————. *Creation and Fall.* London: SCM Press, 1959.

————. *Ethics.* New York: Macmillan, 1973.

————. *Letters and Papers from Prison.* New York: Macmillan, 1971.

————. *Life Together.* London: SCM Press, 1970.

————. *No Rusty Swords.* Translated by E. H. Robertson. London: Collins, Fontana, 1970.

————. *Sanctorum Communio: A Theological Study of the Sociology of the Church*, Minneapolis: Fortress, 1998.

Boswell, John. *Christianity and Social Tolerance: Gay People in Western Europe from the Beginning of the Christian Era to the Fourteenth Century.* Chicago: University of Chicago Press, 1980.

Bromiley, Geoffrey. *God and Marriage.* Grand Rapids, Mich.: Eerdmans, 1981.

Bronfenbrenner, Urie. *The Ecology of Human Development: Experiments by Nature and Design.* Cambridge, Mass.: Harvard University Press, 1979.

Brooten, Bernadette. "Junia . . . Outstanding Among the Apostles." In *Women Priests.* Edited by L. and A. Swidler. New York: Paulist, 1977.

Brown, Colin. "Telos." In *The New International Dictionary of New Testament Theology.* Volume 2. Edited by Colin Brown. Grand Rapids, Mich.: Zondervan, 1976.

Browning, Don. *A Fundamental Practical Theology: Descriptive and Strategic Proposals.* Minneapolis: Fortress, 1991.

————. *The Moral Context of Pastoral Care.* Philadelphia: Westminster Press, 1976.

————, ed. *Practical Theology: The Emerging Field in Theology, Church and World.* San Francisco: Harper & Row, 1983.

Brunner, Emil. *Dogmatics: The Christian Doctrine of the Church, Faith and the Consummation.* Vol. 3. London: Lutterworth, 1962.

————. *Love and Marriage.* London: Collins, Fontana, 1970.

————. *The Misunderstanding of the Church.* London: Lutterworth, 1952.

————. *Natural Theology, Comprising "Nature and Grace."* Translated by Peter Fraenkl. London: Geoffry Blis, Centenary Press, 1946.

Buber, Martin. *Between Man and Man.* London: Collins, Fontana, 1961.

Burr, Chandler. "Homosexuality and Biology." In *Homosexuality in the Church: Both Sides of the Debate.* Edited by Jeffrey S. Siker. Louisville, Ky.: Westminster John Knox, 1994.

Cahill, Lisa Sowle. "Homosexuality: A Case Study in Moral Argument." In *Homosexuality in the Church: Both Sides of the Debate.* Edited by Jeffrey S. Siker. Louisville, Ky.: Westminster John Knox, 1994.

Clark, Stephen. *Man and Woman in Christ.* Ann Arbor, Mich.: Servant, 1980.

Comisky, Andrew. *Pursuing Sexual Wholeness.* Santa Monica, Calif.: Desert Streams Ministries, 1988.

Costos, Orlando. *The Church and Its Mission: A Shattering Critique from the Third World.* Wheaton, Ill.: Tyndale House, 1974.

DeGruchy, John. *Theology and Ministry in Context and Crisis: A South African Perspective.* Grand Rapids, Mich.: Eerdmans, 1987.

Dostoyevsky, Fyodor. *The Brothers Karamazov.* New York: Random House, Modern Library, 1950.

Dueck, Alvin. "Righteousness." *Pastoral Psychology* 35, no. 4 (Summer 1987).

Dykstra, Craig. "Family Promises: Faith and Families in the Context of the Church." In *Faith in Families.* Edited by Lindell Sawyers. Philadelphia: Geneva, 1986.

Edwards, George R. *Gay/Lesbian Liberation: A Biblical Perspective.* New York: Pilgrim, 1984.

Evans, C. Stephen. *Wisdom and Humanness in Psychology: Prospects for a Christian Approach.* Grand Rapids, Mich.: Baker, 1989.

Farley, Edward. *Theologia: The Fragmentation and Unity of Theological Education.* Philadelphia: Fortress, 1983.

Farnsworth, Kirk. *Wholehearted Integration: Harmonizing Psychology and Christianity Through Word and Deed.* Grand Rapids, Mich.: Baker, 1985.

Firet, Jacob. *Dynamics in Pastoring.* Grand Rapids, Mich.: Eerdmans, 1986.

Flanigan, Beverly. *Forgiving the Unforgivable: Overcoming the Bitter Legacy of Intimate Wounds.* New York: Macmillan, 1992.

Ford, David F. "Faith in the Cities: Corinth and the Modern City." In *On Being the Church: Essays on the Christian Community.* Edited by Colin Gunton and Daniel Hardy. Edinburgh: T & T Clark, 1989.

Forrester, Duncan B., ed. *Theology and Practice.* London: Epworth, 1990.

Fowler, James. "Practical Methodology and the Shaping of Christian Lives." In *Practical Theology: The Emerging Field in Theology, Church and World.* Edited by Don Browning. San Francisco: Harper & Row, 1983.

————. "Practical Theology and Theological Education: Some Models and Questions." *Theology Today* 42 (1985): 43-58.

Furnish, Victor P. "The Bible and Homosexuality: Reading the Texts in Context." In *Homosexuality in the Church: Both Sides of the Debate.* Edited by Jeffrey S. Siker. Louisville, Ky.: Westminster John Knox, 1994.

Gadamer, Hans-Georg. *Truth and Method.* Translated by Garrett Borden and John Comming. New York: Continuum, 1975.

Gelwick, Richard. "Discovery and Theology." *Scottish Journal of Theology* 28, no. 4 (1975): 301-21.

Gibbs, Eddie. "Theology, News and Notes." In *Fuller Theological Seminary Alumni Journal.* Pasadena, Calif.: Integrator, June 1986.

Goppelt, Leonhard. *Theology of the New Testament.* Vol. 2. Edited by Jurgen Rolof. Translated by John Allsup. Grand Rapids, Mich.: Eerdmans, 1982.

Gorringe, Timothy J. *Karl Barth: Against Hegemony.* Oxford: Oxford University Press, 1999.

Graham, Elaine L. *Transforming Practice: Pastoral Theology in an Age of Uncertainty.*

New York: Mowbray, 1996.

Grant, George. *Unnatural Affection: The Impuritan Ethic of Homosexuality in the Modern Church*. Franklin, Tenn.: Legacy Communication, 1991.

Green, Clifford. "The Sociality of Christ and Humanity." Ph.D. diss. Ann Arbor, Mich.: University Microfilms International, 1972.

Groome, Thomas. "Theology on Our Feet! A Revisionist Pedagogy for Healing the Gap Between Academia and Ecclesia." In *Formation and Reaction: The Promise of Practical Theology*. Edited by Lewis S. Mudge and James N. Poling. Philadelphia: Fortress, 1987.

Guernsey, Dennis B. and Lucy. *Real Life Marriage*. Waco, Tex.: Word, 1987.

Gundry-Volf, Judy. "Male and Female in Creation and New Creation: Interpretations of Galatians 3:28c in 1 Corinthians 7." In *To Tell the Mystery: Essays on New Testament Eschatology in Honor of Robert H. Gundry*. Edited by Thomas E. Schmidt and Moises Silva. Sheffield, U.K.: Sheffield Academic Press, 1994.

Gunton, Colin. "The Church on Earth: The Roots of Community." In *On Being the Church: Essays on the Christian Community*. Edited by Colin Gunton and Daniel Hardy. Edinburgh: T & T Clark, 1989.

Gustafson, James. "Christian Ethics." In *Religion*. Edited by Paul Ramsey. Englewood Cliffs, N.J.: Prentice-Hall, 1965.

Hall, Douglas John. *Thinking the Faith: Christian Theology in a North American Context*. Minneapolis: Augsburg, 1989.

Halleck, Seymour. L. *The Politics of Therapy*. New York: Harper & Row, 1971.

Hanson, Paul D. *The Diversity of Scripture: A Theological Interpretation*. Philadelphia: Fortress, 1982.

Hart, Trevor. "A Capacity for Ambiguity? The Barth-Brunner Debate Revisited." *Tyndale Bulletin* 44, no. 2 (November 1993).

Hauerwas, Stanley. *A Community of Character: Toward a Constructive Christian Social Ethic*. Notre Dame, Ind.: Notre Dame University Press, 1981.

Hays, R. B. "Awaiting the Redemption of our Bodies: The Witness of Scripture Concerning Homosexuality." In *Homosexuality in the Church: Both Sides of the Debate*. Edited by Jeffrey S. Siker. Louisville, Ky.: Westminster John Knox, 1994.

Heitink, Gerben. *Practical Theology: History; Theory; Action Domains*. Translated by Reinder Bruinsma. Grand Rapids, Mich.: Eerdmans, 1999. Originally published as *Praktische Theologie*. Amsterdam: Kok-Kampen, 1993.

Hiltner, Seward. *Pastoral Counseling*. New York: Abingdon-Cokesbury, 1949.

———. *Preface to Pastoral Theology*. New York: Abingdon, 1958.

Holifield, E. Brooks. *A History of Pastoral Care in America: From Salvation to Self-Realization*. Nashville: Abingdon, 1983.

Hurding, Roger. *The Tree of Healing*. Grand Rapids, Mich.: Zondervan, 1988.

Jeanrond, Werner. "Community and Authority." In *On Being the Church: Essays on the Christian Community.* Edited by Colin Gunton and Daniel Hardy. Edinburgh: T & T Clark, 1989.

Jewett, Paul K. *Man as Male and Female.* Grand Rapids, Mich.: Eerdmans, 1975.

————. *The Ordination of Women.* Grand Rapids, Mich.: Eerdmans, 1982.

Johnson, William Stacy. *The Mystery of God: Karl Barth and the Postmodern Foundations of Theology.* Louisville, Ky.: Westminster John Knox, 1997.

Johnston, Robert. "Homosexuality and the Evangelical: The Influence of Contemporary Culture." In *Evangelicals at an Impasse.* Edited by Robert Johnston. Atlanta: John Knox Press, 1979.

Jones, Stanley L. and D. E. Workman "Homosexuality: The Behavioral Sciences and the Church." In *Homosexuality in the Church: Both Sides of the Debate.* Edited by Jeffrey S. Siker. Louisville, Ky.: Westminster John Knox, 1994.

Kant, Immanuel. *The Critique of Pure Reason.* Translated by Norman Kemp Smith. London: Macmillan, 1929.

Kimmerle, Heinz, ed. *Hermeneutics: The Hand-Written Manuscripts.* Translated by James Duke and Jack Forstman. Missoula, Mont.: Scholars Press, 1977.

König, Adrio. "Covenant and Image: Theological Anthropology, Human Interrelatedness, and Apartheid." In *Incarnational Ministry: The Presence of Christ in Church, Society, and Family.* Edited by Christian D. Kettler and Todd H. Speidell. Colorado Springs, Colo.: Helmers & Howard, 1990.

Kynes, Bill. "Postmodernism: A Primer for Pastors." *The Ministerial Forum* 8, no. 1 (1997).

Loder, James. *The Logic of Spirit: Human Development in Theological Perspective.* San Francisco: Jossey-Bass, 1998.

Loder, James E. and W. Jim Neidhardt. *The Knights Move: The Relational Logic of Spirit in Theology and Science.* Colorado Springs, Colo.: Helmers & Howard, 1992.

Lovin, Robert W. *Christian Faith and Public Choices: The Social Ethics of Barth, Brunner, and Bonhoeffer.* Philadelphia: Fortress, 1984.

Lowe, C. Marshall. *Value Orientation in Counseling and Psychotherapy.* 2nd ed. Cranston, R.I.: Carroll Press, 1976.

MacKinnon, Donald M. "The Relation of the Doctrines of the Incarnation and the Trinity." In *Creation, Christ, and Culture.* Edited by W. A. McKinney. Edinburgh: T & T Clark, 1976.

Mackintosh, Hugh Ross. *The Christian Apprehension of God.* London: Student Christian Movement, 1929.

————. *The Divine Initiative.* London: Student Christian Movement, 1921.

————. *The Doctrine of the Person of Jesus Christ.* Edinburgh: T & T Clark, 1912.

Macmurray, John. *Reason and Emotion.* London: Faber & Faber, 1935.

Mayo, Clara. "Man: Not Only an Individual, but a Member." *Zygon* 3, (March 1968).

McNeill, John J. *The Church and the Homosexual.* Kansas City, Kans.: Sheed & Ward, 1976.

————. "Homosexuality: Challenging the Church to Grow." In *Homosexuality in the Church: Both Sides of the Debate.* Edited by Jeffrey S. Siker. Louisville, Ky.: Westminster John Knox, 1994.

Middleton, J. Richard, and Brian J. Walsh. *Truth Is Stranger Than It Used to Be: Biblical Faith in a Postmodern Age.* Downers Grove, Ill.: InterVarsity Press, 1995.

Miller, Arthur. *After the Fall.* New York: Viking, 1964.

Miskotte, Kornilis. *When the Gods are Silent.* London: Collins, 1967.

Moltmann, Jürgen. *Anthropology in Theological Perspective.* Translated by Matthew J. O'Connell. Philadelphia: Fortress, 1985.

————. *The Church in the Power of the Spirit.* New York: Harper & Row, 1977.

————. *God in Creation: A New Theology of Creation and the Spirit of God.* San Francisco: Harper & Row, 1985.

————. *The Way of Jesus Christ: Christology in Messianic Dimensions.* San Francisco: Harper & Row, 1990.

Moulton, James H. and George Milligan. *The Vocabulary of the Greek New Testament.* London: Hodder & Stoughton, 1972.

Muller, Richard. *The Study of Theology: From Biblical Interpretation to Contemporary Formulation.* Grand Rapids, Mich.: Zondervan, 1991.

Nakpil, Emerito P. *The Human and the Holy: Asian Perspectives in Christian Theology.* Quezon City, Philippines: New Day Publishers, 1978.

Nelson, James B. "Sources for Body Theology: Homosexuality as a Test Case." In *Homosexuality in the Church: Both Sides of the Debate.* Edited by Jeffrey S. Siker. Louisville, Ky.: Westminster John Knox, 1994.

Nelson, Robert. *Human Life: A Biblical Perspective for Bioethics.* Philadelphia: Westminster Press, 1984.

Padgett, Alan. "Paul on Women in the Church: The Contradictions of Coiffure in 1 Corinthians 11:2-16." *Journal for the Study of the New Testament* 20 (1984).

Pannenberg, Wolfhart. *Christian Spirituality and Sacramental Community.* London: Dartman, Longman & Todd, 1983.

————. *The Church.* Philadelphia: Westminster Press, 1983.

————. *Theology and the Philosophy of Science.* Philadelphia: Westminster Press, 1976.

Patton, John. *Is Human Forgiveness Possible? A Pastoral Care Perspective.* Nashville: Abingdon, 1985.

Penn-Lewis, Jessie. *The Magna Carta of Woman.* Minneapolis: Bethany Fellowship, 1975.

Perrin, Norman. *Jesus and the Language of the Kingdom.* Philadelphia: Fortress, 1976.

Peters, George W. *A Theology of Church Growth*. Grand Rapids, Mich.: Zondervan, 1981.

Poling, James N., and Lewis S. Mudge, eds. *Formation and Reaction: The Promise of Practical Theology*. Philadelphia: Fortress, 1987.

Polanyi, Michael. *Personal Knowledge*. London: Routledge & Kegan Paul, 1958.

Pronk, Pim. *Against Nature? Types of Moral Argumentation Regarding Homosexuality*. Grand Rapids, Mich.: Eerdmans, 1993.

Ratzinger, Cardinal Joseph. "Letter to the Bishops of the Catholic Church on the Pastoral Care of Homosexual Persons (1986)." In *Homosexuality in the Church: Both Sides of the Debate*. Edited by Jeffrey S. Siker. Louisville, Ky.: Westminster John Knox, 1994.

Ricoeur, Paul. *Freud and Philosophy: An Essay on Interpretation*. New Haven, Conn.: Yale University Press, 1970.

————. *The Symbolism of Evil*. Translated by Emerson Buchanan. Boston: Beacon, 1967.

Rogers, Jack. "Sex, Philosophy, and Politics: How and What the Church Must Decide in the Debate over Ordination of Homosexuals." In *Homosexuality in the Church: Both Sides of the Debate*. Edited by Jeffrey S. Siker. Louisville, Ky.: Westminster John Knox, 1994.

Roszak, Theodore. *Person/Planet*. New York: Doubleday, Anchor, 1979.

Scanzoni, Letha Q. and Virginia R. Mollenkott. *Is the Homosexual My Neighbor? A Positive Christian Response: Revised and Updated*. 2nd ed. San Francisco: Harper & Row, 1994.

Schillebeeckx, Edward. *The Church with a Human Face: A New and Expanded Theology of Ministry*. New York: Crossroad, 1985.

Schleiermacher, Friedrich. *Hermeneutics: The Hand-Written Manuscripts*: Edited by H. Kinimerle. Translated by James Duke and Jack Forstman. Missoula, Mont.: Scholars Press, 1977.

Scholer, David. "Women in Ministry," *Covenant Companion* 72, no. 21 (1983).

Scroggs, Robin. *The New Testament and Homosexuality*. Philadelphia: Fortress, 1984.

Shults, F. LeRon. *The Task of Theology: A Postfoundationalist Appropriation of Wolfhart Pannenberg*. Grand Rapids, Mich.: Eerdmans, 1999.

Sire, James. *The Universe Next Door: A Basic Worldview Catalog*. 3rd ed. Downers Grove, Ill.: InterVarsity Press, 1997.

Smail, Thomas. *The Forgotten Father*. Grand Rapids, Mich.: Eerdmans, 1980.

Smedes, Lewis B. *The Art of Forgiving: When you Need to Forgive and Don't Know How*. New York: Ballantine, 1996.

————. *Mere Morality: What God Expects of Ordinary People*. Grand Rapids, Mich.: Eerdmans, 1983.

Smith, Steven G. *The Argument to the Other: Reason Beyond Reason in the Thought of Karl Barth and Emmanuel Levinas.* Chico, Calif.: Scholars Press, 1983.

Southard, Samuel. *Theology and Therapy: The Wisdom of God in a Context of Friendship.* Dallas, Tex.: Word, 1989.

Speidell, Todd. "Incarnational Social Ethics." In *Incarnational Ministry: The Presence of Christ in Church, Society and Family,* 140-152. Edited by Christian Kettler and Todd Speidell. Colorado Springs, Colo.: Helmers & Howard, 1990.

Stott, John. *Evangelism and Social Responsibility: An Evangelical Commitment.* London: Paternoster, 1982.

Stott, John and David Edwards, *Evangelical Essentials: A Liberal-Evangelical Dialogue.* Downers Grove, Ill.: InterVarsity Press, 1988.

Stuhlmacher, Peter. *Historical Criticism and Theological Interpretation of Scripture: Towards a Hermeneutic of Consent.* Translated by Roy A. Harrisville. Philadelphia: Fortress, 1977.

Swartley, Willard M. *Slavery, Sabbath, War and Women.* Scottsdale, Penn.: Herald Press, 1983.

Thielicke, Helmut. *Ethics: Foundations.* Vol. 1. Grand Rapids, Mich.: Eerdmans, 1984.

———. *The Evangelical Faith.* Vol. 1. Grand Rapids, Mich.: Eerdmans, 1974.

———. *The Evangelical Faith.* Vol. 2. Grand Rapids, Mich.: Eerdmans, 1977.

Thistleton, Anthony C. *The Two Horizons: New Testament Hermeneutics and Philosphical Description.* Grand Rapids, Mich.: Eerdmans, 1980.

Thurneysen. Eduard. *A Theology of Pastoral Care.* Richmond, Va.: John Knox Press, 1962.

Torrance, James B. "The Vicarious Humanity of Christ." In *The Incarnation: Ecumenical Studies in the Nicene-Constantinopolitan Creed A.D. 381.* Edited by Thomas F. Torrance. Edinburgh: Handsel Press, 1981.

Torrance, Thomas F. *Conflict and Agreement in the Church.* Vol. 2. London: Lutterworth, 1960.

———. *Divine and Contingent Order.* New York: Oxford, 1981.

———. *Reality & Evangelical Theology: The Realism of Christian Revelation.* 1982. Reprint, Downers Grove, Ill.: InterVarsity Press, 1999.

———. "Service in Jesus Christ." In *Theological Foundations for Ministry.* Edited by Ray S. Anderson. Grand Rapids, Mich.: Eerdmans, 1979.

———. *Space, Time, and Resurrection.* Grand Rapids, Mich.: Eerdmans, 1976.

Tracy, David. *The Analogical Imagination: Christian Theology and the Culture of Pluralism.* New York: Crossroad, 1981.

Trible, Phyllis. *God and the Rhetoric of Sexuality.* Philadelphia: Fortress, 1978.

Van Duesen Hunsinger, Deborah. *Theology and Pastoral Counseling: A New Interdisciplinary Approach.* Grand Rapids, Mich.: Eerdmans, 1995.

Verkuyl, Johannes. *Break Down the Walls: A Cry for Racial Justice.* Translated by Lewis B. Smedes. Grand Rapids, Mich.: Eerdmans, 1973.

Wainwright, Geoffrey. *Doxology: The Praise of God in Worship, Doctrine, and Life.* New York: Oxford University Press, 1980.

Weber, Otto. *Foundation of Dogmatics.* Vol. 2. Translated by Darrell Guder. Grand Rapids, Mich.: Eerdmans, 1983.

Wheeler, Barbara and Edward Farley, eds. *Shifting Boundaries: Contextual Approaches to the Structure of Theological Education.* Louisville, Ky.: Westminster John Knox, 1991.

Will, James. *A Christology of Peace.* Louisville, Ky.: Westminster John Knox, 1989.

Williams, Don. *The Apostle Paul and Women in the Church.* Van Nuys, Calif.: BIM Publishing, 1977.

Wright, David F. "Homosexuality: The Relevance of the Bible," *The Evangelical Quarterly* 61 (1989).

Zuendel, Friedrich. *The Awakening: One Man's Battle with Darkness.* Farmington, Penn.: Plough, 1999.

Index of Subjects

Index of Names

Adler, Alfred, 246 n.
Allport, Gordon, 246 n.
Anderson, Herbert, 255 n., 258
Anderson, Ray S., 79 n., 102 n., 141 n., 163 n., 186 n., 194 n., 196 n., 233, 238 n., 252 n., 262 n., 264, 317, 327
Arendt, Hannah, 296
Aristotle, 48, 238-39
Augsburger, David 296, 299 n., 303-4, 307
Ballard, Paul, 17, 26, 29, 32 n., 40 n., 51
Banks, Robert, 12 n., 23 n., 318 n., 324 n.
Barclay, William, 293
Barker, Roger, 235 n.
Bartchy, Scott, 85 n., 91-92 n.
Barth, Karl, 14, 72, 117-19, 132-59, 162-63, 171-73 n., 181, 190 n., 205, 210, 252, 272-78, 321-22
Bella, Robert, 300
Berger, Brigitta, 255
Berger, Peter, 255
Biehl, Amy, 304
Birch, Bruce C., 208 n.
Blumhardt, Johann Christoph, 322 n.
Boisen, A. T., 25
Bolsinger, Todd, 29
Bonhoeffer, Dietrich, 17, 23 n., 117 n., 118, 151, 173 n., 179, 203 n., 222, 263, 295, 299
Boswell, John, 270 n.
Bromiley, Geoffrey, 89 n.
Brooten, Bernadette, 92 n.
Brown, Colin, 240 n.

Browning, Don., 25-29, 35, 47-48, 52
Brunner, Emil, 132, 190 n., 272-73, 319
Buber, Martin, 260 n.
Bultmann, Rudolf, 88 n.
Burr, Chandler, 276 n., 278-79
Cahil, Lisa, 278-80
Calvin, John, 23, 163 n.
Campbell, Alastair, 32
Campbell, John McCleod, 126
Clark, Stephen, 100
Comisky, Andy, 283 n.
Costos, Orlando, 49 n.
De Grutchy, John, 320
Descartes, Rene, 17
Dibelius, Otto, 14
Dilthey, Wilhelm, 246 n.
Dostoyevsky, Fyodor, 88
Dueck, Alvin, 236, 246
Dykstra, Caig, 306
Eagleton, Terry, 20 n.
Edwards, David, 130 n.
Edwards, G. R., 270 n.
Elwood, Douglas J., 171 n.
Farley, Edward, 318 n., 321 n.
Farnsworth, Kirk E., 245
Firet, Jacob, 197-98
Flanigan, Beverly, 292
Ford, David, 191
Foucault, Michael, 19
Fowler, James, 26, 31-34
Fromm, Erich, 246 n.
Furnish, V. P., 266 n., 267 n., 268-69
Gadamer, Hans-Georg, 78 n.
Gelwick, Richard, 65 n.
Gibbs, Eddie, 177 n.
Glasser, William, 246
Goldstein, Kurt, 246
Goppelt, Leonhard, 157 n.
Graham, Elaine L., 48 n.
Grant, George, 268 n.
Groome, Thomas, 31
Grotius, Hugo, 17
Guernsey, Dennis, 207, 252 n., 258
Gundry, Robert, 275 n.

Gundry-Volf, Judith, 275-76
Gunton, Colin, 192
Gustafson, James, 213
Hall, Douglas, 38 n.
Halleck Seymour, L., 236
Hauerwas, Stanley, 242, 257
Hays, Richard B., 269 n., 271 n., 280
Heitink, Gerben, 24-25
Henry, Carl, 88
Hiltner, Seward, 25
Holifield, E. Brooks, 247 n.
Hooker, Evelyn, 278
Horney, Karen, 246 n.
Hunsinger, Deborah van Duesen, 264 n.
Hurding, Roger, 246 n.
Jeanrond, Werner, 196 n.
Jewett, Paul K., 93 n.
Johnson, Stacy, 21
Johnston, Robert, 270 n.
Jones, Stanton L., 276 n.
Kant, Immanuel, 16, 64
Kettler, Christian D., 180 n.
Kierkegaard, Søren, 18-19
Kinimerhe, H., 78 n.
König, Adrio, 180 n.
Kraus, C. Norman, 303
Kynes, Bill, 19, 251-52
Leehan, James, 300
Lewin, Kuert, 235 n., 246 n.
Loder, James, 21 n.
Lovin, Robert, 150
Lowe, C. Marshal, 206
Mackinnon, Donald M., 115 n.
Mackintosh, Hugh Ross, 113, 114 n., 124, 126
MacMurray, John, 74
Mayo, Clara, 260
McNeill, John J., 279 n.
Middleton, Richard, 19, 251 n.
Miller, Arthur, 305
Milligan George, 269 n.
Mollenkott, V. R., 276 n.
Moltmann, Jürgen, 37, 176 n., 184 n., 189-90, 263
Moulton, James H., 269 n.
Muller, Richard, 322 n.